SCHAUM'S OUTLINE OF

THEORY AND PROBLEMS

of

INTERNATIONAL ECONOMICS

Third Edition

DOMINICK SALVATORE, Ph. D.

Professor of Economics
Fordham University

SCHAUM'S OUTLINE SERIES
McGRAW-HILL, INC.

New York   St. Louis   San Francisco   Auckland   Bogotá   Caracas   Hamburg
Lisbon   London   Madrid   Mexico   Milan   Montreal   New Delhi   Paris
San Juan   São Paulo   Singapore   Sydney   Tokyo   Toronto

DOMINICK SALVATORE received his Ph.D. in 1971 and is currently
Professor of Economics at Fordham University in New York. He is the author
of the textbooks *International Economics*, 3rd Ed. (1990), *Microeconomic
Theory*, 2nd Ed. (1991), and *Managerial Economics* (1989). He has also
written Schaum's Outlines in *Microeconomic Theory, Managerial Economics*
and *Statistics and Econometrics*, and coauthored *Principles of Economics* and
Development Economics. His research has been published in numerous
leading scholarly journals and presented at national and international
conferences.

Schaum's Outline of Theory and Problems of
INTERNATIONAL ECONOMICS

1 2 3 4 5 6 7 8 9 10 11 12 13 14 15 16 17 18 19 20 SHP SHP 9 2 1 0

ISBN 0-07-054538-3

Sponsoring Editor, John Aliano
Production Supervisor, Janelle Travers
Editing Supervisors, Meg Tobin, Maureen Walker
Cover design by Amy E. Becker.

Library of Congress Cataloging-in-Publication Data

Salvatore, Dominick.
    Schaum's outline of theory and problems of international
economics
  / Dominick Salvatore. — 3rd ed.
      p.   cm. — (Schaum's outline series)
    ISBN 0-07-054538-3
    1. International economic relations—Outlines, syllabi, etc.
  2. International economic relations—Problems, exercises, etc.
  I. Title.   II. Title: Theory and problems of international
  economics.
  HF1411.S24   1990   89-78160
    337—dc20   CIP

Preface

International Economics deals with the theory and practice of international trade and finance. International economics has great relevance in today's world, but it can get extremely complicated and confusing. The purpose of this book is to present in a clear and systematic way the theoretical and practical core of modern international economics. While primarily intended as a supplement to all current international economics textbooks, the statements of theory and principles are sufficiently complete to enable its use as an independent text as well.

Each chapter begins with a clear statement of theory, principles or background information, fully illustrated with examples. This is followed by a set of multiple-choice review questions with answers. Subsequently, numerous theoretical, numerical and practical problems are presented with their detailed, step-by-step solutions. These solved problems serve to illustrate and amplify the theory, to bring into sharp focus those fine points without which the student continually feels on unsafe ground and to provide the application and the reinforcement so vital to effective learning. There are also sample midterm and final examination questions, with answers.

The topics are arranged in the order in which they are usually covered in international economics courses and texts. As far as content, this book contains more material than is usually covered in most one-semester undergraduate courses in international economics, the level of presentation is somewhat more rigorous and many important practical real-world problems are also analyzed. Thus, while directed primarily at undergraduates, this book can also provide a very useful source of study, review and reference for graduate students at the M.A. and M.B.A. levels as well as for business people. There is no prerequisite for its study other than a prior course in or some knowledge of elementary economics.

The methodology of this book and much of its content has been tested in international economics classes at Fordham University. The students were enthusiastic and made many valuable suggestions for improvements. To all of them, I am deeply grateful. I would like to express my gratitude to the entire Schaum staff of McGraw-Hill for their assistance and especially John Carleo, John Aliano, and Meg Tobin.

This is the THIRD EDITION of a book that has enjoyed gratifying market success and was translated into Spanish, French, Portuguese, Arabic, and Indonesian. All of the features that made the first and second editions successful were retained. Besides a thorough updating, the third edition includes important new theoretical developments and applications. These are the rise of the new protectionism, strategic trade policy, the formation of trading blocks, the U.S. as a debtor nation, exchange rate dynamics, integration of international capital markets and trade negotiations and reforms. Many other changes and additions were also made in response to the numerous helpful comments that I received from the many professors and students who used the first and second editions. One such change is the presentation of the partial equilibrium analysis of tariff before the general equilibrium analysis.

In preparing this third edition, I greatly benefited from comments from Professors John Piderit, Edward Dowling, William Hogan, Patrick O'Sullivan, Reza Barazesh, Francis Colella, Clive Daniel, Nick Gianaris, Thomas Hatcher, Darryl McLeod, George Mungia, Anita Pasmantier, Henry Schwalbengerg, Michael Szenberg and Eden S.H. Yu. Alan Anderson and Emily Tusaneza, my graduate assistants, also provided much help.

PREFACE

Other volumes in the same series authored or coauthored by the same author are: *Microeconomic Theory*, 3rd ed. (1991), *Managerial Economics* (1989), *Statistics and Econometrics* (1982), *Principles of Economics* (1980) and *Development Economics* (1977).

DOMINICK SALVATORE

Contents

CONTENTS

CONTENTS

Chapter 1

Introduction

1.1 INTERNATIONAL ECONOMICS AND ECONOMIC THEORY

International economics deals with the economic relations among nations. The resulting *interdependence* is very important to the economic well-being of most nations of the world and is on the increase (see Example 1).

The economic relations among nations differ from the economic relations among the various parts of a nation (see Example 2). This gives rise to different problems, requiring somewhat different tools of analysis, and justifies International Economics as a distinct and separate branch of "applied" economics.

EXAMPLE 1. Most nations of the world export some goods, services and factors of production in exchange for imports which could only be supplied relatively less efficiently at home, or not at all (as for example, coffee in the U.S., petroleum in Germany, cars in Kenya). Thus, a great deal of the economic well-being of most nations rests crucially on international interdependence. Interdependence has grown during the past decades as indicated by the fact that world trade has grown faster than world output.

EXAMPLE 2. When a U.S. firm wants to export a piece of machinery to Germany, it faces certain restrictions (such as a tariff) imposed by Germany. It must also overcome differences in language, customs and laws. In addition, the U.S. firm may receive payment in the foreign currency which may change in value in relation to the dollar. No such barriers are involved when the U.S. firm sells its machinery domestically. In order to analyze the different problems arising from international as opposed to *interregional* relations, we must modify, adapt, extend and integrate the microeconomic and macroeconomic tools appropriate for the analysis of purely domestic problems.

1.2 THE SUBJECT MATTER OF INTERNATIONAL ECONOMICS

International economics deals with

(1) *The Pure Theory of Trade.* This examines the *basis for trade* and the *gains from trade*.

(2) *The Theory of Commercial Policy.* This studies the reasons for and the results of obstructions to the free flow of trade.

(3) *The Balance of Payments.* This examines a nation's total payments to and total receipts from the rest of the world. These involve the exchange of one currency for others.

(4) *Adjustments in the Balance of Payments.* This deals with the mechanism of adjustment to balance of payments disequilibria under different international monetary systems.

Topics 1 and 2 represent the *microeconomic* aspects of international economics and are covered in the first half of the book. Topics 3 and 4 are the *macroeconomic* aspects and are covered in the second part of the book.

1.3 THE MERCANTILIST VIEW ON TRADE

The economic philosophy known as *mercantilism* (popular from the sixteenth to the middle of the eighteenth century in such countries as Britain, Spain, France and the Netherlands) maintained that the most important way for a nation to become rich and powerful was to export more than it imported. The difference would be

1

settled by an inflow of precious metals—mostly gold. The more gold a nation had, the richer and more powerful it was. Thus mercantilists advocated that the government should stimulate exports and restrict imports. Since not all nations could have an export surplus simultaneously and the amount of gold in existence was fixed at any one time, a nation could only gain at the expense of the other nations (see Problem 1.6).

1.4 ADAM SMITH: ABSOLUTE ADVANTAGE

In 1776, Adam Smith published his famous book, *The Wealth of Nations*, in which he attacked the mercantilist view on trade and advocated instead free trade as the best policy for the nations of the world. Smith argued that with free trade, each nation could specialize in the production of those commodities in which it had an *absolute advantage* (or could produce more efficiently than other nations) and import those commodities in which it had an absolute disadvantage (or could produce less efficiently). This international specialization of factors in production would result in an increase in world output which would be shared by the trading nations. Thus a nation need not gain at the expense of other nations—all nations could gain simultaneously.

EXAMPLE 3. Table 1.1 shows that the U.S. has an absolute advantage over the U.K. in the production of wheat and the U.K. has an absolute advantage in the production of cloth. If the U.S. specialized in the production of wheat and the U.K. in the production of cloth, the combined output of wheat and cloth of the U.S. and the U.K. would be greater, and both the U.S. and the U.K. would share in this increase through (voluntary) exchange (see Problems 1.7 and 1.8).

Table 1.1

	U.S.	U.K.
Wheat (bushels/labor-hour)	6	1
Cloth (yards/labor-hour)	1	2

Smith's theory of absolute advantage is obviously correct, but it does not go very far—it explains only a small portion of international trade. It remained for Ricardo, writing some 40 years later, to explain the bulk of world trade with his law of comparative advantage.

1.5 DAVID RICARDO: COMPARATIVE ADVANTAGE

Ricardo stated that even if a nation had an absolute *disadvantage* in the production of *both* commodities with respect to the other nation, mutually advantageous trade could still take place. The less efficient nation should specialize in the production of and export of the commodity in which its absolute *disadvantage* is *less*. This is the commodity in which the nation has a *comparative advantage*. On the other hand, the nation should import the commodity in which its absolute *disadvantage* is *greater*. This is the area of its *comparative disadvantage*. This is known as the *Law of Comparative Advantage*—one of the most famous and still unchallenged laws of economics.

EXAMPLE 4. Table 1.2 shows that the U.K. has an absolute disadvantage with respect to the U.S. in the production of both wheat and cloth. However, its *disadvantage* is less in cloth than in wheat. Thus the U.K. has a comparative advantage with respect to the U.S. in cloth and a comparative disadvantage in wheat. For the U.S., the opposite is true. That is, the U.S. has an absolute advantage over the U.K. in both commodities, but this advantage is greater in wheat (6:1) than in cloth (3:2). Thus the U.S. has a comparative advantage over the U.K. in wheat and a comparative disadvantage in cloth. Mutually advantageous trade could take place with the U.S. exchanging wheat (W) for cloth (C) with the U.K.

EXAMPLE 5. With reference to Table 1.2, we see that if the U.S. could exchange 6W *for* 6C with the U.K., the U.S. would gain 3C (since the U.S. can only exchange 6W for 3C domestically). To produce 6W itself, the U.K. would require

6 hours of labor (see Table 1.2). Instead, the U.K. can use the 6 labor-hours to produce 12C (see Table 1.2), exchange 6 of these 12C for 6W from the U.S., and end up with 6C more for itself. Thus by exchanging 6W for 6C, the U.S. would gain 3C and the U.K. 6C. There are many other ratios of exchange of W for C (besides 6W for 6C) that would be advantageous to both nations [see Problem 1.13(c)]. The rate at which exchange actually takes place determines how the gains from trade are shared by the two nations. What that rate itself will be depends also on demand conditions in each nation. These will be discussed in Chapter 3.

Table 1.2

	U.S.	U.K.
Wheat (bushels/labor-hour)	6	1
Cloth (yards/labor-hour)	3	2

1.6 EVALUATION OF RICARDO'S LAW OF COMPARATIVE ADVANTAGE

Ricardo based his reasoning on a number of simplifying assumptions (see Problem 1.18). One of these is the so-called *labor theory of value*, which says that the value or price of a commodity is equal to or can be inferred from the amount of labor time going into the production of the commodity. Today we reject the labor theory of value (see Problem 1.21). In so doing, we must also reject Ricardo's *explanation* of comparative advantage, but we need not reject the law of comparative advantage itself. The law of comparative advantage is valid and can be explained in terms of *opportunity costs*. This is done in Chapter 2.

Glossary

Interdependence   The economic relationships among nations.

Pure theory of trade   The theory dealing with the basis for and the gains from trade.

Basis for trade   The forces (absolute advantage for Smith and comparative advantage for Ricardo) that give rise to international trade.

Gains from trade   The increase in each nation's consumption resulting from specialization in production and trade.

Theory of commercial policy   A theory dealing with the reasons for and the results of obstructions to the free flow of trade.

Balance of payments   The measure of a nation's total receipts from and total payments to the rest of the world.

Adjustment in the balance of payments   The mechanisms for correcting balance-of-payments disequilibria.

Microeconomic   Having to do with individual economic units, such as a particular nation and the relative price of a single commodity.

Macroeconomic   Having to do with the whole or the aggregate of an economy, such as the total receipts and payments of a nation and the general price index.

Absolute advantage   The greater efficiency that one nation may have over another in the production of a commodity. According to Adam Smith, this is the basis for trade.

Law of comparative advantage   This law governing trade states that even if a nation has an absolute disadvantage or is less efficient than another nation in the production of commodities, there is still a basis for mutually beneficial trade if the less efficient nation specializes in the production of, and exports, the commodity of its smallest absolute disadvantage (comparative advantage) and exchanges part of its output for the other commodities.

Labor theory of value   A theory purporting that the value or price of a commodity is equal to or can be inferred from the amount of labor time going into the production of the commodity.

Review Questions

1. For which of the following groups of products does the U.S. rely *exclusively* on imports?   (a) Petroleum, coal, natural gas, wood;   (b) coffee, tea, cocoa, tin;   (c) copper, aluminum, iron, steel;   (d) computers, typewriters, airplanes, cars.

   Ans.   (b) Coffee, tea and cocoa can only be produced efficiently in a tropical climate not present in the U.S., and the U.S. has no deposits of tin.

2. One similarity between international and interregional trade is that in general both must overcome   (a) tariffs,   (b) differences in language,   (c) distance or space,   (d) differences in currencies and monetary systems.

   Ans.   (c) See Example 2.

3. In the study of international economics we use the tools of   (a) microeconomic theory only,   (b) macroeconomic theory only,   (c) neither micro nor macro theory,   (d) both micro and macro theory, but we also extend, adapt and integrate them.

   Ans.   (d) See Example 2.

4. With which of the following topics does international economics deal?   (a) The pure theory of trade,   (b) the theory of commercial policy,   (c) the balance of payments,   (d) adjustment to disequilibria in the balance of payments,   (e) all of the above.

   Ans.   (e) See Section 1.2

5. To which of the following would the mercantilists have objected?   (a) Free trade,   (b) stimulating exports,   (c) restricting imports,   (d) accumulation of gold by their nation.

   Ans.   (a) See Section 1.3.

6. We can best understand Smith's views on trade if we regard them as a reaction to   (a) the law of comparative advantage,   (b) the mercantilist view on trade,   (c) Ricardo's views on trade,   (d) all of the above.

   Ans.   (b) Smith objected to the restrictions on trade advocated by the mercantilists on the grounds that these would limit specialization in production, the volume of trade and the benefits that nations receive from trade.

7. What proportion of world trade is based on absolute advantage?   (a) All,   (b) most,   (c) some,   (d) none.

   Ans.   (c) See Example 3.

8. The commodity in which a nation has the least absolute disadvantage represents its area of   (a) comparative disadvantage,   (b) comparative advantage,   (c) absolute advantage,   (d) cannot say without additional information.

   Ans.   (b) See Section 1.5.

9. With reference to Table 1.2 in Example 4, we can say that the U.S. has a comparative advantage over the U.K. in the production of wheat because one labor-hour in the U.S. is   (*a*) twice as productive in C than in W,   (*b*) twice as productive in W than in C,   (*c*) 1.5 times more productive in W but 6 times more productive in C than in the U.K.,   (*d*) 6 times more productive in W but only 1.5 times more productive in C than in the U.K.

   Ans.   (*d*) See Example 4. Note that choice *b* is correct, but it is not sufficient by itself to answer this question.

10. With reference to Table 1.2 and Examples 4 and 5, indicate which of the following statements is correct.   (*a*) The rate at which W exchanges for C in production in the U.S. is 2:1.   (*b*) The rate at which W exchanges for C in production in the U.K. is 1:2.   (*c*) The rate at which W exchanges for C in trade between the U.S. and the U.K. is 1:1.   (*d*) All of the above.

    Ans.   (*d*) See Table 1.2 and Examples 4 and 5.

11. With reference to Example 5, indicate which of the following statements is correct.   (*a*) The U.S. gains 3C by trading 6W for 6C with the U.K.   (*b*) The U.K. gains 6C by exchanging 6 of its 12C for 6W with the U.S.   (*c*) The increase in the combined output of the U.S. and the U.K. when 6W are exchanged for 6C is 9C and 0W.   (*d*) All of the above.

    Ans.   (*d*) See Example 5 and Table 1.2.

12. Ricardo's law of comparative advantage is based on   (*a*) the opportunity cost theory,   (*b*) the labor theory of value,   (*c*) the law of diminishing returns,   (*d*) all of the above.

    Ans.   (*b*) See Section 1.6.

Solved Problems

INTERNATIONAL ECONOMICS AS A SUBJECT

1.1   (*a*) What does international economics deal with?   (*b*) Why do we study it?   (*c*) How can we justify international economics as a special branch of economics?

   (*a*)   International economics deals with the economic relations and interdependence among nations. These influence (and are in turn influenced by) the political, social, cultural and military relations among nations.

   (*b*)   We study international economics primarily in order to analyze the effect of the international flow of goods, services and factors of production on the welfare of domestic consumers. (Remember, consumption is the end of economic activity. Production and exchange are only the means to that end.) We also wish to examine or forecast how national policies directed at regulating these international flows affect domestic welfare. As individuals and voters, we need to study international economics in order to be able to form intelligent opinions on these matters.

   (*c*)   We can justify international economics as a special branch of economics on grounds that international economic relations differ from interregional economic relations and require somewhat different tools of analysis from those used to analyze the domestic economy. International economics has been a special branch of economics for almost two centuries and owes its development to some of the world's most distinguished economists, including Smith, Ricardo, Mill, Marshall, Keynes, Samuelson and many others.

1.2   (*a*) How do international economic relations differ from interregional economic relations?   (*b*) In what way are they similar? How do both differ from the rest of economics?

   (*a*)   Nations impose restrictions on the free international flow of goods, services and factors. Differences in language, customs and laws also hamper these international flows. In addition, international flows may involve receipts and payments in different currencies which may change in value in relation to one another through time. This is to be contrasted with the interregional flow of goods, services and factors which face no such restrictions as tariffs and are conducted in terms of the same currency, usually in the same language and under basically the same set of customs and laws.

(*b*)   Both international and interregional economic relations involve the overcoming of space or distance. Indeed, they both arise from the problems created by distance. This distinguishes them from the rest of economics, which abstracts from space and treats the economy as a single point in space in which production, exchange and consumption take place.

1.3   (*a*) How can we measure the degree of economic interdependence of a nation with the rest of the world?   (*b*) Why does the U.S. rely much less on international trade than any other noncommunist developed nation?   (*c*) What would happen to its standard of living if the U.S. withdrew completely from international trade?

(*a*)   A rough measure of the degree of economic interdependence of a nation with the rest of the world is given by the value of its imports as a percentage of its GNP. For small developed nations such as Belgium, the Netherlands, Switzerland, Denmark and Sweden, the figure ranges from 30 to 60%. For large developed nations such as Germany, England, France and Italy, the figure ranges from 20 to 30%. For the U.S., the figure is about 9%.

(*b*)   The U.S. is a nation of continental size with immense natural and human resources. As such, it can produce with relative efficiency most of the products it needs. Contrasted to this is the position of a small nation like Switzerland which can only specialize in the production of and export of a small range of commodities and imports all the others. In general, and as the figures in part (*a*) indicate, the larger the nation, the smaller its economic interdependence with the rest of the world.

(*c*)   Even though the U.S. relies only to a relatively small extent on foreign trade, a *significant part* of its high standard of living depends on it. For one thing, there are certain commodities such as coffee, tea, cocoa, scotch, cognac, etc. that the U.S. cannot produce at all. In addition, the U.S. has no deposits of certain minerals, such as tin and tungsten, which are important for industrial production. Much more important *quantitatively* to its economic well-being are the many commodities which the U.S. could produce domestically but only at relatively higher costs than the imported commodities. These account for most of the *gains from trade*. However, the U.S. could probably survive without drastic consequences from withdrawing from world trade. The same cannot be said of any other developed nation with the exception of Russia. (In addition to being a huge nation, Russia has, until recently, actively pursued a policy of self-sufficiency for political and military reasons.)

1.4   (*a*) What is the purpose of theory?   (*b*) What are some of the simplifying assumptions made by international economic theorists?   (*c*) What do they seek to accomplish?

(*a*)   The purpose of theory—not just economic theory but theory in general—is to predict and explain. That is, a theory abstracts from the details of an event and focuses on one or two relationships deemed most important in order to predict and explain the event.

(*b*)   International economists *usually* assume a two-nation, two-commodity and two-factor world. They further assume that there is perfect competition, that factors are perfectly mobile interregionally but perfectly immobile internationally, that there are originally no obstructions to the free international flow of goods and services and that transportation costs are zero. They often make additional assumptions. These assumptions may seem unduly restrictive, but it can be proved that most of the conclusions reached on the basis of such simplified models can be extended to a multi-nation, multi-product and multi-factor world— to a world where perfect competition is unusual, where factors are not perfectly mobile interregionally while there is some international mobility, where nations impose restrictions on trade and where transportation costs are not zero.

(*c*)   Using these simplifying assumptions, international economists seek (1) to predict and explain the composition and volume of the international flows of goods and services, (2) to assess their impact on domestic welfare and (3) to predict how national policies affect these flows and, through them, domestic welfare.

1.5   (*a*) Why are the pure theory of international trade and the theory of commercial policy referred to as the microeconomic aspects of international economics?   (*b*) Why are the study of the balance of payments and of the process of adjustment to disequilibria in the balance of payments referred to as the macroeconomic aspects of international economics?

(*a*)   The pure theory of trade examines the basis for and the gains from trade. The theory of commercial policy studies the reasons for and the results of obstructions to the free flow of trade. Since these topics are generally discussed by treating each nation as a *single* unit and by dealing with *individual* (relative) commodity and factor costs and prices, we are in the realm of *microeconomic analysis*.

(*b*)   In the real world, nations normally exchange many goods, services and factors with other nations. The balance of payments summarizes the *total* receipts and payments resulting from all of these international transactions and, as such, it is a *macroeconomic* concept. In addition, trade and the required adjustment to disequilibria in the balance of payments that may result from trade affect the *aggregate* level of output and income and the *general* price index of the trading nations. These are also macroeconomic concepts. Note that this book starts on an abstract and theoretical level and then becomes more applied in nature and more policy oriented. This is because we must understand the problem in order to propose appropriate policies for its solution. In the second part of the book, some integration of the microeconomic and macroeconomic tools of analysis will also be necessary.

PRE-RICARDO VIEWS ON TRADE

1.6   (*a*) How does the mercantilist concept of national wealth differ from today's view?   (*b*) Why did mercantilism advocate the accumulation of gold?   (*c*) How do the mercantilists' views on trade differ from those of Adam Smith?

(*a*)   According to the mercantilists, the wealth of a nation was measured by the stock of precious metals— particularly gold—that is possessed. Today, we measure a nation's wealth by the total stock of human and natural resources that it uses in production. The greater a nation's wealth, the greater the flow of goods and services that can be made available to each person, and the higher the standard of living in that nation.

(*b*)   Mercantilism advocated the accumulation of gold because gold was regarded as the real wealth of the nation. At a more sophisticated level of analysis, there were more rational reasons. With gold, monarchs could equip the armies, buy the supplies and maintain the navies that they needed to consolidate power and acquire colonies. More gold meant more gold coins in circulation and greater business activity. In order to accumulate gold, the nation had to encourage its exports and restrict imports, thus stimulating national output and employment.

(*c*)   The mercantilists advocated strict controls on trade by the government, they tried to show that the aims of nations were basically in conflict, and they preached economic nationalism. In a somewhat more refined and disguised way, some of these views are still alive and even thriving today in a sort of neomercantilism. On the other hand, Adam Smith (and other classical economists) advocated *free trade* as the best policy for the nations of the world. Only few exceptions to this policy of free trade were to be allowed. One of these was the protection of industries important for national defense.

1.7   (*a*) With reference to Table 1.3, indicate in what commodity the U.S. and the U.K. have an absolute advantage.   (*b*) How much would the U.S. and the U.K. gain if 6W were exchanged for 3C? (*c*) What if 6W were exchanged for 6C?

Table 1.3

	U.S.	U.K.
Wheat (bushels/labor-hour)	6	1
Cloth (yards/labor-hour)	1	3

(a)   The U.S. is more efficient than or has an absolute advantage over the U.K. in the production of wheat, while the U.K. has an absolute advantage over the U.S. in the production of cloth.

(b)   If the U.S. exchanged 6W for 3C with the U.K., the U.S. would gain 2C or would save 2 labor-hours (since the U.S. can only exchange 6W for 1C domestically). The 6W which the U.K. receives from the U.S. is equivalent to or would have required 6 labor-hours to produce in the U.K. These same 6 labor-hours can produce 18C in the U.K. (see the table). By exchanging 3C (which require only 1 labor-hour to produce) for 6W, the U.K. thus gains 15C or saves 5 labor-hours.

(c)   If the U.S. exchanged 6W for 6C with the U.K., the U.S. would gain 5C or would save 5 labor-hours. Since 6W is equivalent to 18C in the U.K., and the U.K. need only give up 6C for 6W, the U.K. gains 12C or saves 4 labor-hours.

1.8   (a) How did Adam Smith explain his contention that *all* nations engaged in trade can benefit from trade?   (b) Why do nations usually impose restrictions on the free flow of trade?

(a)   Smith explained that if each nation specialized in (or produced more than it wanted to consume domestically of) the commodity in which it was more efficient, and exchanged this excess for the commodity in which it was less efficient, the output of all commodities entering trade would increase. This increase would be shared by all nations that voluntarily engaged in trade. Thus, the gains from trade would arise from specialization in production and trade. This is simply an extension to the international setting of the gains from specialization or division of labor (and exchange) that Smith showed to occur within the national economy. These gains would be maximized when the government interfered as little as possible with the operation of the domestic economy (*laissez-faire*) and with international trade (free trade).

(b)   Since Smith believed that free trade generally leads to maximum world welfare, it may seem paradoxical that nations invariably impose some restrictions on the free flow of goods, services and factors. Trade restrictions are invariably rationalized in terms of national welfare. In reality, they are usually advocated by and imposed to protect those industries that would be hurt by imports. Thus, trade restrictions generally benefit few at the expense of many (who will have to pay higher prices for domestically produced products).

COMPARATIVE ADVANTAGE

1.9   From Table 1.4, indicate   (a) whether the U.S. has an absolute advantage or disadvantage in wheat and cloth,   (b) the commodity in which the U.S. and the U.K. have a comparative advantage, and (c) the gains to the U.S. and the U.K. if they exchange 6W for 6C.

Table 1.4

	U.S.	U.K.
Wheat (bushels/labor-hour)	6	1
Cloth (yards/labor-hour)	4	3

(a)   The U.S. has an absolute advantage over the U.K. in the production of both commodities. Trade under these circumstances cannot be based on absolute advantage.

(b)   The absolute advantage which the U.S. has over the U.K. is greater in wheat (6:1) than in cloth (4:3). Thus, the U.S. has a comparative advantage over the U.K. in wheat and a comparative disadvantage in cloth. Note that once it is established that the U.S. has a comparative advantage in wheat, it must always follow (by definition) that the U.S. has a comparative disadvantage and the U.K. a comparative advantage in cloth. This is always so in a two-nation, two-commodity world.

(c)   If the U.S. exchanges 6W for 6C with the U.K., the U.S. gains 2C or saves 1/2 labor-hour (since the U.S. can only exchange 6W for 4C domestically). The U.K. would have required 6 labor-hours to produce 6W itself. Instead, the U.K. uses these 6 labor-hours to produce 18C. By then exchanging 6 of these 18C for 6W with the U.S., the U.K. gains 12C or saves 4 labor-hours.

1.10   (a) If a lawyer earns $100 per hour at practicing law but can also type faster than her secretary who receives $10 per hour, does it pay for the lawyer to fire her secretary and do her own typing? (b) The reasoning you employed in answering part (a) is an example of what principle?

(a)   If the lawyer can be fully occupied (for all the hours she wants to work) at practicing law, it would not pay for her to do her own typing. For each hour of typing that she does, she would save $20 (since she can type twice as fast as her secretary who receives $10 per hour). However, in order to type for one hour, the lawyer would have to give up practicing law by one hour and thus forgo earning $100. The lawyer would then lose $80 for each hour that she switches from the practice of law to typing.

(b)   This is an application of the law of comparative advantage to everyday life. The lawyer has an absolute advantage over her secretary in both typing (twice) and the practice of law. However, her absolute advantage is (infinitely) greater in the practice of law than in typing since the secretary cannot practice law. Thus it pays for the lawyer to specialize (i.e., use all of her time) in the practice of law and leave the typing to her secretary. The secretary also gains by not having to look for another job and possibly earning less. (Note that if the lawyer did not have a sufficient number of clients to be fully occupied at practicing law, then she may truly save or *earn $10 per hour* by doing her own typing).

1.11   With respect to each part of Table 1.5, indicate in which commodity the U.S. has an absolute and comparative advantage with respect to the U.K. and which commodity the U.S. should export to England.

Table 1.5

	(a)		(b)		(c)	
	U.S.	U.K.	U.S.	U.K.	U.S.	U.K.
Wheat (bushels/labor-hour)	4	2	4	1	4	2
Cloth (yards/labor-hour)	3	2	1	1	2	1

(a)   The U.S. has an absolute advantage over the U.K. in the production of both commodities. However, since this advantage is greater in wheat (4:2) than in cloth (3:2), the U.S. has a comparative advantage in wheat and a comparative disadvantage in cloth with respect to the U.K. Thus, the U.S. should specialize in the production of and export wheat in exchange for English cloth.

(b)   The U.S. has an absolute advantage in wheat but is equally productive as the U.K. in cloth. Thus, the U.S. has a comparative advantage and should export wheat to the U.K. in exchange for English cloth.

(c)   The U.S. has an absolute advantage over the U.K. in the production of both commodities. But now this advantage is the *same* in wheat (4:2) as in cloth (2:1). That is, the U.S. is exactly *twice as efficient in the production of both wheat and cloth*. In this case we cannot speak of comparative advantage or disadvantage and *there can be no mutually advantageous trade*. For example, in order for the U.S. to gain from trade it would have to get more than 2C for 4W (since the U.S. can exchange 4W for 2C domestically). But the U.K. is not willing to give up more than 2C for 4W from the U.S. since the U.K. can produce 4W domestically by giving up only 2C. This leads to a slight modification to the statement of the law of comparative advantage to read: Even if a nation has an absolute disadvantage in the production of both commodities with respect to the other nation, mutually advantageous trade is still possible, *unless the absolute disadvantage is exactly the same or in the same proportion for the two commodities.*

1.12 With reference to Table 1.6 (the same as Table 1.2 in Example 4), indicate what happens if   (*a*) 6W are exchange for 9C,   (*b*) 6W are exchanged for 3C or   (*c*) 6W are exchanged for 12C.

Table 1.6

	U.S.	U.K.
Wheat (bushels/labor-hour)	6	1
Cloth (yards/labor-hour)	3	2

(*a*) If the U.S. exchanges 6W for 9C with the U.K., the U.S. gains 6C or saves 2 labor-hours. In the U.K., 6W is equivalent to (or requires as many hours to produce as) 12C. Since the U.K. only gives up 9C for 6W, the U.K. gains 3C or saves 1 1/2 labor-hours. Note that while in Example 5, W exchanged for C at a ratio of 1:1, here the ratio of exchange is 1:1 1/2. In either case, *both* nations gain from trade (the gains, however, are shared differently; see Example 5).

(*b*) If the U.S. exchanges 6W for 3C with the U.K., the U.S. gains nothing (since in the U.S. 6W and 3C both require 1 labor-hour to produce). Thus, all of the gains from trade [9C; see Review Question 11(*c*)] accrue to the U.K. In this case, the U.S. is indifferent and may not be willing to trade.

(*c*) If the U.S. exchanges 6W for 12C with the U.K., the U.S. receives all of the gains from trade (9C). The U.K. thus gains (and loses) nothing (since in the U.K., 6W and 12C both require 6 labor-hours to produce). In this case, the U.K. is indifferent and may not be willing to trade.

1.13 With reference to Table 1.6,   (*a*) would the U.S. be willing to exchange 6W for less than 3C with the U.K? Why?   (*b*) Would the U.K. be willing to exchange more than 12C for 6W? Why? (*c*) What quantities of C for 6W represent the limits within which mutually advantageous trade between the U.S. and the U.K. can take place?

(*a*) In the U.S., 1 labor-hour can produce either 6W or 3C. Thus, the U.S. would not be willing to exchange 6W for less than 3C.

(*b*) The U.K. would not be willing to exchange more than 12C (which requires more than 6 labor-hours to produce) for 6W (which requires only 6 labor-hours to produce in the U.K.).

(*c*) In order for both the U.S. and the U.K. to gain from trade, 6W must exchange for more than 3C (for the U.S. to gain) but less than 12C (for the U.K. to gain), or 3C < 6W < 12C. The difference between 12C and 3C (i.e., 9C) represents the total gain from specialization in production and trade. The closer the ratio of exchange settles to 6W for 12C, the greater the proportion of the total gains from trade going to the *U.S.* On the other hand, the closer the ratio of exchange settles to 6W for 3C, the greater the proportion of the total gains from trade going to the *U.K.* Exactly what the ratio of exchange will be (within the possible limits) depends also on demand conditions in each nation. This will be examined in Chapter 3. Also note that in this problem (and chapter), all of the gains from trade are expressed in cloth. We could have expressed the total gains from trade entirely in wheat or partly in wheat and partly in cloth (see Chapter 2). Finally, if at a given ratio of exchange, more than 6W is traded, the combined gains from trade of both nations and of each nation separately would be proportionately greater. This is also shown in Chapter 2.

1.14 If labor is the only factor of production and is homogeneous (i.e., all of one type), as Smith and Ricardo assumed,   (*a*) express the cost *in terms of labor content* of producing wheat and cloth in the U.S. and in the U.K. implied by Table 1.6,   (*b*) express the *cost or price* of wheat (P_W) in terms of labor content *relative* to the cost or price of cloth (P_C) for the U.S. and for the U.K. in the absence of trade and   (*c*) express P_C relative to P_W for both the U.S. and the U.K. in the absence of trade.

(*a*) From Table 1.6, we see that 1 labor-hour produces 6W in the U.S. Therefore, 1W is produced with 1/6 of

1 labor-hour. This is recorded in the top left-hand corner of Table 1.7. The other figures in the table are similarly obtained from Table 1.6.

Table 1.7

	U.S.	U.K.
Cost in labor-hours to produce 1W	1/6	1
Cost in labor-hours to produce 1C	1/3	1/2

(b) In the absence of trade, the U.S. can produce 1W with half the labor-hours required to produce 1C (1/6 is 1/2 of 1/3). This means that in the U.S., the cost or price of producing 1W or P_W (expressed not in dollars but in labor content) is half the cost or price of producing 1C or P_C (also expressed in labor content). That is, $P_W = P_C/2$ or $P_W/P_C = 1/2$ in the U.S. in the absence of trade. This reads: P_W relative to P_C is 1/2, which is what we were asked to find. Turning to the U.K., we find that in the absence of trade, the U.K. requires twice as much labor time to produce 1W than 1C (see Table 1.7), Thus, in the absence of trade, $P_W = 2P_C$ or $P_W/P_C = 2$ in the U.K. It is this difference in relative commodity prices between the U.S. and the U.K. in the absence of trade that is the basis for mutually advantageous trade.

(c) P_C relative to P_W can be rewritten as P_C/P_W. P_C/P_W is the inverse or reciprocal of P_W/P_C. Since $P_W/P_C = 1/2$ in the U.S. in the absence of trade [see part (b)], $P_C/P_W = 2$ in the U.S. For the U.K., we found in part (b) that $P_W/P_C = 2$ in the absence of trade. Therefore, $P_C/P_W = 1/2$ in the U.K. Hence, the U.K. has a *comparative cost or price advantage* over the U.S. in cloth while the U.S. has the comparative advantage in wheat.

1.15 With respect to Problem 1.14, (a) express the limits for mutually advantageous trade in terms of P_W/P_C and P_C/P_W. (b) If P_C/P_W is stabilized at 1 with trade, how can you show the gains from trade for the U.S. and the U.K.?

(a) In Problem 1.14(b), we saw that in the absence of trade, $P_W/P_C = 1/2$ in the U.S. and 2 in the U.K. Thus, the limits for mutually advantageous trade are

$$1/2 < P_W/P_C < 2$$

In Problem 1.14(c), we saw that in the absence of trade, $P_C/P_W = 2$ in the U.S. and 1/2 in the U.K. Thus the limits for mutually advantageous trade are

$$1/2 < P_C/P_W < 2$$

Both results indicate that the U.S. has a *comparative cost or price advantage* over the U.K. in wheat and the U.K. has the comparative advantage in cloth.

(b) If $P_C/P_W = 1$ with trade, the U.S. gains by being able to import cloth from the U.K. at a smaller *relative* price than the U.S. could provide cloth for itself [since $P_C/P_W = 2$ in the U.S. in the absence of trade; see Problem 1.14(c)]. Put differently, this means that the U.S. can import 1C by giving up only 1W, while to produce cloth domestically, it would have to give up 2W for 1C [See Review Question 10(a)]. Since with trade, $P_C/P_W = 1$, $P_W/P_C = 1$ also. In the U.K. in the absence of trade, $P_W/P_C = 2$ [see Problem 1.14(b)]. Thus, the U.K. also gains from trade because it imports *wheat* at the relative price of 1, while to produce 1C domestically, it would have to pay the relative price of 2 [i.e., it would have to give up 2C for 1W domestically; see Review Question 10(b)].

1.16 Given Table 1.8 (the same as Table 1.5), (a) express the cost of producing wheat and cloth in the U.S. and in the U.K. *in terms of labor content*. (b) Find P_C/P_W for both the U.S. and the U.K. in the absence of trade. (c) Express the limits for mutually advantageous trade in terms of P_C/P_W. What does this result indicate?

Table 1.8

	U.S.	U.K.
Wheat (bushels/labor-hour)	4	2
Cloth (yards/labor-hour)	2	1

(a)   **Table 1.9**

	U.S.	U.K.
Cost in labor-hours to produce 1W	1/4	1/2
Cost in labor-hours to produce 1C	1/2	1

(b) For the U.S. in the absence of trade,

$$\frac{P_C}{P_W} = \frac{1/2}{1/4} = 2$$

For the U.K. in the absence of trade, $P_C/P_W = 1/(1/2) = 2$.

(c) $2 < P_C/P_W < 2$. This means that the price of cloth relative to the price of wheat is the same in both the U.S. and the U.K. in the absence of trade. Thus, there is no comparative cost or price advantage or disadvantage, and no mutually advantageous trade is possible.

1.17 With reference to Table 1.6 and assuming that the wage rate per labor-hour is $6 in the U.S. and £1.8 in the U.K. (the symbol £ stands for *pound*, the currency of England), (a) express P_W and P_C in the U.S. in terms of dollars and in the U.K. in terms of pounds, in the absence of trade. (b) Which commodity will the U.S. import and export if the exchange rate between the dollar and the pound is $3 per pound (i.e., £1 = $3)? (c) What if £1 = $0.50? (d) What if £1 = $2? If £1 = $1? (e) When will trade be balanced between the U.S. and the U.K.?

(a) Since 1 labor-hour receives $6 in the U.S. and produces 6W, $P_W = \$1$. Similarly, $P_C = \$2$ in the U.S. In the U.K., $P_W = £1.8$ and $P_C = £0.9$.

(b) If £1 = $3, $P_W = £1.8 = \$5.40$ and $P_C = £0.9 = \$2.70$ in the U.K. in the absence of trade. Since both P_W and P_C (in dollars) are lower in the U.S. than in the U.K., the U.S. will *export* both commodities to the U.K. If these are the only commodities traded, trade will be unbalanced in favor of the U.S. That is, the exchange rate between the dollar and the pound is so high that England's comparative advantage does not show.

(c) If £1 = $0.50, $P_W = £1.8 = \$0.90$ and $P_C = £0.90 = \$0.45$ in the U.K. in the absence of trade. The U.S. would then import both commodities and trade would be unbalanced in favor of the U.K. That is, the exchange rate between the dollar and the pound is so low that the American comparative advantage in wheat does not show.

(d) If £1 = $2, $P_W = £1.8 = \$3.60$ and $P_C = £0.90 = \$1.80$ in the U.K. in the absence of trade. Now P_W (in dollars) is lower and P_C (in dollars) is higher in the U.S. than in the U.K. The difference in relative commodity prices is now reflected in a difference in absolute prices in the U.S. and the U.K. Thus, the U.S. would export wheat to the U.K. and import cloth. If £1 = $1, $P_W = \$1.80$ and $P_C = \$0.90$ in the U.K. in the absence of trade. Therefore, the U.S exports wheat to the U.K. and imports cloth. As this occurs, P_W will rise in the U.S. and fall in the U.K. until P_W (when expressed in terms of a common currency) will be the same in both countries. The opposite occurs in cloth until P_C is the same in both countries. In the absence of transportation costs, trade will stop *expanding* when P_W and P_C (in terms of the same currency) are equalized in the two countries.

(e)   If the exchange rate between the dollar and the pound is free to fluctuate, and wheat and cloth are the only commodities produced and traded, the exchange rate will settle at the point at which the value of the U.S. exports of wheat to the U.K. equals the value of the U.S. cloth imports from the U.K. At this point, trade between the U.S. and the U.K. is balanced. If the exchange rate is fixed by international agreement, then the wage rate in each nation will have to change (rise in the nation with the export surplus and fall in the nation with the import surplus) until trade is balanced.

1.18   State the explicit and implicit assumptions on which Ricardo based his law of comparative advantage.

(1)   Two nations and two commodities

(2)   Free trade

(3)   Perfectly mobile labor within a nation but completely immobile labor internationally

(4)   Constant costs of production

(5)   No transportation costs

(6)   No technological change

(7)   The labor theory of value

Assumption 1 can easily be relaxed (see Problems 1.19 and 1.20). Assumption 7 must be rejected (see Problem 1.21). The main purpose of the modern theory of international trade is to explain the law of comparative advantage on the basis of an acceptable theory of value and to relax most of the assumptions made by Ricardo in explaining the basis and the gains from trade. This is done in the next two chapters.

1.19   If in the absence of trade, $P_W/P_C = 1/2$ in the U.S. and 2 in the U.K., the U.S. has a comparative advantage in and should export wheat to the U.K., while the U.K. has a comparative advantage in and should export cloth to the U.S. If we now add a third nation, Germany, where in the absence of trade $P_W/P_C = 1$, explain how multilateral trade among these three nations can take place.

Since in the absence of trade, P_W/P_C is lower in the U.S. than in the U.K. and Germany, the U.S. has a comparative advantage in and should export wheat. Since in the absence of trade, P_W/P_C is higher (thus P_C/P_W is lower) in the U.K. than in the U.S. and Germany, the U.K. has a comparative advantage in and should export cloth. The limits within which trade can benefit all three nations are $1/2 < P_W/P_C < 2$. If P_W/P_C *with trade* settles at a level greater than 1/2 but smaller than 1, the *U.S. should export wheat to both* the U.K. and Germany and *import cloth from both*. This pattern of trade will benefit all three nations. If on the other hand, P_W/P_C with trade settles at a level greater than 1 but smaller than 2, both the U.S. and Germany should export wheat to the U.K. and both should import cloth from the U.K. In the event that P_W/P_C with trade settles at 1, then, the U.S. should export wheat to the U.K. and the U.K. should export cloth to the U.S. Since P_W/P_C in the trade between the U.S. and the U.K. equals P_W/P_C in Germany *in the absence of trade*, it does not pay for Germany to trade in this case. The trade pattern in wheat and cloth among more than three nations can be determined in a similar fashion.

1.20   With reference to Table 1.10, determine which commodities will be exported and imported by the U.S. if   (a) £1 = $1,   (b) £1 = $2, and   (c) £1 = $0.50.

Table 1.10

Commodity	Price in the U.S. $	Price in the U.K. £
A	1	9
B	4	7
C	6	6
D	8	4
E	12	1

(a) In order to answer this (and the other questions), we must first express the price of all commodities in terms of the same currency and then compare the prices in the two nations. For example, the *dollar* price of the commodities in the U.K. when £1 = $1, are

Commodity	A	B	C	D	E
Dollar Price in the U.K.	9	7	6	4	1

In this case, the U.S. will export commodities A and B to the U.K. and import D and E.

(b) If £1 = $2, the dollar prices in the U.K. are

Commodity	A	B	C	D	E
Dollar Price in the U.K.	18	14	12	8	2

In this case, the U.S. will export commodities A, B and C to the U.K. and import commodity E.

(c) If £1 = $0.50, we have

Commodity	A	B	C	D	E
Dollar Price in the U.K.	4.50	3.50	3	2	0.50

Now the U.S. will export only commodity A to the U.K. and import all the others. This analysis can be extended to many more commodities and to more than two nations.

1.21   (a) What does the labor theory of value state?   (b) Why must we reject it?

(a) The labor theory of value states that the value or price of a commodity is equal to or can be inferred from the amount of labor time going into the production of the commodity. This implies that (1) either labor is the only factor of production or that labor is used in the *same* fixed proportion in the production of all commodities, and (2) labor is homogeneous (i.e., of only one type). Based on these assumptions, in Problem 1.14 we were able to say that since only 1/6 of a labor-hour is required to produce 1 unit of wheat while 1/3 of a labor-hour is required to produce 1 unit of cloth in the U.S. in the absence of trade, then $P_W = P_C/2$ in the U.S.

(b) The labor theory of value must be rejected because (1) labor is neither the only factor of production nor is it used in the same fixed proportion in the production of all commodities (some, such as steel, use much less labor per unit of capital than others, such as textiles; in addition, some substitution of labor for capital in production is usually possible); (2) labor is obviously not all of one type (some, such as doctors, embody much more skill, are much more productive and receive much higher wages than most others). For these reasons, the labor theory of value must be rejected. The modern theory of value overcomes these shortcomings and can be used to explain comparative advantage. This is done in Chapter 2 with the introduction of the opportunity cost theory and the production possibilities curve.

1.22   Figure 1-1 shows the result of an empirical test of the Ricardian trade model. The scales are logarithmic (so that equal distances refer to equal percentage changes). The vertical axis measures the ratio of the productivity of U.S. labor to U.K. labor. The horizontal axis measures the ratio of U.S. exports to

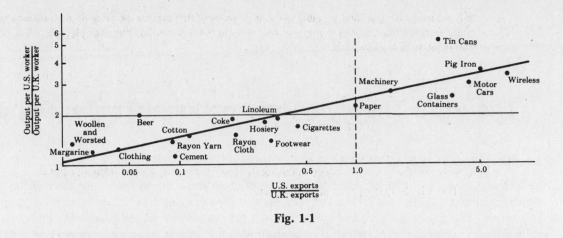

Fig. 1-1

SOURCE: G. D. A. MacDougal, "British and American Exports: A Study Suggested by the Theory of Comparative Costs," *Economic Journal*, December 1951, p. 703.

U.K. exports to the rest of the world in 20 industries. Does the figure tend to support or reject the Ricardian trade model? Why?

The figure supports the Ricardian trade model. That is, the higher the productivity of U.S. labor in relation to U.K. labor, the higher is the ratio of U.S. to U.K. exports. Thus, production costs other than labor costs, demand considerations and so on, did not break the link between relative labor productivities and export shares.

Chapter 2

The Pure Theory of International Trade: Supply

2.1 COMPARATIVE ADVANTAGE AND OPPORTUNITY COSTS

In Section 1.6, we saw that Ricardo based his law of comparative advantage on the labor theory of value, which is unacceptable. However, the law of comparative advantage can be explained in terms of the *opportunity cost theory*. This says that the cost of a commodity is the amount of a second commodity that must be given up in order to release just enough factors of production or resources to be able to produce one additional unit of the first commodity. Note that here labor is neither the only factor of production nor is it assumed that the cost or price of a commodity can be inferred from its labor content, or that labor is homogeneous. The nation with the lower opportunity cost for a commodity has a comparative advantage in that commodity and a comparative disadvantage in the other commodity.

EXAMPLE 1. If to produce one additional unit of cloth, the U.K. must forgo one-half unit of wheat (in order to release just enough resources to produce the additional unit of cloth), the opportunity cost of cloth in the U.K. is one-half unit of wheat. If at the same time, the U.S. (in the absence of trade) must forgo 2W to produce 1C more, the opportunity cost of 1C is 2W in the U.S. Since the opportunity cost of cloth is lower in the U.K. than in the U.S., the U.K. has a comparative cost advantage over the U.S. in cloth and the U.S. has a comparative advantage in wheat.

2.2 THE PRODUCTION POSSIBILITIES CURVE: CONSTANT COSTS

Opportunity costs can be illustrated with the *production possibilities curve* (also called the transformation curve). This shows all the various *alternative* combinations of the two commodities that a nation can produce by fully utilizing all of its factors of production with the best technology available. The slope of the production possibilities curve then refers to the *marginal rate of transformation* (MRT) or to the amount of a commodity that the nation must give up in order to get one more unit of the second commodity. If the nation faces constant costs or MRT, then its production possibilities curve is a straight line with (absolute) slope equal to the *constant opportunity costs* or MRT and to the *relative commodity price* in the nation (see Problem 1.14).

EXAMPLE 2. Table 2.1 gives the maximum amount of wheat *or* cloth that the U.K. and the U.S. could produce if they fully utilized all of the factors of production at their disposal with the best technology available to them.

Table 2.1

	U.K.	U.S.
Wheat (in millions of bushels/year)	60	160
Cloth (in millions of yards/year)	120	80

If, in addition, we were told that the opportunity cost of producing wheat and cloth is constant in each nation, we would get the production possibilities curves shown in Fig. 2-1. Note that each point on the curve represents one combination of wheat and cloth that the nation can produce. For example, at point A, the U.K. produces 40C and 40W. At point A',

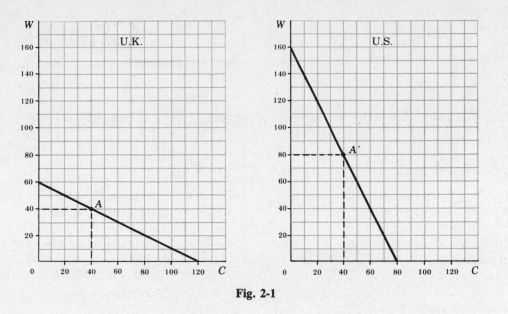

Fig. 2-1

the U.S. produces 40C and 80W. The more of one commodity the nation produces, the less it is able to produce of the other (i.e., the curves are negatively sloped). Moreover, the (absolute) slope of the curve for the U.K. is

$$\frac{60}{120} = \frac{1}{2} = \text{MRT}_{CW} = \frac{P_C}{P_W}$$

and remains constant. For the U.S., the slope is

$$\frac{160}{80} = 2 = \text{MRT}_{CW} = \frac{P_C}{P_W}$$

and remains constant. Note that in the case of constant costs, the internal equilibrium P_C/P_W in each nation is determined exclusively by the supply conditions in each nation.

2.3   THE BASIS FOR TRADE AND THE GAINS FROM TRADE UNDER CONSTANT COSTS

In *autarky* or the absence of trade, a nation's production possibilities curve or frontier also represents its *consumption frontier* (i.e., the nation can consume only a combination of commodities that it can produce). With trade, however, each nation can specialize in the production of the commodity of its comparative advantage, exchange part of this for the commodity of its comparative disadvantage and end up consuming more of both commodities than without trade.

EXAMPLE 3.   Suppose that in the absence of trade, the U.K. consumes (and produces) at point A while the U.S. does so at point A' in Fig. 2-2. (Points A and A' are dictated by tastes or demand conditions in each nation; these will be discussed in Chapter 3). Since in the absence of trade, $\text{MRT}_{CW} = P_C/P_W = 1/2$ (the slope of line AB) in the U.K. while $\text{MRT}_{CW} = P_C/P_W = 2$ (the slope of line $A'B'$) in the U.S., the U.K. has a comparative advantage in cloth and the U.S. has a comparative advantage in wheat. Mutually advantageous trade is possible within the limits: $1/2 < P_C/P_W < 2$ (see Problem 1.15). If P_C/P_W is stabilized at 1 with trade, the U.K. can move from point A to point B in production, exchange 60 of its 120C (produced at point B) for 60W from the U.S., and end up consuming at point E (which involves a gain in consumption of 20C and 20W over its no-trade consumption point, A). The U.S., on the other hand, moves from point A' to point B' in production, exchanges 60 of its 160W (produced at point B') or 60C from the U.K. and ends up consuming at point E' (with a gain of 20C and 20W over point A'). This is one possible outcome showing that each nation can gain by specializing completely in production and then trading.

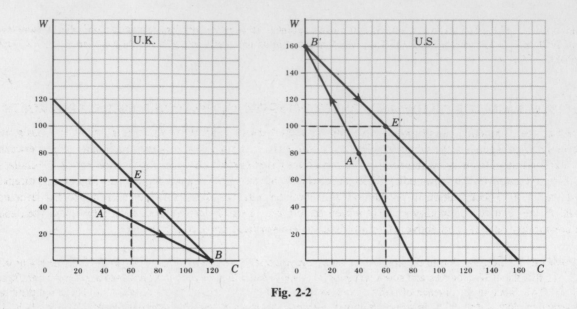

Fig. 2-2

2.4   THE PRODUCTION POSSIBILITIES CURVE: INCREASING COSTS

In the real world, it is more likely for a nation to face *increasing opportunity costs* or MRT in producing more units of a commodity. This is shown by a production possibilities curve that is concave to the origin. The nation will then produce where MRT equals the equilibrium relative commodity price in the nation. In the case of increasing costs, the equilibrium relative commodity price in the nation is determined by supply *and* demand conditions in the nation as shown in detail in Chapter 3. Here, we simply assume an internal equilibrium relative commodity price in each nation and determine where on its production possibilities curve each nation will produce at that price.

EXAMPLE 4.   Figure 2-3 gives hypothetical production possibilities curves for the U.K. and the U.S. showing increasing costs. If in the absence of trade, the internal equilibrium $P_C/P_W = 1/4$ in the U.K., the U.K. would produce at point A, where its $\text{MRT}_{CW} = P_C/P_W = 1/4$. If P_C/P_W rises, it would pay for the U.K. to produce more cloth and less wheat (a movement along the curve in a downward direction). However, as the U.K. does this, its MRT_{CW} rises. Thus, at $P_C/P_W = 1$, the U.K. produces at point B, where its $\text{MRT}_{CW} = P_C/P_W = 1$. Similarly, with $P_C/P_W = 4$, the U.S.

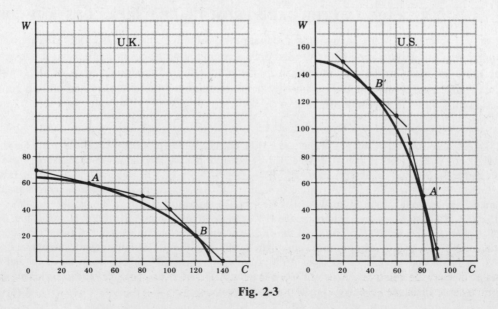

Fig. 2-3

produces at A'. If P_C/P_W falls to 1, the U.S. will move to point B' (thus producing less cloth and more wheat). Note that at point B', the U.S. incurs a lower MRT$_{CW}$, which means that its reciprocal or MRT$_{WC}$ is higher than at point A' (see Problem 2.14).

2.5   THE BASIS FOR TRADE AND THE GAINS FROM TRADE UNDER INCREASING COSTS

Whether the production possibilities curves are straight lines or concave to the origin, there is a basis for mutually advantageous trade whenever there is a difference in the pretrade relative commodity price between the two nations. However, when the production possibilities curves are concave, as each nation specializes in the production of the commodity of its comparative advantage, it incurs higher and higher opportunity costs or MRT. Specialization in production will continue until the rising MRT in each nation has become equal to the relative commodity price at which trade takes place. Through trade, each nation will then end up consuming outside (and above) its no-trade consumption (and production) frontier.

EXAMPLE 5.   Suppose that in the absence of trade, the internal equilibrium $P_C/P_W = 1/4$ in the U.K. and 4 in the U.S., so that the U.K. produces and consumes at point A while the U.S. produces and consumes at point A' (see Figs. 2-3 and 2-4). Since in the absence of trade, P_C/P_W is lower in the U.K. than in the U.S., the U.K. has a comparative advantage in cloth and the U.S. in wheat. Mutually advantageous trade is possible within the limits: $1/4 < P_C/P_W < 4$. If P_C/P_W is stabilized at 1 with trade, the U.K. can move from point A to point B in production, exchange 60 of its 120C (produced at point B) for 60W from the U.S., and end up consuming at point E (with a gain of 20C and 20W over point A; see Fig. 2-4). The U.S., on the other hand, moves from A' to B' in production, and, by exchanging 60W for 60C with the U.K., ends up at point E' (which involves 20C and 20W more than at A'). Note that as the U.K. specializes in the production of cloth, it incurs increasing costs in cloth production (i.e., a higher MRT$_{CW}$). Similarly, as the U.S. specializes in the production of wheat, the U.S. incurs increasing costs in wheat production (i.e., a higher MRT$_{WC}$). Specialization will continue in each country until its MRT$_{CW} = P_C/P_W = 1$. Also note that the U.K. and the U.S. do not specialize completely in the production of one commodity (as in the case of constant costs). Thus, with constant cost we have *complete specialization* in production while with increasing costs we have *incomplete specialization*.

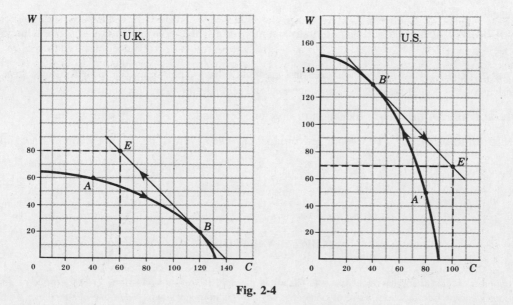

Fig. 2-4

2.6   THE DETERMINANTS OF COMPARATIVE ADVANTAGE

The difference in pretrade relative commodity prices (comparative advantage) between the two nations is based on a difference in factor endowments, technology, or tastes between the two nations. A difference in factor endowments or technology leads to a difference in the shape and location of each nation's production possibilities curve (see Fig. 2-3), which, unless neutralized by difference in tastes, will lead to different relative commodity prices and mutually beneficial trade (see Fig. 2-4). However, even if two nations have exactly the same factor endowments and technology (and thus identical production possibilities curves), a difference in tastes can be the basis for mutually beneficial trade (see Problem 2.21).

Glossary

Opportunity cost theory   This theory states that the cost of one commodity is the amount of another commodity that must be given up in order to release just enough factors of production or resources to enable the production of one additional unit of the first commodity.

Production possibilities curve   A curve that shows the various alternative combinations of the two commodities that a nation can produce by fully utilizing all of its factors of production with the best technology available to that particular nation. This curve is also known as the transformation curve or the production frontier.

Marginal rate of transformation (MRT)   The amount of one commodity that a nation must give up in order to get one more unit of the second commodity. This is another name for the opportunity cost of a commodity.

Constant opportunity costs   The equal amounts of one commodity that a nation must give up in order to release just enough resources to produce each additional unit of another commodity.

Relative commodity price   The ratio of the prices or costs of two commodities.

Autarky   The absence of trade; economic isolation.

Consumption frontier   The various alternative combinations of the two commodities that a nation can consume.

Increasing opportunity costs   The increasing amounts of one commodity that a nation must give up in order to release just enough resources to produce each additional unit of another commodity.

Complete specialization   The production of only one commodity in a nation with trade.

Incomplete specialization   The continued production, even with trade, of both commodities in both nations.

Review Questions

1. The opportunity cost theory assumes that   (a) labor is the only factor of production,   (b) the price or cost of a commodity can be inferred from its labor content,   (c) labor is homogeneous,   (d) none of the above.

   Ans.   (d) See Section 2.1.

2. With respect to a production possibilities curve, we can say that   (a) a point inside or below it implies that the economy is either not utilizing fully all of its resources or not using the best technology available to it,   (b) a point on it involves the full employment of the economy's resources and the use of the best technology available,   (c) a

point above it cannot be reached with the resources and technology presently available to the nation,   (d) all of the above.

Ans.   (d) See Section 2.2.

3. A straight-line production possibilities curve refers to   (a) constant costs,   (b) increasing costs,   (c) decreasing costs,   (d) any of the above.

Ans.   (a) See Example 2.

4. With cloth measured along the horizontal axis and wheat along the vertical axis, the absolute slope of a straight-line production possibilities curve gives   (a) the MRT_{CW},   (b) the P_C/P_W,   (c) both the MRT_{CW} and the P_C/P_W,   (d) neither the MRT_{CW} nor the P_C/P_W.

Ans.   (c) See Example 2.

5. If in the absence of trade, the internal equilibrium P_C/P_W is lower in the U.K. than in the U.S., then   (a) the U.K. has a comparative advantage in cloth with respect to the U.S.,   (b) the U.K. has a comparative disadvantage in wheat,   (c) the U.S. has a comparative advantage in wheat,   (d) the U.S. has a comparative disadvantage in cloth,   (e) all of the above.

Ans.   (e) See Examples 3 and 5.

6. The production frontier for the U.K. in Fig. 2-2 is given by the straight line through points   (a) A and B in the absence of trade, and E and B with trade;   (b) A and B with trade, and E and B without trade;   (c) E and B with and without trade;   (d) A and B with and without trade.

Ans.   (d) See Example 3. Note that the U.K. could have produced at point B even without trade, but the U.K. did not want to consume at point B (i.e., 120C and 0W) without trade.

7. If a nation gains from trade, its consumption point is   (a) on its production possibilities frontier,   (b) inside its production possibilities frontier,   (c) above its production possibilities frontier,   (d) any of the above.

Ans.   (c) See Examples 3 and 5.

8. Increasing opportunity costs to produce more and more units of a commodity is given by a production possibilities curve that is   (a) concave to the origin,   (b) convex to the origin,   (c) a straight line,   (d) any of the above.

Ans.   (a) See Fig. 2-3.

9. With cloth measured along the horizontal axis and wheat along the vertical axis, the absolute slope of a concave production possibilities curve gives   (a) the MRT_{CW},   (b) the internal equilibrium P_C/P_W in isolation,   (c) both the MRT_{CW} and the internal equilibrium P_C/P_W,   (d) neither the MRT_{CW} nor the internal equilibrium P_C/P_W.

Ans.   (a) See Section 2.4.

10. With cloth measured along the horizontal axis and wheat along the vertical axis, a movement down the production possibilities curve results in   (a) a decrease in MRT_{CW},   (b) an increase in MRT_{CW},   (c) an increase in MRT_{WC},   (d) any of the above.

Ans.   (b) See Example 4.

11. With trade, specialization in production is likely to be   (a) complete with increasing costs and incomplete with constant costs,   (b) complete with constant costs and incomplete with increasing costs,   (c) complete with constant and increasing costs,   (d) incomplete with both constant and increasing costs.

Ans.   (b) Compare production points B and B' in Fig. 2-2 with those in Fig. 2-4.

12. A difference in relative commodity prices between two nations can be based upon a difference in   (a) factor endowments,   (b) technology,   (c) tastes,   (d) all of the above.

Ans.   (d) See Section 2.6.

Solved Problems

COMPARATIVE ADVANTAGE AND OPPORTUNITY COSTS

2.1 (a) Compare the explanation of the law of comparative advantage given by Ricardo with that based on the opportunity cost theory. (b) Identify the three main groups of factors of production and some of the major subgroups. (c) Name some of the most important products in which the U.S. has a comparative cost or price advantage and some in which the U.S. has a comparative disadvantage.

(a) Ricardo's explanation of the law of comparative advantage is based on the labor theory of value. This theory holds that labor is the only factor of production (or that labor is used in the same fixed proportion in the production of all commodities), it assumes that labor is homogeneous (i.e., of only one type) and concludes that the cost or price of a commodity is equal to (or can be inferred from) its labor content. Since labor is assumed to be homogeneous within each nation but nonhomogeneous (i.e., of different productivities) in different nations, we have constant costs of production within a nation but comparative advantage and disadvantage between nations. We reject this explanation of the law of comparative advantage because it is based on the unacceptable labor theory of value. The opportunity cost theory, which is acceptable, recognizes that various nonhomogeneous factors of production are usually combined in different proportions to produce various products and also allows for increasing (opportunity) costs in producing more of each product. The law of comparative advantage can then be explained in terms of different opportunity costs or relative commodity prices in different nations.

(b) The three main groups of factors of production, economic resources or inputs are: *labor, capital* and *land*. Each group can be broken down into many subgroups. For example, labor includes unskilled, semiskilled, skilled and entrepreneurial. Capital may be liquid (such as money) and nonliquid (such as machinery, factories, etc.). Land might be subdivided into agricultural, mineral-bearing, industrial and residential areas. Moreover, each of these subgroups can be further subdivided into numerous more detailed types, each commanding a specific price, having a particular productivity in each of its possible uses, and a specific short-run and long-run demand and supply elasticity. It should be evident that there are many nonhomogeneous factors rather than one or a few homogeneous ones.

(c) The U.S. has a comparative advantage in and exports: products with high technological content (such as aircrafts, computers and electronics), construction and mining machinery and equipment; some chemicals and pharmaceuticals, and several agricultural commodities (such as soy beans, grains, tobacco and cotton). On the other hand, the U.S. has a comparative disadvantage in and imports many labor-intensive commodities such as textiles, shoes, bicycles, motorcycles, sewing machines and also some types of machinery, small cars and ships. To be noted is that comparative advantage and disadvantage is not settled once and for all for a nation but changes over time. For example, the U.S. lost the comparative advantage that it once had in textiles and leather goods and, more recently, in steel and automobiles. In this connection, it is often said that the U.S. has a comparative advantage in research and innovation but that it loses it to other nations as products become standardized and other nations learn how to manufacture them through imitation.

THE BASIS FOR TRADE AND THE GAINS FROM TRADE UNDER CONSTANT COSTS

2.2 Table 2.2 gives the maximum amount of wheat *or* cloth that the U.K. and U.S. could produce if they fully utilized all of the factors of production at their disposal with the best technology available to them.

Table 2.2

	U.K.	U.S.
Wheat (in millions of bushels/year)	50	120
Cloth (in millions of yards/year)	150	80

If, in addition, we are told that the (opportunity) cost of producing wheat and cloth is always constant in each nation, (*a*) draw the production possibilities curves of the U.K. and the U.S., (*b*) indicate some of the combinations of wheat and cloth that each nation can produce and (*c*) specify the consumption choices open to each nation in the absence of trade.

(*a*)   See Fig. 2-5.

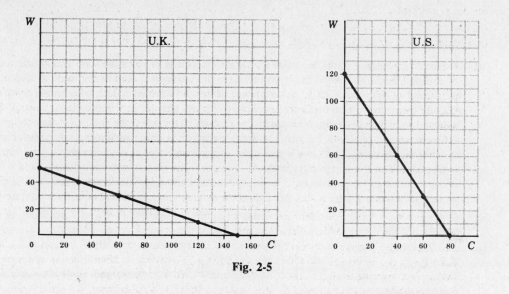

Fig. 2-5

(*b*)   Table 2.3 gives some of the *alternative* combinations of wheat and cloth that the U.K. and the U.S. can produce (all figures are in millions of units per year).

Table 2.3

U.K.		U.S.	
W	C	W	C
50	0	120	0
40	30	90	20
30	60	60	50
20	90	30	60
10	120	0	80
0	150		

Points inside or below the production possibilities curves of Fig. 2-5 are also possible but inefficient. Points above the curves cannot be reached with the present supplies of factors of production and technology available.

(*c*)   In the absence of trade, each nation can only choose to consume from among the alternative combinations of wheat and cloth that it can produce. When this is the case, a nation's production possibilities curve or frontier also represents its consumption frontier. Which one of the many alternative combinations of wheat and cloth the nation will actually produce and consume depends on tastes or demand conditions in the nation (see Section 3.1).

2.3   (*a*) With reference to Fig. 2-5, find MRT$_{CW}$ for the U.K. and the U.S. Does MRT$_{CW}$ vary as we move along each nation's production possibilities curve? Why? (*b*) Under what conditions will a nation face constant costs, constant MRT_{CW} or a straight-line production possibilities curve?   (c) Find P_C/P_W and P_W/P_C for the U.K. and the U.S. from Fig. 2-5. What is the relationship between P_C/P_W and MRT_{CW} in each nation?

(a)   The MRT_{CW} measures by how much the nation must reduce its output of wheat in order to release just enough factors of production to produce exactly one more unit of cloth. MRT_{CW} is given by the (absolute) slope of the production possibilities or transformation curve. Thus for the U.K., $MRT_{CW} = 50/150 = 1/3$. For the U.S., $MRT_{CW} = 120/80 = 3/2$. Since each production possibilities or transformation curve of Fig. 2-5 is a straight line, its slope or MRT_{CW} remains the same throughout the entire length of the curve. Thus, we have a case of constant (opportunity) costs.

(b)   A nation will be facing constant costs only if (1) the factors of production are perfect substitutes for each other or are used in the same fixed proportions in the production of both commodities and (2) all units of each factor of production are homogeneous or of the same quality. Then, as a nation transfers resources from the production of wheat to the production of cloth, the nation will not have to use resources which become less and less suited for the production of cloth. As a result, the nation will have to give up exactly the same amount of wheat for each additional unit of cloth produced—regardless of how far the process has already proceeded. The same is true if the nation wants to produce more wheat. Thus, the cost of each additional unit of the commodity produced in terms of the other is always the same, and we have a case of constant costs. This is seldom, if ever, true in the real world. The constant cost case is discussed first because it provides a good model from which to develop more sophisticated and realistic models.

(c)   As long as each nation produces something of both commodities, P_C/P_W in each nation is given by the (absolute) slope of its (straight-line) production possibilities curve or transformation curve. P_W/P_C is then the reciprocal or inverse of P_C/P_W. Thus, for the U.K., $P_C/P_W = 50/150 = 1/3$ and $P_W/P_C = 3$. For the U.S., $P_C/P_W = 120/80 = 3/2$ and $P_W/P_C = 2/3$. $P_C/P_W = MRT_{CW}$ in each nation and remains constant. Thus, under constant costs, the internal equilibrium P_C/P_W in each nation is determined exclusively by the supply conditions in the nation.

2.4   With reference to Problems 2.2 and 2.3,   (a) indicate in which commodity the U.K. and the U.S. have a comparative advantage.   (b) What are the limits within which mutually advantageous exchange can take place between the U.K. and the U.S.?   (c) If P_C/P_W is stabilized at 1 with trade, explain why the U.K. and the U.S. gain.   (d) How is this problem different from Problem 1.9?

(a)   Since P_C/P_W is lower in the U.K. (1/3) than in the U.S. (3/2) [see Problem 2.3(a)], the U.K. has a comparative advantage over the U.S. in cloth and the U.S. has a comparative advantage in wheat.

(b)   The limits for mutually advantageous trade are: $1/3 < P_C/P_W < 3/2$.

(c)   If P_C/P_W is stabilized at 1 with trade, the U.K. gains because it can get each unit of wheat it wants to consume by giving up only 1 unit of cloth through trade, while it would have to give up 3 units of cloth domestically (i.e., without trade). The U.S. also gains because it can get each unit of cloth it wants to consume by giving up only 1W through trade rather than 1.5W in the absence of trade. Note that in this case the U.K. gains more than the U.S. from trade.

(d)   In Problem 1.9 the explanation of the law of comparative advantage was based on the labor theory of value, while here it is based on the opportunity cost theory. Note that both here and in Problem 1.9, $P_C/P_W = 1/3$ for the U.K. and 3/2 for the U.S. in the absence of trade.

2.5   Starting with Fig. 2-5 and assuming that the U.K. produces 60C and 30W and the U.S. 40C and 60W in the absence of trade, show the point of production and consumption for each nation with trade, if each nation specializes completely in the production of the commodity of its comparative advantage and then trade 50 units of it for 50 units of the commodity of its comparative disadvantage.

In Fig. 2-6, the U.K. produces and consumes at point A in the absence of trade, while the U.S. is at point A'. Since the U.K. has a comparative advantage in cloth and the U.S. in wheat, with complete specialization in production, the U.K. will be at point B and the U.S. at point B'. Since the U.K. exchanges 50C for 50W with the U.S., the U.K. will move to point E in consumption and the U.S. to point E'. Thus both the U.K. and the U.S. gain from specialization and trade.

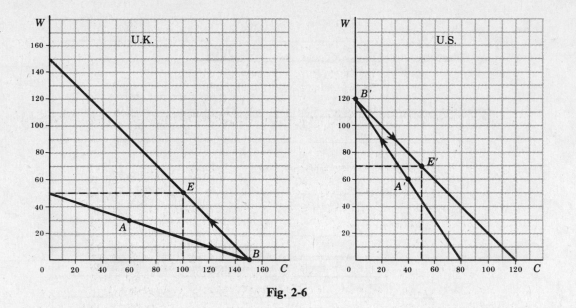

Fig. 2-6

2.6   An alternative to Fig. 2-6 to illustrate the gains from trade under constant costs is obtained by rotating by 180° the U.S. production possibilities curve and superimposing it on the U.K. production possibilities curve in such a way that points B and B' coincide.   (a) Draw such a figure and shade the area showing the total gains from trade.   (b) What does line BE in your figure show?

(a)   See Fig. 2-7.

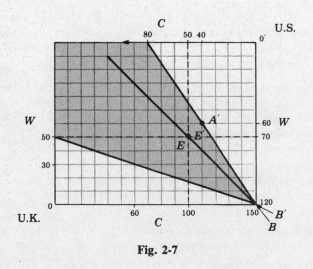

Fig. 2-7

(b)   Line BE (the same as $B'E'$) shows how the total gains from trade are divided between the two nations.

2.7   With reference to Figs. 2-6 and 2-7,   (a) indicate the quantity of wheat and cloth *produced* in the U.K., in the U.S. and in total before and after specialization in production, and the change in the production of each commodity in each nation and in total.   (b) Indicate the quantity of wheat and cloth *consumed* in the U.K., in the U.S. and in total before and after trade, and the gain in the consumption of each commodity in each nation and in total.

(a)

Table 2.4

| | PRODUCTION | | | | | |
| | Before Specialization | | After Specialization | | Change | |
	W	C	W	C	W	C
U.K.	30	60	0	150	−30	+90
U.S.	60	40	120	0	+60	−40
Total	90	100	120	150	+30	+50

(b)

Table 2.5

| | CONSUMPTION | | | | | |
| | Before Trade | | After Trade | | Gains | |
	W	C	W	C	W	C
U.K.	30	60	50	100	20	40
U.S.	60	40	70	50	10	10
Total	90	100	120	150	30	50

2.8   With reference to Problem 2.7,   (a) explain how the combined output of the U.K. and the U.S. for both wheat and cloth can increase without any increase in the quantity of the factors of production available to either the U.S. or the U.K.   (b) Why didn't the U.K. and the U.S. want to specialize in production in the absence of trade?   (c) What is the effect of trade on the relationship between production and consumption in each nation?   (d) What is the ratio of exchange of cloth for wheat between the U.K. and the U.S.?   (e) Why is this the equilibrium ratio of exchange?   (f) What would happen if the exchange ratio was above or below the equilibrium one?

(a)   The combined output of the U.K. and the U.S. for both wheat and cloth increased because each nation specialized in the production of the commodity of its comparative advantage. Note that this involves production on a different point but *on the same production possibilities curve*. The production possibilities curve of each nation remains unchanged because the quantity of factors of production (and technology) were assumed to remain constant in each nation.

(b)   The U.K. and the U.S. did not want to take advantage of specialization in production in the absence of trade because the U.K. did not want to consume only cloth and the U.S. did not want to consume only wheat. Only when the possibility of trade is open will this specialization in production be desirable and advantageous.

(c)   Trade causes an imbalance between the nation's production and consumption. That is, with trade each nation usually ends up consuming a greater range of products than it produces.

(d)   Since 50C are exchanged for 50W, the ratio of exchange or $P_C/P_W = 1$. Note that at this ratio of exchange, the U.K. gains more than the U.S. from trade [see Problem 2.7(b)].

(e)   This is the equilibrium ratio of exchange because at $P_C/P_W = 1$, the quantity of cloth imports *demanded* by the U.S. exactly equals the quantity of cloth exports *supplied* by the U.K. and the quantity of wheat imports *demanded* by the U.K. exactly equals the quantity of wheat exports *supplied* by the U.S.

(f)   At $P_C/P_W > 1$, the quantity of cloth imports demanded by the U.S. *falls short* of the quantity of cloth exports supplied by the U.K. and there will be a pressure on P_C/P_W to fall toward the equilibrium value of 1. At $P_C/P_W < 1$, the quantity of cloth imports demanded by the U.S. *exceeds* the quantity of cloth exports supplied by the U.K. and there will be a pressure on P_C/P_W to rise toward the equilibrium level. The same thing could be expressed in terms of wheat, as follows. At $P_W/P_C > 1$, the quantity of wheat imports demanded by the U.K. falls short of the quantity of wheat exports supplied by the U.S. and so there will be a pressure on P_W/P_C to rise to 1. At $P_W/P_C < 1$, the exact opposite occurs.

2.9 Draw a figure and explain what happens if, starting from points A and A' in Fig. 2-1, the U.K. and the U.S. specialize completely in the production of the commodity of their respective comparative advantage and then exchange 80C for 40W with each other.

In Fig. 2-8, the U.K. moves from point A to point B in production while the U.S. moves from A' to B' (so far this is exactly the same as in Example 3). Since 80C are exchanged for 40W, the equilibrium P_C/P_W or terms of trade = 1/2, which is the same as the pretrade P_C/P_W in the U.K. Thus the U.K. gains nothing from trade (indeed, in this case, point E coincides with point A so that the U.K. consumes exactly the same combination of 40C and 40W with trade as without trade; see Fig. 2-8). The U.S. moves from point B' in production to point E' in consumption and captures all of the gains from trade of 40C and 40W [compare point E' to the no-trade production and consumption point A' in Fig. 2-8; see also Problem 1.12(c)]. If, after specializing completely in production, the U.K. exchanged a different quantity of cloth for wheat at the equilibrium P_C/P_W of 1/2, the U.K. would end up consuming at a different point on its production possibilities curve, but once again it will gain nothing from trade (in the sense that the U.K. could have produced and consumed that combination of wheat and cloth without trade).

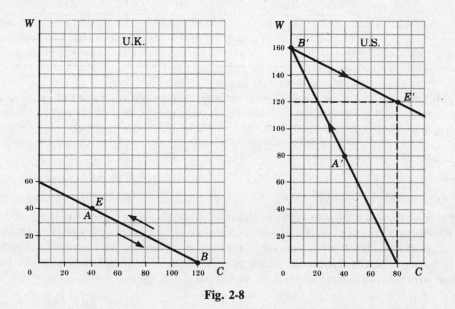

Fig. 2-8

2.10 (a) Draw a figure and explain what happens if, starting from points A and A' in Fig. 2-1, 30C are exchanged for 60W. (b) What generalization can you reach with regard to specialization in production and the distribution of the gains from trade between the two nations by looking at Example 3 and Problems 2.9 and 2.10(a)?

(a) In Fig. 2-9, the U.K. moves from point A to point B in production while the U.S. moves from A' to B'. Note that in this case, the U.K. specializes completely in the production of cloth (point B) but the U.S. does not specialize completely in the production of wheat (i.e., at point B', the U.S. continues to produce some cloth). This occurs because the U.K. is too small a nation to provide all of the cloth demanded by the U.S. at the equilibrium P_C/P_W of 2 (resulting when 30C are exchanged for 60W; see Fig. 2-9). Since the equilibrium P_C/P_W is the same as the pretrade P_C/P_W in the U.S., the U.S. gains nothing from trade (its consumption point with trade, E', coincides with its pretrade consumption point, A'). The U.K. thus captures all of the gains from trade of 50C and 20W [see Fig. 2-9; see also Problem 1.12(b)].

(b) With constant costs, if the equilibrium relative commodity price with trade is *between* the pretrade relative

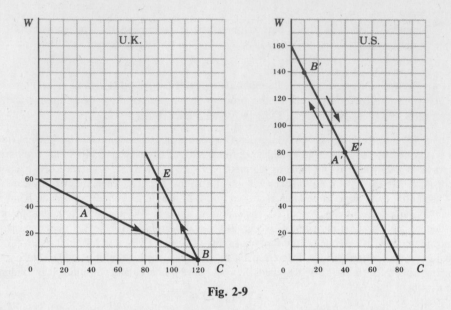

Fig. 2-9

commodity prices in each nation, then each nation specializes completely in production and each gains from trade (see Example 3 and Problem 2.5). If the equilibrium price with trade is the same as the pretrade price in one of the nations, that nation may or may not specialize completely in production (compare Fig. 2-8 with Fig. 2-9) and the nation gains nothing from trade. Its trade partner, on the other hand, will always specialize completely in production (see Figs. 2-8 and 2-9) and will capture all of the gains from trade. The most likely of the two cases when one of the nations gains nothing is that discussed in Problem 2.10(a), where a very small nation (certainly not the U.K.) might trade at the pretrade prices in a large nation, specialize completely in production and capture all of the gains from trade. This is sometimes referred to as "the importance of being unimportant." The large nation then will not be completely specialized in production and gains nothing from trade.

2.11 Starting at points A and A' in Fig. 2-1, suppose that the U.K. and the U.S. specialize in production and then exchange 60C for wheat at the equilibrium P_C/P_W of 4/3.   (a) How much wheat is traded? (b) Will specialization in production be complete in each nation? Why?   (c) Draw a figure showing the pretrade point of production and consumption in each nation, the point of production with specialization, and the new consumption point with trade.   (d) Which nation gains more from trade? Compare the distribution of the gains in this problem with that in Example 3.

(a)   In order for the equilibrium P_C/P_W to be 4/3 when 60C are traded, these 60C must exchange for 80W (so that 1C = 1 1/3W and P_C/P_W = 1 1/3 or 4/3).

(b)   Since the equilibrium P_C/P_W with trade (4/3) lies between the pretrade P_C/P_W in the U.K. (1/2) and in the U.S. (2), each nation will specialize *completely* in the production of the commodity of its comparative advantage [see Problem 2.10(b)]. Specifically, since the U.K. must always give up only 1/2W to produce 1C and can always exchange each 1C for 1 1/3W with the U.S., it pays for the U.K. to specialize completely in the production of cloth. The U.S. also (and for the analogous reason) will want to specialize completely in the production of wheat.

(c)   In Fig. 2-10, the pretrade point of production and consumption for the U.K. is A and for the U.S. is A'. With trade, the U.K. will produce at point B and the U.S. at point B' (so far this is identical to Example 3). From point B, the U.K. exchanges 60C for 80W with the U.S. and reaches point E. The U.S. goes from point B' to E' (see Fig. 2-10).

(d)   In Fig. 2-10, the U.K. consumes 20C and 40W more at point E than at point A. At point E', the U.S. consumes only 20C more than at point A'. Thus the U.K. gains more than the U.S. from trade. This result is to be contrasted to that in Example 3, where at the equilibrium P_C/P_W of 1 with trade, each nation gains exactly the same (20C and 20W; see Fig. 2-2) from trade.

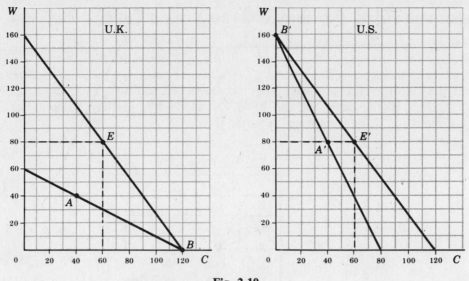

Fig. 2-10

2.12 If one of the values in Table 2.1 were changed as indicated in Table 2.6 and we retained our assumption of constant (opportunity) costs in each nation, would mutually advantageous trade still be possible between the U.K. and the U.S.? Why?

Table 2.6

	U.K.	U.S.
Wheat (in millions of bushels/year)	60	160
Cloth (in millions of yards/year)	30	80

Since the (straight-line) production possibilities curves in Fig. 2-11 have identical (absolute) slopes ($= \text{MRT}_{CW} = $ pretrade P_C/P_W of 1/2), we cannot speak of comparative advantage or disadvantage between the two nations and no mutually advantageous trade is possible [see Problem 1.11(*c*)].

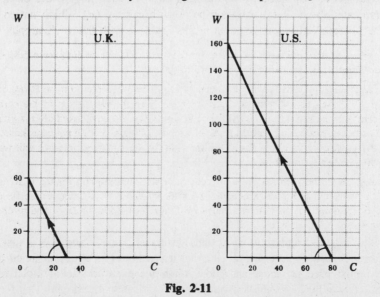

Fig. 2-11

THE BASIS FOR TRADE AND THE GAINS FROM TRADE UNDER INCREASING COSTS

2.13   Table 2.7 gives five alternative combinations of wheat and cloth (in millions of units/year) that the U.K. and the U.S. can produce by fully utilizing all of the factors of production at their disposal with the best technology available to them.   (*a*) Sketch the production possibilities curve for the U.K. and the U.S. What is MRT_{CW} in the U.K. if it produces 60C and 50W? 130C and 20W? What is MRT_{CW} in the U.S. if it produces 80C and 20W? 40C and 90W?   (*b*) Why is the production possibilities curve of the U.K. different from that of the U.S.?

Table 2.7

U.K.		U.S.	
W	C	W	C
52	0	120	0
50	60	90	40
35	110	60	65
20	130	20	80
0	143	0	81

(*a*)   Figure 2-12 gives the production possibilities curves of the U.K. and the U.S. Points below and inside each production possibilities curve are also possible but inefficient. Points above each curve cannot be reached with the present supplies of factors of production and technology available to each nation. At point *A*, MRT_{CW} = the (absolute) slope of the curve = 1/6 in the U.K. (see Fig. 2-12). At *B*, MRT_{CW} = 1. For the U.S., MRT_{CW} = 6 at point *A'* and MRT_{CW} = 1 at point *B'*.

(*b*)   The production possibilities curve for the U.K. is different from that of the U.S. because the U.K. has different factor endowments and may be using a different technology than the U.S. In general, the production possibilities curves of different nations are different. When the supply of factors of production and technology change through time, the production possibilities curves shift. The type and extent of the shift depend on the type and extent of the changes occurring. These are discussed in Chapter 5.

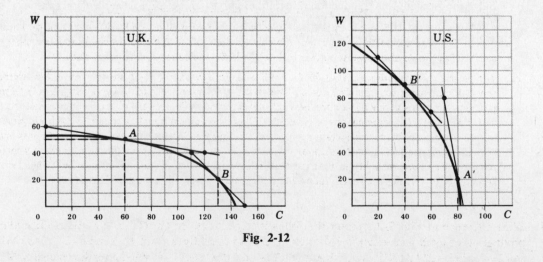

Fig. 2-12

2.14   (*a*) Redraw Fig. 2-3 and show on it that starting at point *A*, the U.K. must give up more and more wheat for each additional batch of 20C that it wants to produce. Also show that starting at point *A'*, the U.S. must give up more and more cloth for each additional batch of 20W that it wants to produce.   (*b*) What does the answer to part (*a*) imply for the MRT_{CW} for a movement down the

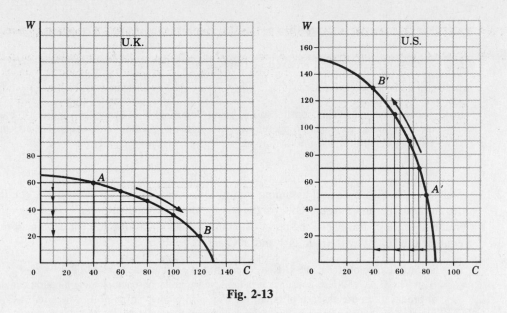

Fig. 2-13

production possibilities curve of the U.K.? For the MRT_{WC} for a movement up the production possibilities curve of the U.S.?   (c) Explain the reason for the shape of the production possibilities curves of the U.K. and the U.S.

(a) See Fig. 2-13.

(b) MRT_{CW} (reads: the marginal rate of transformation of *cloth* for wheat) is given by the (absolute) slope of the production possibilities or transformation curve. It measures how much a nation must reduce its output of *wheat* in order to release just enough factors of production to produce each additional unit of cloth. Thus, the U.K. moves from point A to point B in production, MRT_{CW} increases, indicating that the U.K. faces increasing opportunity costs to produce each additional unit of cloth (see Fig. 2-13). On the other hand, MRT_{WC} (reads: the marginal rate of transformation of *wheat* for cloth) is given by the inverse or reciprocal of the (absolute) slope of the production possibilities or transformation curve. It measures how much a nation must reduce its output of *cloth* in order to release just enough factors of production to produce each additional unit of wheat. Thus, as the U.S. moves from point A' to B' in production, MRT_{WC} increases, indicating that the U.S. faces increasing opportunity costs to produce each additional unit of wheat (see Fig. 2-13). Note that MRT_{WC} would also increase for the U.K. if the U.K. wanted to produce more wheat and MRT_{CW} would also increase for the U.S. if the U.S. wanted to produce more cloth.

(c) The production possibilities curves for the U.K. and the U.S. in Fig. 2-13 are concave to the origin, thus showing increasing (opportunity) costs. This is the usual case. Increasing costs result if (1) factors of production are only partial (rather than perfect) substitutes for each other and (2) each commodity is produced with different factor combinations or intensities. Then, as a nation transfers resources from the production of one commodity to the production of another, the nation will have to use factors that are less and less suitable to the production of the second commodity. As a result, the nation will have to give up more and more of the first commodity to produce each additional unit of the second commodity. Thus, we have increasing opportunity costs and production possibilities curves that are concave to the origin.

2.15   With reference to Fig. 2-3, answer the following questions *for the U.S.:*   (a) What change in the production of cloth and wheat is indicated by a movement from point A' to point B'?   (b) What is MRT_{CW} at point A'? At B'?   (c) What is MRT_{WC} at A'? At B'?   (d) What does the change in MRT_{WC} in moving from point A' to point B' mean for the U.S.? What is this change in MRT_{WC} due to?

(a) At point A', the U.S. produces 80C and 50W (see Fig. 2-3). At point B', the U.S. produces 40C and 130W. Thus, a movement from A' to B' indicates a change of production in the U.S. of −40C and +80W.

(b) At point A', $MRT_{CW} = 4$ (the absolute slope of the U.S. production possibilities curve at point A'; see

Fig. 2-3). At point B', $\text{MRT}_{CW} = 1$. A movement from A' to B' then results in a reduction in MRT_{CW} from 4 to 1.

(c) MRT_{WC} is the reciprocal or inverse of MRT_{CW} [see Problem 2.14(b)]. Thus at point A', $\text{MRT}_{WC} = 1/4$ in the U.S. At point B', $\text{MRT}_{WC} = 1$. A movement from A' to B' then results in an *increase* in MRT_{WC} from 1/4 to 1.

(d) The increase in MRT_{WC} from 1/4 to 1 in going from A' to B' indicates that in order to produce more wheat, the U.S. incurs increasing (opportunity) costs in terms of cloth. This occurs because the production possibilities curve is concave to the origin.

2.16 Starting with Fig. 2-12 and assuming that in the absence of trade, the internal equilibrium $P_C/P_W = 1/6$ in the U.K. and 6 in the U.S., show (a) the point of production and consumption for each nation in the absence of trade, (b) the point of production and consumption for each nation with trade if the equilibrium P_C/P_W with trade is 1 and 50C are traded.

(a) In the absence of trade, the U.K. will produce at point A where its $\text{MRT}_{CW} = P_C/P_W = 1/6$ (see Fig. 2-12). The U.K. will also consume at point A, since in the absence of trade a nation can only consume what it produces. In the absence of trade, the U.S. will produce at point A' where its $\text{MRT}_{CW} = P_C/P_W = 6$. Point A' then also represents the no-trade consumption point for the U.S.

(b) Since in the absence of trade, the internal equilibrium P_C/P_W in the U.K. is different (lower) than in the U.S., mutually advantageous trade is possible. At the equilibrium $P_C/P_W = 1$ with trade, the U.K. moves from point A to point B in production. By then exchanging 50C for 50W with the U.S., the U.K. ends up consuming at point E, which is superior to A (the no-trade consumption point; see Fig. 2-14). With trade, the U.S. moves from A' to B' in production, exchanges 50W for 50C and ends up at E' (which is superior to A'). Note that with increasing costs, specialization in production is incomplete.

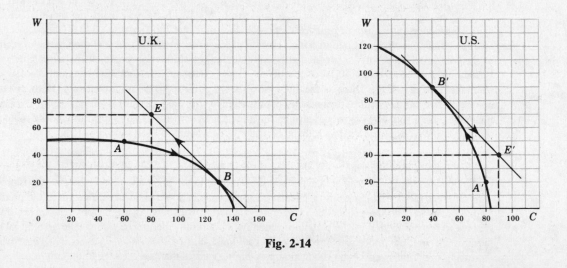

Fig. 2-14

2.17 From Fig. 2-14, (a) explain why it does not pay for the U.K. to continue to specialize in the production of cloth past point B. (b) Construct a table similar to Table 2.4 in Problem 2.7(a). (c) Construct a table similar to Table 2.5 in Problem 2.7(b).

(a) Past point B in Fig. 2-14, MRT_{CW} in the U.K. is higher than P_C/P_W in trade, and so it does not pay for the U.K. to continue to specialize in the production of cloth. Another way of saying this is that past point B, MRT_{WC} in the U.K. is smaller than P_W/P_C in trade, and so it pays for the U.K. to continue to produce some of its wheat (i.e., with increasing costs, specialization in production is incomplete).

(b)

Table 2.8

	PRODUCTION					
	Before Specialization		After Specialization		Change	
	W	C	W	C	W	C
U.K.	50	60	20	130	−30	+70
U.S.	20	80	90	40	+70	−40
Total	70	140	110	170	+40	+30

(c)

Table 2.9

	CONSUMPTION					
	Before Trade		After Trade		Gains	
	W	C	W	C	W	C
U.K.	50	60	70	80	20	20
U.S.	20	80	40	90	20	10
Total	70	140	110	170	+40	+30

Note that in this case, as opposed to Example 5, the gains from trade are not shared equally by the two nations.

2.18 (a) What determines the internal equilibrium P_C/P_W in each nation in the absence of trade? (b) Starting with Fig. 2-12, explain what happens if the U.K. is in internal equilibrium in production *and* consumption at point B in the absence of trade, while the U.S. is in internal equilibrium in production and consumption at point B'. (c) What if the U.K. is in internal equilibrium in production and consumption to the right of B while the U.S. position is to the left of B'?

(a) The internal equilibrium P_C/P_W in each nation in the absence of trade is determined by both the supply conditions in the nation (as summarized by its production possibilities curve) and the tastes or demand conditions in the nation (which determine at which point on its production possibilities curve the nation will consume and produce). This is discussed in detail in Chapter 3. All we need to add here is that the slope of the nation's production possibilities curve at the point where the nation is in equilibrium in production *and* consumption gives the internal equilibrium P_C/P_W in the nation. It is this pretrade, internal equilibrium P_C/P_W in each nation that determines the pattern of specialization in production and in trade.

(b) If tastes or demand conditions are such that the U.K. is in internal equilibrium in production and consumption at point B in the absence of trade, while the U.S. is at point B', the pretrade $\mathrm{MRT}_{CW} = P_C/P_W = 1$ in both the U.K. and the U.S. (see Fig. 2-12), and so no mutually advantageous trade is possible.

(c) If in the absence of trade, the U.K. is in internal equilibrium in production and consumption to the right of B on its production possibilities curve while the U.S. is to the left of B', MRT_{CW} and P_C/P_W (as given by the absolute slope of the production possibilities curve) would be greater in the U.K. than in the U.S. (see Fig. 2-12). By opening trade, the U.K. would then have to specialize in the production of and export *wheat* in exchange for American cloth, while the U.S. would have to specialize in and export cloth in exchange for English wheat. Thus, in this case, the pattern of specialization and trade would be the exact opposite of that in Problem 2.16.

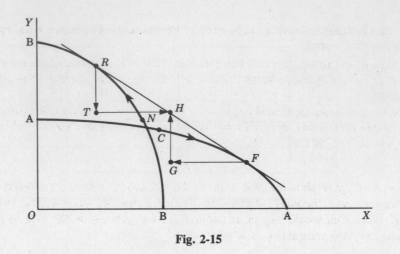

Fig. 2-15

2.19 With reference to Fig. 2-15, assume that nation *A* (with production possibilities curve AA) is in internal equilibrium in production and consumption at point *C* in isolation, while nation B (with production possibilities curve BB) is in internal equilibrium at point *N* in isolation.   (*a*) Explain how with trade each nation ends up consuming at point *H*.   (*b*) Explain how the equilibrium P_X/P_Y and the equilibrium quantities traded are determined.   (*c*) How long will this equilibrium condition persist?

(*a*) At point *C*, the internal equilibrium P_X/P_Y in nation A is smaller than in nation B at point *N*. Thus, A specializes in X and moves along AA in a downward direction until it reaches point *F*, while B specializes in Y until it reaches *R*. At *F* and *R* (and with free trade and no transportation costs), P_X/P_Y is the same in both nations (and is given by line *FHR* in Fig. 2-15). Then, A exports *FG* of X in exchange for *GH* imports of Y and reaches point *H* (see "trade triangle" *FGH* in Fig. 2-15). B exports *RT* of Y for *TH* imports of X and also reaches point *H* (see "trade triangle" *RTH*). Thus with trade, A and B both consume at point *H*, and *H* > *C* and *H* > *N*.

(*b*) The equilibrium P_X/P_Y and the equilibrium quantities of X and Y traded are determined simultaneously by the forces of demand and supply in nations A and B. Only at the equilibrium P_X/P_Y (given by line *FHR* in Fig. 2-15) will the quantity of X exported by A (*FG*) equal the quantity of X imported by B (*TH*), and the quantity of Y exported by B (*RT*) equal the quantity of Y imported by A (*GH*). At $P_X/P_Y > FHR$, A wants to export more of X than B wants to import and P_X/P_Y falls toward *FHR*. At $P_X/P_Y < FHR$, A wants to export less of X than B wants to import and P_X/P_Y rises toward *FHR*. This tendency for P_X/P_Y to be moving toward the equilibrium level given by the line *FHR* could also have been explained in terms of Y.

(*c*) The pattern of specialization in production in nations A and B and the pattern and volume of trade between them will remain the same, time period after time period, unless and until there is a change in supply conditions, in demand conditions, or in both, in either nation or in both (see Chapter 5). Note that in this and in all other trade models discussed in this chapter, the implicit policy conclusions is that free trade is the best policy from the *world's point of view*. This is the same conclusion reached by the classical economists (see Problem 1.8). The effect of interferences to the free flow of trade on the welfare of the world and of each nation separately is discussed in Chapter 6.

THE DETERMINANTS OF COMPARATIVE ADVANTAGE

2.20 (*a*) Why is the production possibilities curve of each nation usually different?   (*b*) Is trade still possible between two nations if they have identical production possibilities curves?   (*c*) Under what conditions can no trade take place between two nations with different production possibilities curves? (*d*) What happens if two nations are identical in every respect?

(*a*) Because each nation has different factor endowments and/or may use a different technology in production, the production possibilities curve will differ from nation to nation.

(b)   Mutually beneficial trade can be based on a difference in tastes between two nations with identical production possibilities curves.

(c)   Even if two nations have different production possibilities curves, no mutually beneficial trade can take place if their different tastes are such as to lead to equal relative commodity prices in the two nations before trade.

(d)   If two nations are identical in every respect (i.e., in factor endowments, technology and tastes) their internal equilibrium relative commodity prices in the absence of trade are identical, and so there is no basis for trade (according to our trade model, as developed so far).

2.21   (a) Draw a figure showing that with increasing costs, even if two nations have identical factor endowments and technology, there is still a basis for mutually advantageous trade if they have different tastes.   (b) What would happen if tastes also were identical in the two nations?   (c) What would happen if we had constant costs in part (a)?

(a)   Since the two nations have identical factor endowments and technology (an unusual situation), their production possibilities curves are identical and can be represented by a single curve, as in Fig. 2-16. Because of different tastes, each nation is in internal equilibrium in production and consumption at a different point on its production possibilities curve in the absence of trade. As a result, the two nations have different internal equilibrium P_X/P_Y (P_X/P_Y is higher in the nation that prefers X to Y). Thus, there is a basis for mutually advantageous trade. For example, nation A might be in internal equilibrium in production and consumption at point A on the production possibilities curve in Fig. 2-16. At point A, its $MRT_{XY} = P_X/P_Y = 1/4$. If nation B has an identical production possibilities curve as nation A but is in internal equilibrium in isolation at point B, its $MRT_{XY} = P_X/P_Y = 4$. Thus, nation A has a comparative advantage in X and nation B in Y. If the equilibrium P_X/P_Y settles at 1 with trade, nation A would move from A to C in production, exchange CG of X for GE of Y and end up at point E, which is superior to A. Nation B moves from B to C in production, exchanges CH of Y for HF of X and ends up at F > B. Note that B's exports of Y (CH) equal A's imports of Y (GE), and A's exports of X (CG) equal B's imports of X (HF).

(b)   If the two nations also had identical tastes, they would produce and consume at the same point on their respective production possibilities curves in isolation. Thus, P_X/P_Y would be the same in both nations and there would be no basis for mutually advantageous trade.

(c)   With constant costs, there would be no basis for trade between A and B if each had identical production possibilities curves but different tastes. This is so because the pretrade P_X/P_Y would be the same in both nations regardless of tastes (i.e., regardless of the pretrade production and consumption point in each nation).

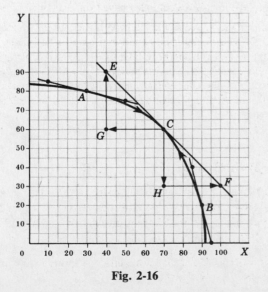

Fig. 2-16

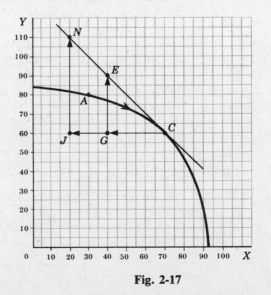

Fig. 2-17

2.22 Suppose that (1) a nation has the production possibilities curve of Fig. 2-16, (2) the nation is in internal equilibrium at point A in isolation and (3) P_X/P_Y on the world market is 1 and is not affected when this nation specializes in production and trades.   (a) Draw a figure showing what happens if this nation exports 30X. If it exports 50X.   (b) Does this nation gain in either case from trade? Why   (c) Under what condition will this nation *not* affect world prices by trading?

   (a)   In Fig. 2-17, the nation moves from point A to point C in production. If it exchanges 30X for 30Y, it ends up consuming at point E [the same as in Problem 2.21(a)]. If it exchanges 50X for 50Y, it ends up consuming at point N.

   (b)   Point E is clearly superior to point A since E involves both more X and more Y than A. Point N, however, would involve more of Y but less of X than at A. Unless the nation does in fact get to point N with trade and does so voluntarily, we cannot say unequivocally whether $N > A$. To answer this question, we need community indifference curves (see Sections 3.1 and 3.2).

   (c)   A nation may not affect world prices by trading if the nation is very small. In that event, the nation receives all of the gains from trade. This is referred to as *the importance of being unimportant* [see Problem 2.10(b)].

Chapter 3

The Pure Theory of International Trade:
Demand and Supply

3.1 COMMUNITY INDIFFERENCE CURVES

So far, we have dealt with the supply conditions in each nation, almost to the complete neglect of the demand side. In this chapter, we expand our model to include explicitly the tastes or demand preferences of each nation. These are introduced by community indifference curves.

A *community indifference curve* shows the various combinations of two commodities which yield equal satisfaction to the community or nation. Higher curves refer to more satisfaction, lower ones to less. Community indifference curves are negatively sloped, they are convex to the origin and, in order to be useful, they must not cross. The (absolute) slope of a community indifference curve at any point gives the *marginal rate of substitution* (MRS) or the amount of a commodity which the nation is willing to give up to obtain one additional unit of the other commodity (and still remain on the same indifference curve).

EXAMPLE 1. Figure 3-1 gives three indifference curves from the indifference map of the U.K. and the U.S. In terms of satisfaction, $N = A < J < E$ for the U.K. For the U.S., $R' = A' < J' < E'$. A movement from point N (20C and 70W) to a point A (40C and 60W) in the U.K. gives an average $\text{MRS}_{CW} = -(\Delta W/\Delta C) = -(-10/20) = 1/2$. At point A, $\text{MRS}_{CW} =$ the (absolute) slope of curve I for the U.K. $= 1/4$. For the U.S., a movement from A' (80C and 50W) to R' (90C and 30W) gives an average $\text{MRS}_{CW} = -(-20/10) = 2$. At point A', $\text{MRS}_{CW} = 4$. Note that as we move down a community indifference curve, its (absolute) slope or MRS_{CW} diminishes (see Problem 3.2). Also note that the indifference curves of the U.K. and the U.S. do not cross (see Problem 3.3).

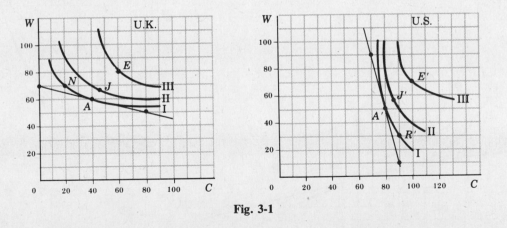

Fig. 3-1

3.2 THE BASIS FOR TRADE AND THE GAINS FROM TRADE RESTATED

In the absence of trade, a nation is in equilibrium when it reaches the highest indifference curve possible with its production possibilities curve. This occurs where a community indifference curve is tangent to the nation's production possibilities curve. The common slope of the two curves at the tangency point gives the internal *equilibrium relative commodity price in isolation* in each nation. When this pretrade relative commodity price differs in the two nations, there is a basis for mutually beneficial trade between them. Specialization in production and trade will then take place as described in Section 2.5.

37

EXAMPLE 2. The production possibilities curve for the U.K. and the U.S. in Fig. 3-2 are those of Figs. 2-3 and 2-4. In the absence of trade, indifference curve I is the highest indifference curve that the U.K. can reach with its production possibilities curve. Thus, the U.K. is in equilibrium (i.e., it produces and consumes) at point A in isolation. At point A, $\mathrm{MRT}_{CW} = \mathrm{MRS}_{CW} = \mathrm{P}_A = 1/4 =$ internal equilibrium P_C/P_W in isolation (see Fig. 3-2). On the other hand, the U.S. is in equilibrium at point A' in isolation, where its $\mathrm{MRT}_{CW} = \mathrm{MRS}_{CW} = \mathrm{P}_{A'} = 4 =$ internal equilibrium P_C/P_W. Since in isolation, P_C/P_W differs in the two nations, there is a basis for mutually advantageous trade. If P_C/P_W is stabilized at

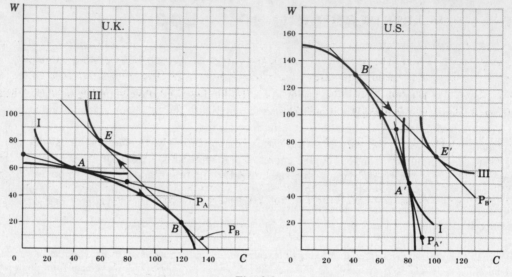

Fig. 3-2

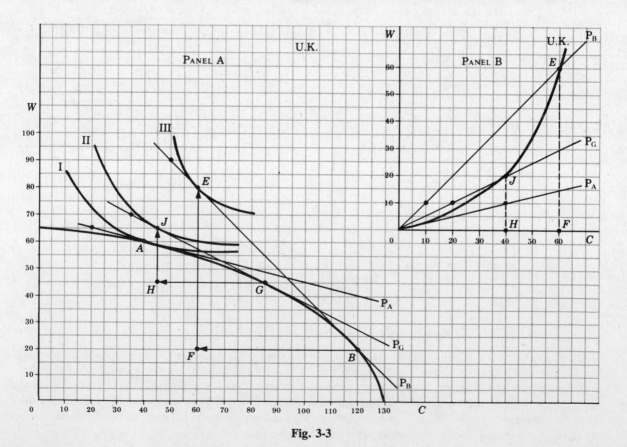

Fig. 3-3

1 with trade, the U.K. will go from point A to point B in production and, by exchanging 60C for 60W with the U.S., reaches point E in consumption on its indifference curve III (see Fig. 3-2 and reread Example 5 in Chapter 2). The U.S. goes from A' to B' in production and, through trade, it reaches point E' on its indifference curve III. Thus, both nations gain 20C and 20W from trade (see Fig. 3-2). Note that in this case, the pretrade difference in P_C/P_W in the two nations is based on a difference in their production conditions reinforced by a difference in their demand preference [see Problem 3.5(b)]. The other cases discussed in Chapter 2 will be examined in Problems 3.5(c) to 3.10.

3.3   THE OFFER CURVE OF ONE NATION

In order to determine the relative commodity price at which trade actually takes place, we must introduce the offer curve of each nation. The *offer curve* of a nation shows how much of its import commodity the nation requires in exchange for various quantities of its export commodity. The offer curve of a nation is derived from the nation's production possibilities curve, its indifference map and the various hypothetical relative commodity prices at which trade could take place.

EXAMPLE 3.   In Panel A of Fig. 3-3, the U.K. starts at pretrade equilibrium point A, as in Fig. 3-2. If trades takes place at $P_B = P_C/P_W = 1$, the U.K. moves to point B in production, trades 60C for 60W with the U.S. and reaches point E (so far this is exactly the same as in Fig. 3-2). This gives point E in Panel B of Fig. 3-3. At $P_C/P_W = P_G = 1/2$ (see Panel A of Fig. 3-3), the U.K. would move from point A to point G in production, exchange 40C for 20W with the U.S. and reach point J on its indifference curve II. This gives point J in Panel B. If we join the origin with points J, E

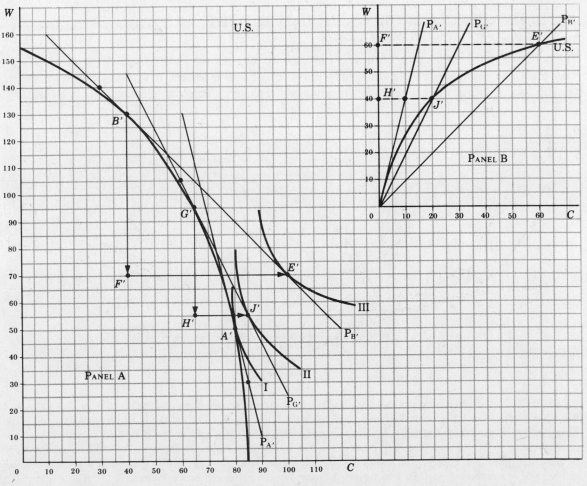

Fig. 3-4

and other points similarly obtained, we generate the offer curve for the U.K. shown in Panel B. This shows how much wheat imports the U.K. requires to be willing to export various quantities of its cloth. Note that P_A, P_G and P_B in Panel B of Fig. 3-3 refer to the same P_C/P_W as P_A, P_G and P_B in Panel A, since they refer to the same *absolute* slope. Also note that in order to induce the U.K. to export more cloth, P_C/P_W must rise, but for a sufficiently small volume of trade, the U.K. would trade at P_A (i.e., over a short range, its offer curve coincides with its no-trade equilibrium P_A line).

3.4   THE OFFER CURVE OF THE OTHER NATION

The offer curve of the trade partner is obtained from its production possibilities curve, its indifference map and the various relative commodity prices at which trade can take place—in a completely analogous way.

EXAMPLE 4.   In Panel A of Fig. 3-4, the U.S. starts at the pretrade equilibrium point A', as in Fig. 3-2. If trade takes place at $P_B' = P_C/P_W = 1$, the U.S. moves to B' in production, trades 60W for 60C with the U.K. and reaches point E'. This gives point E' in Panel B of Fig. 3-4. At $P_C/P_W = P_G' = 2$, the U.S. would move from point A' to point G' in production, exchange 40W for 20C with the U.K. and reach point J' on its indifference curve II. This gives point J' in Panel B. If we join the origin with the points J', E' and other points similarly obtained, we generate the offer curve of the U.S. shown in Panel B. This shows how much cloth imports the U.S. requires to export various quantities of wheat. Note that in order to induce the U.S. to export more wheat, P_C/P_W must fall (i.e., P_W/P_C must rise), but for a sufficiently small volume of trade, the U.S. would trade at $P_{A'}$.

3.5   OFFER CURVES AND THE EQUILIBRIUM RELATIVE COMMODITY PRICE WITH TRADE

The point where the offer curves of the two nations intersect gives the *equilibrium relative commodity price with trade*. At any other relative commodity price, the *desired* quantities of imports and exports of each commodity are not equal. This results in a pressure on the relative commodity price to move to its equilibrium level.

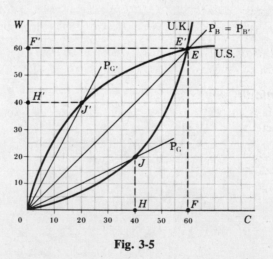

Fig. 3-5

EXAMPLE 5.   The offer curves of the U.K. and the U.S. in Fig. 3-5 are those of Panel B in Figs. 3-3 and 3-4. The two offer curves intersect at point E, giving equilibrium $P_C/P_W = P_B = 1$. At P_B, the U.K. offers 60C for 60W (point E on the U.K. offer curve) and the U.S. offers exactly 60W for 60C (point E' on the U.S. offer curve). Thus, trade is in equilibrium at P_B. At any other P_C/P_W, trade is not in equilibrium. For example, at P_G, the 40C of exports *supplied* by the U.K. (point J in Fig. 3-5) falls short of the cloth imports *demanded* by the U.S. (given by the point, not shown in Fig. 3-5, where the extended P_G line crosses the extended U.S. offer curve; see Problem 3.15). This excess demand tends to drive P_C/P_W up. As this occurs, the cloth exports supplied by the U.K. rise and the cloth imports demanded by the U.S. fall, until they are equalized at P_B. The pressure on P_G to move to P_B could also have been explained in terms of wheat (see Problem 3.15) and arises at any other $P_C/P_W \neq P_B$. By *determining* the equilibrium $P_B = 1$ (this is the same equilibrium P_C/P_W that we *assumed* in Example 5 in Chapter 2), we have thus completed our simple trade model.

3.6 THE TERMS OF TRADE OF A NATION

In a world of two traded commodities, the ratio of the price of a nation's export good to the price of its import good or P_X/P_M at equilibrium, is called the nation's *terms of trade*. Since in a two-nation world, the imports of a nation are the exports of its trade partner, the terms of trade of the partner is the inverse or the reciprocal of the terms of trade of the other nation. Thus, the terms of trade of the U.K. in Fig. 3-5 is given by $P_C/P_W = P_B = 1$, while the terms of trade of the U.S. equals P_W/P_C or the inverse of P_C/P_W and is also equal to 1 in this case. When more than two commodities are traded, the terms of trade are given by the ratio of the index of export to import prices. The terms of trade are usually given in percentages.

Glossary

Community indifference curve A curve showing the various combinations of two commodities that yield equal satisfaction to the community or nation.

Marginal rate of substitution (MRS) The amount of a commodity that a nation is willing to give up to obtain one additional unit of the other commodity and still remain on the same indifference curve. It is given by the slope of the community indifference curve at the point of consumption and declines as the nation consumes more of the commodity.

Equilibrium relative commodity price in isolation The relative commodity price at which a nation maximizes its welfare in the absence of trade. It is given by the slope of the common tangent to the nation's production possibilities curve and indifference curve at the autarky point of production and consumption.

Offer curve A curve that shows how much of its import commodity a nation requires in exchange for various quantities of its export commodity. This curve is also known as reciprocal demand curve.

Equilibrium relative commodity price with trade The common relative commodity price in two nations at which trade is balanced. It is given by the slope of the line from the origin to the point where the offer curves of the nations intersect.

Terms of trade The ratio of the price of a nation's export commodity to the price of its import commodity. When more than two commodities are traded, we use the index of export to import prices. The terms of trade are usually given in percentages.

Review Questions

1. Community indifference curves introduce (*a*) the production conditions in the nation, (*b*) the tastes or demand preferences of the nation, (*c*) both the production conditions and the tastes of the nation. (*d*) neither the production conditions nor the tastes of the nation.

    Ans. (*b*) See Section 3.1.

2. As we move down a community indifference curve in Fig. 3-1, MRS$_{CW}$ (a) declines,   (b) rises,   (c) remains unchanged,   (d) may decline, rise or remain unchanged.

   Ans.   (a) See Example 1.

3. The internal equilibrium relative commodity price in a nation in the absence of trade is determined by the nation's   (a) production possibilities curve,   (b) indifference map,   (c) production possibilities curve or indifference map,   (d) production possibilities curve and indifference map.

   Ans.   (d) See P$_A$ and P$_{A'}$ in Fig. 3.2.

4. At point A in Fig. 3-2 (i.e., at the pretrade equilibrium point in production and consumption in the U.K.),   (a) MRT$_{CW}$ = P$_A$ = MRS$_{CW}$,   (b) MRT$_{CW}$ = P$_A$ ≠ MRS$_{CW}$,   (c) MRT$_{CW}$ ≠ P$_A$ = MRS$_{CW}$,   (d) MRT$_{CW}$ ≠ P$_A$ ≠ MRS$_{CW}$.

   Ans.   (a) See Example 2.

5. When the U.K. is in equilibrium with trade in Fig. 3-2,   (a) MRT$_{CW}$ = P$_B$ = MRS$_{CW}$,   (b) MRT$_{CW}$ = P$_B$ ≠ MRS$_{CW}$,   (c) MRT$_{CW}$ ≠ P$_B$ = MRS$_{CW}$,   (d) MRT$_{CW}$ ≠ P$_B$ ≠ MRS$_{CW}$.

   Ans.   (a) See Points B and E in Fig. 3-2. Note that with trade, production and consumption occur at different points, but at equilibrium in production and consumption MRT$_{CW}$ = P$_B$ = MRS$_{CW}$.

6. The offer curve of a nation shows what the nation   (a) can do,   (b) must do,   (c) is willing to do,   (d) any of the above.

   Ans.   (c) See Sections 3.3 and 3.4.

7. Trade triangle *BFE* in Panel A of Fig. 3-3 corresponds in Panel B to trade triangle   (a) *OFE*,   (b) *OHJ*,   (c) either *OHJ* or *OFE*,   (d) neither *OHJ* nor *OFE*.

   Ans.   (a) See Example 3.

8. Trade triangle *G'H'J'* in Panel A of Fig. 3-4 corresponds in Panel B to trade triangle   (a) *OF'E'*,   (b) *OH'J'*,   (c) either *OF'E'* or *OH'J'*,   (d) neither *OF'E'* nor *OH'J'*.

   Ans.   (b) See Example 4.

9. The offer curve of a nation bulges or bends toward the axis that measures its   (a) export commodity,   (b) import commodity,   (c) export or import commodity,   (d) nontraded commodity.

   Ans.   (a) See Panel B in Figs. 3-3 and 3-4.

10. At point E in Fig. 3-5,   (a) the U.K. is willing to exchange 60C for 60W,   (b) the U.S. is willing to exchange 60W for 60C,   (c) the U.S. is willing to export 60W and the U.K. is willing to import 60W,   (d) the U.K. is willing to export 60C and the U.S. is willing to import 60C,   (e) all of the above statements are correct.

    Ans.   (e) See Example 5.

11. At P$_{G'}$ in Fig. 3-5,   (a) the wheat exports of the U.S. fall short of the wheat imports demanded by the U.K.,   (b) the wheat exports of the U.S. exceed the wheat imports demanded by the U.K.,   (c) the cloth exports of the U.S. exceed the cloth imports demanded by the U.K.,   (d) the cloth exports of the U.S. fall short of the cloth imports demanded by the U.K.

    Ans.   (a) See Example 5.

12. If a nation's terms of trade is 2, its trade partner's terms of trade is   (a) 4,   (b) 2,   (c) 1,   (d) 1/2.

    Ans.   (d) See Section 3.6.

Solved Problems

COMMUNITY INDIFFERENCE CURVES

3.1   Table 3.1 gives points on four community indifference curves from the indifference maps of the U.K. and the U.S.   (*a*) Sketch the indifference curves of the U.K. on one set of axes and those of the U.S. on another set of axes; also draw a tangent at the middle point of indifference curves II, III and IV and label these points, respectively, *A, J* and *E* for the U.K. and *A', J'* and *E'* for the U.S. (*b*) What do community indifference curves show?   (*C*) Why are the indifference curves of the U.K. and the U.S. in part (*a*) different?   (*d*) For what are community indifference curves needed? (*e*) What are their characteristics?

Table 3.1

U.K.								U.S.							
I		II		III		IV		I		II		III		IV	
W	C	W	C	W	C	W	C	W	C	W	C	W	C	W	C
70	10	70	30	80	50	90	70	60	73	60	77	60	80	60	85
50	40	50	60	55	70	70	80	25	75	20	80	30	85	40	90
35	110	45	110	50	110	60	110	2	90	5	90	15	105	30	105

(*a*)   See Fig. 3-6.

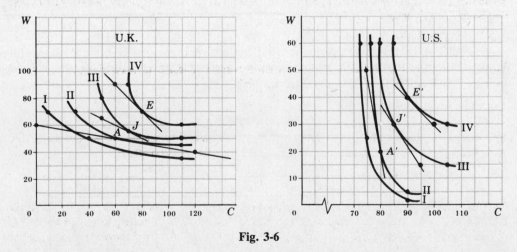

Fig. 3-6

(*b*)   Community indifference curves show the tastes or demand preferences of a community or nation. They are almost completely analogous to a consumer's indifference curves (see Problem 3.3) except that they refer to an entire community. Points on the same community indifference curve show the combinations of the two commodities that yield equal satisfaction to the nation. Higher curves refer to the greater satisfaction, lower ones to less. Thus, in Fig. 3-6, $E > J > A$ for the U.K., and $E' > J' > A'$ for the U.S.

(*c*)   The fact that the indifference curves of the U.K. in Fig. 3-6 differ in shape and location from those of the U.S. implies that the U.K. and the U.S. have different tastes or demand preferences for wheat and cloth. Only if the U.K. and the U.S. had identical tastes would their indifference map and indifference curves be identical.

(*d*)   Community indifference curves, together with the nation's production possibilities curve, are needed to determine the internal equilibrium point in production and consumption and the equilibrium relative commodity price in the nation in the absence of trade (*autarky*). Community indifference curves are also needed to determine the nation's point of consumption with trade.

(*e*)   Community indifference curves are negatively sloped, they are convex to the origin and, to be useful, they must not cross (see Section 3.1 and Fig. 3-6).

3.2   (*a*) Why are community indifference curves negatively sloped?   (*b*) Find the average MRS_{CW} between consecutive points on indifference curves II and IV for the U.K. and the U.S. in Fig. 3-6. (*c*) Find MRS_{CW} at points *A, J* and *E* and *A', J'* and *E'* on the community indifference curves in Fig. 3-6. What happens to MRS_{CW} as we move down a community indifference curve?   (*d*) Why are community indifference curves convex to the origin?

(*a*)   Since we are dealing with economic (i.e., scarce) goods, if the nation consumes more of one good, it must consume less of the other to remain at the same level of satisfaction (i.e., on the same indifference curve). Therefore, community indifference curves must be negatively sloped.

(*b*)   The average MRS_{CW} between any two points on a community indifference curve is given by $-\Delta W/\Delta C$.

Table 3.2

U.K.						U.S.					
II			IV			II			IV		
W	C	MRS_{CW}	W	C	MRS_{CW}	W	C	MRS_{CW}	W	C	MRS_{CW}
70	30	—	90	70	—	60	77	—	60	85	—
50	60	2/3	70	80	2	20	80	40/3	40	90	4
45	110	1/10	60	110	1/3	5	90	3/2	30	105	2/3

(*c*) MRS_{CW} at any point on a community indifference curve is given by the (absolute) slope of the (tangent to the) curve at that point. As we move down a community indifference curve, its (absolute) slope or MRS_{CW} declines (see Fig. 3-6).

Table 3.3

U.K.			U.S.		
Indifference			Indifference		
Point	Curve	MRS_{CW}	Point	Curve	MRS_{CW}
A	II	1/6	*A'*	II	6
J	III	1/2	*J'*	III	3/2
E	IV	1	*E'*	IV	1

(*d*)   As a nation moves down an indifference curve, it is willing to give up less and less of its wheat in order to obtain each additional unit of cloth (i.e., MRS_{CW} declines). This is so because the less wheat and the more cloth a nation has (i.e., the lower point on the indifference curve), the more valuable is each remaining unit of wheat and the less valuable is each additional unit of cloth to the nation. A declining MRS_{CW} results in community indifference curves that are convex to the origin.

3.3   (*a*) Why must community indifference curves not cross in order to be useful?   (*b*) Why can community indifference curves cross when we open up trade or increase the volume of trade?   (*c*) How can we overcome the problem raised by the possibility of intersecting community indifference curves?

(a) When two community indifference curves cross, one of them is above the other (implying a higher level of satisfaction) at one side of the point of intersection, and below the other (implying a lower level of satisfaction) on the other side of the point of intersection. Thus, we cannot say unequivocally which of the two community indifference curves refers to a greater level of satisfaction.

(b) While an individual's indifference curves, by definition, *cannot* cross, community indifference curves *may* cross. This is because the indifference map of a nation refers to a particular income distribution within the nation. For a different income distribution, we have a different community indifference map, whose indifference curves may cross those of the previous indifference map. This is precisely what happens between two trade situations. That is, when we open up trade or expand its volume, domestic producers of the importable commodity are hurt while producers of the exportable commodity benefit. Thus, the income distribution of the nation changes, and we get a new and different community indifference map with indifference curves that may cross those of the previous community indifference map. In that case, we cannot use them to determine if the opening or the expansion of trade increased the nation's welfare.

(c) One way we can overcome the problem raised by intersecting community indifference curves is by the so-called *compensation principle*. This says that if those who gain from trade can compensate the losers entirely for their losses and still have something of the gain left over, and if at the same time, the losers are not willing to bribe the gainers into forgoing trade, then trade is beneficial to the nation—whether compensation actually occurs or not. While the compensation principle is not sufficient to overcome all of the conceptual difficulties inherent in the use of community indifference curves, the concept of such curves is a neat device that continues to be used (albeit cautiously) in trade theory.

THE BASIS FOR TRADE AND THE GAINS FROM TRADE RESTATED

3.4 Using the production possibilities curve of Fig. 2-12 and the community indifference curves of Fig. 3-6, determine   (a) the equilibrium point of production and consumption in the U.K. and in the U.S. in autarky, and   (b) the equilibrium P_C/P_W in the U.K. and in the U.S. in autarky.   (c) What conditions hold at the autarky equilibrium point?   (d) What do points of intersection of a community indifference curve with the nation's production possibilities curve indicate?

(a) In the absence of trade, the U.K. is in equilibrium at point A and the U.S. at A', where the production possibilities curve of each nation is tangent to its community indifference curve II—the highest each nation can reach in autarky (see Fig. 3-7). Since community indifference curves are convex to the origin and are drawn as nonintersecting, the equilibrium point is unique (i.e., there is only one such tangency or equilibrium point). Also, the fact that community indifference maps are dense (i.e., they are made up of an infinite number of indifference curves) always ensures the existence of an equilibrium point.

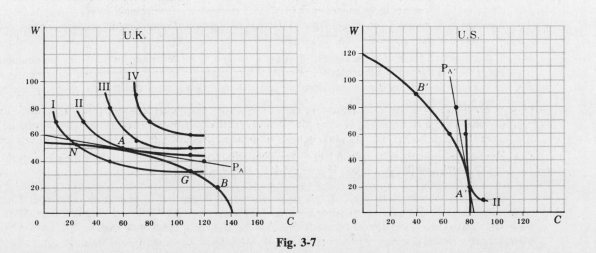

Fig. 3-7

(b) The autarky equilibrium $P_C/P_W = P_A = 1/6$ in the U.K. and $P_{A'} = 6$ in the U.S. (see Fig. 3-7). These are given by the (absolute) slope of the tangent to the production possibilities curve and community indifference curve II at points A and A', respectively. Thus, the nation's supply conditions (as summarized by its production possibilities frontier) and demand preferences (as summarized by its indifference map) *together* determine the equilibrium relative commodity price in the nation in autarky.

(c) At point A, the U.K. is in equilibrium both in production (because $MRT_{CW} = P_A$) and in consumption (because $MRS_{CW} = P_A$). Thus, at point A, $MRT_{CW} = P_A = MRS_{CW} = 1/6$ in the U.K. (see Fig. 3-7). At point A', $MRT_{CW} = P_{A'} = MRS_{CW} = 6$ in the U.S.

(d) Points of intersection of a community indifference curve with the nation's production possibilities curve are attainable but do not maximize the nation's satisfaction. For example, at point N in Fig. 3-7, $MRS_{CW} > MRT_{CW}$. This means that the U.K. is willing to give up more wheat in consumption than it needs to give up in production to obtain one more unit of cloth. Thus, it pays for the U.K. to produce (and consume) more cloth and less wheat. As it does this, the U.K. moves down its production possibilities frontier and reaches higher and higher indifference curves until point A on indifference curve II—the highest the U.K. can reach with its production constraint. The exact opposite is true at the other intersection point (i.e., point G) in Fig. 3-7. Points on higher indifference curves are beyond the present production capacity of the U.K.

3.5 With reference to Fig. 3-7,   (a) indicate in which commodity the U.K. and the U.S. have a comparative advantage.   (b) On what is the difference in P_A and $P_{A'}$ based?   (c) What would happen if community indifference curve II was tangent to the production possibilities curve at point B in the U.K. and at point B' in the U.S.?   (d) If the tangency point was to the right of B in the U.K. and to the left of B' in the U.S.?

(a) Since in isolation, $P_A < P_{A'}$ (see Fig. 3-7), the U.K. has a comparative price advantage over the U.S. in cloth and the U.S. in wheat. It follows that with trade between the two nations, the U.K. should specialize in cloth and import wheat while the U.S. specializes in wheat and imports cloth.

(b) The indifference in P_A and $P_{A'}$ is based on *both* the difference in supply conditions and demand conditions in the U.K. and the U.S. From the supply side (i.e., from the shape of the production possibilities curve), we see that the U.K. has a production bias in favor of cloth and the U.S. in favor of wheat (see Fig. 3-7). From the demand side (i.e., from the shape and location of the community indifference curves), we see that the U.K. has a consumption bias in favor of wheat and the U.S. in favor of cloth. More specifically, the U.K. can supply a large quantity of cloth in *relation* to its small taste or demand for cloth, while it can supply a small quantity of wheat in relation to its taste for wheat. Thus, both supply and demand conditions in the U.K. reinforce each other in making the pretrade equilibrium P_C/P_W low in the U.K. The exact opposite is true in the U.S., thus making the pretrade equilibrium P_C/P_W higher in the U.S.

(c) When the tangency point is at B in the U.K. and at B' in the U.S., the equilibrium $P_C/P_W = 1$ in autarky in both nations (see Fig. 3-7) and no mutually advantageous trade is possible between them. This occurs only if the English demand for its own cloth in isolation is so strong that to produce that large quantity of cloth, the U.K. incurs the relatively high $MRT_{CW} = 1 = P_C/P_W$ (see point B in Fig. 3-7). At the same time, the U.S. consumption bias in favor of wheat is so high that it neutralizes its production bias in favor of wheat and gives a $P_C/P_W = MRT_{CW} = 1$.

(d) If the tangency point is to the right of B in the U.K. and to the left of B' in the U.S., the equilibrium $P_C/P_W > 1$ in the U.K. and $P_C/P_W < 1$ in the U.S. in autarky. In this case, demand considerations within each nation overwhelm supply considerations and lead to a trade pattern which is the reverse of the more usual case discussed in part (b).

3.6 Starting at the autarky points A and A' in Fig. 3-7, draw a figure showing the points of production and consumption for the U.K. and the U.S., if trade takes place at $P_C/P_W = 1$. Is this the equilibrium price with trade? Why? How much does each nation gain from trade?

At $P_C/P_W = 1$ with trade, the U.K. moves from point A to point B in production, exchanges 50C for 50W with the U.S. and ends up at point E on its indifference curve IV (thus gaining 20C and 20W; see Fig. 3-8). This is the highest level of satisfaction that the U.K. can reach with trade at $P_C/P_W = 1$, since MRT_{CW} at $B = MRS_{CW}$ at $E = P_C/P_W = P_B = 1$.

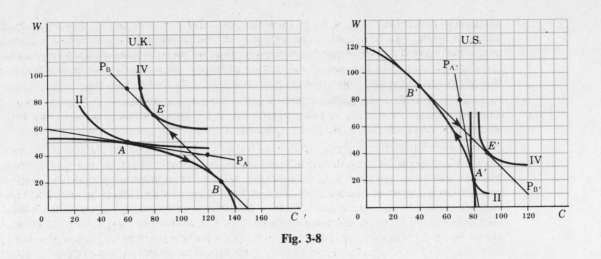

Fig. 3-8

On the other hand, the U.S. moves from A' to B' in production, exchanges 50W for 50C with the U.K. and reaches E' on its indifference curve IV (thus gaining 10C and 20W). This is the highest indifference curve the U.S. can reach with trade at $P_C/P_W = 1$, since MRT_{CW} at $B' = MRS_{CW}$ at $E' = P_C/P_W = P_{B'} = 1$. Since the quantities traded are in equilibrium, $P_C/P_W = P_B = P_{B'} = 1$ is the equilibrium price with trade. Note that while in Problem 2.16(b) we had to be told that 50C and 50W were traded, we can now determine that volume of trade at $P_C/P_W = 1$ with the aid of community indifference curves.

3.7   (a) Add the hypothetical community indifference curves for nation 1 and nation 2 to Fig. 2-16 so that we get the results reached in Problem 2.21(a).   (b) What conditions are now *determined* but had to be assumed or given in Problem 2.21(a)?

(a)   In Fig. 3-9, indifference curves I and II refer to nation 1, and I$'$ and II$'$ to nation 2. In autarky, nation 1 is in equilibrium at point A, where $MRT_{XY} = MRS_{XY} = P_A = 1/4$ and nation 2 at point B, where $MRT_{XY} = MRS_{XY} = P_B = 4$. With trade, nation 1 moves from A to C in production, exchanges 30X

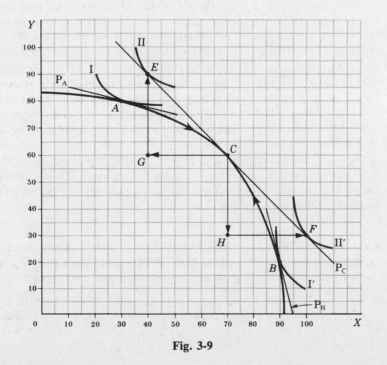

Fig. 3-9

for 30Y with nation 2 and reaches point E on indifference curve II. Nation 2 moves from B to C in production, exchanges 30Y for 30X with nation 1 and reaches point F on indifference curve II'. Thus, at equilibrium in production and consumption with trade, $MRT_{XY} = MRS_{XY} = P_C = 1$ in both nations. The two nations will be able to reach higher indifference curves than II and II' only as the supply of their factors of production rises and technology improves through time. This model is the reverse of the more usual case, where nations face more or less identical tastes but different factor endowments or production possibilities curves. If the indifference map of each nation were also the same in Fig. 3-9, then their autarky points of production and consumption would coincide, P_X/P_Y would be the same in each nation, and no mutually advantageous trade would be possible between them.

(b)   With the introduction of community indifference curves for nations 1 and 2, we can now determine the autarky equilibrium of production and consumption in each nation. We can also determine exactly what quantities of X and Y are traded at $P_X/P_Y = 1$. Both of these conditions had to be assumed or given in Problem 2.21(a). Note, however, that in order for this trade model to be complete, we still must show how the equilibrium $P_X/P_Y = 1$ with trade is determined.

3.8   Draw a set of indifference curves for the nation in Problem 2.22 and Fig. 2-17 showing that A is the autarky equilibrium point, $A < N < E$, and E is the equilibrium point of consumption with trade.

   In Fig. 3-10, the nation is in equilibrium in autarky at point A, where its indifference curve I is tangent to its production possibilities curve. Thus, the autarky $P_X/P_Y = P_A = 1/4$ in the nation. Since we are told in Problem 2.22 that $P_X/P_Y = P_W = 1$ on the world market and is not affected when this nation specializes in the production of X and trades, the nation moves to point C in production (where its $MRT_{XY} = P_W = 1$), exchanges 30X for 30Y, and reaches point E on its indifference curve III (see Fig. 3-10). At point E, the nation's $MRS_{XY} = P_W = 1$, and indifference curve III is the highest the nation can reach. The nation could reach point N by exchanging 50X for 50Y. Point N (on community indifference curve II) is superior to point A (on I) but inferior to point E

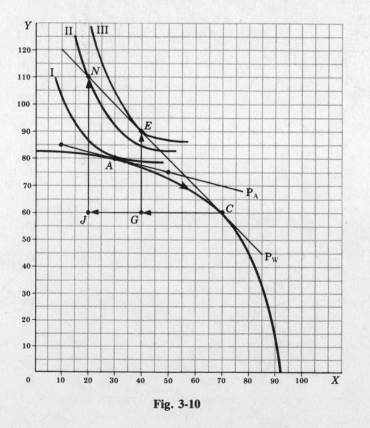

Fig. 3-10

(on III). At point N, $MRS_{XY} > P_W$ and the nation would be consuming too much of Y and too little of X to be in equilibrium in consumption with trade (reread the solution to Problem 2.22). The fact that the rest of the world is passively willing to trade any quantity of Y in exchange for X at $P_W = 1$ with this nation has an important implication for the shape of the world's offer curve from this nation's point of view (see Problem 3.16).

3.9 For the nation of Problem 3.8, show the breakdown of the total gains from trade into the gains from exchange alone and the gains from specialization in production.

In Fig. 3-11, the change in consumption from point A (on indifference curve I) to point T (on indifference curve II') measures the gains from exchange alone if the nation, for whatever reason, cannot move to point C in production but continues to produce at point A even with trade. The change in consumption from point T to point E (on indifference curve III) measures the gains from specialization in production.

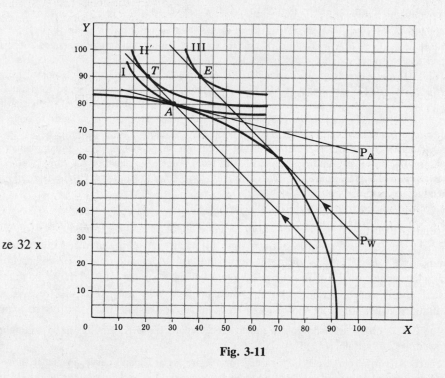

ze 32 x

Fig. 3-11

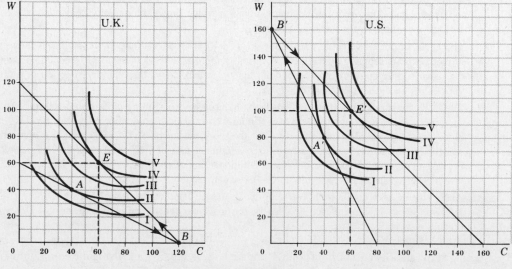

Fig. 3-12

3.10 Add hypothetical community indifference curves for the U.K. and the U.S. to Fig. 2-2, so that we get the results reached in Example 3 of Chapter 2.

The commentary for Fig. 3-12 is the same as in Example 3 in Chapter 2, except for the fact that by adding community indifference curves for the U.K. and the U.S. to Fig. 2-2, we can now determine rather than assume the autarky equilibrium point of production and consumption for each nation and the equilibrium point of consumption with trade [see also Problem 2.21(c)]. Still to be assumed, however, is the equilibrium $P_X/P_Y = 1$ at which trade takes place.

OFFER CURVES AND THE EQUILIBRIUM RELATIVE COMMODITY PRICE WITH TRADE

3.11 Starting at the autarky equilibrium point A for the U.K. in Fig. 3-7 and using the community indifference curves of the U.K. in Fig. 3-6, derive the offer curve of the U.K.

In Panel A of Fig. 3-13, the U.K. starts at the autarky equilibrium point A, as in Fig. 3-7. If trade takes place at $P_B = P_C/P_W = 1$, the U.K. moves to point B in production, exchanges 50C for 50W with the U.S. and reaches point E (so far this is exactly as in Fig. 3-8 in Problem 3.6). Trade triangle BFE in Panel A of Fig. 3-13 corresponds to trade triangle OFE in Panel B and we get point E on the U.K.'s offer curve. At $P_C/P_W = P_G = 1/2$ (see Panel A of Fig. 3-13), the U.K. would move instead to point G in production, exchange 40C for 20W with the U.S. and reach point J on its indifference curve II. Note that P_G is less favorable to the U.K. than P_B and so the U.K. gains less from trade (i.e., $J < E$). Trade triangle GHJ in Panel A corresponds to triangle OHJ in Panel B, and we get point J as another point on the U.K.'s offer curve. By starting with other P_C/P_W at which trade could take place, we would obtain in a similar manner other points on the U.K.'s offer curve. By joining the origin with these points, we generate the U.K.'s offer curve shown in Panel B. Note that P_A, P_G and P_B in Panel B of Fig. 3-13 refer to the same P_C/P_W as P_A, P_G and P_B in panel A, since they refer to the same absolute slope.

3.12 With reference to the U.K.'s offer curve in Panel B of Fig. 3-13, answer the following questions. (a) What does the offer curve show? (b) In what way can the offer curve be regarded as a demand curve? How is this different from the usual demand curve of microeconomic theory? (c) In what way can the offer curve be regarded as a supply curve? How is this different from the usual supply curve of microeconomic theory? (d) Why must the U.K. receive a higher P_C/P_W to be induced to export more cloth? (e) How much cloth is the U.K. willing to export at P_A?

(a) The U.K.'s offer curve shows how much wheat imports the U.K. requires to be willing to export various quantities of its cloth.

(b) The U.K.'s offer curve can be regarded (in a sense) as a demand curve, in that it shows the quantity of wheat imports demanded by the U.K. at various *total expenditures in terms of cloth*. This is different from the usual demand curve of microeconomic theory, which shows the quantity demanded of a commodity at various *per unit prices in terms of money*.

(c) The U.K.'s offer curve could also be regarded (in a sense) as a supply curve, in that it shows the quantity of cloth exports supplied by the U.K. at various *total expenditures in terms of wheat*. This is different from the usual supply curve of microeconomic theory, which shows the quantity supplied of a commodity at various *per unit prices in terms of money*.

(d) The U.K. must receive a higher P_C/P_W to be induced to export more cloth because to produce more cloth for export, the U.K. incurs increasing opportunity costs in cloth production. Also, as the U.K. exports more cloth, the U.K. receives more wheat. But the more wheat the U.K. consumes, the lower the extra (or marginal) satisfaction it receives from each additional unit of (imported) wheat. Thus, P_C/P_W must rise because (1) it costs more to produce each additional unit of cloth for export and (2) each additional unit of wheat received in exchange results in less extra satisfaction.

(e) At P_A (the autarky equilibrium P_C/P_W in the U.K., see Panels A and B of Fig. 3-13), the U.K. is willing to export about 15C (see Panel B). That is, for this small quantity of cloth exports, the U.K.'s offer curve coincides with P_A.

3.13 Starting at the autarky equilibrium point A' for the U.S. in Fig. 3-7 and using the community indifference curves of the U.S. in Fig. 3-6, derive the offer curve of the U.S.

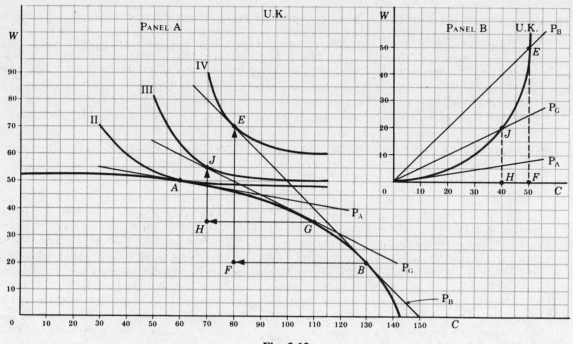

Fig. 3-13

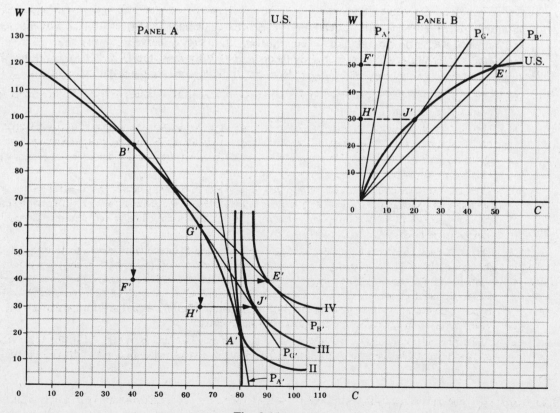

Fig. 3-14

In Panel A of Fig. 3-14, the U.S. starts at the autarky equilibrium point A', as in Fig. 3-7. If trade takes place at $P_{B'} = P_C/P_W = 1$, the U.S. moves to B' in production, exchanges 50W for 50C with the U.K. and reaches point E' (as in Fig. 3-8). Trade triangle $B'F'E'$ in Panel A of Fig. 3-14 corresponds to trade triangle $OF'E'$ in Panel B, and we get point E' on the U.S. offer curve. Using another P_C/P_W (in the range: $1/6 < P_C/P_W < 6$, at which trade can take place between the U.S. and the U.K.), say $P_C/P_W = P_{G'} = 3/2$, we get trade triangle $G'H'J'$ in Panel A which corresponds to trade triangle $OH'J'$ in Panel B, and we get point J' on the U.S. offer curve. By joining the origin with such points as J' and E', we get the U.S. offer curve of Panel B. This shows how much cloth imports the U.S. requires to export various quantities of wheat. In a sense, the U.S. offer curve can be regarded as the U.S. demand curve for cloth and also as the U.S. supply curve of wheat. Note that in order to induce the U.S. to export more wheat, P_C/P_W must fall (i.e., P_W/P_C must rise), but the U.S. is willing to export about 5W at $P_{A'}$ (see Panel A of Fig. 3-14).

3.14 Using the offer curve of the U.K. in Panel B of Fig. 3-13 and the offer curve of the U.S. in Panel B of Fig. 3-14, determine   (*a*) the equilibrium P_C/P_W at which trade takes place between them and (*b*) the terms of trade of the two nations.

(*a*)   In Fig. 3-15, the offer curves intersect at point E (which coincides with point E'), giving equilibrium $P_C/P_W = P_B = P_{B'} = 1$. P_B is the equilibrium relative commodity price because at P_B, the 50W of imports demanded by the U.K. exactly matches the 50W of exports supplied by the U.S., and the 50C of imports demanded by the U.S. exactly matches the 50C of exports supplied by the U.K.

(*b*)   The terms of trade of the U.K. = $P_X/P_M = P_C/P_W = 1$. The terms of trade of the U.S. = $P_X/P_M = P_W/P_C = 1$ also in this case. If a nation exports and imports more than one commodity, then P_X and P_M refer to price index numbers of exports and imports, respectively. These terms of trade are sometimes referred to as the *net barter terms of trade* or as the *commodity terms of trade* to distinguish them from other terms of trade to be discussed in Problems 5.23 and 5.24 in connection with trade and development. The terms of trade of nations and the volume of trade change through time as their offer curves shift due to changes in factor endowments, technology and tastes (see Chapter 5).

3.15 Starting from Fig. 3-15,   (*a*) extend the P_G price line and the U.S. offer curve so that they cross at 60W from 160C; also extend the $P_{G'}$ price line and the U.K. offer curve so that they cross at 120W and 60C.   (*b*) With reference to the figure in part (*a*), explain in terms of the quantities of *cloth* traded, why P_G and $P_{G'}$ are not the equilibrium P_C/P_W. How is P_B reached?   (*c*) Do the same thing as in part (*b*) in terms of *wheat* traded.

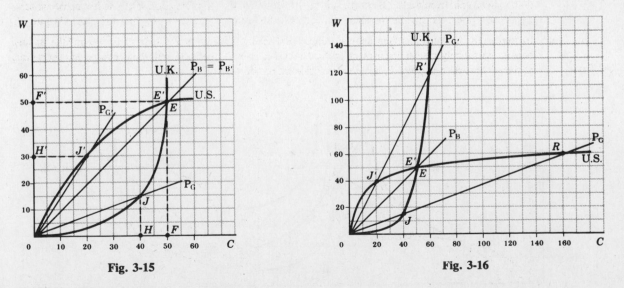

Fig. 3-15   **Fig. 3-16**

(*a*)   See Fig. 3-16.

(*b*)   At P_G, the 40C exports *supplied* by the U.K. (point J in Fig. 3-16) falls far short of the 160C imports *demanded* by the U.S. (point R in Fig. 3-16). This excess demand tends to drive P_C/P_W up from P_G. As this occurs, the U.K. moves up its offer curve and supplies more cloth for export while the U.S. moves down its offer curve and demands less cloth imports. This continues until, at P_B, the *desired* quantities of cloth exports and imports are equalized (see points E and E' in Fig. 3-16). At $P_{G'}$, the 20C imports demanded by the U.S. (point J') falls short of the 60C exports supplied by the U.K. (point R'). This excess supply causes P_C/P_W to fall from $P_{G'}$. As this occurs, the U.S. moves up its offer curve and demands more cloth imports while the U.K. moves down its offer curve and supplies less cloth for export. This continues until P_B, where the desired quantities of cloth imports and exports are the same.

(c)   At P_G, the 15W imports demanded by the U.K. (point J) falls short of the 60W exports supplied by the U.S. (point R). This causes P_C/P_W to rise—which means that P_W/P_C falls. As this occurs, the U.K. moves up its offer curve and demands more wheat imports, while the U.S. moves down its offer curve and supplies less wheat for export. This continues until P_B, where the desired quantities of wheat imports and exports are the same. At $P_{G'}$, the U.S. is willing to export 40W (point J') but the U.K. wants to import 120W (point R'). This excess demand causes P_W/P_C to rise from $P_{G'}$ to P_B, where the desired quantities of wheat imports and exports are equal. Thus, P_B is the *unique* equilibrium P_W/P_C in the sense that only at P_B does the market clear itself.

3.16   (a) Using offer curves, show that nation 2—a "very small" nation—may trade at the autarky $P_C/P_W = P_1$ prevailing in nation 1—a "very large" nation.   (b) Under what condition would a nation's offer curve be represented by a (positively sloped) straight line through the origin? At what relative commodity price would trade take place if the partner's offer curve took the usual shape?   (c) What would happen if both nations operate under constant conditions throughout?

(a)   In Fig. 3-17, nation 2 is so small that its offer curve crosses the straight-line segment of the large nation's (i.e., nation 1) offer curve. Thus, the equilibrium volume of trade (given by point E in Fig. 3-17) takes place at P_1 (the autarky equilibrium P_C/P_W in nation 1) and nation 2 captures all of the gains from trade.

(b)   A nation's offer curve is portrayed by a straight line through the origin when the nation operates under constant cost conditions. The slope of the offer curve is then given by the absolute slope of the (negatively sloped) production possibilities curve of the nation. With the trade partner's offer curve taking the usual shape, trade will take place at the autarky relative commodity price prevailing in the nation facing constant costs, and the trade partner captures all of the gains from trade. This is to be contrasted to the more usual case, where trade takes place between the autarky relative commodity prices in the two nations, and so both nations gain from trade. Of course, the closer the terms of trade of a nation settles to its autarky relative commodity price, the smaller the share of the total gains from trade accruing to the nation (see Chapter 1).

(c)   In Fig. 3-18, both nations face constant costs, and their offer curves are straight lines until the nations become completely specialized in production. The offer curves then assume their regular shape and determine, at their intersection at point E, the equilibrium relative commodity price P_E.

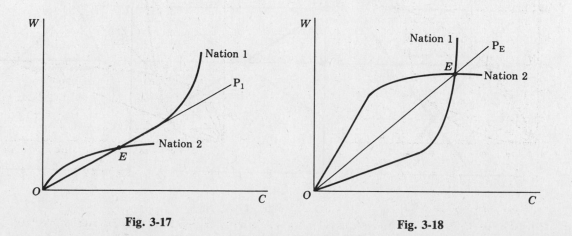

Fig. 3-17   Fig. 3-18

3.17 (*a*) Explain, in general, the forces which determine the equilibrium relative commodity price at which trade takes place.   (*b*) In what way does the trade model presented in this chapter represent a general equilibrium model? In what way does it not?

(*a*) The equilibrium relative commodity price at which trade takes place is determined by the conditions of demand and supply for each commodity in both nations. "Other things being equal," the nation with the more intense demand for the other nation's exported good will gain less from trade than the nation with the less intense demand. This is sometimes referred to as the *law of reciprocal demand*, first expounded numerically by John Stuart Mill (another English classical economist), and subsequently extended and generalized by F. Y. Edgeworth and Alfred Marshall with the introduction of offer curves or reciprocal demand curves, as shown in Problems 3.11 to 3.14.

(*b*) The trade model presented in this chapter represents a simple general equilibrium model. As such, it summarizes clearly and concisely a remarkable amount of information. It shows the conditions of production in the two nations (with the production possibilities curves), their tastes or demand preferences (with the community indifference maps), the autarky equilibrium point and relative commodity price in each nation, the basis for trade, the pattern of trade, the equilibrium relative commodity price with trade, the degree of specialization in production with trade, the quantity traded of each commodity that clears markets, and the gains from specialization in production and trade. Our trade model is not, of course, a completely general equilibrium model since it deals only with two nations, two commodities, two factors, relative prices and perfect competition, among other things. However, most economists believe that this simple trade model can be extended and made more realistic—and complicated. In any event, our simple model *is* useful, since the purpose of theory is to abstract from details, to simplify, and to predict and explain—in our case, the basis for trade and the gains from trade.

3.18 From Panel A of Fig. 3-19 (which shows nation 1's demand and supply curves for commodity X) and Panel C (which shows nation 2's demand and supply curves for commodity X), explain   (*a*) how the demand and supply curves for exports of commodity X in Panel B are derived and   (*b*) how equilibrium P_X/P_Y is determined.   (*c*) How does the process of determining the equilibrium relative price for commodity X with trade in Panel B differ from the method used in Figs. 3-5 and 3-15?

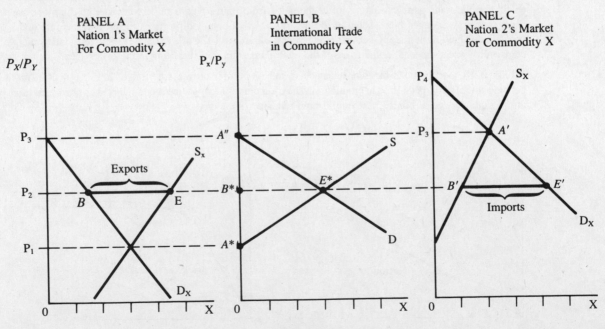

Fig. 3-19

(a) At P_X/P_Y larger than P_1, nation 1's excess supply of commodity X in Panel A gives rise to nation 1's supply curve of exports of commodity X (S) in Panel B. On the other hand, at P_X/P_Y lower than P_3, nation 2's excess demand for commodity X in Panel C gives rise to nation 2's demand for imports of commodity X (D) in Panel B.

(b) Panel B shows that only at P_2 does the quantity of imports of commodity X demanded by nation 2 equal the quantity of exports supplied by nation 1. Thus, P_2 is the equilibrium P_X/P_Y with trade. At $P_X/P_Y > P_2$, there will be an excess supply of exports of commodity X and this will drive P_X/P_Y down to P_2. At $P_X/P_Y < P_2$, there will be an excess demand for imports of X and this will drive P_X/P_Y up to P_2.

(c) Figure 3-19 refers to partial equilibrium analysis, while Figs. 3-5 and 3-15 refer to general equilibrium analysis. Specifically, Fig. 3-19 examines only the market for commodity X, while Figs. 3-5 and 3-15 examine simultaneously the market for commodities X and Y. Thus, Fig. 3-19 provides only a partial analysis or approximation to the general equilibrium analysis shown in Figs. 3-5 and 3-19.

Chapter 4

The Heckscher-Ohlin Theory and Extensions

4.1 THE HECKSCHER-OHLIN THEORY

We have seen in Section 2.6 that comparative advantage and trade are based on a difference in factor endowments, technology or tastes between nations. The *Heckscher-Ohlin* (*H-O*) *theory* focuses on the difference in relative *factor endowments* and *factor prices* between nations as the most important determinants of trade (on the assumption of equal or similar technology and tastes). The *H-O theorem* postulates that each nation will export the commodity intensive in its relatively abundant and cheap factor and import the commodity intensive in its relatively scarce and expensive factor. The *factor-price equalization theorem* (actually, a corollary of the H-O theorem) postulates that trade will lead to the elimination or reduction in the pretrade difference in relative and absolute factor prices between nations.

EXAMPLE 1. Figure 4-1 shows the production possibilities curves of the U.K. and the U.S. on the same set of axes. Technology is assumed to be the same in both nations. Production is skewed toward the cloth axis in the U.K. because cloth is labor (L)-intensive and the U.K. has a relative abundance of labor. Production is skewed toward the wheat axis in the U.S. because wheat is capital (K)-intensive and the U.S. has a relative abundance of capital. The same indifference map refers to both nations because of the assumption of equal tastes or demand preferences. In the absence of trade (left panel of Fig. 4-1), the U.K. produces and consumes at point A on its indifference curve I with $P_C/P_W = P_A$, while the U.S. is at A' on I with $P_{A'}$. With trade (right panel of Fig. 4-1), the U.K. produces at point B (i.e., it specializes in the production of cloth) and consumes at point E on indifference curve II; while the U.S. produces at B' and consumes at E' on II at $P_{B'} = P_B$. As the U.K. specializes in cloth (the L-intensive commodity) and produces less wheat (the K-intensive commodity), its demand for and price of labor time (the wage rate) rises while its demand for and price of capital (the interest rate) falls. The exact opposite occurs in the U.S., with the wage rate falling and the interest rate rising. This continues until relative and absolute factor prices are equalized in the two nations [under highly restrictive assumptions; see Problem 4.3(*b*)].

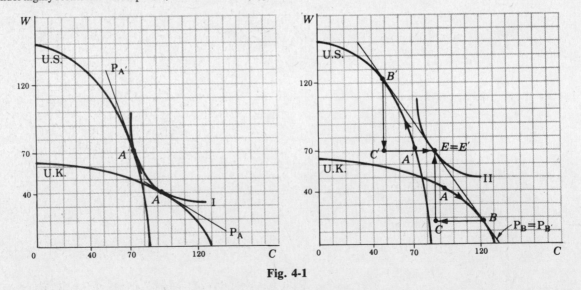

Fig. 4-1

4.2 EMPIRICAL TESTS AND FACTOR-INTENSITY REVERSAL

The first empirical test of the H-O theory was conducted by Leontief in 1951 using U.S. data for 1947. Leontief found that U.S. *import substitutes* were about 30 percent more K-intensive than U.S. exports. Since the U.S. was the most K-abundant nation, this result was the opposite of what the H-O theory predicted and became known as the *Leontief paradox*. While subsequent refinements of the test seem to have resolved the paradox (see Problems 4.5 and 4.6), more recent empirical studies found only partial support for the H-O theory. Another possible reason for Leontief's results is *factor-intensity reversal* (FIR). This refers to the situation where a commodity is the *L-intensive commodity* in the *L-abundant nation* and the *K-intensive commodity* in the *K-abundant nation*. This would lead to the rejection of the H-O theory. Empirical tests indicate that FIR is not very prevalent in the real world.

EXAMPLE 2.   If cloth is the L-intensive commodity in the U.K. (the L-abundant and L-cheap nation) and the K-intensive commodity in the U.S. (the K-abundant and K-cheap nation), we have FIR. Note that we would expect cloth and wheat to be more L-intensive in the U.K. than in the U.S. because the ratio of wage of labor to interest on capital (w/r) is lower in the U.K.; but to have FIR, cloth would have to be the L-intensive commodity in the U.K. and the K-intensive commodity in the U.S. With FIR, the H-O theorem would fall because it would predict that the U.K. should export cloth (the L-intensive commodity in the U.K.) because the U.K. is the L-abundant nation, and the U.S. should also export cloth (the K-intensive commodity in the U.S.) because the U.S. is the K-abundant nation. As the U.K. and the U.S. cannot export the same (homogeneous) commodity to each other, the U.S. may end up exporting wheat. Since wheat is the L-intensive commodity in the U.S., the demand for L and w (wage of labor) would rise in both the U.K. and the U.S., and so w may move apart rather than closer in the two nations. Thus, the factor-price equalization theorem would also not hold. FIR results when *factor substitution* is much greater in the production of one commodity (say, cloth) than in the other (see Problem 4.9).

4.3   TRADE BASED ON DIFFERENTIATED PRODUCTS

Although the Heckscher-Ohlin theory is retained, there is a substantial portion of international trade that the basic H-O model does not explain. Some of this is *intra-industry trade* or trade in differentiated products. *Differentiated products* refer to similar, but not identical, products (such as automobiles, typewriters and cigarettes) produced by the same industry or broad product group in various nations. Intra-industry trade arises as producers cater to "majority" tastes within their nation, leaving "minority" tastes to be satisfied by imports. Related to this is the sharp increase in international trade in product parts and components as multinational corporations produce parts and assemble them in different nations in order to minimize production costs.

EXAMPLE 3.   The U.S. both imports and exports automobiles, typewriters, cigarettes, chemicals and many other industrial products. Another example is the European Common Market. The formation of the European Common Market led to a surge in the volume of trade among member nations, but most of the increase involved the exchange of differentiated products. For example, German automobiles appeal to the majority of car buyers in Germany, but an important minority in Germany still prefers French, Italian or British cars. Trade in parts and components arises when, for example, German and Japanese camera manufacturers ship parts to be assembled in Singapore to take advantage of much cheaper labor there.

4.4   TRADE BASED ON ECONOMIES OF SCALE

Even if two nations are identical in every respect (so that the H-O model would predict no trade), there is still a basis for mutually beneficial trade based on economies of scale. *Economies of scale* refer to the production situation where output grows proportionately more than the increase in the use of inputs or factors of production.

EXAMPLE 4.   If the two nations are identical in every respect (i.e., in factor endowments, technology and tastes), relative commodity prices would be the same in two nations in isolation and no trade would be possible according to the H-O model. However, if both commodities face economies of scale in production, each nation could specialize in the production of one of the two commodities and, by exchanging some of its output for the output of the other nation, reach a higher level of satisfaction (consumption) than in isolation. The gains with trade arise from the increase in the total output of both commodities resulting from economies of scale (see Problem 4.11).

4.5 TRADE BASED ON TECHNOLOGICAL GAPS AND PRODUCT CYCLES

According to the *technological gap model*, great deal of the exports of industrial nations are based on the introduction of new products and new production processes. These give the nation a temporary monopoly until other nations copy the technology and undersell the nation that introduced the newer technology. In the meantime, the technological leader may have introduced still newer products and new production processes. A generalization and extension of the technological gap model is Vernon's *product cycle model*. According to this model, the introduction of a new product usually requires highly skilled labor in the production process. As the product matures and acquires mass acceptance, its production becomes standardized, requiring only unskilled labor. The comparative advantage then shifts from the nation that introduced the product to the nation with the cheaper labor. A great deal of the exports of the U.S. (often the technological leader) involve the continuous introduction of new products.

EXAMPLE 5.   Immediately after World War II, the U.S. dominated the world market for radios based on vacuum tubes developed in the U.S. A few years later, Japan copied the technology and undersold the U.S. because of lower wages in Japan. The U.S. recaptured the technological leadership and market with the development of transistors. But again, in a few years, Japan copied the technology and undersold the U.S. The U.S. then introduced the printed circuit and reacquired its ability to successfully compete with Japan. It remains to be seen if Japan can quickly copy this new technology and once again take the market away from the U.S. or whether both nations will be displaced by still cheaper producers in Korea, Taiwan or Singapore.

4.6 TRANSPORTATION COSTS

So far we have abstracted from transportation costs (i.e., we have implicitly assumed that they were zero). Their inclusion modifies our trade model slightly, as follows. A commodity will be traded only if the pretrade price difference between the two nations exceeds the cost of transporting it between them. In addition, when trade is in equilibrium, the price of the traded commodity in the importing nation exceeds the price of the same commodity in the exporting nation by the cost of transportation (see Problems 4.14 to 4.16).

Glossary

Heckscher-Ohlin (H-O) theory   A theory that is based on the H-O theorem and the factor-price equalization theorem.

Factor endowments   The availability of such factors of production and resources as labor and capital.

Factor prices   The wage of labor (w) and the interest rate on capital (r) to hire or use a unit of labor and capital, respectively.

Heckscher-Ohlin (H-O) theorem   This theorem postulates that each nation will export the commodity intensive in its relatively abundant and cheap factor and import the commodity intensive in its relatively scarce and expensive factor.

Factor-price equalization theorem   This theorem postulates that trade leads to the equalization of relative and absolute factor prices between nations (under highly restrictive assumptions).

Import substitutes   Commodities (such as cars) produced at home and imported because of incomplete specialization.

Leontief paradox   The empirical results obtained by Leontief that showed U.S. import substitutes in 1947 to be about 30% more K-intensive than U.S. exports. Since the U.S. was the most K-abundant nation, this result was the opposite of what the H-O theory predicted.

Factory-intensity reversal (FIR)   The situation where a commodity is the L-intensive commodity in the L-abundant nation and the K-intensive commodity in the K-abundant nation. If prevalent, it would lead to the rejection of the H-O theory.

Labor-intensive commodity   The commodity that requires a higher ratio of labor to capital (L/K), or lower K/L, in production.

L-abundant nation   The nation with the higher ratio of total labor to total capital (L/K) and lower ratio of wages to interest rate (w/r), or higher r/w.

Capital-intensive commodity   The commodity that requires a higher ratio of capital to labor (K/L), or lower L/K in production.

K-abundant nation   The nation with the higher ratio of total capital to total labor (K/L) available and lower ratio of interest to wages (r/w), or higher w/r.

Factor substitution   The possibility of reducing the amount of one factor by increasing the amount of another factor to produce a unit of a commodity.

Intra-industry trade   International trade in differentiated products of the same industry or broad product group.

Differentiated products   Similar, but not identical, products (such as cars, typewriters and cigarettes) produced by the same industry or broad product group.

Economies of scale   The production situation where output grows proportionately more than the increase in the use of inputs or factors of production.

Technological gap model   This model postulates that a great deal of the exports of industrial nations are based on the introduction of new products and new production processes.

Product cycle model   This generalization and extension of the technological gap model postulates that the comparative advantage in introducing new products lies in the high-technology nations but shifts to cheap-labor nations once the product acquires mass acceptance. The premise underlying this model is that highly skilled labor is initially required to produce a new product; but upon mass acceptance and standardization of the product, production can be carried out by unskilled labor, and hence the comparative advantage shifts to cheap-labor nations.

Review Questions

1. For Heckscher and Ohlin, the most important cause of the difference in relative commodity prices and trade between nations is a difference in   (a) factor endowments,   (b) technology,   (c) tastes,   (d) demand conditions.

   Ans.   (a) See Section 4.1.

2. The H-O theory postulates that as a result of trade, the difference in *factor* prices between nations   (a) diminishes,   (b) increases,   (c) remains unchanged,   (d) any of the above are possible.

   Ans.   (a) See Section 4.1.

3. The Leontief paradox refers to the result that U.S.   (a) exports are more K-intensive than U.S. imports,   (b) exports are more K-intensive than U.S. import substitutes,   (c) imports are more K-intensive than U.S. exports,   (d) import substitutes are more K-intensive than U.S. exports.

   Ans.   (d) See Section 4.2.

4. Factor-intensity reversal refers to the situation where (a) both commodities are more L-intensive in one nation than in the other nation,   (b) one commodity is the L-intensive commodity in one nation and the K-intensive commodity

in the other nation,   (c) the same commodity is more L-intensive in one nation than in the other nation,   (d) any of the above.

Ans.   (b) See Example 2.

5. Which type of trade is not explained by the Heckscher-Ohlin trade model?   (a) Intra-industry trade,   (b) trade based on economies of scale,   (c) trade based on imitation gaps and product cycles,   (d) all of the above.

Ans.   (d) See Sections 4.3 to 4.5.

6. Trade in differentiated products refers to   (a) inter-industry trade,   (b) intra-industry trade,   (c) trade based on economies of scale,   (d) trade based on imitation gaps and product cycles.

Ans.   (b) See Section 4.3.

7. Trade in differentiated products results from domestic producers catering to   (a) majority tastes in the nation,   (b) majority tastes abroad,   (c) minority tastes in the nation,   (d) any of the above.

Ans.   (a) See Section 4.3.

8. Economies of scale is a term that refers to the production situation where the growth of output in relation to the increase in the use of inputs is   (a) greater,   (b) less,   (c) equal,   (d) any of the above.

Ans.   (a) See Section 4.4.

9. The technological gap model represents an extension of the H-O model because the H-O model   (a) did not consider technology,   (b) viewed technology statically (i.e., at one point in time),   (c) viewed technology dynamically (i.e., over time),   (d) any of the above.

Ans.   (b) Compare Section 4.5 with Section 4.1.

10. According to the product cycle trade model   (a) when a new product is introduced, it usually requires highly skilled labor to produce;   (b) after the product acquires mass acceptance and is standardized, it can be produced with unskilled labor;   (c) comparative advantage shifts to cheap-labor nations after the product is standardized;   (d) all of the above.

Ans.   (d) See Section 4.5.

11. If the cost of transporting a good between two nations exceeds the pretrade difference for the good between the two nations, then trade in that good is   (a) possible,   (b) impossible,   (c) reversed,   (d) cannot say.

Ans. (b) See Section 4.6.

12. Which of the following statements is not true with respect to transportation costs?   (a) The price of the traded commodity in the importing nation exceeds the price of the same commodity in the exporting nation by the cost of transportation.   (b) Some commodities are not traded because of transportation costs.   (c) Consideration of transportation costs invalidates the H-O theory.   (d) Transportation cost is not what distinguishes international from interregional trade.

Ans.   (c) See Section 4.6 and Problem 1.2(b).

Solved Problems

THE HECKSCHER-OHLIN THEORY

4.1   (a) Identify the conditions that may give rise to trade between two nations.   (b) What are some of the assumptions on which the Heckscher-Ohlin theory of trade is based?   (c) What does this theory say about the pattern of trade and effect of trade on factor prices?

(a) Trade can be based on a difference in factor endowments, technology or tastes between two nations. A difference either in factor endowments or technology results in a different production possibilities curve for each nation, which, unless neutralized by a difference in tastes [see Problem 2.18(b)], leads to a difference in relative commodity price and mutually beneficial trade (see Problem 2.16). If two nations face increasing costs and have identical production possibilities curves but different tastes, there will also be a difference in relative commodity prices and the basis for mutually beneficial trade between the two nations (see Problem 2.21). The difference in relative commodity prices is then translated into a difference in absolute commodity prices between the two nations, which is the *immediate* cause of trade (see Problem 1.20).

(b) The Heckscher-Ohlin theory (sometimes referred to as the modern theory—as opposed to classical theory—of international trade) assumes that nations have the same tastes, use the same technology, face constant returns to scale (i.e., a given percentage increase in all inputs increases output by the same percentage) but differ widely in factor endowments. It also says that in the face of identical tastes or demand conditions, this difference in factor endowments will result in a difference in relative *factor* prices between nations, which in turn leads to a difference in relative *commodity* prices and trade (see Example 1). Thus, in the Heckscher-Ohlin theory, the international difference in supply conditions alone determines the pattern of trade. To be noted is that the two nations need not be identical in other respects in order for international trade to be based primarily on the difference in their factor endowments (see Section 3.2 and Fig. 3-2).

(c) The Heckscher-Ohlin theorem postulates that each nation will export the commodity intensive in its *relatively* abundant and cheap factor and import the commodity intensive in its *relatively* scarce and expensive factor. As an important corollary, it adds that under highly restrictive assumptions [see Problem 2.33(c)], trade will completely eliminate the pretrade relative and absolute differences in the price of homogeneous factors among nations. Under less restrictive and more usual conditions, however, trade will reduce, but not eliminate, the pretrade differences in relative and absolute factor prices among nations (see Problem 4.3). In any event, the Heckscher-Ohlin theory does say something very useful on how trade affects factor prices and the distribution of income in each nation. Classical economists were practically silent on this point.

4.2 Suppose that (1) the capital-labor ratio (i.e., K/L) to produce 1 unit of wheat is greater than the K/L to produce 1 unit of cloth (i.e., wheat is K-intensive relative to cloth) in both the U.S. and the U.K.; (2) the *ratio* of *total* capital to *total* labor available in the U.S. is greater than in the U.K.; (3) the taste for wheat and cloth is the same in both nations; (4) each nation faces increasing costs of production; and (5) the same technology is available to both nations. (a) Indicate how the U.S. production possibilities curve would differ from that of the U.K. (b) In which nation is the price of capital (i.e., the interest rate, r) relative to the price of labor time (i.e., the wage rate, w) lower? Why? (c) Which nation in isolation will have the lower equilibrium P_W/P_C? Why?

(a) Since (1) the same technology is available to both nations, (2) the ratio of total capital to total labor is greater in the U.S. than in the U.K. and (3) wheat is K-intensive relative to cloth, the U.S. production possibilities curve is skewed toward the wheat axis while that of the U.K. is skewed toward the cloth axis, as in Fig. 4-1.

(b) Since the ratio of total capital to total labor (i.e., the relative supply of capital) is greater in the U.S. than in the U.K. in the face of identical tastes for wheat and cloth in both nations, r/w is lower in the U.S. than in the U.K. This lower r/w in the U.S. translates into a lower dollar interest rate and a higher dollar wage rate in the U.S. than in the U.K. (just as the lower P_W/P_C in the U.S. translates into a lower dollar price of wheat but a higher price for cloth in Problem 1.20).

(c) Since r/w is lower in the U.S. than in the U.K. and wheat is K-intensive, the equilibrium P_W/P_C in isolation is lower in the U.S. than in the U.K. (see Fig. 4-1). This means that the U.S. has a comparative advantage in wheat and the U.K. in cloth.

4.3 With reference to Problem 4.2, explain (a) how trade causes a reduction in the difference in r and w between the U.S. and the U.K. (b) Under what conditions will the return to homogeneous factors become completely equalized with trade?

(a)   Since in Problem 4.2(c) we said that P_W/P_C is lower in the U.S. than in the U.K., the U.S. specializes in the production of wheat and exports wheat for English cloth. As the U.S. produces more wheat and less cloth, the U.S. demand for capital rises while that for labor falls. Given the U.S. supply of capital, the increase in the U.S. demand for capital causes an increase in the equilibrium rate of interest in the U.S. Given the U.S. supply of labor, the decrease in the U.S. demand for labor results in a decrease in the equilibrium wage rate in the U.S. The exact opposite occurs in the U.K. Since the pretrade r was lower in the U.S. than in the U.K. and as a result of trade r rises in the U.S. and falls in the U.K., trade causes a reduction in the pretrade difference in r between the two nations. On the other hand, since before trade, w was higher in the U.S. than in the U.K. and trade reduces w in the U.S. and increases it in the U.K., the pretrade difference in w is reduced with trade. Thus, international trade reduces the international difference in the return to *homogeneous* factors.

(b)   According to the H-O theory, international trade will bring about equalization in the returns to homogeneous factors only if trade proceeds until P_W/P_C has become identical in both nations. This is so because as long as there is a difference in r/w in the two nations, there will be a difference in P_W/P_C and the volume of trade will expand. But as this occurs, the difference in P_W/P_C and thus the difference in r/w will be reduced. If the volume of trade stops expanding when P_W/P_C has become identical in both nations, then r/w and r and w will also be equalized. This would occur if we had no transportation costs and no trade barriers (such as tariffs, quotas, etc.). Since in the real world, transportation costs and trade barriers do exist, trade stops expanding before P_W/P_C is equalized (see Section 4.6 and Chapter 6). Thus, r/w, r and w also are not equalized. However, actual differences in factor prices around the world today seem to be too great to be explained by transportation costs and trade barriers alone. The greater part of the difference may result because the assumptions of the same technology in all nations, no economies of scale and perfect competition made by the H-O theory are not met in the real world.

4.4   With reference to Problem 4.2, explain   (a) how the international flow of factors would reduce the difference in r and w between the U.S. and the U.K.   (b) Under what conditions would the international flow of labor and capital equalize r and w?   (c) How do international factor mobility and trade affect the earnings of the nation's scarce factor? What does this lead to?

(a)   If factors are free to move from the nation of low return to that of high return and we have no trade, labor will leave the U.K. (the nation with the lower w), attracted by the higher w in the U.S. This increases the U.S. supply of labor. In the face of an unchanged U.S. demand for labor, the equilibrium w will fall in the U.S. The exact opposite occurs in the U.K. Since w falls in the high-wage nation (i.e., the U.S.) and rises in the low-wage nation (i.e., the U.K.), the pretrade difference in the wage of homogeneous labor in the U.S. and the U.K. is reduced. On the other hand, capital leaves the U.S. (the low-interest nation) for the higher returns in the U.K. The supply of capital then falls in the U.S. and rises in the U.K. With unchanged demand conditions for capital in the U.S. and the U.K., r rises in the U.S. and falls in the U.K., reducing the pretrade difference in r. Thus, international factor movements can be an alternative to international trade in causing a reduction in the international difference in the return to homogeneous factors. Note that while trade operates on the demand for factors, factor mobility operates on the supply of factors; however, the outcome as far as factor prices are concerned is the same.

(b)   With factor movements but no trade, factor prices in the two nations would be equalized only if there were no restrictions to the free international flow of factors, all factors had perfect knowledge of costs and opportunities in each nation, and there were no transportation costs or costs of transferring factors from one nation to another. Because these and the previous conditions are not met, wide differences remain in returns as evidenced, say, by the difference in doctors' salaries in the U.S. and India but also between the U.S. and U.K. If we had some factor movements, a smaller volume of trade would be needed to bring about equality in factor returns between the two nations.

(c)   International factor mobility and trade reduce the earnings of the nation's scarce factor and increase the earnings of the nation's abundant factor [see Problems 4.3(a) and 4.4(a)]. Since labor is a relatively scarce factor in the U.S. and other industrial nations, the earnings of labor fall. Thus, labor unions in these nations generally oppose immigration and free trade.

EMPIRICAL TESTS AND FACTOR-INTENSITY REVERSAL

4.5 (*a*) What is meant by the Leontief paradox? What is its significance for the H-O theory? (*b*) Could the fact that Leontief used U.S. data on import substitutes instead of foreign data on U.S. imports explain the paradox? (*c*) What are some of the possible criticisms of the Leontief study that would explain the paradox?

(*a*) The Leontief paradox refers to the empirical results obtained by Leontief using 1947 data that U.S. import substitutes were about 30% more *K*-intensive than U.S. exports. Since the U.S. is the most *K*-abundant nation, this result was the opposite of what the H-O theory predicted.

(*b*) Leontief used data on U.S. import substitutes because foreign data on U.S. imports were not available. Even though U.S. production techniques could be expected to be more *K*-intensive than abroad (since the U.S. was the most *K*-abundant and *K*-cheap nation), U.S. import substitutes should still have been more *L*-intensive than U.S. exports for the H-O theory to hold. Thus, the fact that Leontief used U.S. data on import substitutes rather than foreign data on U.S. imports does not explain the paradox.

(*c*) Some possible criticisms of Leontief's study that could explain the paradox are: (1) the year 1947 was too close to World War II to be representative; (2) some commodities are intensive in natural resources so that classifying them as either *L*- or *K*-intensive, as Leontief did, is inappropriate; (3) U.S. tariffs are generally higher on *L*-intensive commodities, and this distorted the flow of trade; (4) Leontief included in his measure of capital only physical capital (machinery, buildings, etc.) and completely ignored human capital.

4.6 (*a*) What is meant by human capital? (*b*) How does the knowledge that wages are higher in U.S. export industries than in U.S. import-competing industries help resolve the Leontief paradox? (*c*) What is the status of the controversy on the Leontief paradox?

(*a*) Human capital refers to expenditures on education, job training, health, and so on, all of which increase the productivity of labor. It is very useful for analytical purposes to consider expenditures on human capital as investments involving costs that are justified by the resulting increased productivity of labor (just like the investment in a piece of machinery).

(*b*) Since U.S. labor in export industries receives higher wages than U.S. labor in import-competing industries, it can be inferred that the former embody more human capital than the latter. Thus, if the relatively greater amount of human capital embodied in U.S. exports is added to the physical or material capital (and the same is also done for U.S. import substitutes), U.S. exports might become more *K*-intensive than U.S. import substitutes, thus eliminating the Leontief paradox.

(*c*) Subsequent empirical tests that addressed the paradox resulting from Leontief's study seem to weigh in favor of eliminating the paradox, so that the H-O theory can be tentatively retained while we await results of additional tests.

4.7 (*a*) What is meant by factor-intensity reversal (FIR)? (*b*) Why would the prevalence of FIR lead to the rejection of the H-O theorem? (*c*) Why would the prevalence of FIR lead to the rejection of the factor-price equalization theorem?

(*a*) FIR refers to the situation where a commodity (say cloth) is the *L*-intensive one in relation to the other commodity (wheat) in the *L*-abundant nation (say the U.K.) and is the *K*-intensive commodity in the *K*-abundant nation (the U.S.).

(*b*) The H-O theorem postulates that the *L*-abundant nation (say the U.K.) would have to export its *L*-intensive commodity and the *K*-abundant nation (the U.S.) would have to export its *K*-intensive commodity. However, with FIR, the same product (cloth, in this instance) is the *L*-intensive commodity in the U.K. and the *K*-intensive commodity in the U.S. Thus, according to the H-O theorem, both the U.K. and the U.S. would have to export cloth to each other. Since this is impossible, the H-O theorem can no longer predict the pattern of trade in the presence of FIR.

(*c*) Since with FIR the H-O theorem no longer predicts the pattern of trade, the factor-price equalization theorem (a corollary of the H-O theorem) also falls. Specifically, since the U.K. and the U.S. cannot export (homogeneous) cloth to each other, either the U.K. or the U.S. would have to export wheat and the other nation cloth. Suppose that the U.K. exports cloth and the U.S. exports wheat. Since cloth is the L-intensive commodity in the U.K. (the low-wage nation) and wheat is the L-intensive commodity in the U.S. (the high-wage nation), the demand for labor and w rises in both nations. Thus, the difference in w between the U.K. and the U.S. may fall, remain unchanged or increase, depending upon whether w rises faster, at the same rate or less in the U.K. than in the U.S. Thus, the factor-price equalization theorem can no longer predict the effect of trade on factor prices in the two nations. The same would be true if the U.K. exported wheat and the U.S. cloth.

4.8   (a) Explain how, to some extent, capital and labor can be substituted for each other in the production of wheat and cloth.   (b) What determines the K/L ratio actually used in the production of wheat and cloth in the U.S. and U.K.?   (c) If capital and labor can be substituted for each other so that wheat and cloth can be produced with different K/L ratios, when can we say unequivocally that wheat is K-intensive in relation to cloth?

    (a)   A given amount of wheat can be produced on a given amount of land, either by using many workers and very simple and cheap equipment (i.e., with a low K/L ratio) or with fewer workers using more sophisticated and expensive equipment (i.e., with a higher K/L ratio). The same is true for cloth. Within certain limits, factors of production can be substituted for one another in the production of most commodities.

    (b)   The K/L ratio actually used in the production of wheat and cloth is determined by the cost of using capital in relation to the cost of hiring labor of r/w in the U.S. and U.K. Each nation will use the particular combination of capital and labor that will enable it to produce the desired level of output of each commodity at the lowest possible cost. If the U.S. has a relative abundance of capital and the r/w ratio is lower than in the U.K., the U.S. will use more K-intensive techniques (i.e., a higher K/L) ratio) in the production of both wheat and cloth *in relation to the U.K.*

    (c)   Even though the U.S. uses more K-intensive techniques in the production of both wheat and cloth than the U.K., we can say unequivocally that wheat is K-intensive in relation to cloth, if the K/L ratio in wheat production is higher than the K/L ratio in cloth production *in both the U.S. and the U.K.* In this case, the Heckscher-Ohlin theory holds intact, as stated in Section 4.1 and Example 1.

4.9   (a) Explain the condition necessary for FIR to occur.   (b) How prevalent is FIR in the real world? What overall conclusion can you reach as to the acceptability of the H-O theory?

    (a)   FIR may result when the possibility of factor substitution is much greater in the production of one commodity (say cloth) than in the production of the other commodity (wheat). This means that it is much easier to substitute L for K in cloth production than in wheat production. As a result, cloth is produced with L-intensive techniques in the L-cheap nation (say the U.K.) and with K-intensive techniques in the K-cheap nation (the U.S.). If at the same time the possibility of substituting L for K is very low in wheat production, the U.K. and the U.S. will be forced to use similar techniques in wheat production. As a result, cloth will be the L-intensive commodity in the U.K. and the K-intensive commodity in the U.S. and we have a case of FIR.

    (b)   That FIR sometimes occurs in the real world is a known fact. However, only if FIR is fairly prevalent would the H-O theory have to be rejected. Recent empirical research indicates that FIR occurs infrequently; hence, FIR can be treated as an exception and the H-O theory can be retained.

EXTENSIONS OF THE HECKSCHER-OHLIN TRADE MODEL

4.10   (a) Why does the Heckscher-Ohlin (H-O) trade model need to be extended?   (b) In what important ways can the H-O trade model be extended?   (c) What is meant by differentiated products and intra-industry trade?

    (a)   The H-O trade model needs to be extended because, while generally correct, it fails to explain a significant portion of international trade, particularly the trade in manufactured products among industrial nations.

(b)   The international trade left unexplained by the basic H-O model can be explained by (1) intra-industry trade, (2) trade based on economies of scale and (3) trade based on imitation gaps and product differentiation.

(c)   Differentiated products refer to similar, but not identical, products (such as cars, typewriters, cigarettes, soaps and so on) produced by the same industry or broad product group. Intra-industry trade refers to the international trade in differentiated products.

4.11   Draw a figure showing that even if two nations, say the U.K. and Germany, have identical factor endowments, technology and tastes, there is still a basis for mutually beneficial trade between them if both nations face economies of scale in the production of more wheat and more cloth.

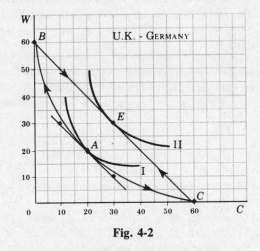

Fig. 4-2

Since the two nations have identical factor endowments and technology, the production possibilities curves are identical. Since both nations face economies of scale, or operate under decreasing costs, the production possibilities curves are *convex* from the origin. For example, in Fig. 4-2, *BAC* is the production possibilities curve for both the U.K. and Germany. Since both nations also have identical tastes, they have identical indifference maps as well. In isolation, both nations consume at point *A* on indifference curve I. Even though $P_W/P_C = 1$ in both nations at point *A*, there is still a basis for trade based on decreasing costs. For example, Germany could specialize completely in the production of wheat (i.e., move from *A* to *B* in production, thus taking advantage of economies of scale, or decreasing costs, in wheat production), exchange 30W for 30C with the U.K. and reach point *E* on indifference curve II in consumption. The U.K. would then specialize completely in the production of cloth (i.e., move from *A* to *C* in production, thus taking advantage of decreasing costs in cloth production), exchange 30C for 30W with Germany and reach point *E* in consumption. By doing this, both nations gain 10W and 10C.

Related to trade based on economies of scale is the hypothesis advanced by Linder that a nation exports those manufactured products that appeal to the majority taste within the nation and for which a large domestic market exists. While confirmed for his native Sweden, Linder's hypothesis was not confirmed for other nations. For example, it cannot explain why Korea exports Christmas cards in the absence of a domestic market for this product.

4.12   (*a*) How do economies of scale arise?   (*b*) In what way can we say that in Fig. 4-2 equilibrium point *A* in each nation in isolation is unstable?   (*c*) In the case described in Problem 4.11, how does each nation determine the export commodity in which it will specialize in production?   (*d*) Need the two nations be identical in every respect for trade to be based on economies of scale?   (*e*) What happens within each nation if economies of scale persist over a sufficiently large range of outputs?

(*a*)   Economies of scale arise because division of labor and specialization become possible when the scale of operation is sufficiently great. That is, each worker can specialize in performing a simple repetitive task, with a resulting increase in productivity. In addition, more specialized and productive machinery can be introduced at a large scale of operation.

(b) Point A is unstable in the sense that if, for whatever reason, the U.K. or Germany moves away from point A in production, the nation will not return to point A in production but will continue to specialize even more in the commodity in which it started to specialize. The other nation will then specialize in the production of the other commodity.

(c) It is a matter of complete indifference as to which nation specializes in the production of wheat and which in cloth. This may be agreed upon by the two nations or be the result of an historical accident.

(d) The two nations need not be identical for trade to be based on economies of scale. This is left as an exercise for the more advanced student to show graphically.

(e) If economies of scale persist over a sufficiently long range of outputs, then a single or few firms will capture the entire market for the commodity, leading to monopoly or oligopoly, respectively.

4.13 (a) What is meant by the technological gap model? What is a shortcoming of this model? (b) What is meant by the product cycle model? Is there empirical support for this model in the real world? (c) In what way do the technological gap and product cycle models differ from trade theory, presented in Chapters 2 and 3, in which a difference in technology is clearly recognized as a basis for trade?

(a) The technological gap model postulates that a great deal of the exports of industrial nations are based on the introduction of new products and new production processes, which nations with cheaper labor imitate to capture the market. In the meantime, the technological leader may have introduced still newer products and newer production processes. One disadvantage of this model is that it does not explain how technological gaps arise in the first place and exactly how they are eliminated over time.

(b) The product cycle model, fully developed by Vernon in 1966, represents a generalization and extension of the technological gap model. According to this model, the initial production of a new product usually requires skilled labor, which can be replaced by unskilled labor once the product acquires mass acceptance and is standardized. Thus, the comparative advantage held by the high-technology nations that introduce new products shifts to lower-wage nations. Considerable support for this model exists in the real world, where a strong correlation has been found between expenditures on research and development (R & D) as a proxy for temporary comparative advantage in new products and export performance in these products.

(c) Traditional trade theory (as presented thus far) takes technology as given. Even if this model could be extended to incorporate changes in technology (see Chapter 5), the model still would not deal with the dynamic process (i.e., the process over time) by which a change in technology affects trade. This gap is filled by the technological gap and product cycle models.

4.14 The U.K.'s and the U.S.'s portions of Fig. 4-3 share a common vertical axis which measures the (absolute) price of cloth in terms of dollars. Increasing quantities of cloth per year are measured by a movement from the common origin to the right (as usual) for the U.S. and a movement from the origin to the left for the U.K. Note that D_C is negatively sloped and S_C is positively sloped for the U.K. if we move from left to right, as we should. With regard to Fig. 4-3, (a) what are the equilibrium price and quantity of cloth in the absence of trade in the U.K. and the U.S.? (b) If we assume zero transportation costs, what price of cloth will bring about equilibrium in trade? How much cloth is traded? How much cloth is produced and consumed in each nation with trade?

(a) The equilibrium price and quantity of cloth in each nation in the absence of trade are given by the intersection of the market demand curve and market supply curve in the nation. Thus, $P_C = \$3$ and $Q_C = 60$/year in the U.K., while $P_C = \$6$ and $Q_C = 60$/year in the U.S. (see Fig. 4-3).

(b) When trade is allowed, the U.K. will export cloth to the U.S., and P_C rises in the U.K. and falls in the U.S. (from their respective autarky levels). The equilibrium P_C with trade (the same in both nations) is the one that clears the market. This is given by $P_C = \$4.50$, because at this price, the U.K. wants to export 60C per year and the U.S. wants to import 60C per year (see Fig. 4-3). That is, at $P_C = \$4.50$, the U.K. produces 90C, consumes 30C and exports 60C, while the U.S. produces 30C, imports 60C and consumes 90C. The same thing could be done for wheat.

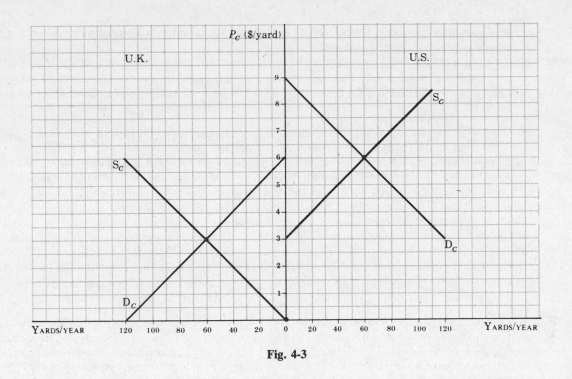

Fig. 4-3

4.15 With reference to Fig. 4-3, (*a*) what would P_C be in each nation if the cost of transporting each yard of cloth from the U.K. to the U.S. were $1? How much would be produced, consumed and traded by the U.K. and the U.S. in this case? (*b*) What if the cost of transporting one yard of cloth were $2? $3? $4? (*c*) What can you then say in general about the effect of transportation costs on the price of the traded commodity in each of the trading nations? The level of production? Consumption? Trade?

(*a*) With transportation costs equal to $1/yard, P_C in the U.S. (the importing nation) will exceed P_C in the U.K. (the exporting nation) by $1. This cost will be shared by the two nations in such a way that the volume of trade is in equilibrium. This occurs when $P_C = \$4$ in the U.K. and $5 in the U.S. At $P_C = \$4$, the U.K. produces 80C, consumes 40C and *exports 40C*. At $P_C = \$5$, the U.S. produces 40C, *imports 40C* and consumes 80C (see Fig. 4-3). Note that in this case the cost of transportation is shared *equally* by each nation. This is due to the way we have drawn Fig. 4-3. In other cases, the more steeply inclined the D and S curves for the traded commodity of one nation in relation to the D and S curves of the other nation, the greater the share of the transportation costs falling on the first nation.

(*b*) With transportation costs of $2/yard, $P_C = \$3.50$ in the U.K. and $5.50 in the U.S. The U.K. produces 70C, consumes 50C and exports 20C. The U.S. produces 50C, imports 20C and consumes 70C. With transportation costs of $3/yard, $P_C = \$3$ in the U.K. and $6 in the U.S., and both the U.K. and the U.S. produce and consume 60C and trade nothing. Transportation costs of more than $3/yard exceed the difference in the pretrade P_C in the two nations and result in no trade in cloth between the two nations. In this case, cloth would be a purely domestic commodity in both nations rather than an international commodity. Note that transport costs include not only freight charges but also loading and unloading charges, insurance premiums and the interest cost while the goods are in transit.

(*c*) Parts (*a*) and (*b*) show that transportation costs will make the price of the traded commodity higher in the importing nation than in the exporting nation. Compared to the case where there is free trade and there are no transportation costs, the exporting nation will produce less, consume more and export less. The importing nation, on the other hand, will produce more, consume less and import less. Thus, specialization in production and the volume of trade are less—and so are the gains from trade.

4.16 On the same set of axes, draw a hypothetical offer curve for the U.K. and the U.S. and explain how this figure can be used to analyze the effect of transportation costs on the equilibrium relative commodity price with trade, and on the volume of trade.

In Fig. 4-4, the equilibrium relative commodity price with trade in the absence of transportation costs is P_2 and the equilibrium volume of trade is given by point E. With transportation costs considered, the relative price of each commodity will be higher in the importing nation than in the exporting nation, by the amount of the transportation costs expressed as a quantity of one of the traded commodities. For example, in Fig. 4-4, the U.S. imports OH units of cloth at $P_C/P_W = P_3$ while the U.K. exports OH of cloth at P_1. $P_3 > P_1$ by the cost of transporting OH units of cloth from the U.K. to the U.S. This equals FG of wheat. Viewed in terms of wheat, we can say that the U.S. exports FH of wheat at $P_W/P_C = P_3$ while the U.K. imports GH of wheat at the higher P_W/P_C of P_1. P_W/P_C of $P_1 > P_W/P_C$ of P_3 by the cost of transporting GH of wheat from the U.S. to the U.K. This equals FG of wheat. The introduction of transportation costs also reduces the volume of trade (see Fig. 4-4). Needless to say, the general equilibrium approach which measures transportation costs in terms of the amount of a commodity is very awkward. A better and simpler method is by the *partial equilibrium approach* discussed in Problem 4.15.

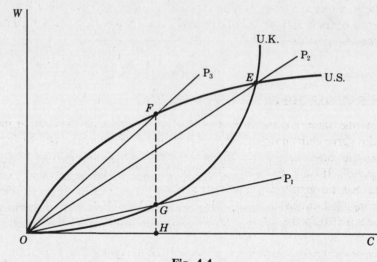

Fig. 4-4

Chapter 5

Dynamic Factors in International Trade: Growth and Development

5.1 DYNAMIC FACTORS

So far, we have assumed that each nation has given and unchanging factor endowments and technology (hence a given production possibilities curve) and given and unchanging tastes (hence a given community indifference map). On this premise, we examined the basis and the gains from trade. However, over time, a nation's factor endowments change and its technology may improve. These changes cause its production possibilities curve to shift. Similarly, a nation's tastes may change and result in a different indifference map. All of these changes affect the terms of trade and the volume of trade. How much these are altered depends on the actual type and degree of the changes occurring.

5.2 GROWTH IN FACTOR SUPPLIES THROUGH TIME

If technology remains the same but the factors of production available to a nation increase, the nation's production possibilities curve shifts outward. This shift is uniform or symmetrical (so that the new production possibilities curve has the same shape as the old one) if labor and capital grow in the same proportion. This is called *balanced growth*. If only the nation's supply of labor increases or if its supply of labor increases proportionately more than its supply of capital, then the nation's production possibilities curve shifts more along the axis measuring the L-intensive commodity than along the axis measuring the K-intensive commodity. The opposite shift occurs if only the nation's supply of capital increases or if its supply of capital increases proportionately more than its supply of labor.

According to the *Rybczynski theorem,* at constant relative commodity prices, the growth of only one factor leads to the absolute expansion in the output of the commodity using the growing factor intensively and to the absolute reduction in the output of the commodity using the nongrowing factor intensively.

EXAMPLE 1.   If only the supply of labor increases in the U.K., or if the supply of labor increases proportionately more than the supply of capital and its technology remains the same, then the U.K.'s production possibilities curve or transformation curve in Fig. 2-3 might shift outward from TT to T'T' as shown in Fig. 5-1. Note that the shift is greater along the horizontal axis, which measures cloth (the L-intensive commodity) than along the vertical axis, which measures wheat (the K-intensive commodity). The shift along the cloth axis in Fig. 5-1 is exaggerated for pedagogical reasons. Even if the supply of labor alone increases in the U.K., the U.K. production possibilities curve will nevertheless shift slightly upward since labor is also used in the production of wheat (the K-intensive commodity). However, according to the Rybczynski theorem, the output of cloth would rise while the output of wheat would fall in the U.K. at constant P_C/P_W. For the effect of other types of factor changes on the production possibilities curve of the U.K. and the U.S. and for graphical illustrations and an intuitive proof of the Rybczynski theorem, see Problems 5.5 to 5.8.

5.3 TECHNICAL PROGRESS

Technical progress increases the productivity of a nation's factors of production and has the same general effect on the nation's production possibilities curve as an increase in the supply of its factors. There are at least three types of technical progress:

69

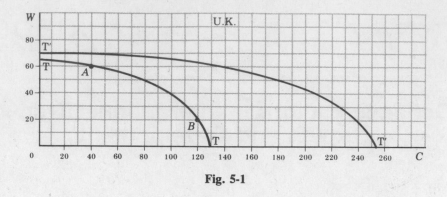

Fig. 5-1

(1) *K-saving technical progress* throughout the economy increases the productivity of labor proportionately more than that of capital. As a result, *L* is substituted for *K* in production at constant *w/r*, and *K/L* falls in the production of both commodities. This means that a given output can now be produced with fewer units of *L* and *K* but also with lower *K/L* (higher *L/K*). *K*-saving technical progress is equivalent to a proportionately greater increase in the supply of labor than of capital (with unchanged technology). For example, *K*-saving technical progress in the U.K. equally applicable to cloth and wheat production might cause an outward shift in the U.K. production possibilities curve from TT to T'T' in Fig. 5-1. Note that technical progress is defined at constant *w/r*, and constant returns to scale are assumed in production.

(2) *L-saving technical progress* is exactly the opposite of *K*-saving technical progress (see Figs. 5-4 and 5-7).

(3) *Neutral technical progress* increases the productivity of *L* and *K* by the same proportion and results in a uniform or symmetrical outward shift in the nation's production possibilities curve (see Figs. 5-5 and 5-8).

5.4   CHANGE IN FACTOR SUPPLIES AND TECHNOLOGY, AND TRADE

When there is an increase in a nation's supply of factors of production and/or technical progress, the nation's production possibilities curve shifts outward. With unchanged tastes, this causes a change in the terms of trade, the volume of trade and in the distribution of the gains from trade between the two nations. The actual result depends on the type and degree of the changes occurring.

EXAMPLE 2. In Panel A of Fig. 5-2, we see that before any change in factor endowments and/or technology, the U.K. produces at point *B* on TT, exports 60C for 60W, and consumes at point *E* on III (as in Fig. 3-2). This gives point *E* on the U.K. offer curve in Panel B (as in Fig. 3-3). With unchanged tastes and at the same terms of trade of P_B but after TT shifted to T'T', the U.K. would like to produce at point *M* on T'T', export 150C for 150W, and consume at point *U* on VII. This gives point *U* on offer curve U.K.* in Panel B. If nothing changed in the U.S. (so that the U.S. offer curve in Panel B of Fig. 5-2 is the same as that in Fig. 3-4), we see that at P_B the U.K. would like to export more of its cloth and import more American wheat than the U.S. is willing to trade at P_B (see Panel B of Fig. 5-2). Thus, the terms of trade move against the U.K. from P_B to P_G. At P_G, the U.K. produces at point *N* on T'T', exports 140C for 70W, and consumes at point *R* on V (see Panel A of Fig. 5-2). This corresponds to the new equilibrium point *R* in Panel B, where the U.K.* and the U.S. offer curves cross. Thus, the U.S. shares in the benefit of the growth taking place in the U.K. The general rule is that if, at unchanged terms of trade, the nation wants to trade more after growth, its terms of trade will usually deteriorate and the nation shares part of the benefit of its growth with its trade partner. If the nation wants to trade less, the nation not only retains all of the benefits of its growth, but is also likely to gain from better terms of trade (see Problems 5.9 to 5.13).

5.5   CHANGE IN TASTES AND TRADE

A nation's *offer curve* also shifts if the nation's supply of factors and technology remain unchanged but its tastes change. Thus, a change in tastes also alters the volume of trade and the nation's terms of trade. More

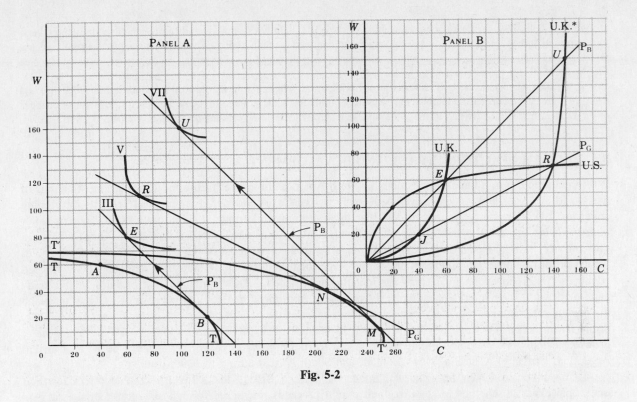

Fig. 5-2

specifically, if a nation's tastes shift away from its *importable* and toward its *exportable commodity* (other things equal), the volume of trade declines and the nation's terms of trade improve. The reverse occurs with an opposite change in the nation's tastes. However, since the nation's indifference map is altered by the change in tastes, we can no longer determine how the nation's welfare is affected.

EXAMPLE 3. If the U.K.'s tastes shift away from wheat (its importable commodity) and toward cloth (its exportable commodity—other things being equal), offer curve U.K. in Fig. 5-3 shifts up or rotates counterclockwise, say, to offer curve U.K.' This is because the U.K. now wants wheat less intensely and is willing to offer less of its cloth than before for each quantity of wheat imported. Thus, with offer curve U.K.', the U.K. exchanges only 20C for 40W at the new equilibrium point J' and the terms of trade of the U.K. improve to $P_{G'} = 2$ (from $P_B = 1$). This improvement in the terms of trade, by itself, tends to improve the welfare of the U.K. The reduction of specialization in production and in the volume of trade, by itself, tends to reduce the welfare of the U.K. (from the previous free trade position before the

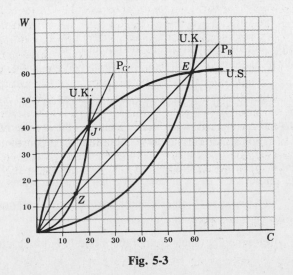

Fig. 5-3

change in tastes). Whether on balance the welfare of the U.K. improves or not depends on the relative strength of these two opposing forces. However, we can no longer use commodity indifference curves to answer this question because when tastes change in the U.K., the entire indifference map of the U.K. changes and indifference curves cross (see Problem 5.16).

If, on the other hand, the U.K.'s tastes shift from cloth to wheat, the U.K. offer curve would rotate clockwise and result in a greater volume of trade but reduced terms of trade for the U.K. (see Problem 5.17). For the effect of changes in the U.S. tastes, separately and at the same time as changes in the U.K.'s tastes occur, see Problems 5.18 to 5.20.

5.6 DYNAMIC FACTORS, TRADE AND DEVELOPMENT

With the exception of a handful of nations in North America, in Western Europe and Japan, most nations of the world are classified as less developed countries (LDCs) or, to put it more positively, as developing countries. LDCs presently account for less than one-fourth of world trade. Aside from a small group of *newly industrializing countries* or *NICs* (especially South Korea, Singapore, Taiwan, and Hong Kong) which are growing very rapidly based on the export of manufactured goods, most of the trade of other LDCs involves the export of raw materials, fuels, minerals and some food products to the industrialized, rich and developed countries (DCs), in exchange mostly for manufactured goods. LDCs complain that because of this trade pattern, because their internal conditions differ widely from those in DCs and because of the way in which the present international monetary system operates, most of the benefit of their own growth accrues to DCs, primarily in the form of secularly improving terms of trade. Thus, trade can no longer serve as an *engine of growth* for today's developing countries, as it did for the *regions of recent settlement* (the U.S., Canada, Argentina, Uruguay, Australia, New Zealand, and South Africa) during the 19th century.

LDCs advocate a *New International Economic Order* (NIEO), which involves higher prices for their traditional exports, schemes to stabilize their export proceeds, increased foreign aid, preferential treatment for their manufactured exports to DCs, and reforms of the international monetary system that would take their interests into consideration (see Problems 5.21 to 5.36).

For a discussion of multinational corporations and international labor migration, see Problems 5.27 and 5.28.

Glossary

Balanced growth Equal rates of factor growth and technical progress in the production of both commodities.

Rybczynski theorem The theorem that postulates that at constant relative commodity prices, the growth of only one factor leads to the absolute expansion in the output of the commodity using the growing factor intensively and to the absolute reduction in the output of the commodity using the nongrowing factor intensively.

K-saving technical progress Technical progress that increases the productivity of labor proportionately more than the productivity of capital and results in an increase in L/K at constant relative factor prices.

L-saving technical progress Technical progress that increases the productivity of capital proportionately more than the productivity of labor and results in an increase in K/L at constant relative factor prices.

Neutral technical progress Technical progress that increases the productivity of labor and capital in the same proportion so that K/L remains the same at constant relative factor prices.

Importable commodity A commodity (such as cars in the U.S.) that a nation produces at home and also imports (because of incomplete specialization in production).

Exportable commodity A commodity (such as aircrafts in the U.S.) that a nation produces for domestic use and for export.

Newly industrializing countries (NICs)   Countries such as South Korea, Singapore, Taiwan and Hong Kong which are growing very rapidly based mostly on export growth.

Engine of growth   The driving force behind economic growth. In the 19th century, for example, exports were the leading sector that propelled the economies of the regions of recent settlement into rapid growth and development.

Regions of recent settlement   The mostly empty and resource-rich lands, such as the U.S., Canada, Argentina, Uruguay, Australia, New Zealand and South Africa, that Europeans settled during the 19th century.

New International Economic Order (NIEO)   The demands made by developing nations as a group at the United Nations for the removal of the alleged injustices in the operation of the present international economic system and for the implementation of specific measures to facilitate the development of these nations.

Review Questions

1. Dynamic factors in trade theory refer to changes in   (a) factor endowments,   (b) technology,   (c) tastes,   (d) all of the above.

   Ans.   (d) See Section 5.1.

2. If a nation's technology remains unchanged but its supplies of labor and capital grow in the same proportion, then the nation's production possibilities curve shifts outward   (a) evenly along its entire length,   (b) more along the axis measuring the L-intensive commodity,   (c) more along the axis measuring the K-intensive commodity,   (d) any of the above is possible.

   Ans.   (a) See Section 5.1.

3. If a nation's technology remains unchanged but its supply of labor grows proportionately more than its supply of capital, then the nation's production possibilities curve shifts outward   (a) evenly along its entire length,   (b) more along the axis measuring the L-intensive commodity,   (c) more along the axis measuring the K-intensive commodity,   (d) any of the above is possible.

   Ans.   (b) See Example 1 and Fig. 5-1.

4. If a nation's supply of labor increases but its supply of capital and technology remain unchanged, then the nation's production possibilities curve shifts outward   (a) only along the axis measuring the L-intensive commodity,   (b) mostly along the axis measuring the L-intensive commodity but also a little along the axis measuring the K-intensive commodity,   (c) mostly along the axis measuring the K-intensive commodity,   (d) any of the above is possible.

   Ans.   (b) This is so because even in the production of the K-intensive commodity some labor is used.

5. According to the Rybczynski theorem, the growth of only one factor, at constant relative commodity prices, leads to the absolute expansion in the output of   (a) both commodities,   (b) the commodity using the growing factor intensively,   (c) the commodity using the nongrowing factor intensively,   (d) any of the above.

   Ans.   (b) See Section 5.2.

6. Technical progress   (a) increases the productivity of the nation's factors of production,   (b) reduces the amount of factors of production required to produce any output level,   (c) is equivalent to an increase in the nation's supply of factors and unchanged technology,   (d) causes an outward shift in the nation's production possibilities curve,   (e) all of the above.

   Ans.   (e) See Section 5.3.

7. K-saving technical progress   (a) increases the productivity of capital proportionately more than that of labor,   (b) is equivalent to a proportionately greater increase in the supply of capital than in the supply of labor,   (c) causes a greater outward shift in the nation's production possibilities curve along the axis measuring the K-intensive commodity than along the axis measuring the L-intensive commodity,   (d) all of the above.

   Ans.   (d) See Section 5.3.

8. If, at unchanged terms of trade, a nation wants to trade more after growth, then the nation's terms of trade can be expected to   (a) deteriorate,   (b) improve,   (c) remain unchanged,   (d) any of the above.

   Ans.   (a) See Example 2.

9. A proportionately greater increase in the nation's supply of labor than of capital is likely to result in a deterioration in the nation's terms of trade if the nation exports   (a) the K-intensive commodity,   (b) the L-intensive commodity,   (c) either commodity.

   Ans.   (b) See Example 2 and Fig. 5-2.

10. Starting with the original offer curves of the U.K. and the U.S. that cross at point E in Fig. 5-3, if the U.K.'s tastes shift from cloth to wheat, then the U.K. offer curve will rotate   (a) up and the U.K. terms of trade improve,   (b) up and the U.K. terms of trade worsen,   (c) down and the U.K. terms of trade improve,   (d) down and the U.K. terms of trade worsen.

    Ans.   (d) This is exactly the opposite of Example 3.

11. Starting with the original offer curves of the U.K. and the U.S. that cross at point E in Fig. 5-3, if U.S. tastes shift from wheat to cloth, then the   (a) U.K. offer curve rotates up,   (b) U.K. offer curve rotates down,   (c) U.S. offer curve rotates up,   (d) U.S. offer curve rotates down.

    Ans.   (c) Since the change in tastes occurs in the U.S. it is the U.S. offer curve that rotates. Since the U.S. tastes shift from wheat to cloth, the U.S. offer curve rotates up. This means that the U.S. is now willing to offer more of its wheat than before for each quantity of cloth imported.

12. Developing nations complain that   (a) their terms of trade deteriorate,   (b) their export proceeds are very unstable,   (c) their industrialization is discouraged,   (d) the present international monetary system favors developed countries,   (e) all of the above.

    Ans.   (e) See Section 5.6.

Solved Problems

DYNAMIC FACTORS

5.1   (a) On what does the *size* of a nation's production possibilities curve depend?   (b) On what does the *shape* of a nation's production possibilities curve depend?

   (a)   The *size* of a nation's production possibilities curve depends on the availability of factors of production and technology in the nation. The greater the amount of factors of production available to a nation and the more advanced the technology with which they are combined in production, the greater the amounts of both commodities that the nation is able to produce, and the greater the size of (i.e., the farther out from the origin) the nation's production possibilities curve.

   (b)   The *shape* of a nation's production possibilities curve depends on:

      (1)   The ratios with which different factors of production are available to the nation. For example, the greater the total L/K ratio in a nation, the greater the quantity of cloth in relation to the quantity of wheat that

the nation can produce, if cloth is L-intensive in relation to wheat, and the more stretched out and lower the nation's production possibilities curve, if cloth is measured on the horizontal axis (see Fig. 5-1).

(2) The relationship in the productivity of the nation's technology in the two commodities. For example, the greater the productivity of the nation's technology in cloth as opposed to wheat, the more stretched out and lower the nation's production possibilities curve (if cloth is measured along the horizontal axis).

(3) The greater substitutability of factors in production, the less concave or "bulging out" (i.e., the smaller the curvature of) the nation's production possibilities curve. At one extreme, the substitutability of factors in production is perfect (i.e., all units of each factor are homogeneous or are equally suitable in the production of both commodities) and the nation's production possibilities curve is a straight line (see Fig. 2-5 and Problem 2.3).

5.2 (*a*) Why do nations have different production possibilities curves? (*b*) What changes occur through time in a nation that affect its ability to produce goods and services? (*c*) What happens to a nation's production possibilities curve through time? To its indifference map?

   (*a*)   Since different nations have different factor endowments and may be using different technologies in production, it is natural to expect that they have different production possibilities curves. For example, the U.S., being much larger in natural, human and fabricated resources than a nation such as Switzerland, has a production possibilities curve for wheat and cloth that is much larger (further out from the origin) than Switzerland. Also, since the U.S. has a much greater proportion of factors suited for the production of wheat than for the production of cloth than a nation like the U.K., the production possibilities curve of the U.S. is much more stretched out along the wheat (vertical axis) than along the cloth (horizontal axis) *relative* to the production possibilities curve of the U.K. (see Fig. 2-3).

   (*b*)   Through time, the amounts of factors of production available to a nation change. For example, a nation's population increases, and with it, its labor supply. The level of education and skills in the nation (*human capital*) may also increase, and so does its amount of *physical* capital (the number of factories and machinery, office buildings and equipment, electric generating plants, trucks and roads, ships and harbors, aircrafts and airports, etc.). On the other hand, some natural resources, such as mineral deposits and agricultural land, may be depleted, while others may be found through new discoveries and new uses. Thus, the amounts of factors of production available to a nation change (usually increase) through time. Technology also improves through time.

   (*c*)   A nation's production possibilities curve at any one point in time or in any one year depends on the availability of factors of production and technology at that point in time or in that year. Through time, as these factors change, the nation's production possibilities curve shifts. The type of shift occurring depends on the type and degree of changes that occur in the nation. Through time, and partly due to international trade, a nation's tastes may also change, and so its indifference map will also be altered.

5.3 (*a*) Does a nation's comparative advantage remain the same through time? (*b*) How can we incorporate changes in factor endowments, technology and tastes into our trade theory?

   (*a*)   In Chapters 2 and 3, we determined a nation's comparative advantage on the basis of given and unchanging factor endowments, technology and tastes. However, these generally change through time. Thus, a nation's comparative advantage is not determined once and for all but may change through time. For example, the U.S. was losing its comparative advantage in agriculture during the 1920s and the 1930s, but regained it in the 1940s and 1950s, when technological advance in U.S. agriculture outstripped that in other nations. In the 1970s the U.S. lost its comparative advantage in cars and steel (as evidenced by the calls for trade protection by these industries). Japan today is losing its comparative advantage in simple L-intensive commodities to such other lower-wage nations as Korea, Singapore and Hong Kong. Even when the changes in factor endowments, technology and tastes are not sufficiently great to reverse a nation's comparative advantage, they will alter its terms of trade, the volume of trade and its gains from trade (see Example 2).

   (*b*)   Different types of factor growth and technological progress can be incorporated into the classical theory of comparative advantage by changing the size and/or shape of the nation's production possibilities curve. Changes in the structure of demand can be incorporated by changing the nation's indifference map. We can then trace the effects of these dynamic growth factors on the nation's offer curve, and on its terms of trade, volume of trade, gains from trade and comparative advantage in general.

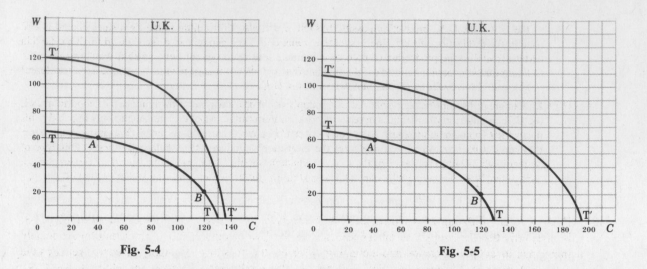

Fig. 5-4   Fig. 5-5

5.4   (*a*) What is meant by *static analysis?* Give an example of static analysis from Chapter 3.   (*b*) What is meant by *comparative static analysis?* Give an example of comparative static trade analysis from the text of this chapter.   (*c*) What is meant by *dynamic analysis?* Is the analysis in the text of this chapter dynamic? Why?

(*a*)   Static analysis examines the equilibrium position of a specific economic unit (e.g., the entire nation, an industry, an individual) under given and unchanging conditions. For example, in Chapter 3, based on a given production possibilities curve and community indifference map for each nation, we determined comparative advantage, the terms of trade and the equilibrium volume of trade. Thus, the theory of comparative advantage, as presented thus far (with the exception of Section 4.5), is completely static in nature.

(*b*)   When one or more of the underlying conditions on which equilibrium is based change, the equilibrium position will be disturbed until a new equilibrium position is established. Comparative static analysis studies and compares these equilibrium positions, without regard to the transitional period and process involved in the adjustment. For example, in Fig. 5-2, the change in factor endowments and/or technology in the U.K. shifted the U.K. production possibilities curve outward and disturbed the original equilibrium condition. We then examined the new equilibrium position established and compared it to the previous one. Thus, we conducted a comparative static analysis. Note that comparative statics implies an instantaneous adjustment to disturbances of equilibrium.

(*c*)   Dynamic analysis, on the other hand, studies the movement *over time* of the variables involved in the analysis, as one equilibrium position evolves into another. Thus, dynamic trade theory would study the time path of change in the terms of trade, volume of trade and gains from trade. In this chapter, we deal almost exclusively with the comparative statics of trade. Dynamic trade theory is still in its infancy.

GROWTH IN FACTOR SUPPLIES AND TECHNOLOGY THROUGH TIME

5.5   Draw a figure showing a hypothetical shift in the production possibilities curve of the U.K. in Fig. 2-3,   (*a*) if only the U.K. supply of capital increases or the U.K. supply of capital increases proportionately more than its supply of labor and technology remains the same. To what type of technical progress in the U.K. is this equivalent?   (*b*) If the U.K. supply of labor and capital grow in the same proportion. To what type of technical progress in the U.K. is this equivalent?

(*a*)   If only the supply of capital increases in the U.K. or if the supply of capital increases proportionately more than the supply of labor and its technology remains the same, then the U.K. production possibilities curve or transformation curve in Fig. 2-3 might shift outward from TT to T'T' as shown in Fig. 5-4. Note that the shift is greater along the vertical axis, which measures wheat (the *K*-intensive commodity) than along the horizontal axis, which measures cloth (the *L*-intensive commodity). The degree of the shift along the wheat axis in Fig. 5-4 was exaggerated for pedagogical reasons. Even if only the supply of capital increases in the U.K., the U.K. production possibilities curve will also shift a little to the right since capital is also used in the production of cloth (the L-intensive commodity) and capital can be substituted for labor (within certain limits) in the production of both commodities. The same type of outward shift would result in the U.K. production possibilities curve if the supply of factors did not change but there was an L-saving technical progress in the production of cloth and wheat in the U.K.

(b) If technology remains the same but the U.K. supply of labor and capital grow in the same proportion, then the U.K. production possibilities curve shifts outward uniformly along its entire length, as in Fig. 5-5. This means that (with constant returns to scale) TT and T'T' have the same slope or MRT_{CW} at the point where they are cut by any straight-line ray from the origin and is referred to as balanced growth. This type of outward shift would also result in the U.K. production possibilities curve if the supply of factors did not change but there was a neutral technical progress in the production of cloth and wheat in the U.K.

5.6 Draw a figure showing a hypothetical shift in the U.S. production possibilities curve of Fig. 2-3, if (a) only the U.S. supply of labor increases, or the U.S. supply of labor increases proportionately more than its supply of capital and technology remains the same, or the supply of factors remains the same but there is K-saving technical progress in the production of wheat and cloth in the U.S.; (b) only the U.S. supply of capital increases, or the U.S. supply of capital increases proportionately more than its supply of labor or there is L-saving technical progress; (c) the U.S. supply of labor and capital grow in the same proportion or there is neutral technical progress in the U.S.

(a) See Fig. 5-6.

(b) See Fig. 5-7.

(c) See Fig. 5-8.

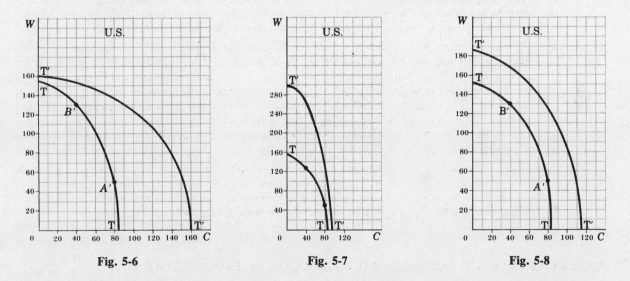

Fig. 5-6   Fig. 5-7   Fig. 5-8

5.7 (a) What is meant by an export-biased, import-biased and unbiased or neutral technical progress? (b) Classify the shifts from TT to T'T' in the U.K. and the U.S. production possibilities curves in Figs. 5-1 and 5-4 to 5-8, as export-biased, import-biased or neutral.

(a) Export-biased (X-biased) technical progress is one that increases the output of the nation's export commodity more than that of its import-competing commodity. An import-biased (M-biased) innovation is just the opposite. Unbiased or neutral technical progress is one that increases the output of the nation's export- and import-competing commodities by the same proportion.

(b) Since the U.K. exports cloth (the L-intensive commodity), K-saving technical progress (which causes the U.K. production possibilities curve to shift from TT to T'T') in Fig. 5-1 is X-biased from the U.K. point of view. L-saving technical progress in Fig. 5-4 is M-biased from the U.K. viewpoint, while that shown in Fig. 5-5 is unbiased or neutral for the U.K. On the other hand, since the U.S. imports cloth (the L-intensive commodity), the K-saving technical progress in Fig. 5-6 is M-biased from the U.S. point of view. L-saving technical progress in Fig. 5-7 is X-biased for the U.S., while that shown in Fig. 5-8 is unbiased or neutral.

5.8 Starting with the free-trade equilibrium position of the U.K. and the U.S. in Fig. 2-4, illustrate the Rybczynski theorem for an increase in the supply of (*a*) labor in the U.K. and (*b*) capital in the U.S. (*c*) Explain why the Rybczynski theorem holds.

(*a*) See Fig. 5-9. Note that with free trade, P_C/P_W will fall below 1 after growth as the U.K. attempts to export more cloth at $P_C/P_W = 1$ (see Example 2). The Rybczynski theorem tells us only that *at constant P_C/P_W*, the U.K. output of cloth (the L-intensive commodity) rises and that of wheat (the K-intensive commodity) falls as a result of an increase in only the supply of L in the U.K.

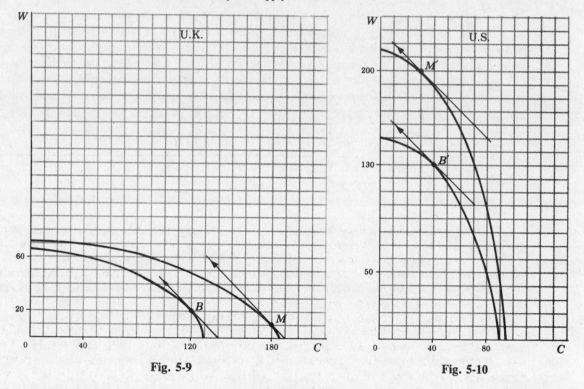

Fig. 5-9   Fig. 5-10

(*b*) See Fig. 5-10. Note that with free trade, P_W/P_C will fall below 1 after growth as the U.S. attempts to export more wheat at $P_W/P_C = 1$ (see Problem 5.11). The Rybczynski theorem tells us only that at constant P_W/P_C, the U.S. output of wheat rises and that of cloth falls as a result of an increase in only the supply of K in the U.S.

(*c*) The Rybczynski theorem states that at constant relative commodity prices, the growth of only one factor leads to an increase in the output of the commodity using that factor intensively and a decrease in the output of the commodity using the nongrowing factor intensively. This is, in fact, what happens, for the only way for K/L to remain unchanged and also absorb all of the increase in L in the U.K. is for the U.K. to reduce its output of wheat (so as to release K and L at the greater K/L used in wheat production) and combine the released K with the additional L at the lower K/L used in cloth production. Similarly, at constant P_W/P_C, the U.S. would have to reduce its cloth output and increase its wheat output in order to fully employ an increase in its supply of K only.

CHANGE IN FACTOR SUPPLIES AND TECHNOLOGY, AND TRADE

5.9 With reference to Fig. 5-11, and starting with the U.K. production possibilities curve TT in Panel A, explain the sequence of events shown in Panels A and B.

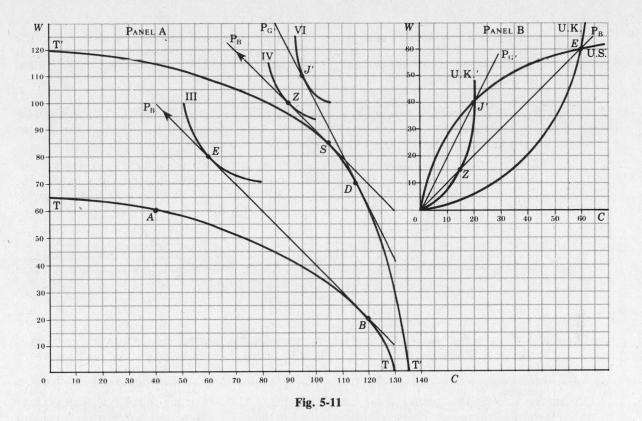

Fig. 5-11

In Panel A of Fig. 5-11, we see that before any change in factor endowments and/or technology, the U.K. produces at point *B* on TT, exports 60C for 60W, and consumes at point *E* on III. This gives point *E* on the U.K. offer curve in Panel B (so far this is the same as in Fig. 5-2). After the U.K. production possibilities curve shifted to T'T' (as in Fig. 5-4), at the same terms of trade of P_B, the U.K. would like to produce at point *S* on T'T', export 15C for 15W, and consume at point *Z* on IV. This gives point *Z* on offer curve U.K.' in Panel B. But at P_B, the U.K. wants to export less cloth and import less wheat than the U.S. is willing to trade at P_B (see Panel B). Thus, the U.K. terms of trade improve from P_B to $P_{G'}$. At $P_{G'}$, the U.K. produces at point *D* on T'T', exports 20C for 40W and consumes at point *J'* on VI (see Panel A). This corresponds to the new equilibrium point *J'* in Panel B, where the unchanged U.S. offer curve and the new U.K. offer curve (i.e., U.K.') cross. Thus, if only the supply of capital increases in the U.K., or if its supply of capital increases proportionately more than its supply of labor, or if there is *L*-saving and M-biased technical progress in the U.K. (so that TT shifts to T'T'), the U.K. will want to trade less at P_B. Therefore, the U.K. not only retains all the benefits of its growth, but also gains from better terms of trade (compare points *E*, *Z* and *J'* in Panel A).

5.10   With reference to Fig. 5-12, and starting with the U.S. production possibilities curve TT in Panel A, explain in detail the sequence of events shown in Panels A and B.

In Panel A of Fig. 5-12, we see that before any change in factor endowments and/or technology, the U.S. produces at point *B'* on TT, exports 60W for 60C and consumes at point *E* on III (the same as point *E'* in Fig. 3-2). This gives point *E* on the U.S. offer curve in Panel B (the same as point *E'* in Figs. 3-4 and 3-5). After the U.S. offer curve shifted to T'T' (as in Fig. 5-6), at $P_C/P_W = P_B$, the U.S. would like to produce at point *M'* on T'T', export 15W for 15C and consume at point *Z* on IV. This gives point *Z* on offer curve U.S.' in Panel B. But at P_B, the U.S. wants to export less wheat and import less cloth than the U.K. wants to trade at P_B (see Panel B). Thus, the U.S. terms of trade improve from $1/P_B = 1$ to $1/P_G = 2$. At P_G, the U.S. produces at point *N'* on T'T', exports 20W for 40C, and consumes at point *J* on VI (see Panel A). This corresponds to the new equilibrium point *J* in Panel B, where the unchanged offer curve of the U.K. and the new U.S. offer curve (i.e., U.S.') cross. Thus, if only the supply of labor increases in the U.S., or if its supply of labor increases proportionately more than its supply of capital, or if there is *K*-saving and M-biased technical progress in the U.S. (so that TT

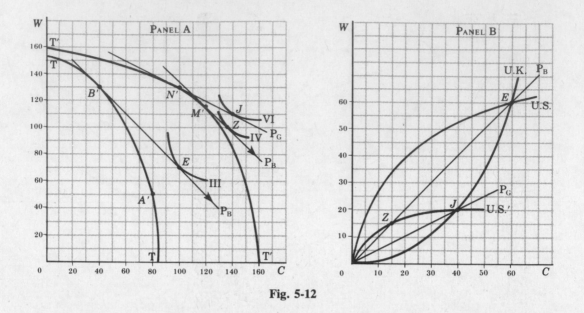

Fig. 5-12

shifts to T'T' as in Fig. 5-6), the U.S. will want to trade less at P_B. Therefore, the U.S. not only retains all of the benefits of its growth, but also gains from better terms of trade (compare points E, Z and J in Panel A).

5.11 Starting with the U.S. position under free trade in Fig. 3-2, draw a figure and explain what happens if there is L-saving or X-biased technical progress in the U.S. or if its total K/L increases in such a way as to shift its production possibilities curve outward as in Fig. 5-7.

After the U.S. production possibilities curve shifts to T'T' in Panel A of Fig. 5-13, at P_B, the U.S. will want to produce at point S' on T'T' (note that this involves more wheat but less cloth than at B') and trade along P_B until price line P_B is just tangent to a U.S. indifference curve. If this occurs at point U on VII, the U.S. will want to export 150W for 150C (see panel A). This gives point U on offer curve U.S.* in Panel B. But at P_B, the U.S. will want to trade much more than the U.K. (see Panel B), and so the U.S. terms of trade deteriorate. If the U.S. terms of trade deteriorate from $1/P_B = 1$ to $1/P_{G'} = 1/2$, the U.S. will produce at D' on T'T' and trade along P_G until price line P_G is just tangent to a U.S. indifference curve. If this occurs at point H on V, the U.S. will export 140W for 70C (see panel A). This corresponds to the new equilibrium point H in Panel B, where the unchanged offer curve of the U.K. and the new U.S. offer curve (i.e., U.S.*) cross. In this case, the U.S. shares part of the benefit of its growth with the U.K. in the form of worsening terms of trade.

5.12 Starting with the U.K. free-trade position in Fig. 3-2, draw a figure and explain what happens if (1) TT for the U.K. shifts to T'T' as shown in Fig. 5-5, and (2) as income rises, the U.K. will continue to consume wheat and cloth in the same proportion as at point E in Fig. 3-2.

At P_B and with T'T' in Panel A of Fig. 5-14, the U.K. would like to produce at B' on T'T' [see Problem 5.5(b)] and consume at E' (along a straight-line ray from the origin through point E) by exchanging 90C for 90W. This gives point E' on offer curve U.K." in Panel B. Since at P_B, the U.K. now wants to trade more than the U.S. is willing to trade, the U.K. terms of trade deteriorate. The new U.K. terms of trade of P_F ($<P_B$) are given by the new equilibrium point F, where the unchanged U.S. offer curve crosses offer curve U.K." (see Panel B). Thus, the U.K. would end up producing along T'T' to the left of B', where P_F is tangent to T'T' (not shown in Panel A) and exchange about 84C for 64W (see point F in Panel B) so as to consume below point E' along the ray from the origin through points E and E' (see Panel A). Thus, even in this case of neutral technical progress or proportionate increase in the supply of labor and capital in the U.K., the U.K. shares part of the benefit of its growth with the U.S. in the form of deteriorating terms of trade. Remember, this results because at the unchanged terms of trade of P_B, the U.K. would like to trade more than before its growth. This is the usual case [see Problem 5.13(b)].

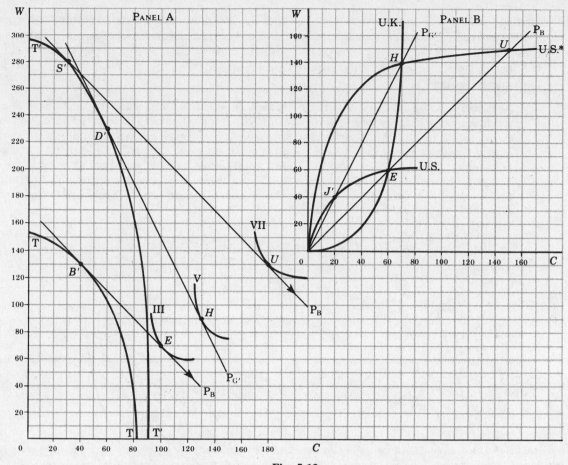

Fig. 5-13

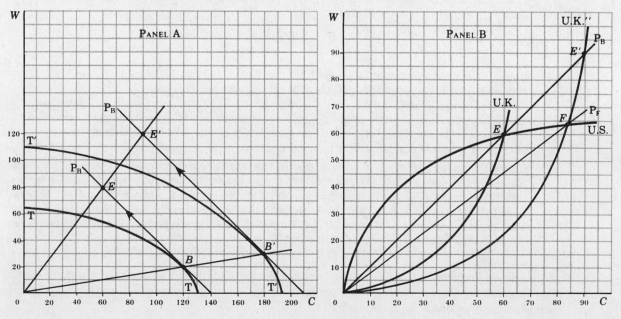

Fig. 5-14

5.13 Starting with the U.S. free-trade position in Fig. 3-2, (*a*) draw a figure and explain what happens if TT shifts to T'T' for the U.S. as shown in Fig. 5-8, and if, as income rises, the U.S. continues to consume wheat and cloth in the same proportion. (*b*) How would the result in part (*a*) differ if the U.S. decided to consume 110C at P_B, after its TT curve shifted to T'T'? (*c*) What if the U.S. decided to consume less than 110C at P_B?

(*a*) At P_B and with T'T' in Panel A of Fig. 5-15, the U.S. would like to produce at point B'' on T'T' and consume at point E'' by exchanging about 72W for 72C. This gives point E'' on offer curve U.S." in Panel B. Since at P_B, the U.S. wants to trade more than the U.K. is willing to trade (see Panel B), the U.S. terms of trade deteriorate from $1/P_B$ to $1/P_{F'}$. $P_{F'}$ is given by the new equilibrium point F', where the unchanged U.K. offer curve crosses offer curve U.S." (see Panel B). Thus, the U.S. would end up producing along T'T' to the right of B'', where $P_{F'}$ is tangent to T'T' (not shown in Panel A) and exchange about 71W for 61C (see point F' in Panel B) so as to consume below point E'' along the ray from the origin through points E and E'' (see Panel A).

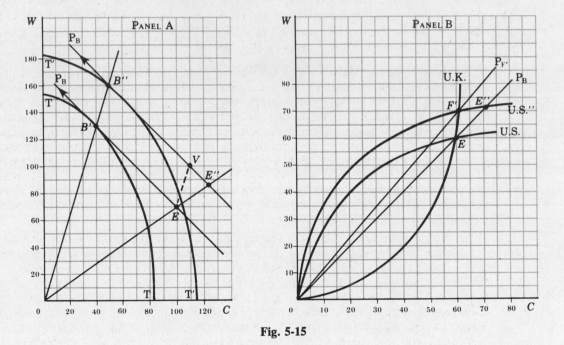

Fig. 5-15

(*b*) If the U.S. decided to consume 110C (and 100W; see point V in Panel A), at P_B, the U.S. would produce at point B'' in Panel A and would exchange 60W for 60C, *the same as before TT shifted to T'T'* (because EV is parallel to $B'B''$ and so $B'E = B''V$). In this case, the U.S. offer curve would remain unchanged as the result of its neutral technical progress or proportional increase in its supply of labor and capital. Thus, the terms of trade, the volume of trade and the gains from trade would remain completely unchanged after this type of growth in the U.S. This is possible but unusual.

(*c*) If the U.S., on the other hand, decided to consume less than 110C and more than 100W at P_B (i.e., to the left of point V on P_B in Panel A), the U.S. would want to trade less than 60W for 60C and its terms of trade would improve. The rest is qualitatively identical to L-saving technical progress in the U.S. Note that if the U.S. consumed less than 100C (and more than 110W) along P_B in Panel A, it would mean that cloth is an inferior good for the U.S. since the U.S. would be consuming less cloth than at point E (i.e., before growth occurred and real income rose in the U.S.).

5.14 (*a*) How do Problems 5.9 to 5.13 bring forth the general equilibrium character of our trade model? (*b*) How can we analyze the effect of more than one change in the conditions of production occurring simultaneously in one or both nations?

(a) The general equilibrium character of our basic trade model is brought forth by the fact that we traced the effect of a change in the condition of production in one nation on the terms of trade, the volume of trade, the level of consumption and the distribution of the gains between the two nations.

(b) So far, we have used comparative statics to trace the effect of a single change in the conditions of production in a single nation. However, it should be obvious that we can extend this type of analysis to examine the effect of more than one change occurring simultaneously in one or both nations. For example, if changes in both factor endowments and technology occur in one or both nations, we can find their *net* effect on each nation's production possibilities and offer curves. The point where these new offer curves cross will determine the new terms of trade and equilibrium volume of trade. We could then go back to each nation's production possibilities curve to find its new equilibrium point of production and consumption.

5.15 (a) Discuss what would happen if at the same time that there is *L*-saving technical progress in the U.K. that shifts the U.K. offer curve to U.K.' in Panel B of Fig. 5-11 the supply of capital or the supply of labor also increases in the U.K. (while nothing changes in the U.S.). (b) Draw a figure and explain what happens if at the same time that there is *L*-saving technical progress in the U.K. that shifts the U.K. offer curve to U.K.' in Panel B of Fig. 5-11, *K*-saving technical progress also occurs in the U.S. that shifts the U.S. offer curve to U.S.' in Panel B of Fig. 5-12.

(a) If, in addition to the *L*-saving technical progress, the supply of capital also increases in the U.K., the U.K. offer curve would shift to the left (past offer curve U.K.') and intersect the unchanged U.S. offer curve to the left of J' in Panel B of Fig. 5-11. Thus, the new U.K. terms of trade will be better than $P_{G'}$ and the volume of trade even less than that indicated by point J'. Therefore, *L*-saving technical progress and the simultaneous increase in the supply of capital in the U.K. operate in the same direction and reinforce each other. On the other hand, an increase in the supply of labor in the U.K. operates in the opposite direction as the *L*-saving technical progress. Thus, the U.K. offer curve would move back to the right from offer curve U.K.'. How far back depends on how much the supply of labor increases in the U.K. In either case, once the new equilibrium terms of trade are established, we can determine on the new U.K. production possibilities curve its new equilibrium point of production, and, with the use of the nation's indifference map, its new equilibrium point of consumption.

(b) In Fig. 5-16, offer curve U.K.' crosses offer curve U.S.' at point Z. Thus, the new terms of trade remain at P_B for the U.K. and at $1/P_B$ for the U.S., while the volume of trade dwindles to 15C for 15W (from 60W for 60C at point E, before the technical progress in the U.K. and the U.S.). From Panel A of Fig. 5-11, we can then see that in the U.K., the new production point is at S on $T'T'$ while the new consumption point is at Z on IV. From Panel A of Fig. 5-12, we see that the U.S. now produces at N' at $T'T'$ and consumes at Z on IV. Note that these M-biased innovations in the U.K. and in the U.S. reduce the U.K. comparative advantage in cloth and the U.S. comparative advantage in wheat, and if they continue to occur, they could conceivably reverse the pattern of trade between the two countries. Of course, the same thing would eventually happen if, through time, the U.K. supply of capital continued to grow proportionately more than its supply of labor, while the opposite occurred in the U.S. Other simultaneous changes in the conditions of production in both nations could be similarly analyzed.

CHANGE IN TASTES AND TRADE

5.16 (a) Explain how a shift in tastes from wheat to cloth in the U.K. affects the U.K.'s indifference map. (b) From Fig. 5-3, draw a figure showing the points of production and consumption in the U.K. before the change in tastes described in part (a), and after.

(a) If wheat is measured along the vertical axis and cloth along the horizontal axis, a shift in tastes from wheat to cloth in the U.K. will cause the community indifference curves of the U.K. to shift down and to the right and become steeper. They shift down and to the right because at each level of real income and unchanged P_C/P_W, the U.K. demands a smaller quantity of wheat and a larger quantity of cloth than before. They become steeper (i.e., MRS_{CW} rises in the U.K.; see Section 3.1) because cloth is now worth more in terms of wheat than before to the U.K. If on the other hand, the U.K. tastes shifted from cloth to wheat, the U.K. indifference curves would shift up and to the left and become flatter. In any event, when tastes

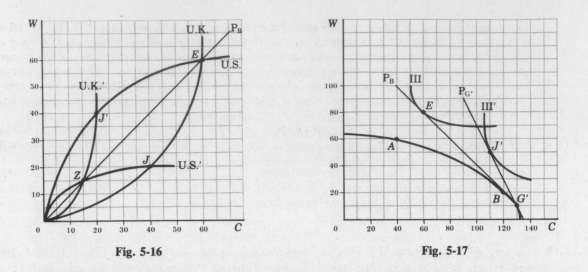

Fig. 5-16   Fig. 5-17

change, a nation's indifference curves change shape and cross the original indifference curves of the nation (i.e., those referring to the conditions before the change in tastes). This makes welfare comparison impossible.

(b) In Fig. 5-17, the U.K. produces at point B, exchanges 60C for 60W, and consumes at point E on III (as in Fig. 3-2) before the change of tastes. This is how point E in Fig. 5-3 was derived. Since the U.K. tastes shifted from wheat to cloth, the U.K. demands a smaller quantity of wheat and a larger quantity of cloth than before at unchanged income and P_C/P_W. This will cause P_C/P_W (i.e., the U.K. terms of trade) to rise, thus moderating the decline in the quantity of wheat and the increase in the quantity of cloth demanded by the U.K. per time period. From Fig. 5-3, we know that $P_{G'}$ is the new and higher U.K. terms of trade and that the U.K. exchanges 20C for 40W at $P_{G'}$. Thus, the U.K. must be producing at point G' and consuming at point J' in Fig. 5-17. At J', a new community indifference curve (III'), which is below, to the right and steeper than III, must be tangent to $P_{G'}$. Since III and III' are part of two different U.K. indifference maps (III refers to before the change in tastes in the U.K., and III' to after), we cannot determine the effect of the change in tastes on the welfare of the U.K. (i.e., whether $J' \gtreqless E$). Note that since the U.K. technology and supply of factors remained unchanged, the U.K. production possibilities curve has not changed.

5.17 Starting with the original U.K. and U.S. offer curves that cross at point E in Fig. 5-3, draw a figure and explain what happens if the U.K. tastes shift from cloth to wheat, while there is no change in supply or demand conditions in the U.S.

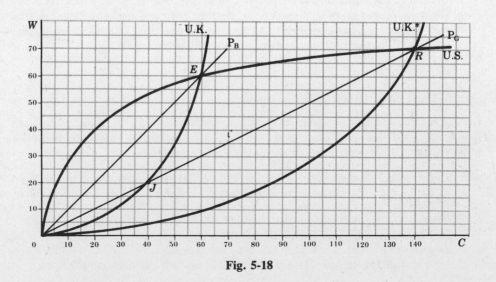

Fig. 5-18

If the U.K. tastes shift from cloth to wheat (other things being equal), offer curve U.K. in Fig. 5-3 shifts down or rotates clockwise, say to offer curve U.K.* in Fig. 5-18. This happens because the U.K. now wants wheat more intensely and is willing to offer more of its cloth than before for each quantity of wheat imported or, equivalently, the U.K. requires less wheat imports for each quantity of cloth exported than before. This causes the volume of trade to rise and the U.K. terms of trade to fall. In Fig. 5-18, the volume of trade rises from 60C for 60W to 140C for 70W, and the U.K. terms of trade decline from P_B to P_G. However, we cannot determine whether or not the U.K. is better off now than before (i.e., whether $R \gtreqless E$).

Point R in Fig. 5-18 is to be contrasted with point R in Panel B of Fig. 5-2, which was also reached by the U.K. exchanging 140C for 70W, but which resulted from a change in the conditions of production in the U.K. with unchanged tastes. Since tastes were unchanged in Fig. 5-2, we were able to determine that $R > E$. Note, however, that the assumption of unchanged tastes in the U.K. in the face of significant changes in its production conditions is unrealistic. We made that assumption in Example 2 in order to isolate the effect of only one change, before moving on to the more complicated cases of multiple changes.

5.18 Starting with the original U.K. and U.S. offer curves crossing at point E in Fig. 5-3, draw a figure and explain what happens (1) if the U.S. tastes for cloth decline and/or tastes for wheat increase, while there is no change in the U.K. and (2) if the U.S. tastes change in the opposite direction.

If U.S. tastes for cloth decline and/or tastes for wheat increase (other things being equal), the U.S. offer curve in Fig. 5-3 shifts down or rotates clockwise, say to offer curve U.S.' in Fig. 5-19. This is because the U.S. now wants cloth less intensely and is willing to offer less of its wheat than before for each quantity of cloth imported or, equivalently, for each quantity of wheat exported, the U.S. now requires more cloth. With offer curve U.S.' in Fig. 5-19, the volume of trade declines from 60W for 60C to 20W for 40C (see point J) and the U.S. terms of trade improve from $1/P_B = 1$ to $1/P_G = 2$, but we cannot tell whether $J \gtreqless E$ for the U.S. If the opposite changes occur in U.S. tastes, the U.S. offer curve rotates in the opposite direction. If it moves to offer curve U.S.* in Fig. 5-19, the volume of trade rises to 140W for 70C (see point H) and the U.S. terms of trade decline to $1/P_G = 1/2$, but once again, we cannot say whether $H \gtreqless E$ for the U.S.

5.19 (a) Draw a figure and show what happens if, *because of a change in tastes,* offer curve U.K. shifts to offer curve U.K.* (as in Panel B of Fig. 5-2), while offer curve U.S. shifts to offer curve U.S.* (as in Fig. 5-19).   (b) What would happen if at the same time that tastes change in the U.K. and the U.S., the conditions of production also change in both nations?

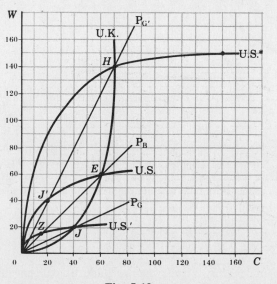

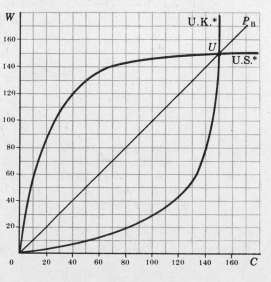

Fig. 5-19   Fig. 5-20

(a) In Fig. 5-20, we see that with offer curves U.K.* and U.S.*, 150C are exchanged for 150W between the U.K. and the U.S. at $P_C/P_W = P_B = 1$. Other simultaneous changes in tastes in the U.K. and in the U.S. can be similarly examined.

(b) If tastes, factor endowments and technology change at the same time and in both nations, anything can happen (even the pattern of trade can be reversed) and our comparative statistics approach would become very complicated, if not impossible.

5.20 (a) Draw a figure and explain what would happen if because of changes in tastes, offer curve U.K. of Fig. 5-19 shifted to offer curve U.K.' of Fig. 5-3, or to offer curve U.K.* of Fig. 5-20, *and* the U.S. offer curve was a straight-line ray from the origin with a slope of 1 and remained unchanged. (b) What general rule can you deduce from Example 3 and Problems 5.16 to 5.20(a) as to the effect of changes in the nation's tastes on the volume of trade, on the nation's terms of trade and on its welfare?

(a) A straight-line U.S. offer curve as in Fig. 5-21 would mean that the U.S. is willing to export any quantity of wheat at $P_W/P_C = P_C/P_W = 1$ (i.e., the U.S. offer curve is infinitely elastic). Thus, with offer curve U.K., England exchanges 60C for 60W with the U.S. at $P_C/P_W = 1$ (see point E in Fig. 5-21). With offer curve U.K.', England trades 15C for 15W at $P_C/P_W = 1$ (see point Z), and with offer curve U.K.*, England trades 150 C for 150W also at $P_C/P_W = 1$ (see point U). The terms of trade would also remain unchanged for both nations (but the volume of trade would change) if the offer curve of a very small nation shifted in such a way as to continue to intersect the straight-line segment of an otherwise bending offer curve of a very large nation (the reader is left to sketch this out for him- or herself, starting with a figure such as Fig. 3-17).

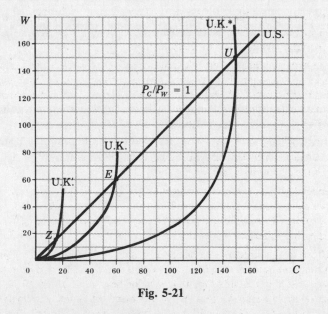

Fig. 5-21

(b) If a nation shifts from its importable to its exportable commodity, the volume of trade declines and the nation's terms of trade improve—unless the offer curve of its trade partner is infinitely elastic (see Figs. 5-3, 5-21 and 5-19). With the opposite changes in the nation's tastes, the results are the reverse (see Figs. 5-18, 5-19 and 5-21). In either case, however, we cannot determine whether the nation is better off after the change in tastes than before (see Problem 5.16 and Fig. 5-17).

DYNAMIC FACTORS, TRADE AND DEVELOPMENT

5.21 (a) Explain why LDCs in general feel that traditional trade theory is irrelevant as a guide to development. (b) How would you counter such a charge?

(*a*) LDCs attack traditional trade theory as completely static. More specifically, they feel that traditional trade theory might be useful to determine a nation's comparative advantage and pattern of trade under existing conditions. But development involves changing, not adjusting to existing conditions, and for this, a truly dynamic theory is required. For example, with the present distribution of factor endowments and technology between LDCs and DCs, traditional trade theory prescribes that LDCs should continue to specialize in the production of and export raw materials, fuel, minerals and food to DCs in exchange for manufactured products. LDCs feel that though this trade pattern may maximize their welfare in the short run, it would continue to relegate them to a subordinate position vis-à-vis DCs and would prevent them from reaping the dynamic benefits of industry and from maximizing their welfare and development in the long run.

(*b*) It is true that traditional trade theory is static in nature. However, it can readily be extended to incorporate changes in factor endowments, technology and tastes by the technique of comparative statics, as shown in this chapter. What this means is that a nation's comparative advantage and trade pattern are not determined once and for all, but must be recomputed as the underlying conditions change *or are anticipated to change*. Thus, LDCs are not necessarily relegated by traditional trade theory to be exporters of primary commodities and importers of manufactured goods. If capital accumulation, the acquisition of skills and technology proceed faster in some LDCs than in other nations, their comparative advantage will eventually shift away from primary products to simple manufactured goods first and then to more sophisticated ones. This process may be occurring today in Brazil and in many other LDCs. Thus, comparative statics can carry us a long way toward incorporating dynamic changes in the economy into traditional trade theory. However, it must be recognized that this is still far short of a truly dynamic trade theory.

5.22 State briefly the problems which LDCs face in their trade relations with DCs and the ways in which they seek to overcome these problems.

(1) Though the empirical evidence available gives conflicting results, LDCs believe that in general (and except for petroleum-exporting LDCs), they face declining terms of trade. They have thus banded together to demand higher prices for their traditional exports.

(2) LDCs complain that their export prices and export receipts fluctuate too widely, and that this hinders their development plans. Empirical evidence seems to support their first contention, but there are conflicting results as to the second. In any event, LDCs advocate so-called *international commodity agreements* to stabilize their export prices and receipts. These are in general very expensive to operate and often unmanageable. There are only a few of them presently in operation.

(3) Since LDCs' demand for manufactured imports increases faster than their earnings from primary exports, LDCs feel the need to industrialize. Most LDCs believe that the natural way to begin their process of industrialization is through import-substitution.

(4) DCs in general give a great deal of protection (see Chapter 6) to their relatively simple L-intensive industries such as textiles, shoes, bicycles, etc. These are the industries in which many LDCs already have or can soon be expected to achieve a comparative advantage. Therefore, LDCs advocate that DCs import these commodities from them on a preferential basis.

(5) LDCs believe that the international monetary system was created by DCs primarily to reflect and serve DCs' needs. Among the reforms that LDCs are asking is the distribution of new international monetary reserves to LDCs so that they can spend them on development (see Section 12.7).

Most of these demands, including the demand for increased foreign aid (which in recent years has stagnated), are part of LDCs' call for a New International Economic Order (NIEO).

5.23 A nation's commodity or *net barter* terms of trade, $N = (P_X/P_M)100$, where P_X is an index of export prices, P_M is an index of import prices, and we multiply by 100 in order to express N as a percentage. If we take 1990 as the base year ($N = 100$) and we find that by the end of 1991 a nation's P_X has fallen by 5% (to 95) while its P_M has risen by 10% (to 110), (*a*) determine by how much N changes for this nation during 1991. (*b*) If during 1991, this nation's export volume index increased by 20% (from 100 to 120), determine by how much this nation's capacity to import changed during 1991.

(*a*) Since $N = (P_X/P_M)100 = (95/110)100 \cong 86.36$, this nation's terms of trade declined about 14% during 1991.

(b)   A nation's capacity to import or income terms of trade (I) equals P_X/P_M times Q_X, where Q_X is an index of export volume. Thus,

$$I = \frac{P_X}{P_M} \cdot Q_X = (0.8636)(120) \cong 103.63$$

This means that during 1991, this nation's capacity to import increased by 3.63% over 1990 (even though P_X/P_M declined). I is very important for LDCs, since they rely to an important degree on imported capital goods for their development.

5.24   A nation's *single factoral terms of trade*, $S = (P_X/P_M) \cdot Z_X$, where Z_X is an export productivity index. If during 1991, the productivity of the nation in Problem 5.23 rose by 30% (from 100 to 130) in its export sector,   (a) determine how much S changed for this nation during 1991.   (b) Which of the different terms of trade defined here and in Problem 5.23 do you think is most significant for a LDC?

(a)   Since

$$S = \frac{P_X}{P_M} \cdot Z_X = (0.8636)(130) \cong 112.27$$

in 1991, the nation gets 12.27% more imports per unit of factors of production embodied into its exports than in 1990. Thus, the nation is better off, even if it shares the benefit of the productivity increase in its export sector with its trade partner. This concept of single factoral terms of trade could be extended to define the nation's *double factoral terms of trade*, $D = N/(Z_X/Z_M)$, where Z_M is an import productivity index. Thus, D measures how many units of *domestic* factors embodied into this nation's exports exchange per unit of *foreign* factors embodied into this nation's imports.

(b)   Of the four different terms of trade defined (i.e., N, I, S, D), D is the most cumbersome and difficult to measure. In addition, it does not seem very relevant and so it is rarely, if ever, calculated (it was only included here for the sake of completeness). The most relevant, especially for LDCs, are S and I, but it is N that is used most often because it is the simplest to calculate. Indeed, N is often referred to simply as the "terms of trade." However, as we have seen in Problems 5.23 and 5.24(a), N can deteriorate at the same time as I and S are improving. This situation is normally interpreted as being beneficial of the LDC. Obviously, the most favorable situation for a LDC occurs when N, I, S and D all improve.

5.25   (a) Explain how international trade operated as an "engine of growth" for the "regions of recent settlement" (such as the U.S., Canada, Argentina, Uruguay, Australia, New Zealand and South Africa) in the 19th century.   (b) Explain from the supply point of view and   (c) from the demand point of view, why international trade is not an engine of growth for today's LDCs.

(a)   In the 19th century, workers with various skills and capital moved in great waves from the highly populated areas of Europe to the mostly empty and natural-resource-rich lands in the "new world." This, together with a very rapidly growing demand for food and raw materials, particularly from industrializing but resource-poor England, resulted in rapid and sustained export-led growth in the economies of these new lands. Thus, international trade was truly an engine of growth in these new lands in the 19th century.

(b)   Today's LDCs believe that this experience is not applicable to them in the 20th century. On the supply side, they cite the fact that today's LDCs are in general overpopulated and resource poor (except for some petroleum-exporting LDCs) and so even if the demand for food and raw materials were growing very rapidly, they would be unable to expand their outputs of these products greatly and thus experience significant export-led growth.

(c)   More importantly, LDCs feel that the world demand for food and some raw materials is not growing as rapidly today as it grew for the regions of recent settlement in the 19th century and as required for export-led growth. They give several reasons for this: the income elasticity of demand in DCs for many of the food exports of LDCs is quite low; agricultural protectionism in most DCs; the center of world production shifted to some extent from resource-poor Europe to the U.S. and Russia, both of which are of continental size and rich in natural resources; the development of synthetic raw materials such as synthetic rubber; new technological breakthroughs which increased the amount of output per unit of raw material input (such as tin-plated cans, microcircuits, etc.); a more rapid increase in the output of services than commodities in

DCs. For these reasons, today's LDCs believe (and to a large extent, justifiably so) that they cannot rely on their exports of traditional products to grow and develop rapidly.

5.26 Draw a figure and explain how a LDC can be worse off with free trade after growth than before growth.

The LDC in Fig. 5-22 produces and consumes at point A on TT and I in autarky and before growth. With free trade and terms of trade of P_B, the nation produces at point B on TT and consumes at point E on III. The movement from A to E represents the LDC's gains from trade before growth. With export-biased growth, the LDC produces at point F on T'T' and consumes at point G on II. Since $G < E$, the LDC is worse off with free trade after growth than before. This is referred to as *immiserizing growth*. Immiserizing growth occurs only rarely, when as a result of X-biased growth in the LDC, the terms of trade of the LDC deteriorate so much that the LDC *exports* more than the entire benefit of its growth (compare Fig. 5-22 with Fig. 5-2, where $R > E$ and we did not have immiserizing growth).

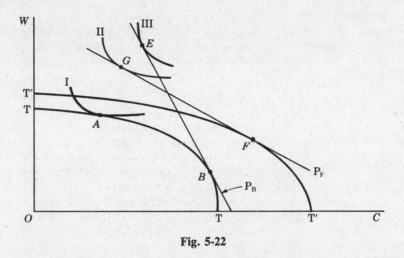

Fig. 5-22

5.27 One of the most significant international economic developments of the postwar period is the proliferation of multinational corporations (MNCs). These are firms that own, control or manage production facilities in several countries. With regard to MNCs, explain   (*a*) the reason for their existence,   (*b*) some of the alleged problems that they create for the home country and   (*c*) some of the alleged problems that they create for the host country.

(*a*)   The basic reason for the existence of MNCs is the competitive advantage that they have over other forms of economic organization based on economies of scale in production, financing, research and development (R & D), and in gathering market information, resulting from a global network of production and distribution. Today, MNCs account for over 20% of world output, and the trade between the parent firms and their foreign affiliates accounts for more than 25% of world trade in manufactured goods.

(*b*)   The most controversial of the alleged harmful effects of MNCs on the home nation is the loss of domestic jobs resulting from foreign direct investments. However, it must be pointed out that the home nation may have lost some of these jobs anyway to foreign competitors. A related problem stems from the export of advanced technology. Countering this harmful effect, however, is the tendency of MNCs to concentrate their R & D in the home nation. Finally, easy accessibility of MNCs to the international capital market reduces the effectiveness of domestic monetary policy.

(*c*)   Host countries have even more serious complaints against MNCs. First is the alleged domination by the MNCs of the hosts' economy. The largest MNCs have yearly sales greater than the GNP of all but a handful of nations. It is further alleged that MNCs absorb local savings and local entrepreneurial talent, use excessively K-intensive production techniques inappropriate for developing nations and do not train local labor. Most of these complaints are to some extent true especially for host LDCs and have led these nations to regulate foreign direct investments in order to mitigate the harmful effects and increase the possible benefits.

5.28 (*a*) In what way can the economic decision to migrate to other nations be regarded as an investment in human capital?   (*b*) What are the effects of international labor migration on the nation of immigration?   (*c*) What are its effects on the nation of emigration?

(*a*) The economic decision to migrate can be regarded as an investment in human capital because, just as any other investment, it involves a cost (transportation, job search and so on) and confers certain economic benefits (the higher earnings over the remaining working life of the migrant, better education opportunities for the migrant's children and so on).

(*b*) Migration generally increases the output of the nation of immigration while it prevents real wages from being as high as they would have been in the absence of immigration. For this reason, immigration is generally opposed by organized labor. Since migrants are usually young workers, the age structure of the nation of immigration improves.

(*c*) Migration reduces output and increases real wages in the nation of emigration (unless the migrants were unemployed or not part of the labor force in the nation of emigration). To the extent that emigrants are young workers, the age structure of the nation of emigration worsens. Since the 1950s and 1960s, concern has increased about the great number of scientists, technicians, doctors, nurses and other highly skilled personnel migrating from LDCs to DCs and from Europe to the U.S. This is referred to as the *brain drain*. The problem arises because the nation of emigration incurs the cost of training these workers but the benefits accrue to the nation of immigration. This is of particular concern to LDCs, which have a great need for skilled people.

Chapter 6

Trade Restrictions:
Tariffs and Other Commercial Policies

6.1 RESTRICTIONS ON THE FLOW OF INTERNATIONAL TRADE

So far we have established that free trade is better than autarky for each nation. However, a nation can try to increase its welfare at the expense of other nations by restricting trade. Trade restrictions are classified as tariff and nontariff. The *ad valorem import tariff* has received the most attention. This is expressed as a percentage of the value of the imported commodity and is usually imposed to limit the volume of imports. An *import quota* is a direct quantitative restriction on the importation of a commodity and has many of the effects of an import tariff (see Problem 6.9). Tariffs have generally declined since World War II and are now only about 6% on manufactured goods [see Problem 6.21(c)]. Since the mid-1970s, however, the number and importance of nontariff restrictions on trade or *new protectionism* in the form of voluntary export restraints, technical, administrative, and other regulations have increased significantly (see Problem 6.3). Trade in agricultural commodities is also subject to many direct quantitative restrictions and other nontariff trade barriers.

6.2 PARTIAL EQUILIBRIUM ANALYSIS OF TARIFFS

The effects of a tariff can be studied with partial equilibrium analysis when the industry and the nation are small. Partial equilibrium analysis of a tariff shows: (1) that a tariff usually results in a higher domestic price for the importable commodity, lower domestic consumption, higher domestic production and thus smaller imports of the commodity; (2) the revenues collected by the government; (3) the redistribution of income from consumers (who must pay a higher price for the commodity) to producers (who receive the higher price) and from the nation's abundant factor(s) of production, which produce exportables, to the nation's scarce factors, which produce import-competing products; (4) the inefficiencies, called *protection costs,* resulting from the tariff.

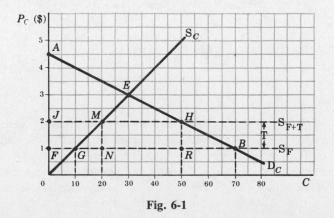

Fig. 6-1

EXAMPLE 1. Assume that in Fig.6-1 D_C stands for the U.S. demand for cloth and S_C for the U.S. supply of cloth (the importable commodity of the U.S.) and that the cloth industry and the U.S. are small. At the free-trade price of cloth of $1, the U.S. demands 70 units of cloth (FB), of which 10 units are produced domestically (FG) and the remainder

91

of 60 units (GB) is imported. The horizontal dashed line S_F represents the infinitely elastic free-trade foreign supply of cloth to the U.S. If the U.S. imposes a 100% *ad valorem* tariff on the importation of cloth, then $P_C = \$2$ (OJ) in the U.S. At $P_C = \$2$, the U.S. demands 50C ($JH$), of which 20 units ($JM$) are produced domestically and 30 (MH) are imported. The horizontal dashed line S_{F+T} represents the new tariff-inclusive foreign supply curve of cloth to the U.S. Thus, the consumption effect equals $-20C$ (BR), the production effect equals $+10C$ (GN), imports decline by 30C ($BR + GN$) and the government collects $30 in revenue ($NMHR$). The consumers' surplus (measured by the area under the demand curve and above the going price for the commodity) is $122.50 (the area of triangle ABF) under free trade and $62.50 (the area of triangle AHJ) with that tariff. Of the $60 reduction in consumers' surplus ($122.50 − $62.50 = area of $FJHB$), $30 ($NMHR$) is collected by the government as tariff revenue, $15 ($FJMG$) is redistributed to producers in the form of rent (see Problem 6.7), and the remaining $15 ($GMN + BHR$) represents the protection cost to the economy (see Problem 6.8).

6.3 NOMINAL VERSUS EFFECTIVE TARIFF RATE

So far, we have discussed the *ad valorem* or *nominal* tariff on imports. When the domestic import-competing industry uses imported inputs subject to a different nominal tariff rate than that on the final commodity, then the nominal tariff rate differs from the effective protective rate. The latter measures the actual rate of protection that the nominal tariff rate actually provides to the import-competing industry. The *rate of effective protection* is the tariff on value added and is measured by the following formula:

$$f = \frac{t - ai}{1 - a}$$

where f = the rate of effective protection
     t = the nominal tariff rate on the final commodity
     a = the ratio of the value of the imported input to the value of the final commodity
     i = the nominal tariff rate on the imported input

EXAMPLE 2. If $t = 100\%$, $a = 0.5$ and $i = 0\%$ (i.e., the imported input is allowed in duty free), then

$$f = \frac{100\% - (0.5)(0\%)}{1 - 0.5} = \frac{100\% - 0}{0.5} = 200\%$$

That is, since the imported input represents 50% of the value of the final commodity, a nominal tariff of 100% computed on the value of the final commodity represents a 200% tariff on the *value added* of the import-competing industry and gives a measure of the actual or effective rate of tariff protection provided to domestic producers. If t had instead equalled 10%, f would have been 20%. The average values of t and f on manufactured imports in the world today are about 6% and 9% respectively.

6.4 GENERAL EQUILIBRIUM ANALYSIS OF TARIFFS

Tariff in a Small Nation

The imposition of an import tariff by a small nation has the following general equilibrium results: (1) prices on the world market remain unchanged; (2) the domestic price of the importable commodity rises by the full amount of the tariff *for individual producers and consumers in the small nation*; (3) domestic production of the importable commodity rises, while domestic consumption and imports fall in the small nation; (4) the price of the importable commodity *for the small nation as a whole* remains unchanged since the small nation itself collects the tariff; (5) the welfare of the small nation declines; and (6) the real income of the nation's scarce factor increases (this is called the *Stolper-Samuelson theorem*).

EXAMPLE 3. At the free-trade $P_C/P_W = P_B = 1$ on the world market, the U.S. (now assumed to be a small nation) produces at point B and consumes a point E in Fig. 6-2 (as in the right panel of Fig. 3-2, but omitting for simplicity the

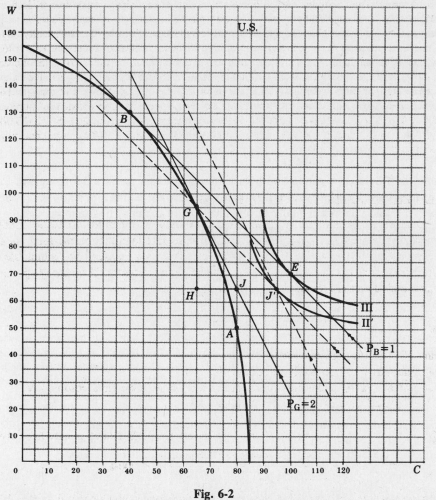

Fig. 6-2

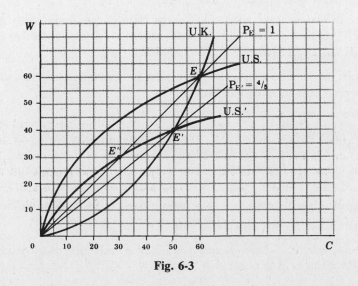

Fig. 6-3

primes attached to the letters). If the U.S. imposes a 100% *ad valorem* tariff on its cloth imports, P_C/P_W remains unchanged at the free-trade price of $P_B = 1$ on the world market because the U.S. is now assumed to be a small nation. However, for individual producers and consumers in the U.S., $P_C/P_W = 2$ (i.e., rises by the full amount of the tariff). At $P_C/P_W = P_G = 2$, the U.S. produces at point G and exports 30W (GH) for 30C (HJ'), of which 15C (HJ) goes directly to U.S. consumers and the remaining 15C (JJ') is collected as a tariff (in kind) by the U.S. government. For the U.S. as a whole, $P_C/P_W = P_B = 1$ since the U.S. itself collects the tariff. The U.S. consumption point with the tariff (point J') is given at the intersection of the two dashed lines and is inferior to the U.S. free-trade consumption point (point E). However, the real income of labor (the scarce factor in the U.S.) rises (for an intuitive proof, see Problem 6.16).

Tariff in a Large Nation

The imposition of a tariff by a large nation improves its terms of trade, reduces the volume of trade and may improve the nation's welfare. However, since the improvement in the nation's position comes at the expense of its trade partner, the trade partner is likely to retaliate and, in the end, both nations usually lose. These effects are best analyzed with offer curves (see Example 4).

The Stolper-Samuelson theorem also holds for large nations in the vast majority of the cases.

EXAMPLE 4.   Assume that both the U.S. and the U.K. are now large nations and affect world prices. Under free trade, offer curves U.S. and U.K. in Fig. 6-3 cross at point E giving the equilibrium $P_C/P_W = P_E = 1$, at which 60C are exchanged for 60W. If the U.S. now imposes a 100% import tariff on cloth, offer curve U.S. rotates down to offer curve U.S.', which is at all points twice as distant from the wheat axis as offer curve U.S. This happens because with a 100% tariff on cloth imports, the U.S. now wants 100% more, or twice as much, cloth as before for each quantity of wheat exported. With offer curve U.S.', the terms of trade of the U.S. improve to $P_W/P_C = 1/P_{E'} = 5/4 = 1.25$, but the volume of trade declines to 40W for 50C. If the positive effect on the U.S.'s welfare resulting from the better terms of trade overwhelms the negative effect from the reduced volume of trade, the U.S.'s welfare will also be greater. Starting from the free-trade position, as the U.S. imposes higher tariffs, the U.S.'s welfare will increase up to a point (the *optimum tariff*) and decline thereafter. However, since the improved position of the U.S. comes at the expense of the U.K., the U.K. is likely to retaliate. If the U.K. imposed a 100% import tariff on wheat, the offer curve of the U.K. would rotate up and cross offer curve U.S.' at point E''. Then both nations would be worse off than under free trade (see Problem 6.21). The other effects of the tariff are more easily analyzed with partial equilibrium analysis.

6.5   SOME ARGUMENTS FOR TRADE PROTECTION

Trade protection is sometimes advocated to:

(1)   Protect domestic labor against cheap foreign labor.

(2)   Make the price of the imported good equal to the price of the domestically produced good (the "scientific tariff") so as to enable domestic producers to compete with foreign rivals.

(3)   Reduce domestic unemployment (by producing at home some of the goods previously imported).

(4)   Cure a deficit in the nation's balance of payments (i.e., to eliminate the excess of the nation's expenditures abroad over its foreign earnings).

(5)   Improve the nation's terms of trade and welfare.

(6)   Protect domestic producers against dumping (*dumping* refers to selling in a foreign market at below cost or below the price charged domestically).

(7)   Allow domestic industries to be established and grow until they become efficient (*the infant-industry argument*).

(8)   Take advantage of oligopoly power and external economies (*strategic trade policy*).

(9)   Protect industries important for national defense.

The first five arguments listed above are generally invalid (see Problem 6.24). The last four can be valid with qualifications (see Problems 6.25 to 6.28).

6.6 ECONOMIC INTEGRATION

Economic integration refers to the formation of a free-trade area, a customs union, a common market or an economic union among a group of nations. In a *free-trade area,* all tariffs are removed on trade between the member nations, but each nation retains its own tariff rates against nonmembers. A *customs union* is the same as a free-trade area except that a common tariff rate is applied against nonmembers. A *common market* goes beyond a customs union by also allowing for the free movement of labor and capital among the member nations. An *economic union* goes still further by harmonizing the monetary, fiscal and tax policies of the member nations as well.

Most of the theoretical discussion revolves around the customs union. The static welfare effects of a customs union are measured in terms of trade creation and trade diversion. *Trade creation* results when domestic production is replaced by imports from a lower-cost and more efficient producer within the customs union. This increases welfare. *Trade diversion* results when imports from a lower-cost supplier from outside the union are replaced by a higher-cost supplier from within. This usually reduces welfare [see Problem 6.30(*b*)]. For a graphic representation of a trade-creating and a trade-diverting customs union, see Problem 6.31. The dynamic welfare effects are more important and result from greater competition, economies of scale and the higher level of investments made possible by economic integration (see Problem 6.33).

EXAMPLE 5. In 1960, the European Free Trade Association (EFTA) was formed by England, Sweden, Denmark, Switzerland, Norway, Austria and Portugal. The complete elimination of tariffs on trade in industrial goods was achieved in 1967. By far the most successful and talked about case of economic integration is the European Economic Community (EEC) or Common Market. It was formed in 1958 by West Germany, France, Italy, the Netherlands, Belgium and Luxembourg. The common external tariff was set at the average of the 1957 tariffs of the six nations. Free trade in industrial goods within the EEC and common prices for agricultural products were achieved in 1968. Restrictions on the free movement of labor and capital were reduced by 1970. In 1973, England and Denmark left the EFTA and together with Ireland joined the EEC. Greece joined in 1981 and Spain and Portugal in 1986. The enlarged EEC has a population greater than that of the U.S. and represents the largest trading block in the world. The formation of the EEC resulted in net trade creation in industrial goods but trade diversion in agricultural products. The static welfare benefits appear to be very small. The dynamic welfare benefits are presumed to be larger but measurement is very difficult. Recently many nations in Europe and Africa have become associated with the EEC. So far, attempts at economic integration in Latin America, Asia and Africa have not been very successful (see Problem 6.34). In 1988, the U.S. negotiated a free-trade agreement with Canada.

Glossary

Ad valorem import tariff   A tariff expressed as a fixed percentage of the value of the imported commodity.

Import quota   A direct quantitative restriction on imports.

New protectionism   The proliferation since the mid-1970s of such nontariff trade barriers as voluntary export restraints and technical, administrative, and other regulations.

Nominal tariff   A tariff expressed as a percentage of the value of the traded commodity.

Rate of effective protection   The actual rate of protection that a nominal tariff rate actually confers to the import-competing industry. It is the tariff on value added.

Protection cost of a tariff   The real losses in a nation's welfare because of inefficiencies in production and consumption resulting from a tariff.

Stolper-Samuelson theorem   The theorem that postulates that tariff protection leads to an increase in the income of the nation's scarce factor.

Optimum tariff　The rate of tariff that maximizes the benefit resulting from the improvement in the nation's terms of trade against the negative effect resulting from the reduction in the volume of trade.

Dumping　The export of a commodity at below cost or its sale abroad at a lower price than at home.

Infant-industry argument for tariffs　The argument that tariff protection is required to allow for the establishment and growth of domestic industries until they become efficient and can withstand foreign competition.

Strategic trade policy　Trade policies that a nation can use to increase its welfare by taking advantage of oligopolistic power and external economies.

Free-trade area　The form of economic integration that removes all barriers on trade among members, but each nation retains its own tariff rates against nonmembers.

Customs union　The form of economic integration that removes all barriers on trade among member nations and harmonizes trade policies toward the rest of the world.

Common market　The form of economic integration that removes all barriers on trade among member nations, harmonizes trade policies toward the rest of the world, and also allows for the free movement of labor and capital among member nations.

Economic union　The form of economic integration that removes all barriers on trade among member nations, harmonizes trade policies toward the rest of the world, allows for the free movement of labor and capital among member nations, and also harmonizes the monetary, fiscal and tax policies of its members.

Trade creation　The replacement of domestic production by imports from a lower-cost producer within the customs union.

Trade diversion　The replacement within a customs union of imports from a lower-cost supplier by goods from a higher-cost supplier belonging to the union.

Review Questions

1. When a nation imposes an import tariff,　(*a*) the domestic price of the importable commodity rises,　(*b*) domestic consumption of the importable commodity falls,　(*c*) domestic production of the import-competing commodity increases,　(*d*) the volume of imports of the importable commodity falls,　(*e*) all of the above.

   Ans.　(*e*) See Section 6.2.

2. The cost of protection is equal to the reduction in consumers' surplus minus　(*a*) the increase in the rent to producers,　(*b*) the revenue effect of the tariff,　(*c*) the increase in rent to producers and the revenue effect of the tariff.

   Ans.　(*c*) See Example 1 and Fig. 6-1.

3. When no imported inputs are used in the production of a commodity, the effective tariff rate on the commodity is　(*a*) equal to the nominal tariff rate on the commodity,　(*b*) greater than the nominal rate,　(*c*) smaller than the nominal rate,　(*d*) any of the above is possible.

   Ans.　(*a*) That is, since $a = 0$, $f = t$ (see the formula in Section 6.3).

4. With reference to the formula for the effective tariff rate in Section 6.3, we can say that if $a > 0$ and $t > i$, then　(*a*) $f = t$,　(*b*) $f < t$,　(*c*) $f > t$,　(*d*) $f \gtreqless t$.

   Ans.　(*c*) See Example 2 and Problem 6.10.

5. Which of the following is not a general equilibrium result of the imposition of an import tariff by a small nation: (*a*) prices on the world market remain unchanged; (*b*) prices for individuals in the nation rise by the full amount of the tariff; (*c*) prices for the nation as a whole remain unchanged; (*d*) domestic production of the commodity falls, while consumption and imports rise; (*e*) the nation's welfare declines.

    Ans.   (*d*) See Section 6.4.

6. The Stolper-Samuelson theorem postulates that the imposition of a tariff by a nation causes the real income of the nation's (*a*) scarce factor to rise, (*b*) scarce factor to fall, (*c*) abundant factor to rise, (*d*) scarce and abundant factors to rise.

    Ans.   (*a*) See Section 6.4.

7. When a nation imposes an import tariff, the nation's offer curve will (*a*) shift away from the axis measuring its export commodity, (*b*) shift away from the axis measuring its import commodity, (*c*) not shift, (*d*) any of the above is possible.

    Ans.   (*a*) See Fig. 6-3 and Example 4.

8. The imposition of an import tariff by a large nation (*a*) usually improves the nation's terms of trade and increases the volume of trade, (*b*) worsens the nation's terms of trade but increases the volume of trade, (*c*) worsens the nation's terms of trade and reduces the volume of trade, (*d*) usually improves the nation's terms of trade but reduces the volume of trade.

    Ans.   (*d*) See Section 6.4.

9. The imposition of an import tariff by a nation will increase the nation's welfare. (*a*) Always, (*b*) never, (*c*) sometimes.

    Ans.   (*c*) See Example 4.

10. The only arguments in favor of a tariff which could be valid (when qualified) are (*a*) protection of domestic labor against cheap foreign labor, the scientific tariff, and the reduction of domestic unemployment; (*b*) correction of a deficit in the nation's balance of payments and improvement of the nation's terms of trade; (*c*) the infant-industry argument, strategic trade, and protection against dumping and for industries important for national defense; (*d*) all of the above.

    Ans.   (*c*) See Section 6.5.

11. The form of economic integration in which the member nations eliminate tariffs on trade among themselves, adopt a common external tariff wall, and allow for the free movement of labor and capital within the union is the (*a*) free-trade area, (*b*) customs union, (*c*) common market, (*d*) economic union.

    Ans.   (*c*) See Section 6.6.

12. When imports from a lower-cost supplier from outside the union are replaced by goods from a higher-cost supplier from within, we have (*a*) dynamic welfare effects, (*b*) trade creation, (*c*) trade diversion, (*d*) all of the above.

    Ans.   (*c*) See Section 6.6.

Solved Problems

RESTRICTIONS ON THE FLOW OF INTERNATIONAL TRADE

6.1   Does free trade maximize world welfare? Explain.

   Free trade leads to the most efficient use of world resources and thus to maximum world output. Because of this, classical economists such as Adam Smith believed that free international trade also maximized world welfare (see Problem 1.8). There is no question (and it was proved in Chapter 3) that free trade is better than autarky for each trading nation and thus for the world as a whole. However, free trade is a necessary but not sufficient condition for maximizing world welfare, since the distribution of income among people and nations is also important. Even when free trade does maximize world welfare, not every step toward *freer* trade *when free trade itself cannot be achieved* will necessarily increase world welfare. This somewhat startling conclusion follows from the "Theory of the Second Best," which is studied in detail in a more advanced course.

6.2   (*a*) Why do nations restrict international trade?   (*b*) How do they restrict it?

(*a*)   Practically all nations of the world impose some restrictions on the flow of international trade. Trade restrictions are invariably rationalized in terms of national welfare. In reality, they are usually advocated by and imposed to protect those industries and workers that would be hurt by imports. Thus, trade restrictions generally benefit a few at the expense of many (who will have to pay higher prices for the domestically produced product).

(*b*)   There are two types of trade restrictions: tariffs and nontariff restrictions. A *tariff* is a tax on the traded commodity. The import tariff is much more common than the export tariff. The latter is prohibited by the U.S. Constitution but is applied by some LDCs on their traditional exports in order to get better prices and raise revenues. The *ad valorem* tariff (expressed as a percentage of the value of the traded commodity) is more common than the *specific* tariff (expressed as a charge per unit of the traded commodity). The most important of the nontariff restrictions on the flow of trade is *the quota*. This is a direct quantitative restriction on the quantity of a commodity allowed to be imported or exported. Though a quota has many of the same effects as a tariff, it is generally more restrictive [see Problem 6.9(*c*)].

6.3   (*a*) What is meant by the "new protectionism"?   (*b*) To what problems does it give rise?

(*a*)   The new protectionism refers to the proliferation since the mid-1970s of voluntary export restraints and technical, administrative and other regulations. *Voluntary export restraints* (VERs) refer to situations whereby an importing nation induces an exporting nation to "voluntarily" restrict its exports of a commodity for a specific period of time under the threat of higher all-round trade restrictions. The U.S. and other industrial countries have negotiated VERs with Japan, newly industrializing countries (such as South Korea, Singapore, Taiwan, and Hong Kong) and other less developed countries to limit their exports of textiles, apparel, steel, automobiles, consumer electronics and other products.

     Technical, administrative, and other regulations refer to health regulations, pollution standards, labeling and packaging regulations, which though serving legitimate purposes have also (and sometimes primarily) been used to restrict imports.

(*b*)   The spread of the new protectionism restricts the flow of international trade and the benefits from specialization in production and trade. This has coincided with (and to some extent has neutralized) the benefits resulting from the sharp tariff reductions that have been negotiated since the end of World War II. The spread of the new protectionism now represents the greatest threat to the liberal trading system that has been so painstakingly been put together during the postwar period and which so well served the world economy.

PARTIAL EQUILIBRIUM ANALYSIS OF TARIFFS

6.4   Figure 6-4 (which is the same as Fig. 4-3) shows that with free trade and zero transportation costs, the U.S. imports 60C/year from the U.K. at $P_C = \$4.50$/yard (reread Problem 4.14). If the U.S. now imposes an import tariff of \$1 on each yard of cloth it imports from the U.K.,   (*a*) what will P_C be in the U.S. and the U.K.? How much cloth will be traded?   (*b*) What happens to the U.S. terms of trade?   (*c*) What would happen instead if the S_C curve of the U.K. had been infinitely elastic (i.e., horizontal) at $P_C = \$4.50$?

(*a*) P_C in the U.S. will exceed P_C in the U.K. by \$1 (the import tariff), and in such a way that the volume of trade will be in equilibrium. This occurs when $P_C = \$4$ in the U.K. and \$5 in the U.S. and 40C are traded (see Fig. 6-4). This result is exactly the same as when we had free trade but transportation costs of \$1/yard [see Problem 4.15(*a*)].

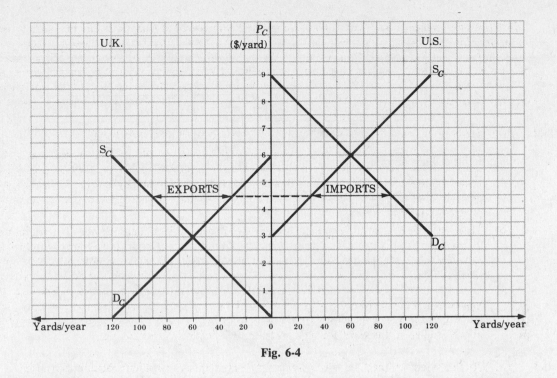

Fig. 6-4

(b) Since the U.S. government collects the tariff of $1 per yard of cloth imported, the U.S. is essentially paying a price of $4 for each yard of cloth imported rather than the price of $4.50 under free trade. Thus, by imposing an import tariff on cloth, the U.S. reduced its demand of cloth imports and was able to import cloth at a lower price. If the price that the U.S. receives for its wheat exports remains unchanged in the face of this reduction in the price of its cloth imports, then the U.S. terms of trade (i.e., $P_X/P_M = P_W/P_C$) improve. This is the usual result. In general, the more elastic the S_C curve of the U.K., the smaller the fall in the P_C to the U.S., and the less the improvement in the U.S. terms of trade (this result is left for the more advanced reader to prove for him- or herself on Fig. 6-4).

(c) If the S_C curve of the U.K. were infinitely elastic (i.e., horizontal) at $P_C = \$4.50$, the imposition of the $1 tariff would leave the price at which the U.S. imports cloth from the U.K. unchanged at the free-trade $P_C = \$4.50$. Then, the P_C to U.S. consumers would rise by the full amount of the tariff to $5.50, the U.S. cloth imports would fall to 20C (see Fig. 6-4), and the U.S. terms of trade would remain unchanged. Though this is an extreme and unusual result, it was used in Example 1 and will be used in Problems 6.5 to 6.9 because it greatly simplifies the analysis.

6.5 Suppose that the U.S. market demand and supply functions for cloth are given, respectively, by: $QD_C = 140 - 20P_C$ and $QS_C = 20P_C - 20$, where P_C is given in dollars. (a) Derive the U.S. demand and supply schedules for cloth. (b) Plot the U.S. demand and supply curves for cloth and indicate the equilibrium price and quantity for cloth in the U.S. in the absence of trade. (c) If the U.S. now allows free trade and $P_C = \$2$ on the world market, the world supply of cloth is infinitely elastic at $P_C = \$2$ and we assume no transportation costs, what will P_C be in the U.S.? How much cloth will the U.S. consume, produce and import with free trade?

(a) The U.S. demand and supply schedules for cloth are obtained by substituting various alternative P_C into the U.S. demand and supply functions of cloth, as in Table 6.1.

Table 6.1

$P_C(\$)$	0	1	2	3	4	5	6	7
QD_C	140	120	100	80	60	40	20	0
QS_C	−20	0	20	40	60	80	100	120

(b) In the absence of trade, $P_C = \$4$ and the U.S. produces and consumes 60C (see point E in Fig. 6-5).

(c) With free trade, $P_C = \$2$ in the U.S. (the same as on the world market). At $P_C = \$2$, the U.S. consumes 100C, produces 20C and imports 80C (see Fig. 6-5).

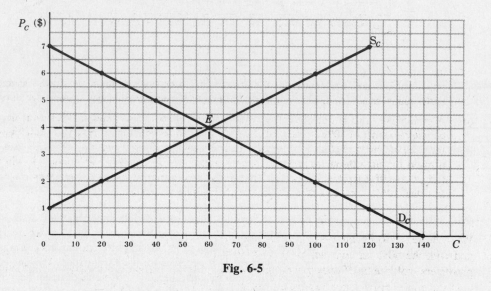

Fig. 6-5

6.6 If, from the free-trade position in Fig. 6-5, the U.S. imposed a 50% *ad valorem* (nominal) tariff on its cloth imports,   (a) draw a figure showing the new P_C in the U.S. and the consumption, production, trade and revenue effects of the tariff, as well as the world supply of cloth to the U.S. without and with the tariff.   (b) On what do the size of the consumption, production, trade and revenue effects depend?   (c) What would constitute a prohibitive tariff on cloth in part (a)?

(a) Since the free-trade $P_C = \$2$, the 50% *ad valorem* tariff is equal to \$1 per unit of cloth imported. Since we assumed (in Problem 6.5) that the world supply of cloth to the U.S. is infinitely elastic, P_C to domestic consumers in the U.S. will rise by the full \$1 amount of the tariff to \$3 [see Problem 6.5(c)]. At $P_C = \$3$, the U.S. consumes 80C (*JH* in Fig. 6-6), of which 40 (*JM*) are produced domestically and 40 (*MH*) are imported. Thus, the consumption effect of the tariff equals −20C (*BR*), the production effect (i.e., the expansion of domestic production resulting from the tariff) equals 20C (*GN*), the trade effect (i.e., the reduction in imports) equals 40C (*BR + GN*) and the revenue effect (i.e., the revenue collected by the government) equals \$40 (\$1 on each of the 40C imported, or *NMHR*). In Fig. 6-6, dashed lines S_F and S_{F+T} are the world supply curves of cloth to the U.S. without and with the tariff, respectively.

(b) For the same \$1 increase in P_C in the U.S. as a result of the tariff, the consumption effect will be greater, the more elastic and flatter the D_C curve of the U.S. in Fig. 6-6. Similarly, the more elastic the S_C curve of the U.S., the greater the production effect. Thus, the more elastic the D_C and the S_C curves of the U.S., the greater the trade effect (i.e., the greater the reduction in U.S. imports), and the *smaller* the revenue effect of the tariff. Today, import tariffs are imposed by DCs primarily for their protection effect rather than for their revenue effect. Revenues are today more efficiently raised in DCs through income taxes and

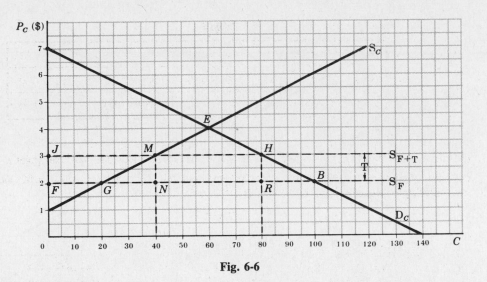

Fig. 6-6

other forms of taxation. However, this has not always been so. In the early days of national states and in LDCs today, tariffs were and are imposed primarily to generate revenues, since they are easiest to collect.

(c) A prohibitive tariff is one high enough to stop all imports of a commodity. For example, in Fig. 6-6, an *ad valorem* tariff of 100% (equal to $2/unit) or more imposed by the U.S. on its cloth imports would make the price of imported cloth to domestic consumers equal to $4 or more. Since the U.S. can satisfy its entire demand for cloth through domestic production at $P_C = \$4$ (see Fig. 6-6), the U.S. will import no cloth (i.e., the tariff is a prohibitive one). If transportation costs are considered, then an *ad valorem* tariff of even less than 100% (i.e., less than $2/unit) can be prohibitive.

6.7 With reference to Problem 6.6 indicate (a) the total revenue of U.S. cloth producers under free trade and with the 50% *ad valorem* tariff. (b) How much of the increase in the total revenue of U.S. cloth producers with the tariff over their total revenue under free trade is absorbed by their higher production cost for cloth? How much represents an increase in their rent?

(a) Under free trade, U.S. cloth producers sell 20C (*FG* in Fig. 6-6) at the free-trade price of $P_C = \$2$, and so their total revenue is $40. With the tariff, U.S. cloth producers sell 40C (*JM*) at $P_C = \$3$ and receive $120, or $80 more than under free trade.

(b) The increase in production costs incurred by U.S. cloth producers to produce the 20 additional units of cloth (*GN*) with the tariff is given by the area under the S_C curve from point *G* to point *M* and equals $50 (see Fig. 6-6). Thus, of the additional $80 received by U.S. cloth producers, $50 is absorbed by their higher costs of production, and the remaining $30 (*FJMG*) represents an increase in their rent (i.e., an increase in their total revenue which is not required in the long run to induce them to supply these extra 20 units of cloth).

6.8 With reference to Fig. 6-6 (redrawn below as Fig. 6-7) and Problem 6.6, indicate   (a) the reduction in the consumers' surplus as a result of the tariff and   (b) the redistribution effect and the protection cost of the tariff.   (c) To what is the protection cost of the tariff due?

(a) Consumers' surplus refers to the difference between what consumers are willing to pay to obtain a specific amount of the commodity and what they actually pay. What U.S. consumers are willing to pay for 100C is given by the area under the D_C curve up to point $B = 0ABK = \$450$ in Fig. 6-7. Since they pay only $0FBK = \$200$ under free trade, the consumers' surplus $= FAB = \$250$ under free trade. With the tariff, the U.S. consumes 80C. To get 80C, U.S. consumers are willing to pay $0AHL = \$400$. Since they pay only $0JHL = \$240$, the consumers' surplus $= JAH = \$160$ with the tariff. Thus, as the result of the tariff, the consumers' surplus falls from $FAB = \$250$ to $JAH = \$160$ or by $FJHB = \$90$.

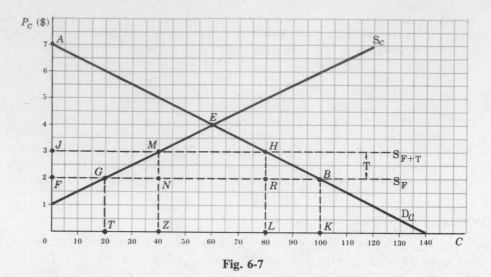

Fig. 6-7

(b) Of the fall in the consumers' surplus of $FJHB$ = $90 resulting from the tariff, $NMHR$ = $40 is the revenue effect of the tariff and $FJMG$ = $30 is redistributed to U.S. cloth producers and represents an increase in their rent (see Problem 6.7 and Fig. 6-7). The remainder of $20 (i.e., GMN = $10 plus BHR = $10) represents the protection cost of the tariff to the U.S. economy.

(c) The protection cost of the tariff arises from the inefficiencies associated with the reduced volume of trade—the terms of trade remaining constant by assumption (see Problem 6.5). More specifically, when the U.S. imposes the tariff, it produces 20 additional units of cloth (GN in Fig. 6-7) at the cost of $TGMZ$ = $50 [see Problem 6.7($b$)]. But the U.S. could have imported these 20 additional units of cloth (GN) at the free-trade price of P_C = $2 for a total expenditure of $TGNZ$ = $40. This extra $10 ($GNM$ in Fig. 6-7) expenditure represents the production component of the protection cost of the tariff. It arises because less efficient domestic cloth production is substituted for more efficient foreign cloth production and represents a real cost for the U.S. economy. The consumption component of the protection cost of the tariff to the U.S. is also $10 ($BHR$ in Fig. 6-7). It arises because the import tariff on cloth artificially increases P_C in relation to other prices to U.S. consumers and causes a distortion in consumption in the U.S.

6.9   Starting at the free-trade price P_C = $2 in the U.S. in Figs. 6-6 and 6-7,   (a) find the consumption, production and redistribution effects of a quota of 40C imposed by the U.S. on its cloth imports. (b) What is the revenue effect of the import quota? Who captures it?   (c) Which is a more restrictive barrier to trade, an import quota or an "equivalent" import tariff?

(a) The U.S. import quota of 40C raises P_C for U.S. consumers to $3 (the same as with the 50% *ad valorem* import tariff on cloth, which also allowed 40C of imports into the U.S., see Fig. 6-7). Thus, the consumption effect of the import quota (BR = $-20C$), the production effect (GN = 20C) and the redistribution effect ($FJMG$ = $30) are exactly the same as with the "equivalent tariff" of 50% *ad valorem* on cloth imports.

(b) If the government auctions off import licenses at $1 for each of the 40C imports allowed, the revenue effect of the import quota is also the same as that of the equivalent import tariff (i.e., $NMHR$ = $40 in Fig. 6-7). However, the government seldom auctions off import licenses. In that case, the revenue effect will be captured by importers, exporters or shared by both in the form of higher prices and profits, and represents a rent for them. The revenue effect will be captured by U.S. importers (and so the U.S. terms of trade remain unchanged) if U.S. importers are organized and behave as a monopolist while exporters are not organized. This is the most likely result. The revenue effect will be captured by foreign cloth exporters (and the U.S. terms of trade deteriorate) if they are organized while U.S. cloth importers are not. If both importers and exporters are organized, we have a case of bilateral monopoly where the revenue effect is shared by both, but the actual result is theoretically indeterminate. Note that when the government does not auction off import licenses, it faces the problem of how to allocate these import licenses among potential importers of the commodity.

(c)   An import tariff increases the price of the imported commodity to domestic consumers and reduces the volume of imports [see Problem 6.4 and 6.6(a)]. However, foreign producers, by increasing their production efficiency and by being able to export the commodity at a lower price, can overcome the import tariff and increase their exports. They cannot do this with an import quota, since this fixes the quantity of imports allowed, regardless of price. Thus, an import quota is a more restrictive barrier to trade than the "equivalent" import tariff. With tariff barriers having been reduced to their present low levels as the result of successful international negotiations, quantitative restrictions on trade have increased in relative importance, especially in agriculture. GATT rules forbid the imposition of quantitative restrictions on trade except for nations in balance of payments difficulties and for those imposing similar quotas on domestic production as, for example, in agriculture. Recently, the U.S. government induced foreign exporters of textiles, shoes, steel and automobiles (under the threat of higher all-around trade restrictions) to impose *voluntary* quotas on their exports of these commodities to the U.S.

NOMINAL VERSUS EFFECTIVE TARIFF RATE

6.10   Suppose that t (the nominal tariff rate on the final commodity) = 0.5 or 50%, i (the nominal tariff rate on the imported input used in the production of the final commodity) = 0.2 or 20%, and a (the ratio of the value of the imported input to the value of the final commodity) = 0.4. Find f, the effective protective rate given to the domestic producers of the commodity.

$$f = \frac{t - ai}{1 - a} = \frac{0.5 - (0.4)(0.2)}{1 - 0.4} = \frac{0.5 - 0.08}{0.6} = \frac{0.42}{0.6} = 0.7$$

Note that while the *nominal tariff* rate is computed on the value of the final commodity (as, for example, the *ad valorem* tariff) and, by affecting the price of the final commodity to consumers, is important for consumers in their consumption decisions, the *effective tariff* is important for producers in their production decision. Specifically, the theory of effective protection implies that those industries given a higher rate of effective protection will expand, or expand more than the industries given a lower rate of effective protection—regardless of the level of the nominal tariff rate.

6.11   Prove that if no imported inputs go into the domestic production of the final commodity, then $f = t$.

If no imported inputs go into the domestic production of the final commodity, $a = 0$. When $a = 0$, the formula for f [i.e., $(t - ai)/(1 - a)$] becomes

$$\frac{t - (0)(i)}{1 - 0} = t$$

Thus, when there are no imported inputs, the entire value of the final commodity represents value added in the nation, and so $f = t$.

6.12   Suppose there is no tariff on imported inputs and the ratio of the value of imported inputs to the value of the final commodity is 0.25, 0.5, or 0.75. Find the effective protective rate in terms of the nominal tariff rate, in each of these three alternative cases.

When $a = 0.25$,

$$f = \frac{t - (0.25)(0)}{1 - 0.25} = \frac{t}{0.75} = \frac{t}{3/4} = \frac{4}{3}t$$

When $a = 0.5$,

$$f = \frac{t - (0.5)(0)}{1 - 0.5} = \frac{t}{0.5} = \frac{t}{1/2} = 2t$$

When $a = 0.75$,

$$f = \frac{t - (0.75)(0)}{1 - 0.75} = \frac{t}{0.25} = \frac{t}{1/4} = 4t$$

Thus, when $i = 0$, the higher a, the greater f for any given t.

6.13 Given $a = 0.5$ and $t = 0.4$, find f when $(a)\ i = 0.6$, $(b)\ i = 0.8$ and $(c)\ i = 1$.

   (a) When $i = 0.6$,

$$f = \frac{0.4 - (0.5)(0.6)}{1 - 0.5} = \frac{0.4 - 0.3}{0.5} = \frac{0.1}{0.5} = 0.2, \text{ or } 20\%$$

   Thus, if $i > t$, $f < t$.

   (b) When $i = 0.8$,

$$f = \frac{0.4 - (0.5)(0.8)}{1 - 0.5} = \frac{0.4 - 0.4}{0.5} = \frac{0}{0.5} = 0$$

   This means that the domestic, import-competing industry is given no protection whatsoever, even though $t > 0$.

   (c) When $i = 1$,

$$f = \frac{0.4 - (0.5)(1.0)}{1 - 0.5} = \frac{0.4 - 0.5}{0.5} = \frac{-0.1}{0.5} = -0.2, \text{ or } -20\%$$

   This means that not only is the domestic, import-competing industry not protected, but that it is actually discouraged. From the formula for the rate of effective protection, we can see that this will occur whenever $t < ai$.

6.14 (a) Summarize the results of Section 6.3, Example 2, and Problems 6.10 to 6.13. (b) Derive the formula for finding f when more than one input enters into the domestic production of the final commodity and each input is subject to a different nominal import tariff. (c) What is the limitation of the theory of effective protection?

   (a)

$$f = \frac{t - ai}{1 - a}$$

   (See Section 6.3.) If $t > i$ and $i \geqq 0$, then $f > t$, and the greater the value of a, the more f exceeds t for any value of t (see Example 2 and Problems 6.10 and 6.12). If $a = 0$, then $f = t$, regardless of the value of i (see Problem 6.11). If $ai > t$, then f is negative regardless of the value of t.

   (b) When there is more than one imported input, each subject to a different import duty, then

$$f = \frac{t - \Sigma ai}{1 - \Sigma a}$$

   where $\Sigma ai = a_1 i_1 + a_2 i_2 + \cdots + a_n i_n$, while $\Sigma a = a_1 + a_2 + \cdots + a_n$, and the subscripts $1, 2, \ldots,$ n refer to the n imported inputs. Thus, Σai is the *weighted average* of the ai values, one for each of the imported inputs, while Σa is the sum of the ratios of the value of each imported input to the value of the final commodity.

   (c) The limitation of the theory of effective protection is its partial equilibrium nature. That is, the theory assumes a fixed relationship between each input and the final commodity (i.e., a constant value of a for each input) in computing f. However, these a values usually change as relative factor prices change, and so a reliable value of f cannot be readily found.

GENERAL EQUILIBRIUM ANALYSIS OF TARIFFS

Tariff in a Small Nation

6.15 Explain how the first five effects listed in Section 6.4 arise when a small nation imposes an import tariff.

   (1)   A small nation is by definition one that does not affect world prices by its trading. Thus, the imposition of an import tariff by the small nation reduces the volume of trade by an amount too small to affect world prices.

(2)   The imposition of a tariff by a nation in the face of unchanged world prices represents a tax that has to be paid in full (in the form of higher prices) by individuals in the nation.

(3)   With higher domestic prices for the importable commodity, domestic producers expand the production of the importable commodity until its price rises to the level of the world price plus the tariff. Domestic consumers will purchase less of the importable commodity at the higher tariff-inclusive price that they must pay. With domestic production of the importable commodity rising and domestic consumption falling, the imports of the commodity by the small nation falls. Note that with a 300% tariff on cloth imports, the U.S. would return to its autarky production point A in Fig. 6-2. Thus, a tariff of 300% or more on cloth imports represents a *prohibitive tariff* for the U.S.

(4)   Since domestic consumers pay a price for the importable commodity which is higher than the world price by the amount of the import tariff but the tariff is collected by the government of the nation, the price of the importable commodity remains unchanged at the world price level *for the nation as a whole*. It is assumed that the government then uses the tariff revenue to reduce taxes or provide additional services.

(5)   With less specialization in production and a smaller volume of trade at unchanged commodity prices for the nation as a whole, the small nation's welfare declines. Note that indifference curve II' in Fig. 6-2 is different from indifference curve II in the right panel of Fig. 3-2 because the tariff changed the distribution of income in the U.S.

6.16   Explain why the real income of labor (the scarce factor in the U.S.) rises when the U.S. imposes a tariff on its cloth imports.

When the U.S. imposes a tariff on its cloth imports, P_C/P_W rises and the U.S. produces more cloth and less wheat (compare point G with point B in Fig. 6-2). Since cloth is the L-intensive commodity, the relative demand for L rises. As a result, w/r rises and K is substituted for L, so that K/L rises in the production of both commodities. As more K is used with each unit of L, the productivity and the real wages of L rise in the U.S. Since it is assumed that L and K are fully employed before and after the imposition of the tariff, the real *income* of L also rises in the U.S. Thus, labor unions in the U.S. and in other industrial nations generally favor trade restrictions. With the gain of labor usually smaller than the loss of owners of capital (the abundant factor in the U.S.), the welfare of the U.S. as a whole falls (compare point J' to point E in Fig. 6-2).

Though we examined exclusively the effects of an import tariff, the results would generally be the same for an export tariff or any other trade restriction since they all shift production away from the commodity in which the nation has a comparative advantage and toward the commodity in which the nation has a comparative disadvantage.

6.17   Starting with the U.K. free-trade model in the left panel of Fig. 3-2, but assuming that the U.K. is now a small nation, draw a figure analogous to Fig. 6-2 showing the effect of the U.K. imposing a 100% tariff on its wheat imports.

At the free-trade $P_C/P_W = P_B = 1$ on the world market, the U.K. (now a small nation) produces at point B and consumes at point E in Fig. 6-8 (as in the left panel of Fig. 3-2). When the U.K. imposes a 100% tariff on its wheat imports: (1) P_C/P_W remains unchanged at $P_B = 1$ on the world market; (2) $P_W/P_C = 2$ and $P_C/P_W = 1/2$ for individuals in the U.K.; (3) the U.K. produces 25W more and 35C less than with free trade (compare point G to point B in Fig. 6-8), consumption declines to 75W and 55C (point J') and imports of wheat decline from 60W to 30W; (4) $P_C/P_W = P_B = 1$ for the nation as a whole because the U.K. government collects the 100% tariff on its wheat imports in the form of 15W (JJ'); (5) the consumption point of the U.K. with the tariff (point J') is inferior to its consumption point under free trade (point E); (6) the real income of owners of capital (the scarce factor in the U.K.) increases.

Tariff in a Large Nation

6.18   (*a*) Sketch the U.K. and the U.S. offer curves given in Table 6.2.   (*b*) What is the volume of trade between the U.K. and the U.S.? What is the equilibrium P_C/P_W with trade? What are the terms of trade of the U.K. and the U.S.?

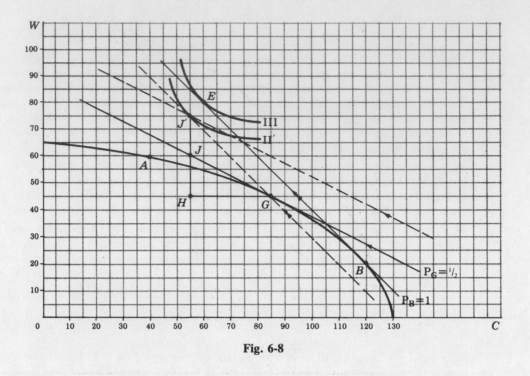

Fig. 6-8

Table 6.2

U.K.	C	15	25	40	60	75	90
	W	5	10	20	40	60	90
U.S.	W	20	30	40	60	80	90
	C	6.25	12.5	20	37.5	60	90

(*a*) See Fig. 6-9.

(*b*) The U.K. exchanges 90C for 90W with the U.S. (point *E* in Fig. 6-9). With trade, the equilibrium $P_C/P_W = P_E = 1$. The U.K. terms of trade = $P_X/P_M = P_C/P_W = P_E = 1$. The U.S. terms of trade = $P_X/P_M = P_W/P_C = 1/P_E = 1$.

6.19 Starting with the U.K. and the U.S. offer curves in Table 6.2.   (*a*) show in tabular form what happens if the U.K. imposes a 100% tariff on its wheat imports and   (*b*) redraw Fig. 6-9 to show the effect of the 100% tariff on wheat imports imposed by the U.K.   (*c*) What is the new volume of trade? What are the new terms of trade of the U.K. and the U.S.?   (*d*) How does the imposition of the 100% import tariff by the U.K. affect the welfare of the U.K. and the U.S.?   (*e*) How does the tariff effect the real income of capital owners in the U.K.?

(*a*) Since it is the U.K. that imposes the tariff, it is the U.K. offer curve that is affected. By imposing a 100% tariff on its wheat imports, the U.K. now wants 100% more, or twice as much, wheat as before for each quantity of cloth exported. The original offer curve of the U.K. and its new offer curve (U.K.′) are given in Table 6.3.

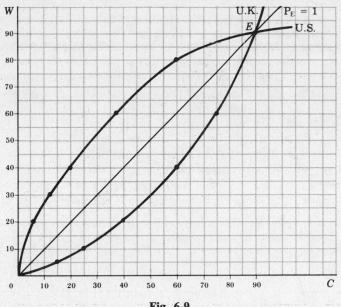

Fig. 6-9

Table 6.3

U.K.	C	15	25	40	60	75	90
	W	5	10	20	40	60	90
U.K.'	C	15	25	40	60	75	90
	W	10	20	40	80	120	180

(b) See Fig. 6-10.

(c) The U.K. now exchanges 60C for 80W with the U.S., down from 90C for 90W (compare point E' with point E in Fig. 6-10). The new terms of trade of the U.K. equals $P_X/P_M = P_C/P_W = P_{E'} = 4/3$ and exceeds the original terms of $P_E = 1$. On the other hand, the U.S. terms of trade deteriorates from $1/P_E = 1$ to $1/P_{E'} = 1/(4/3) = 3/4$.

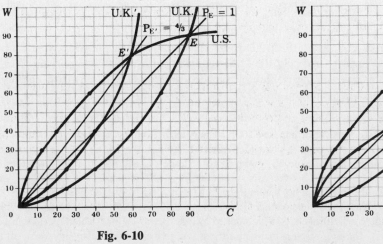

Fig. 6-10

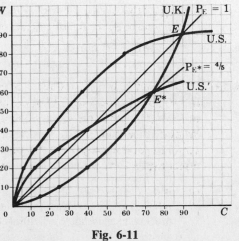

Fig. 6-11

(d) The welfare of the U.K. is greater at point E' than at point E, if the positive effect of the tariff on the U.K. terms of trade exceeds the negative effect on the volume of trade. Starting from a zero tariff, as the U.K. imposes higher and higher import tariffs, the welfare of the U.K. rises up to a point and then declines. The tariff that maximizes a nation's welfare is called the *optimum tariff*. On the other hand, the U.S. is definitely worse off at point E' than at point E, because its terms of trade deteriorated and the volume of trade declined.

(e) According to the Stolper-Samuelson theorem, the real income of owners of capital (the scarce factor in the U.K.) rises in the U.K.

6.20 Starting with the U.S. offer curve in Table 6.2, (a) show in tabular form what happens if the U.S. imposes a 100% import tariff. (b) Redraw Fig. 6-9 and show on it the effect of the 100% import tariff imposed by the U.S. (c) What is the new volume of trade? What are the new terms of trade of the U.K. and the U.S.? (d) How does this tariff affect the welfare of the U.K. and the U.S.?

(a) Since the U.S. imposes a 100% import tariff, the U.S. now wants 100% more, or twice as much, cloth as before for each quantity of wheat exported. The original offer curve of the U.S. and its new offer curve (U.S.') are given in Table 6.4.

Table 6.4

U.S.	W	20	30	40	60	80	90
	C	6.25	12.5	20	37.5	60	90
U.S.'	W	20	30	40	60	80	90
	C	12.5	25	40	75	120	180

(b) See Fig. 6-11.

(c) The U.S. now exchanges 60W for 75C with the U.K., down from 90W for 90C (compare point E^* with point E in Fig. 6-11). The new terms of trade of the U.K. deteriorates from $P_E = 1$ to $P_{E^*} = 4/5$, while the new terms of trade of the U.S. improve from $1/P_E = 1$ to $1/P_{E^*} = 1/(4/5) = 5/4 = 1.25$.

(d) The U.K. will be worse off at point E^* than at point E, because its terms of trade deteriorated and the volume of trade declined. The welfare of the U.S. increases if the positive effect of the U.S. import tariff on the U.S. terms of trade exceeds the negative effect on the volume of trade. If the 100% import tariff imposed by the U.S. represented the optimum tariff for the U.S., increases in the U.S. tariff rate up to the 100% level increase U.S. welfare. Still higher tariffs reduce the U.S. welfare, until a prohibitive tariff ends all trade (and all gains from trade) and the origin of Fig. 6-11 is reached. To measure the size of the optimum tariff, *trade indifference curves* are needed. These are discussed in more advanced courses and texts.

6.21 Starting with offer curves U.S. and U.S. in Fig. 6-9, (a) draw a figure showing what happens if the U.K. imposes a 100% import tariff and the U.S. retaliates with a 100% import tariff of its own. (b) What effect does this have on the welfare of the U.K. and the U.S.? (c) How can both nations move back to the free-trade equilibrium point?

(a) See Fig. 6-12.

(b) After the U.K. and the U.K. have imposed 100% import tariffs, we get offer curves U.K.' and U.S.' in Fig. 6-12. These offer curves cross at point E'', where 40C are exchanged for 40W and the terms of trade of each nation equals 1. Since, at point E'', the terms of trade of each nation are the same as at point E (the free-trade equilibrium point) but the volume of trade is greatly reduced, both nations are worse off at point E'' than at point E. Thus, if either nation imposes an import tariff in an attempt to increase its welfare, it causes a loss of welfare to its trade partner (see Problems 6.19 and 6.20). The trade partner is then likely to retaliate and impose a tariff of its own in order to recoup part of its loss. This process can be repeated any number of times. The final result is that both nations lose in the end (i.e., they are worse off than under free trade).

(c) Starting at point E'', both nations can increase their welfare by a reciprocal reduction of tariffs. Their joint output and welfare (assuming "retaliation") is maximized when all tariffs have been completely removed (i.e., at point E, the free-trade equilibrium point). Such a reciprocal reduction of tariffs (from their all-time high reached in the U.S. under the *Smoot-Hawley Tariff Act* of 1930) was the aim of the U.S. *Reciprocal Trade Agreement Act,* first passed in 1934 and then regularly renewed. With the U.S. *Trade Expansion Act* of 1962, and bargaining at the international forum known as the *General Agreement on Tariffs and Trade* (GATT), (nominal) tariff rates on manufactured goods were lowered by about 35% in the so-called "Kennedy Round" of negotiations that was completed in 1967. Under the authority of the *Trade Reform Act* of 1974, the U.S. negotiated tariff reductions averaging 31% in the "Tokyo Round" completed in 1979, so that today tariff rates on manufactured goods are only about 6%. Under GATT rules, reductions of tariffs agreed to by two nations are extended to all other nations with which the bargaining nations have "most-favored-nation" agreements. The "Uruguay Round" of multilateral trade negotiations (1986–1990) sought to reverse the trend of rising nontariff trade barriers, bring services and agriculture into GATT and improve GATT dispute-settlement mechanisms.

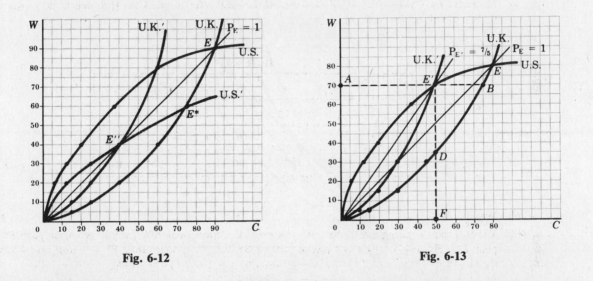

Fig. 6-12   Fig. 6-13

6.22 With reference to Fig. 6-13,   (a) what are the volume of trade and the terms of trade with offer curves U.K. and U.S.? With offer curves U.K.' and U.S.?   (b) What import tariff on wheat must the U.K. have imposed in order to go from offer curve U.K. to offer curve U.K.'?   (c) What *export tariff* on cloth could the U.K. impose in order to go from offer curve U.K. to offer curve U.K.'?

(a) With offer curves U.K. and U.S., the U.K. exchanges 80C for 80W with the U.S. (see point E in Fig. 6-13), and the terms of trade are $P_E = 1$ for the U.K. and $1/P_E = 1$ for the U.S. With offer curves U.K.' and U.S., the U.K. exchanges 50C for 70W with the U.S. (see point E'), and the terms of trade are $P_{E'} = 7/5$ for the U.K. and $1/P_{E'} = 5/7$ for the U.S.

(b) For each quantity of cloth exports, offer curve U.K.' involves twice as much wheat imports as offer curve U.K. (see Fig. 6-13). Thus, the U.K. must have imposed a 100% import tariff on wheat, or DE'/FD. If, instead, we had used FE' as the base for computing the percentage, the tariff of DE', collected by the U.K. in wheat, represents a 50% import tariff on wheat, or DE'/FE' (see Fig. 6-13).

(c) We would also get offer curve U.K.' and the results of part (a) if the U.K., instead of an import tariff on wheat, imposed an export tariff on cloth of $BE'/AE' = 25/50 = 1/2$ or 50% (see Fig. 6-13). Note, however, that now the tariff of BE' is collected by the U.K. in cloth, England's export commodity, rather than in wheat (its import commodity). Thus, the U.K. can shift its offer curve up and to the left and improve its terms of trade and welfare (assuming no retaliation by the U.S.) by the use of an import tariff on wheat, an export tariff on cloth or a combination of the two. Our discussion has been entirely in terms of import tariffs because the Constitution of the United States prohibits export tariffs, and import tariffs are much more widespread than export tariffs elsewhere in the world [see Problem 6.2(b)].

6.23 (*a*) Draw a figure showing the shifts in the U.K. offer curve in Table 6.2, if the U.K. imposes a 50%, a 100% or a 150% import tariff on its wheat imports. On the same set of axes, draw the U.S. offer curve as a straight-line ray from the origin with a slope of 1.   (*b*) What happens to the volume of trade, the terms of trade and welfare of the U.K. and the U.S. when the U.K. imposes the 50%, the 100% or the 150% import tariff on wheat?   (*c*) What is the level of the optimum tariff for the U.K. in this case? On what does the size of the optimum tariff depend?

(*a*)   In Fig. 6-14, offer curve U.K.$_1$ is that of Table 6.2. Offer curves U.K.$_2$, U.K.$_3$ and U.K.$_4$ result when the U.K. imposes a 50%, a 100% or a 150% import tariff on wheat, respectively. The straight-line offer curve of the U.S. indicates that the U.S. is willing to export any quantity of wheat at $P_C/P_W = 1$ (i.e., the U.S. offer curve is infinitely elastic; see Problem 5.20).

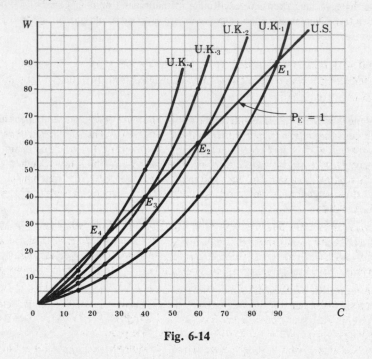

Fig. 6-14

(*b*)   Under free trade, offer curves U.K.$_1$ and U.S. in Fig. 6-14 cross at point E_1, indicating that 90C are exchanged for 90W at the terms of trade of 1 for both nations. With offer curves U.K.$_2$, U.K.$_3$ and U.K.$_4$, the volume of trade falls to 60C for 60W, 40C for 40W, and 25C for 25W, respectively, but the terms of trade of both nations remain unchanged at the value of 1 (see equilibrium points E_2, E_3 and E_4). Thus, the higher the level of the tariff imposed by the U.K., the smaller the volume of trade at unchanged terms of trade, and so the smaller the welfare of both nations. We would get the same result if, before a very small nation imposes a tariff, its offer curve intersected the straight-line segment of the otherwise bending offer curve of its trade partner (see Problems 5.20 and 3.16).

(*c*)   Even in the absence of retaliation from the U.S., the U.K. cannot increase its welfare from the free-trade level by imposing a tariff. Indeed, by imposing any tariff, the U.K. would cause a reduction in its welfare. Also, the greater the tariff level, the greater the reduction in welfare. Thus, when the offer curve of the trade partner (here the U.S.) is infinitely elastic, the optimum tariff for a nation (here the U.K.) is zero. By extension, we can say that the more elastic (i.e., the smaller the curvature of) the offer curve of the trade partner, the smaller the level of the optimum tariff for a nation, and vice versa.

SOME ARGUMENTS FOR TRADE PROTECTION

6.24 Of the arguments for trade protection listed in Section 6.5, explain why   (*a*) arguments 1 and 2 are wrong outright and   (*b*) arguments 3, 4, and 5 are usually invalid.

(a) Argument 1 states that trade protection is needed in order to protect domestic labor against cheap foreign labor. However, even if U.S. wages are higher than abroad, if the productivity of U.S. labor is sufficiently higher than abroad, the labor component of the U.S. costs of production is less than abroad and no protection is needed for domestic labor. Even if this is not the case, mutually advantageous trade based on comparative advantage can still take place and tariff protection is still not justified. Argument 2 (the scientific tariff) is wrong because it would eliminate all price differences and trade between nations (and the gains from trade).

(b) Arguments 3, 4 and 5 are beggar-thy-neighbor arguments for trade protection and, as such, are usually invalid. Specifically, by imposing a tariff, a nation can reduce domestic unemployment and improve its balance of payments, terms of trade and welfare. However, since this nation's gains come at the expense of other nations (which suffer increased unemployment and worsened balance of payments, terms of trade and welfare), other nations are likely to retaliate, and all nations lose in the end. Domestic unemployment and deficits in the nation's balance of payments should be corrected by appropriate monetary and fiscal policies (see Chapter 10) rather than by import tariffs designed to cut specific imports.

6.25   (a) Explain why trade protection may be justified in the case of dumping.   (b) Are export subsidies a form of dumping? Why?   (c) How can trade protection be justified by national defense? How must this argument be qualified?

(a) Dumping is sometimes carried on for the specific purpose of driving foreign producers of a given commodity out of business, after which the price is greatly increased. This is referred to as *predatory* dumping. Here, trade protection is justified to protect the domestic industry; however, predatory dumping is often not easy to prove. If, on the other hand, the dumping is *persistent,* domestic consumers benefit from the continuing lower prices for the imported items, and so a case against this type of dumping can hardly be made. Dumping can also be *sporadic* in order to sell an unforeseen and temporary surplus abroad without having to reduce domestic prices.

(b) *Export subsidies* are direct payments or the granting of tax relief and subsidized loans to the nation's exporters or potential exporters and/or low-interest loans to foreign buyers so as to stimulate the nation's exports. As such, export subsidies can be regarded as a form of dumping. Although they are illegal by international agreement, many nations provide them in disguised and not-so-disguised forms.

(c) Trade protection sometimes is advocated to protect industries important for national defense. This is a noneconomic argument for protection, and the economist has no particular competence to evaluate its validity, except to point out that even in this case, a direct production subsidy is generally a better method of aiding an industry important for national defense than trade protection. Something more can be said. That is, in case of localized wars (e.g., the Korean and Vietnam wars), the needed material for the war effort (such as cargo vessels, military clothing and shoes, etc.) might easily be provided for and much more cheaply from abroad than by producing it in the U.S. In the case of a total war today, there would hardly be the time to utilize the protected industries.

6.26   (a) Explain why and under what conditions the infant-industry argument for an import tariff is valid. (b) How must this argument be qualified?

(a) The infant-industry argument for tariffs is generally valid, especially for LDCs. It holds that a LDC may have a potential comparative advantage in a particular commodity, say textiles, but that because its initial production costs are too high (due to lack of know-how and the initial small level of output), this industry cannot be established or grow in the LDC in the face of foreign competition. An import tariff is then justified to help the LDC establish the industry and protect it during its "infancy," until the industry has grown in size and efficiency and is able to meet foreign competition. At that time, the tariff is to be removed.

(b) In order for the infant-industry argument to be valid, not only must the tariff eventually be removed and the "grown up" industry be able to compete with foreign firms without protection, but the extra return in the industry (after the removal of the protection) must be high enough to justify the costs involved during the period of protection. These costs arise because the commodity is produced domestically rather than imported for less. It may also be difficult a priori to determine which industry or potential industry qualifies for this treatment, and to eventually remove the tariff once it is imposed. Economists also agree that what a tariff can do here, a direct subsidy to the infant industry can do better. This is because a subsidy can be varied so as to provide the infant industry with the same degree of protection as an equivalent import tariff but without distorting relative prices and domestic consumption. However, a subsidy requires revenue, rather than generating it as the tariff does.

6.27 (*a*) Draw a figure showing the infant-industry argument for trade protection. (*b*) What is the relationship between the desire of LDCs to industrialize, infant industry, import substitution and the theory of effective protection?

(*a*) In Fig. 6-15, P_W is the world price of a commodity in which the LDC has a potential comparative advantage. However, since the cost of producing this commodity in the LDC initially exceeds P_W, this industry could not be established in the LDC without sufficient protection against foreign competition. This protection can be provided, and this industry established in the LDC with an import tariff on this commodity which exceeds $P_W P_Z$. As time passes and the industry acquires know-how, and as output expands and the industry reaps the benefits of economies of scale, domestic costs begin to fall (at output Q_1 in Fig. 6-15) and so the rate of protection can be reduced, until it can be completely eliminated at Q_2 (where domestic costs equal P_W). Past output Q_2, this commodity becomes an exportable for the LDC. However, as pointed out in Problem 6.26(*b*), an equivalent production subsidy is better than tariff protection.

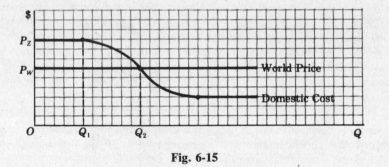

Fig. 6-15

(*b*) LDCs see industrialization as the key to their economic development (see Problem 5.21). However, industry can often not be established in a LDC without some initial protection against foreign competition (the infant-industry argument for protection). With sufficient protection, the industry can be established and grow, at least for a while, by replacing imports of the commodity with domestic production (i.e., by import substitution). However, once all imports of the commodity have been replaced by domestic production, the process of industrialization may become stagnant (as occurred in Argentina in the late 1930s), unless the domestic industry can increase its efficiency to the point where it can compete with foreign firms without protection and actually succeed in entering the world market as an exporter of the commodity. But here, the higher effective than nominal tariff rates that DCs maintain against *L*-intensive manufactured imports may prevent LDCs from entering the world market as exporters of these commodities. At a series of United Nations Conferences on Trade and Development (UNCTAD) held in 1964, 1968, 1972, 1976, 1980, 1984 and 1988, LDCs raised this and many other complaints against the trade policies of DCs and demanded, among other things, preferential access for their manufactured exports to DCs as part of their call for NIEO (see Section 5.6). Recently, LDCs have achieved some degree of success along these lines in their negotiations with the EEC and the U.S.

6.28 (*a*) How can strategic trade policy justify trade protection? (*b*) What difficulties arise in carrying out a strategic trade policy?

(*a*) According to strategic trade policy, a nation can create a comparative advantage through temporary trade protection in such fields as semiconductors, computers, telecommunications, and other industries that are deemed crucial to future growth in the nation. These high-technology industries are subject to high risks, require large-scale production to achieve economies of scale and give rise to extensive external economies when successful. Strategic trade policy suggests that by encouraging such industries, the nation can enhance its future growth prospects. This is similar to the infant-industry argument in developing nations, except that it is advanced for industrial nations to acquire a comparative advantage in crucial high-technology industries. Most nations do some of this. Indeed, some economists would go so far as to say that a great deal of the postwar industrial and technological success of Japan is due to its strategic industrial and trade policies.

(b) There are three serious difficulties in carrying out strategic trade policy. First, it is extremely difficult to pick winners (i.e., choose the industries that will provide large external economies in the future) and devise appropriate policies to successfully nurture them. Second, since most leading nations undertake strategic trade policies at the same time, their efforts are largely neutralized so that the potential benefits to each may be small. Third, when a country does achieve substantial success with strategic trade policy, this comes at the expense of other countries (i.e., it is a beggar-thy-neighbor policy) and so other countries are likely to retaliate. Faced with all these practical difficulties, even supporters of strategic trade policy grudgingly acknowledge that *free trade is still the best policy, after all*.

ECONOMIC INTEGRATION

6.29 With reference to Table 6.5, (a) indicate whether we have trade creation or trade diversion when country A, which initially imposes a nondiscriminatory *ad valorem* import tariff of 100% on commodity X, t_X (column 3 in Table 6.5), forms a customs union with country B.   (b) What if country A initially imposed a nondiscriminatory *ad valorem* import tariff of 50% on commodity X (column 4) before forming a customs union with country B?

Table 6.5

(1) Country	(2) P_X = Cost of producing X	(3) P_X to A when t_X = 100%	(4) P_X to A when t_X = 50%
A	$10	$10	$10
B	8	16	12
C	6	12	9

(a) Before the formation of the customs union and with t_X = 100%, country A produces commodity X domestically. When country A forms a customs union with country B (and removes the 100% import tariff on commodity X from country B but retains it on country C), country A will import commodity X from country B at P_X = $8, rather than supplying it domestically at P_X = $10. This is a case of trade creation. Less efficient domestic production is replaced here by more efficient production in the union partner.

(b) Before the formation of the customs union and with t_X = 50%, country A imports commodity X from country C at P_X = $9, rather than supplying it itself at P_X = $10. When country A forms a customs union with country B (and removes the 50% import tariff on commodity X from country B but retains it on country C), country A will now import commodity X from country B at P_X = $8, rather than from country C at P_X = $9. Before the formation of the customs union, country A imported commodity X from country C at P_X = $9 but country A collected the revenue of $3 per unit of X imported. Thus, country A was really paying a P_X = $6 to import commodity X from country C. After the formation of the customs union with country B, country A imports commodity X from country B at the higher P_X of $8. Thus, the formation of the customs union diverted trade from a more efficient, lower-cost source outside the union to a less efficient, higher-cost source from within the union. This is a case of trade diversion.

6.30 (a) Explain why a trade-creating customs union increases the welfare of the nations forming it as well as the welfare of the rest of the world.   (b) Explain why a trade-diverting customs union will reduce the welfare of the rest of the world and may reduce the welfare of the nations forming the customs union.

(a) We saw in Problem 6.29(a) that trade creation leads to more rational and efficient production within the customs union. Assuming that full employment of all economic resources is maintained within the trade-creating customs union, this leads to an increase in the output and welfare of union members. Part of the increase in the real income of the trade-creating customs union spills over into a greater demand for imports from the rest of the world, leading to an increase in the welfare of the rest of the world as well.

(b) We saw in Problem 6.29(b) that with trade diversion, more efficient production outside the union is replaced with less efficient production within the union. Since the released resources in the rest of the world can only be absorbed into less productive uses, the welfare of the rest of the world will fall. Similarly, if all economic resources were fully employed before the formation of the union, the trade-diverting customs union can only lead to reduced welfare for the union members (because of the less efficient use of resources). However, this reduction in welfare within the trade-diverting customs union is moderated or even reversed by the lower price paid by consumers and their resulting greater consumption of the commodity. For example, in Problem 6.29(b), consumers pay a P_X of \$9 before the formation of the trade-diverting customs union and a P_X of \$8 afterward. In general, the formation of a customs union is likely to lead to trade creation in some commodities and trade diversion in others, making it even more difficult to determine its net effect on welfare. It was primarily to avoid trade diversion from the EEC that the U.S. initiated (with the passage of the Trade Expansion Act of 1962 and under the auspices of GATT), the Kennedy Round of negotiations. Since this dealt primarily with manufactured goods, the U.S. has demanded and recently obtained some relief from the diversion of trade that it suffered in agricultural products vis-à-vis the EEC.

6.31   In Fig. 6-16, D_C and S_C represent nation 2's domestic demand and supply curves of cloth. Nation 2 is assumed to be a small nation. S_{1+T} and S_{3+T} are the foreign supply curves of cloth to nation 2 from nation 1 and nation 3, respectively, with a 100% nondiscriminatory *ad valorem* tariff (T) imposed by nation 2 on its cloth imports. With reference to Fig. 6-16, answer the following questions: (a) What will be the price of cloth in nation 2 when nation 2 imposes a 100% nondiscriminatory *ad valorem* tariff on its cloth imports? How much cloth will nation 2 consume, produce and import? From which nation will nation 2 import cloth? (b) What happens if nation 2 forms a customs union with nation 1? Is this a trade-creating or a trade-diverting customs union? What is the welfare gain or loss for nation 2? (c) What happens if nation 2 forms a customs union with nation 3 instead? Is this a trade-creating or a trade-diverting customs union? What is the welfare gain or loss for nation 2?

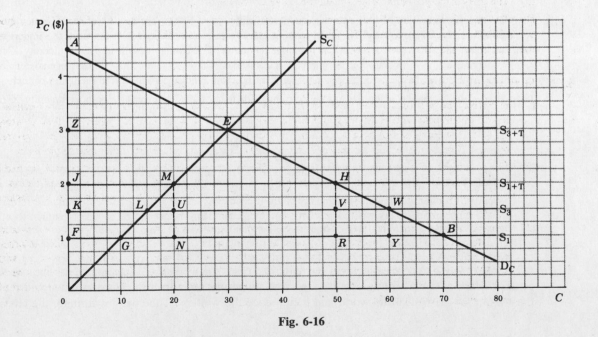

Fig. 6-16

(a) $P_C = \$2$ in nation 2. At $P_C = \$2$, nation 2 consumes 50C (JH), with 20C (JM) produced in nation 2 and 30C (MH) imported from nation 1. Nation 2 collects a tariff revenue of \$30 (NMHR). Nation 2 does not import cloth from nation 3 because the tariff-inclusive $P_C = \$3$ (UZ). So far this is the same as in Fig. 6-1.

(b) If nation 2 forms a customs union with nation 1, $P_C = \$1$ in nation 2. At $P_C = \$1$, nation 2 consumes 70C (FB), with 10C (FG) produced domestically and 60C (GB) imported from nation 1. The tariff revenue disappears and area FGMJ represents a transfer from domestic producers to domestic consumers. This leaves net static gains to nation 2 as a whole of \$15, given by the sum of the areas of triangles GMN and BHR. This is a trade-creating customs union. Note that the analysis is of a partial equilibrium type and, as such, it faces the shortcoming mentioned in Problem 6.14(c).

(c) If nation 2 forms a customs union with nation 3 instead (i.e., it removes the tariff on cloth imports from nation 3 only), $P_C = \$1.50$ in nation 2. At $P_C = \$1.50$, nation 2 consumes 60C (KW), with 15C (KL) produced domestically and 45C (LW) imported from nation 3. Trade is diverted from nation 1 to nation 3 because the tariff-inclusive $P_C = \$2$ for imports from nation 1. There is also some trade creation since nation 2 now imports 45C (from nation 3) instead of the 30C (from nation 1) before the formation of any customs union. The welfare gain in nation 2 from pure trade creation is \$3.75 (given by the sum of the areas of triangles LMU and WHV). The welfare loss from trade diversion proper is \$15 (the area of rectangle NUVR). This results from the higher cost of the imports of 30C diverted from nation 1 to nation 3. This is a trade-diverting customs union that reduces the welfare of nation 2 by \$11.25 (\$15 − \$3.75). Note that the more elastic or flatter are D_C and S_C, the more likely it is that even a trade-diverting customs union increases the welfare of the nation joining such a union. The theory of customs unions is an example of the theory of the second best (see Problem 6.1), which states (in this context) that not every step in trade liberalization (when the first best of free trade cannot be achieved) will necessarily increase welfare.

6.32 What conditions are likely to lead to a trade-creating customs union?

(1) The higher the pre-union import duties of the member countries (see Problem 6.29).

(2) The larger the size and the greater the number of countries in the union (since it is then more likely that the low-cost producers will fall within the union).

(3) The more competitive rather than complementary the pre-union economies (since there is then more room for specialization in production—and trade creation—with the formation of the union).

(4) The closer geographically the member nations forming the union (since transportation costs would then be less of an obstruction to trade creation).

(5) The greater the pre-union trade among the member nations.

Note that conditions 3, 4 and 5 are some of the reasons for the greater degree of success of the EEC as opposed to the EFTA. However, even the EEC has resulted in extremely small static gains for the member nations (very rough estimates put these static gains at less than 1% of their GNP).

6.33 State and discuss the dynamic gains to the nations forming a customs union.

(1) *Increased competition*. That is, with the formation of a customs union, firms in each member nation are forced to compete with other firms within the customs union without the trade protection they previously enjoyed. The result is that the less efficient firms are forced to increase their efficiency, merge or go out of business. Consumers within the customs union benefit from lower prices and better-quality products.

(2) The possibility of *economies of scale* made possible by the enlargement of the free-trade area beyond the national boundaries of the member nations. However, it must be pointed out that even a small nation, not a member of any customs union, can overcome the smallness of its domestic market and achieve substantial economies of scale in production by exporting to the rest of the world.

(3) *Stimulus to investment*. This may arise from the internal expansion of firms taking advantage of economies of scale and from greater investments by outsiders to set up factories within the customs union in order to avoid the tariff wall. These are referred to as *tariff factories*. A great many of these have been set up within the EEC by the U.S. during the last two decades. Though these dynamic gains are presumed to be very significant in the EEC (indeed, the U.K. joined the EEC primarily because of them), they have eluded even rough measurement thus far.

6.34   Explain why economic integration among a group of LDCs may have difficulty succeeding.

Perhaps the greatest stumbling block to successful economic integration among a group of LDCs is that the resulting static and dynamic benefits will not be evenly distributed among the member nations. The more advanced nations gain most of the benefit, giving rise to fears in the lagging nations that economic integration will retard rather than stimulate their economic development. Thus, there is a strong compulsion for these less advanced nations to withdraw from a union, causing its collapse. This could be avoided by investment assistance and industrial planning (i.e., assigning certain industries to each country within the union).

Another difficulty is that many LDCs are wary of relinquishing any part of their newly acquired national sovereignty to a supernational union body, as required for successful economic integration. This is particularly true in Africa. Other difficulties are the lack of good transportation and communications among the member nations, the great geographical distance separating them and the competition for the same world markets for their agricultural exports.

These difficulties, particularly the first one (i.e., the uneven distribution of the benefits), may explain the failure or slow progress toward economic integration in LDCs. For example, the Central American Common Market (CACM) including Costa Rica, El Salvador, Guatemala, Honduras, Nicaragua and Panama, after some initial success, dissolved in 1969. The East Africa Common Market also dissolved. Others, such as the Latin American Free Trade Association or LAFTA (which was superseded in 1980 by the Latin American Integration Association or LAIA) and the Economic Community of West Africa are still in their formative stages, and their success and economic significance remain in doubt. However, the Caribbean Free Trade Association (CARAFTA), set up in 1968, was transformed into a common market (CARICOM) in 1973.

Midterm Examination

1. (a) State the law of comparative advantage for the case of two nations and two commodities.

   (b) State the Heckscher-Ohlin theory for the case of two nations and two commodities.

   (c) In what way is the Heckscher-Ohlin theory superior to classical trade theory?

   (d) Explain under what conditions the Heckscher-Ohlin theory would not be valid. Are these conditions common today?

   (e) In what ways must the Heckscher-Ohlin theory be extended in order to fully explain international trade today?

2. *Given:* (1) two nations (1 and 2) which have the same technology but different factor endowments and tastes, (2) two commodities (X and Y) produced under increasing costs conditions, and (3) no transportation costs, tariffs or other obstructions to trade.

   Prove geometrically that mutually advantageous trade between the two nations is possible. [*Note:* Your answer should show the autarky (no-trade) and free-trade points of production and consumption for each nation, the gains from trade of each nation and express the equilibrium condition that should prevail when trade stops expanding.]

3. *Given:* (1) two nations, the U.S. (the capital-abundant nation) and the U.K. (the labor-abundant nation); (2) two commodities, wheat (the capital-intensive commodity) and cloth (the labor-intensive commodity); and (3) free trade.

   Show graphically with (a) production possibilities curves and community indifference curves and (b) offer curves the effect of capital-biased technical progress in the U.K. on the U.K. terms of trade when all else remains constant in both nations.

4. (a) Draw a figure showing the consumption, production, trade, revenue and redistribution effects of an import tariff when the nation is assumed to be too small to affect world prices. What is the protection cost of the tariff?

   (b) What is the difference between the nominal and the effective tariff rate on imports? What is the significance of each?

   (c) Can a nation increase its welfare by imposing a tariff? Why do nations impose tariff and other trade restrictions? What are the meaning and importance of the rise of the new protectionism?

   (d) What is meant by strategic trade policy? What difficulties arise in carrying out a strategic trade policy?

ANSWERS

1. (a) The law of comparative advantage states that even if a nation has an absolute disadvantage (i.e., is less efficient) in the production of both commodities with respect to the other nation, mutually advantageous trade could still take place between them. The less efficient nation should specialize in the production of and export the commodity in which its absolute disadvantage is less. This is the commodity in which the nation has a comparative advantage. On the other hand, the nation should import the commodity in which its absolute disadvantage is greater. This is the area of its comparative disadvantage. The only exception occurs when the absolute disadvantage which a nation has with respect to another nation is the same in both commodities. This is rather unusual.

   (b) The H-O theory can be expressed in the form of two theorems. (1) The H-O theorem seeks to explain the pattern of trade by postulating that each nation will export the commodity intensive in its abundant and cheap factor and import the commodity intensive in its scarce and expensive factor. (2) The factor-price equalization theorem postulates that trade will lead to the equalization of relative and absolute factor prices between the two nations (under highly restrictive assumptions).

117

(*c*) The H-O theory is superior to classical theory because it seeks to explain (1) the pattern of trade (based on the difference in factor endowments among nations), and (2) the effect of trade on factor prices and on the distribution of income. Classical theory assumed rather than explained comparative advantage and could not say much on the distribution of income among and within nations.

(*d*) The Heckscher-Ohlin theory would not be valid if factor-intensity reversal (FIR) were prevalent. FIR refers to the situation where a commodity is the *L*-intensive commodity in the *L*-abundant nation and the *K*-intensive commodity in the *K*-abundant nation. Then, the H-O theorem would no longer accurately predict the pattern of trade. Similarly, the factor-price equalization theorem would also fall. As a result, the H-O theory would have to be rejected. To date, empirical studies show that FIR is not a common occurrence.

(*e*) The H-O theory, while generally acceptable, leaves a great deal of international trade unexplained, particularly the trade in manufactured products among industrial nations. The gap can be filled by such concepts and models as (1) intra-industry trade or trade in differentiated products, (2) trade based on economies of scale and (3) trade based on imitation gaps and product cycles.

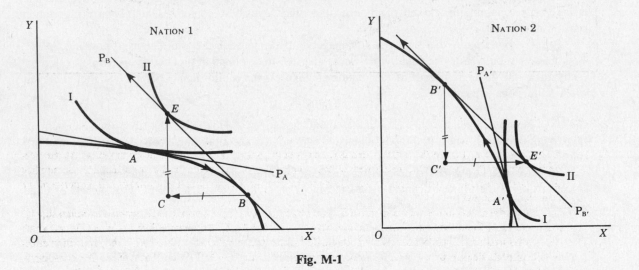

Fig. M-1

2. Nations 1 and 2 have different production possibilities curves and different community indifference maps. With these, they will usually end up with different relative commodity prices in autarky, thus making mutually beneficial trade possible. In Fig. M-1, nation 1 produces and consumes at point *A* and $P_X/P_Y = P_A$ in autarky, while nation 2 produces and consumes at point *A'* and $P_X/P_Y = P_{A'}$.

   Since $P_A < P_{A'}$, nation 1 has a comparative advantage in X and nation 2 in Y. Specialization in production proceeds until point *B* in nation 1 and point *B'* in nation 2, at which $P_B = P_{B'}$ and the quantity supplied for export of each commodity exactly equals the quantity demanded for import. Thus, nation 1 starts at point *A* in production and consumption in autarky, moves to point *B* in production, and by exchanging *BC* of X for *CE* of Y reaches point *E* in consumption. $E > A$ since it involves more of both X and Y and lies on a higher community indifference curve. Nation 2 starts at *A'* in production and consumption in autarky, moves to *B'* in production, and by exchanging *B'C'* of Y for *C'E'* of X reaches *E'* in consumption (which exceeds *A'*). At $P_X/P_Y = P_B = P_{B'}$, nation 1 wants to export *BC* of X for *CE* of Y, while nation 2 wants to export *B'C'* (=*CE*) of Y for *C'E'* (=*BC*) of X. Thus, $P_B = P_{B'}$ is the equilibrium relative commodity price because it clears both (the X and Y) markets.

3. *K*-biased technical progress in the U.K. is one that increases the cloth output of the U.K. proportionately more than its wheat output. In panel A of Fig. M-2, the U.K. produces at point *B* on TT and consumes at point *E* at terms of trade P_B, before the technical progress. At the same terms of trade of P_B after *K*-biased technical progress, the U.K. would produce at point *M* on T'T' and consume at point *U* on community indifference curve III. However, to reach *U*, the U.K. has to export much more cloth than before technical progress. This causes the terms of trade of the U.K. to fall until trade between the U.S. and the U.K. is once again balanced. This occurs at P_G, at which the U.K. produces at point *N* on T'T' and consumes at point *R*. To see that P_G is the new equilibrium P_C/P_W and trade is balanced, we turn to panel B. In panel B, trade was originally in equilibrium at point *E* at terms of trade of P_B. After

technical progress in the U.K., the U.K. offer curve shifts to U.K.* and trade equilibrium is reached at point R at $P_G < P_B$. Since at unchanged terms of trade the U.K. wants to trade more after growth, in terms of trade deteriorate and the U.K. shares part of the benefit of its growth with the U.S.

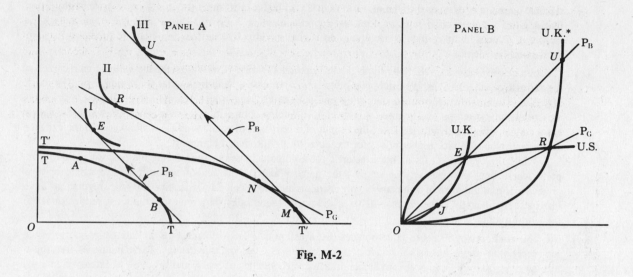

Fig. M-2

4. (a) In Fig. M-3, D and S are the nation's demand and supply curves for the importable commodity. At the free-trade price of P_1, the quantity demanded of the commodity in the nation is AG, of which AB is supplied domestically and BG is imported. Dashed line S_F represents the nation's free-trade foreign supply curve of the importable commodity.

When the nation imposes an import tariff, T, dashed line S_{F+T} represents the tariff-inclusive foreign supply. As a result, the commodity price in the nation rises, say to P_2. At P_2, the quantity demanded is HM, of which HL is produced domestically and LM is imported. Thus, the consumption effect is $(-)GF$, the production effect is BC, imports decline by GF plus BC and the government collects $MLCF$ in tariff revenues. The consumers' surplus falls by $AGMH$, of which $ABLH$ is redistributed to domestic producers and BCL plus GFM represent the protection cost of the tariff to the nation.

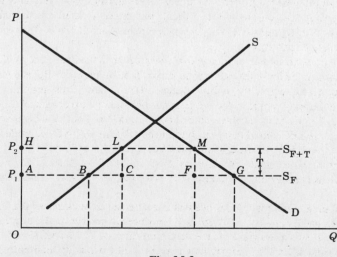

Fig. M-3

(b) The nominal tariff rate is computed on the total value of the final commodity imported while the effective tariff rate is computed on the domestic value added embodied into the import-competing final commodity. If there are no imported inputs into the domestically produced commodity or if there are imported inputs subject to the same nominal tariff rate as on the final commodity, the nominal and effective tariff rates on the final commodity are identical. When the domestic import-competing industry uses imported inputs subject to no import tariff or to a lower nominal tariff rate than on the final commodity (the usual case), then the effective tariff rate on the final commodity exceeds the nominal tariff rate. The effective tariff rate measures the actual rate of protection that a given nominal tariff rate provides the import-competing industry. Thus, while the nominal tariff is important to consumers in their consumption decisions, the effective tariff is important to producers in their production decisions.

(c) A nation can increase its welfare by imposing an "optimum" tariff. However, since the nation's gain comes at the expense of other nations, we can expect other nations to retaliate and impose tariffs of their own. The result is that the volume of trade shrinks and, in the end, all nations usually lose. Tariffs and other trade restrictions are usually advocated by and imposed to protect from foreign competition those industries in which the nation has a comparative disadvantage. Thus, the benefit of a few industries and workers is purchased at the expense of the rest, who will face higher prices for the domestically produced commodity.

While the average tariffs on manufactured goods imports have declined during the postwar period to the point where they average only about 6%, the number and importance of nontariff trade barriers or new protectionism in the form of voluntary export restraints and technical, administrative and other regulations have increased significantly since the mid-1970s to the point where today they represent the most serious threat to the world trading system.

(d) Strategic trade policy refers to trade policies that a nation can use to increase its welfare by promoting such high-technology industries as semiconductors, computers, and telecommunications. These industries are subject to high risks, require large-scale production to achieve economies of scale, and give rise to extensive external economies when successful. Strategic trade policy suggests that by encouraging such industries, the nation can enhance its future growth prospects.

There are serious difficulties in carrying out strategic trade policy. First, it is extremely difficult to pick winners (i.e., choose the industries that will provide large external economies in the future) and devise appropriate policies to successfully nurture them. Second, since most leading nations undertake strategic trade policies at the same time, their efforts are largely neutralized so that the potential benefits to each may be small. Third, when a country does achieve substantial success with strategic trade policy, this comes at the expense of other countries (i.e., it is a beggar-thy-neighbor policy), and so other countries are likely to retaliate.

Chapter 7

The Foreign Exchange Markets

7.1 DEFINITION AND FUNCTIONS

The *foreign exchange market* is the organizational framework within which individuals, firms and banks buy and sell foreign currencies or foreign exchange. The foreign exchange market for any currency, say the dollar, is composed of all the locations, such as London, Zurich, Paris, Frankfurt, Singapore, Hong Kong, Tokyo, as well as New York, where dollars are bought and sold for other currencies. By far, the principal function of the foreign exchange market is the transfer of funds or purchasing power from one nation and currency to another (see Problem 8.14). Other functions are to provide short-term credits to finance trade [see Problem 8.13(*a*)] and the facilities for avoiding foreign exchange risks or hedging (see Section 7.4).

7.2 THE FOREIGN EXCHANGE RATES

The *foreign exchange rate* is the domestic currency price of the foreign currency. This exchange rate is kept the same in all parts of the market by arbitrage. *Foreign exchange arbitrage* refers to the purchasing of a foreign currency where its price is low and selling it where the price is high. A rise in the exchange rate refers to a *depreciation* or a reduction in the value of the domestic currency in relation to the foreign currency. A fall in the exchange rate refers to an *appreciation* or an increase in the value of the domestic currency. Since a nation's currency can depreciate against some currencies and appreciate against others, an *effective exchange rate* is usually calculated. This is a weighted average of the nation's exchange rates [see Problem 7.3(*d*)].

EXAMPLE 1. The exchange rate between the dollar (the domestic currency) and the pound refers to the number of dollars required to purchase one pound, or $/£. If this rate is $1.99 in London and $2.01 in New York, foreign exchange arbitrageurs will purchase pounds in London and resell them in New York, making a profit of 2¢ on each pound. As this occurs, the price of pounds in terms of dollars rises in London and falls in New York until they are equal, say at $2.00, in both places. Then the possibility of earning a profit disappears and arbitrage comes to an end. If through time, the exchange rate (R) rises from $2.00 to $2.10 (in both New York and London), we say that the dollar has depreciated with respect to the pound because we now need more dollars to purchase each pound. On the other hand, when R falls, the dollar appreciates. This is equivalent to a depreciation of the pound (see Problem 7.3).

7.3 THE EQUILIBRIUM FOREIGN EXCHANGE RATE

In general, the foreign exchange rate is determined by the intersection of the market demand curve for and the market supply curve of the foreign currency. The demand for foreign exchange arises primarily in the course of importing goods and services from abroad and making foreign investments and loans (see Chapter 8). The supply of foreign exchange arises in the course of exporting goods and services and receiving foreign investment and loans.

EXAMPLE 2. Figure 7-1 shows the foreign exchange market for pounds from the U.S. point of view, in a simplified two-nation world. The intersection of the U.S. market demand curve for pounds ($D_£$) and the U.S. market supply curve for pounds ($S_£$) determines the *equilibrium exchange rate* of $2.00 = £1 and the equilibrium quantity of pounds demanded and supplied per year of £6 billion. $D_£$ is negatively sloped because at lower R's, England becomes a cheaper and more attractive place in which to buy and invest and so U.S. residents demand a greater quantity of pounds. On the other hand, $S_£$ is usually positively sloped because at lower R's, U.K. residents find it more expensive to buy and invest in the U.S. and, as a result, they spend fewer pounds in the U.S. If for some reason, $D_£$ shifts up, the U.S. will face an excess

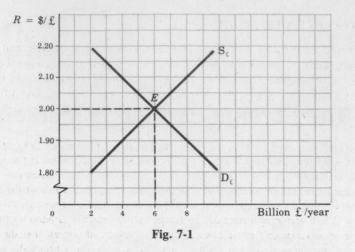

Fig. 7-1

quantity demanded of pounds (a deficit in the U.S. balance of payments) at the original equilibrium exchange rate. This can be corrected if the U.S. allows the dollar to depreciate (i.e., R to rise to its new equilibrium level; see Problem 7.6). The opposite occurs if $D_£$ decreases or $S_£$ increases (see Problem 7.7).

7.4 HEDGING

Since foreign exchange rates usually fluctuate through time, anyone who has to make or receive a payment in a foreign currency at a future date runs the risk of having to pay more or receiving less *in terms of the domestic currency* than originally anticipated. These foreign exchange risks can be avoided or "covered" by *hedging*. This usually involves an agreement today to buy or sell a certain amount of foreign exchange at some future date (usually three months hence) at a rate agreed upon today (the *forward* exchange rate).

EXAMPLE 3.   Suppose that a U.S. firm owes £1,000 to a British exporter payable in three months. At today's exchange rate or *spot rate* of $2.00 = £1, the U.S. firm owes an equivalent of $2,000. If the spot rate in three months rose to $2.10, the U.S. firm would have to pay an equivalent of $2,100, or $100 more. But if the three-month forward rate were $2.01, the U.S. could buy today £1,000 at $2.01 per pound for delivery in three months and avoid any further foreign exchange risk. After three months, when the payment is due, the U.S. firm would get the £1,000 it needs for $2,010, regardless of what the spot rate is at that time. Similarly, if a U.S. exporter is to receive £1,000 in three months, he or she can sell this £1,000 for delivery in three months at today's three-month forward rate, and avoid the risk that the spot rate in three months will be very much below today's spot rate.

7.5 SPECULATION

Speculation is the opposite of hedging. While a hedger seeks to avoid or cover a foreign exchange risk for fear of a loss, the speculator accepts or even seeks a foreign exchange risk or an open position in the hope of making a profit. If the speculator correctly predicts the market, he or she makes a profit. Otherwise, the speculator incurs a loss. Speculation usually occurs in the forward exchange market.

EXAMPLE 4.   If the forward rate on pounds for delivery in three months is $2.00 and a speculator believes that the spot rate of the pound in three months will be $2.10, he can enter today into a forward contract to buy £1,000 in three months at $2.00 per pound. After three months, he will pay $2,000 for the £1,000, and if at that time the spot rate on the pound is indeed $2.10 (as he anticipated), he can resell the £1,000 in the spot market for $2,100 and earn $100 on the transaction. If, on the other hand, his expectations prove to be wrong and the spot rate of the pound after three months is instead $1.95, he will still have to pay $2,000 for the £1,000 that he receives on the matured forward transaction, but he can only resell this £1,000 for $1,950 in the spot market, thus losing $50 on the transaction.

7.6 COVERED INTEREST ARBITRAGE

Interest arbitrage refers to the transfer of liquid funds from one monetary center and currency to another to take advantage of higher rates of returns (interest). The resulting foreign exchange risk is usually covered or hedged by a forward sale of the foreign currency to coincide with the maturity of the foreign investment. There is an incentive for *covered interest arbitrage* as long as the positive interest differential in favor of the foreign monetary center exceeds the forward discount on the foreign currency.

EXAMPLE 5. If the return on three-month treasury bills is 12% (on a yearly basis) in London and 8% in New York, a U.S. resident can exchange her dollars for pounds at the current spot rate and invest them in London where she earns 4% more per year or 1% more for the quarter. However, in three months, the U.S. resident may want to reconvert pounds into dollars and collect the extra interest earned. Since in three months, the spot rate of the dollar with respect to the pound may be lower, her extra interest gained may be wiped out or more than wiped out. To cover this exchange risk, at the same time that the U.S. investor exchanges dollars for pounds to invest in London for three months, she will also engage in a forward sale of an equal amount of pounds (plus the amount of interest that she will earn) for dollars for delivery in three months. If the forward discount on the pound is 1% on a yearly basis, she will lost 1/4 of 1% for the quarter on the foreign exchange transaction, but will gain an extra 1% interest for the quarter, for a net riskless return of about 3/4 of 1% on her foreign investment.

   However, as covered interest arbitrage proceeds, the positive interest differential in favor of London tends to decline while the forward discount on the pound tends to increase, until they are equal (interest parity; see Problem 7.21). At *interest parity*, there is no further possibility of gain and covered interest arbitrage comes to an end.

7.7 EXCHANGE RATE DYNAMICS

During the past two decades, there has been a great deal of exchange rate volatility (variability) and over-shooting. *Exchange rate overshooting* refers to the tendency of exchange rates to immediately depreciate or appreciate by more than required for long-run equilibrium and then to partially reverse their movement as they move toward their new long-run equilibrium level (see Example 6). The reason for this is that financial markets adjust much more quickly than trade flows to market disequilibria (see Problems 7.23 to 7.25).

EXAMPLE 6. Suppose that from the initial long-run equilibrium exchange rate between the dollar and the pound, the supply of money increases in the U.S. This will lower exchange rates in the U.S. and results in an outflow of investment funds to the U.K. as U.S. investors seek to take advantage of the now relatively higher interest rates in the U.K. This will lead to a quick increase in the U.S. demand for pounds and depreciation of the dollar. Over time, however, as U.S. exports increase and U.S. imports decline in response to the dollar depreciation, the dollar appreciates. The only way for the U.S. dollar to first depreciate and then appreciate as it moves toward its new long-run equilibrium level is for the dollar to first depreciate past its new long-run equilibrium level and then gradually appreciate toward its long-run equilibrium level.

7.8 THE EUROCURRENCY MARKETS

The Eurocurrency markets are the markets where Eurocurrencies are bought and sold. *Eurocurrencies* refer to commercial bank deposits outside the country of issue of the currency. For example, a deposit denominated in U.S. dollars in a British commercial bank (or even in a British branch of a U.S. bank) is called a Eurodollar. Similarly, a pound sterling deposit outside the U.K. is called a Eurosterling, and so on. The Eurocurrency market consists mostly of short-term funds with maturity of less than six months.

EXAMPLE 7. The Eurocurrency market has grown from less than $10 billion in the early 1960s to over $1 trillion in 1990. More than half of the total value of Eurocurrencies is in Eurodollars. This market grew very rapidly, especially after 1973, as petroleum-exporting countries deposited outside the U.S. huge dollar amounts accumulated from the sharp increase in petroleum prices. Starting in December 1981, U.S. banks were exempted from federally imposed interest ceilings and reserve and insurance requirements and were allowed to compete directly in the Eurodollar market.

Glossary

Foreign exchange market The organizational framework within which individuals, firms and banks buy and sell foreign currencies or foreign exchange.

Foreign exchange rate The domestic currency price of the foreign currency.

Foreign exchange arbitrage Purchasing of a foreign currency where its price is low and selling it where the price is high. This keeps the exchange rate equal in all parts of the market.

Depreciation An increase in the domestic currency price of the foreign currency.

Appreciation A decrease in the domestic currency price of the foreign currency.

Effective exchange rate A weighted average of the exchange rates between the domestic currency and the currency of the nation's most important trade partners.

Equilibrium exchange rate The exchange rate determined by the intersection of the market demand curve for and the market supply curve of the foreign currency.

Hedging The avoidance or the covering of a foreign exchange risk.

Forward exchange rate The exchange rate in foreign exchange transactions that calls for the payment or receipt of the foreign exchange one, three or six months (usually three months) after the contract is agreed upon.

Spot exchange rate The exchange rate in foreign exchange transactions that calls for the payment or receipt of the foreign exchange within two business days of the transaction.

Speculation The acceptance of a foreign exchange risk, or open position, in the hope of making a profit.

Interest arbitrage The transfer of liquid funds from one monetary center (and currency) to another in order to take advantage of the higher rates of return or interest.

Covered interest arbitrage The transfer of liquid funds from one monetary center to another to earn higher returns or interest, with the foreign exchange risk covered by a forward sale of the foreign currency to coincide with the maturity of the foreign investment.

Interest parity The situation where the positive interest differential in favor of the foreign monetary center is equal to the forward discount on the foreign currency.

Exchange rate overshooting The tendency of exchange rates to immediately depreciate or appreciate by more than required for long-run equilibrium and then to partially reverse their movement as they move toward their long-run equilibrium levels.

Eurocurrencies Commercial bank deposits outside the country of issue of the currency.

Review Questions

1. The function of the foreign exchange market is to   (a) transfer funds from one nation to another,   (b) provide short-term credits to finance trade,   (c) provide the facilities for hedging,   (d) all of the above.

   Ans.   (d) See Section 7.1

2. If $3.60 is needed to purchase £2, the exchange rate is   (a) $3.60 = £ 2,   (b) $1.80 = £1,   (c) £0.50 = $1,   (d) £0.40 = $1.

   Ans.   (b) See Section 7.2 and Problem 7.4(a).

3. The exchange rate is kept the same in all parts of the market by   (a) exchange arbitrage,   (b) interest arbitrage,   (c) hedging,   (d) speculation.

Ans.   (a) See Section 7.2 and Example 1.

4. A change from $3 = £1 to $2 = £1 represents   (a) a depreciation of the dollar,   (b) an appreciation of the dollar,   (c) an appreciation of the pound,   (d) none of the above.

Ans.   (b) See Section 7.2 and Example 1.

5. Under a flexible exchange system, the exchange rate is determined by   (a) the nation's monetary authorities,   (b) the price of gold,   (c) the forces of demand and supply in the foreign exchange market,   (d) exchange arbitrage.

Ans.   (c) See Section 7.3.

6. When the U.S. demand for pounds increases under a flexible exchange rate system,   (a) the dollar depreciates,   (b) the pound depreciates,   (c) the dollar appreciates,   (d) none of the above.

Ans.   (a) See Example 2 and Fig. 7-1. Note that an increase in demand refers to an upward shift in $D_£$.

7. Hedging refers to   (a) the acceptance of a foreign exchange risk,   (b) the covering of a foreign exchange risk,   (c) foreign exchange speculation,   (d) foreign exchange arbitrage.

Ans.   (b) See Section 7.4.

8. A U.S. exporter scheduled to receive £1,000 three months from today can hedge his foreign exchange risk by   (a) buying today £1,000 in the forward market for delivery in three months,   (b) buying £1,000 in the spot market three months from today,   (c) selling £1,000 in the spot market three months from today,   (d) selling today £1,000 in the forward market for delivery in three months.

Ans.   (d) See Example 3.

9. If a foreign exchange speculator expects the spot rate of the pound three months from today to be lower than today's forward rate on the pound for delivery in three months, she will   (a) buy pounds forward today and resell them in the spot market three months from today,   (b) buy pounds in the spot market three months from today,   (c) sell pounds in the spot market three months from today,   (d) sell pounds forward today and buy them in the spot market three months from today.

Ans.   (d) This is the opposite of Example 4.

10. Covered interest arbitrage involves   (a) the transfer of liquid funds from one monetary center and currency into another to take advantage of higher interest rates in the latter,   (b) hedging,   (c) earning extra interest in a riskless way,   (d) all of the above.

Ans.   (d) See Section 7.6.

11. A liquid capital outflow from New York to London under covered interest arbitrage can take place if the positive interest differential in favor of London   (a) is smaller than the forward discount on the pound,   (b) is equal to the forward discount on the pound,   (c) is larger than the forward discount on the pound,   (d) is equal or larger than the forward discount on the pound.

Ans.   (c) See Example 5.

12. An example of a Eurocurrency is   (a) a dollar deposit outside the U.S.,   (b) a pound sterling deposit outside the U.K.,   (c) a mark deposit outside Germany,   (d) all of the above.

Ans.   (d) See Section 7.8.

Solved Problems

THE FOREIGN EXCHANGE MARKETS

7.1   (*a*) In what way is domestic trade different from foreign trade?   (*b*) How is the foreign exchange market organized?   (*c*) What is its principal function? How is this accomplished?   (*d*) What are the other functions of the foreign exchange market? How are these accomplished?

   (*a*)   Domestic trade involves payments made and received in terms of the national currency. Foreign trade, on the other hand, usually involves payments and receipts in foreign currencies (see Section 1.1). Thus, foreign trade involves the exchange of the national currency for foreign currencies and the exchange of foreign currencies for the national currency.

   (*b*)   The foreign exchange market for any currency is composed of all the locations or cities where the currency is traded for other currencies. These different monetary centers are connected by a telephone network. Individuals and firms buy and sell foreign currencies from banks and brokers, who then deal with other banks and brokers in these monetary centers.

   (*c*)   The principal function of the foreign exchange market is to transfer purchasing power from one nation and currency to another. Today, this is accomplished primarily by the telegraphic transfer, which is a check that is radioed or wired rather than mailed. With it, a bank instructs its correspondent in a foreign monetary center to pay a specific amount of the local currency to a designated person, firm or account.

   (*d*)   Another function of the foreign exchange market is the credit function. Credit is needed as goods move from seller to buyer and also to allow some time for the buyer to resell the goods and be able to make the payment. The exporter usually allows 90 days to pay, but he then often rediscounts the importer's obligation to pay at the foreign department of his bank, which will eventually collect the payment from the importer when due. Thus, in general, it is the foreign department of a bank that extends the credit or finances trade. The foreign exchange market also provides the facilities for hedging (and speculation). This is accomplished in the forward exchange market (which is part of the foreign exchange market; see Problems 7.9 to 7.18).

7.2   (*a*) How can a U.S. importer pay a British exporter?   (*b*) How can a U.S. exporter receive payment from a British importer?   (*c*) How can these be accomplished in the foreign exchange market?

   (*a*)   The U.S. importer could exchange dollars for pounds in New York, London or elsewhere and make the payment in pounds to the British exporter. Or, she could pay in dollars, which the British exporter would then exchange for pounds in London, New York or elsewhere.

   (*b*)   A U.S. exporter can receive payment in pounds which he would then exchange for dollars in New York, London or elsewhere. Or he can receive payment in dollars which the British importer bought with pounds in London, New York or elsewhere.

   (*c*)   If U.S. exporters are paid in pounds, these pounds can be sold in the foreign exchange market to U.S. importers who want or have to make payments in pounds. Similarly, if British exporters are paid in dollars, these dollars can be sold in the foreign exchange market to British importers who want or have to make payments in dollars. Or, U.S. exporters who are paid in pounds can sell them for dollars to British exporters who have received payment in dollars. Similarly, U.S. importers who need pounds can buy them with dollars from the British importer who needs dollars. Thus, the foreign exchange market operates as a clearinghouse, where imports are essentially paid with exports and only the net balances are settled in currencies.

THE FOREIGN EXCHANGE RATES

7.3   (*a*) What is meant by the exchange rate between the dollar and the pound?   (*b*) If the exchange rate between the dollar and the pound changes from \$2.00 = £1 to \$2.20 = £1, what does this mean for the dollar? For the pound?   (*c*) If the exchange rate between the dollar and the pound changes from \$2.00 = £1 to \$1.98 = £1, what does this mean for the dollar? For the pound?   (*d*) What is meant by an effective exchange rate? How is it measured?

(a) The exchange rate between the dollar and the pound refers to the number of dollars required to get one pound. For example, at one point in time, $2.00 might be required to purchase one pound. Then, the exchange rate between the dollar and the pound could be expressed as $2.00 = £1. This is the formulation preferred by the U.S. and the one we will continue to use in this book. However, the exchange rate between the dollar and the pound could also be expressed as the number of pounds required to purchase one dollar. Thus, the above exchange rate of $2.00 = £1 could also be expressed as £0.50 = $1. Similarly, the exchange rate between the dollar and the French franc (F) could be expressed either as $0.20 = F1 or as F5 = $1. The exchange rate between the dollar and the German mark (DM) might be quoted as $0.40 = DM1 or as DM2.5 = $1. There is an exchange rate between the dollar and every other traded currency.

(b) An increase in the exchange rate from $2.00 = £1 to $2.20 = £1 refers to a (10%) depreciation of the dollar with respect to the pound, since (10%) more dollars are now required to purchase one pound. This is equivalent to an appreciation of the pound with respect to the dollar (since a smaller quantity of pounds is now required to purchase one dollar).

(c) A decrease in the exchange rate between the dollar and the pound from $2.00 = £1 to $1.98 = £1 represents a (1%) appreciation of the dollar, or conversely, a (1%) depreciation of the pound.

(d) An effective exchange rate refers to a weighted average of the exchange rates between the domestic currency and the currency of the nation's most important trade partners, with weights given by the relative value of the nation's trade with each of these trade partners.

7.4 (a) How can foreign exchange arbitrage take place if $1.98 = £1 in New York and at the same time $2.00 = £1 in London?   (b) What happens as arbitrage takes place?

(a) Foreign exchange arbitrageurs will buy pounds in New York at $1.98 per pound and immediately resell them in London for $2.00, making a profit of 2 cents or 1% on each pound so exchanged (minus the interest charge on the money during the time it is tied up in arbitrage and the cost of the telegraphic transfer—both of which are very small). This profit margin may seem very small indeed, but on a transaction of one million dollars, it means a gain of almost $10,000 for only a few minutes work! Note also that the arbitrageur does not incur a foreign exchange risk, except momentarily, because he or she buys and immediately resells an equal amount of the foreign currency.

(b) As arbitrage continues, the dollar price of the pound tends to increase in New York (because of the increase in demand for pounds) and to fall in London (because of the increased supply of pounds). This tends to reduce the profitability of arbitrage and to result in approximately the same dollar price for the pound in New York, London and in every other monetary center where the two currencies are traded for each other. When foreign exchange arbitrage does not occur either because of lack of knowledge or because it is forbidden, wide differences can exist in different monetary centers in the exchange rate between the same two currencies. What we have described above is two-point arbitrage. Three-point arbitrage rests on essentially the same principle but involves three monetary centers and three currencies and occurs much less frequently.

THE EQUILIBRIUM FOREIGN EXCHANGE RATE

7.5 With reference to Fig. 7-1,   (a) what lies behind the U.S. demand for pounds?   (b) Why is the U.S. demand curve for pounds ($D_£$) negative sloped?   (c) What lies behind the U.S. supply of pounds? (d) Why is the U.S. supply curve of pounds ($S_£$) positively sloped?   (e) Why is $2.00 = £1 the equilibrium exchange rate?

(a) Behind the U.S. demand for pounds lies the U.S. desire to import goods and services from the U.K. (in a two-nation world), to make transfer payments to the U.K., and to invest in and extend loans to the U.K. (see Chapter 8). In addition, a demand for pounds may arise for speculation.

(b) $D_£$ is negatively sloped because at lower exchange rates (so that fewer dollars are required to get each pound), England becomes a cheaper and more attractive place in which to buy and invest. So, U.S. residents buy and invest more in England and demand a greater quantity of pounds. In addition, speculators could also enter the (spot) market for pounds and buy greater quantities of pounds the lower the exchange rate (if they expect the exchange rate to rise in the future; see Problem 7.22).

(c) Behind the U.S. supply of pounds lies the U.K. desire to import goods and services from the U.S. and to invest in and make loans to the U.S. (see Chapter 8). In addition, a supply of pounds may also arise from speculators.

(d) $S_£$ is positively sloped because at higher exchange rates (R's), it becomes cheaper and more attractive for U.K. residents to buy and invest in the U.S. (since they now receive more dollars for each pound) and so the quantity of pounds that they supply to the U.S. *usually* increases (see Chapter 9). In addition, the higher the exchange rate (and the greater the expectation that it will fall in the future), the greater the quantity of pounds supplied by speculators (see Problem 7.22).

(e) At exchange rates higher than $2.00 = £1, the quantity supplied of pounds exceeds the quantity demanded of pounds (see Fig. 7-1) and the exchange rate tends to fall. At exchange rates below $2.00 = £1, $QD_£ > QS_£$ and the exchange rate tends to rise. Only At $2.00 = £1 does $QD_£ = QS_£$ (at £6 billion per year) and is the exchange rate in equilibrium.

7.6 In Fig. 7-2, $D_£$ and $S_£$ are the same as in Fig. 7-1. With reference to Fig. 7-2, (a) explain what happens when $D_£$ shifts up to $D'_£$ and U.S. monetary authorities keep the exchange rate fixed at $2.00 = £1. (b) What happens if the exchange rate is allowed to vary? (c) What can cause the U.S. $D_£$ to shift to $D'_£$?

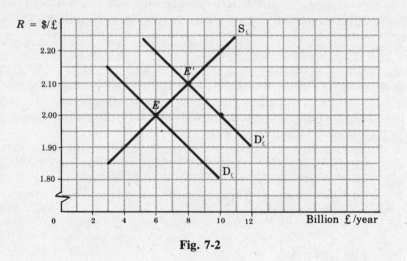

Fig. 7-2

(a) With $D_£$ and $S_£$, the equilibrium exchange rate is $2.00 = £1 and the equilibrium quantity demanded and supplied of pounds is £6 billion per year (point E in Fig. 7-2). When $D_£$ shifts up to $D'_£$, we see from the figure that at the unchanged exchange rate of $2.00 = £1, $QD'_£ = (10) > QS_£ = (6)$ by £4 billion per year (equal to $8 billion at the exchange rate of $2.00 = £1).

(b) If, on the other hand, the exchange rate is allowed to vary (as under a freely fluctuating exchange rate system), the exchange rate will rise to its new equilibrium level of $2.10 = £1, at which £8 billion per year are demanded and supplied (point E' in Fig. 7-2). Thus, the depreciation of the dollar (and the appreciation of the pound) automatically corrects the U.S. excess of expenditures over earnings in the U.K. (and the equal U.K. excess of earnings over expenditures in the U.S.).

(c) $D_£$ shifts up (i.e., the U.S. demands more pounds at each exchange rate) if the U.S. tastes for English goods increase, as the GNP of the U.S. rises (see Chapter 9), and if the price of traded commodities in terms of the domestic currency rises faster in the U.S. than in the U.K.

7.7 With reference to Fig. 7-3, (a) explain what happens when the U.S. $S_£$ shifts down to $S'_£$ and U.S. monetary authorities keep the exchange rate fixed at $2.00 = £1, (b) What happens if the exchange rate is allowed to vary? (c) What can cause the U.S. $S_£$ to shift down?

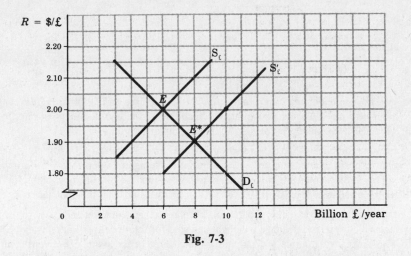

Fig. 7-3

(a) When $S_£$ shifts down to $S_£'$, we can see from Fig. 7-3 that at the unchanged rate of $2.00 = £1, $QS_£' = (10) > QD_£ = (6)$ by £4 billion ($9.8 billion) per year.

(b) If, on the other hand, the exchange rate is allowed to vary, the exchange rate will fall to its new equilibrium level of $1.90 = £1, at which £8 billion per year are demanded and supplied (point E^* in Fig. 7-3). Thus, the appreciation of the dollar (and the depreciation of the pound) automatically corrects the excess expenditures of the U.S. in the U.K. (and the equal excess earnings of the U.K. in the U.S.).

(c) $S_£$ shifts down (i.e., the U.K. supplies more pounds to the U.S. at each exchange rate) if U.K. tastes for American products increase, as the GNP of the U.K. rises (see Chapter 9), and if the increase in the domestic price of traded commodities is greater in the U.K. than in the U.S.

7.8 Draw a figure and explain what happens if $D_£$ shifts up to $D_£'$ (as in Fig. 7-2) and at the same time, $S_£$ also shifts down to $S_£'$ (as in Fig. 7-3).

In Fig. 7-4, the new equilibrium exchange rate with $D_£'$ and $S_£'$ is $2.00 = £1 (the same as with $D_£$ and $S_£$), but the new equilibrium quantity demanded and supplied is £10 billion per year (point E'' in Fig. 7-4). Note that in this case, the result would be the same whether the U.S. operated under a flexible or a fixed exchange rate system. In the real world, the demand and supply of each currency in terms of others are constantly changing, causing exchange rates to fluctuate continuously (see the daily quotations of the most important currencies in terms of dollars in the financial pages of any leading newspaper). Exchange rates also fluctuate (though to a much lesser extent), even under relatively fixed exchange rate systems (see Chapter 9). These continuous fluctuations in exchange rates give rise to the need for hedging and the opportunity for speculation in the foreign exchange market.

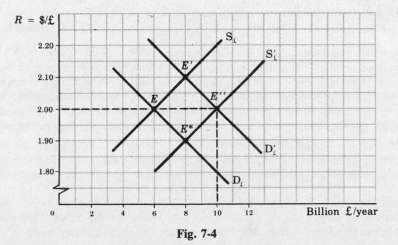

Fig. 7-4

HEDGING

7.9   (*a*) What is meant by a spot foreign exchange transaction? The spot exchange rate? Give an example. (*b*) What is meant by a forward foreign exchange transaction? The forward exchange rate? Give an example.   (*c*) What is the forward exchange market?

(*a*)   A spot foreign exchange transaction refers to the purchase or sale of foreign exchange for delivery within two business days. The exchange rate at which this occurs is called the spot rate. For example, £100 could be obtained immediately by paying $2.00 per pound for a total of $200.

(*b*)   A forward foreign exchange transaction involves an agreement today to buy or sell a specific amount of foreign exchange, at a specified future date, at a rate agreed upon today (the forward exchange rate). For example, I could enter into an agreement today to purchase £100 three months from today at $2.02 = £1. After three months, I get the £100 for $202, regardless of what the spot rate is at that time.

(*c*)   The forward exchange market is part of the foreign exchange market and refers to the institutional framework within which foreign exchange is bought and sold for future delivery at rates agreed upon today. The usual forward exchange contract and rate are for one, three or six months. Forward contracts for longer periods are rare because of the great uncertainty involved. However, forward contracts can usually be renegotiated for one or more periods when they become due. The following problems will deal with three-month contracts and rates exclusively.

7.10   (*a*) How is the equilibrium forward exchange rate determined?   (*b*) What is meant by the pound being at a three-month forward premium? At a three-month forward discount?

(*a*)   Just as the spot exchange rate is determined by the intersection of the market demand curve for and the market supply curve of foreign exchange for delivery within two business days (see Example 2), so the forward exchange rate is determined by the intersection of the market demand curve for and the market supply curve of foreign exchange for future delivery. The demand and supply of forward foreign exchange arise in the course of hedging, covered interest arbitrage, and foreign exchange speculation (see the following problems). The equilibrium forward rate may be equal to, above or below the corresponding equilibrium spot rate.

(*b*)   The pound is said to be at a three-month *forward premium* when the three-month forward rate is greater than the corresponding spot rate. For example, if the spot rate of the pound is $2.00 and the three-month forward rate is $2.02, we say that the pound is at a three-month forward premium of 2¢ or 1% (or at a 4% forward premium per year) with respect to the dollar. On the other hand, if the pound spot rate is still $2.00 but the three-month forward rate is $1.98, the pound is said to be at a *forward discount* of 2¢ or 1% for the three months or 4% per year. Unless otherwise indicated, forward premiums and discounts are expressed as percentages per year (from the corresponding spot rate).

7.11   (*a*) What is meant by hedging? What gives rise to it? Who should hedge?   (*b*) Can hedging take place in the spot market? How?   (*c*) Why does hedging usually take place in the forward market?

(a)   Hedging refers to the act of avoiding or covering a foreign exchange risk. The need for hedging arises because (spot) exchange rates fluctuate continuously through time. As a result, people who expect to make or receive payments in terms of a foreign currency at a future date face the risk that they will have to pay more or will receive less in terms of the domestic currency than they anticipated. Except for foreign exchange speculators who actually seek foreign exchange risks, everyone else with foreign exchange payables or receivables at a future date should (and usually does) hedge these foreign exchange risks.

(b)   Hedging can take place in the spot market. For example, a U.S. importer who anticipates making a future payment in pounds, and who worries that the spot rate of the pound will rise in the future (so that she will need more dollars than presently to buy the pounds she needs), can buy the pounds she needs in the spot market today at today's spot rate and leave them on deposit (and earn interest) in a London bank until needed to make the payments. Similarly, a U.S. exporter who anticipates receiving a future payment in pounds can borrow pounds in London today, exchange them for dollars at today's spot rate, and then repay the loan in pounds when he receives the payment (in pounds) for his exports.

(c) Hedging usually takes place in the forward market because it is simpler and, at the same time, it does not tie up the individual's or firm's capital or funds. For example, the above U.S. importer, by purchasing pounds today and holding them until the payment is due is, in effect, paying cash for her imports (the interest she receives on her pound deposits could be earned in the form of a price discount from the exporter by paying cash).

7.12 Suppose that the spot rate of the pound today is $2.00 while the three-month forward rate is $2.02. (a) How can a U.S. importer who has to pay £10,000 in three months hedge his foreign exchange risk? (b) What happens if the U.S. importer does not hedge and the spot rate of the pound in three months is $2.22? $1.95?

(a) The U.S. importer can hedge by buying £10,000 today for delivery in three months at today's three-month forward rate of the pound of $2.02. Thus, he willingly pays on his forward contract 2¢ more per pound (or $200 for the £10,000) than today's spot rate in order to insure himself against the risk that the spot rate of the pound in three months will be much higher than $2.02. After three months, when his payment becomes due, the U.S. importer will pay $20,200 and get the £10,000 he needs to make the payment, regardless of what the spot rate of the pound is at that time.

(b) If the U.S. importer does not hedge and the spot rate of the pound in three months is $2.22, he has to pay $22,200, or $2,000 more than if he had hedged, to get the £10,000 he needs to make the payment. On the other hand, if the spot rate of the pound in three months is instead $1.95, he only has to pay $19,500 or $700 less than if he had hedged to get the £10,000 he needs. Thus, by hedging, the U.S. importer will not only avoid the risk of having to pay more in terms of dollars than he anticipated, but he will also and at the same time forgo the chance that he will have to pay less. However, since he is not a speculator, he is satisfied with this situation.

7.13 Suppose that the spot rate of the pound today is $2.00 while the three-month forward rate is $1.98. (a) How can a U.S. exporter or investor who is to receive £100,000 in three months hedge her foreign exchange risk? (b) What happens if the U.S. exporter or investor does not hedge and the spot rate of the pound in three months is $1.90? $2.01?

(a) The U.S. exporter or investor can hedge by selling £100,000 today for delivery in three months at today's three-month forward rate of the pound of $1.98. Thus, she willingly sells pounds for future delivery at 2¢ less per pound than today's spot rate in order to insure herself against the risk that the spot rate of the pound in three months will be much less than $1.98. After three months, the U.S. exporter or investor will get $198,000 for the £100,000 she receives, regardless of what the spot rate of the pound is at that time.

(b) If the U.S. exporter or investor does not hedge and the spot rate in three months is $1.90, she gets only $190,000, or $8,000 less than if she had hedged, for the £100,000 she receives. On the other hand, if the spot rate of the pound in three months is instead $2.01, she gets $201,000, or $3,000 more than if she had hedged, for the £100,000 she receives. Thus, by hedging, the U.S. exporter or investor will not only avoid the risk of receiving less in terms of dollars than she anticipated, but she will also and at the same time forgo the chance that she will receive more. However, since she is not a speculator, she is satisfied with this state of affairs.

SPECULATION

7.14 (a) What is meant by foreign exchange speculation? (b) How can speculation take place in the spot market? (c) Why does speculation usually occur in the forward market?

(a) Foreign exchange speculation refers to the taking of a foreign exchange risk or an open position in hopes of making a profit. It is the opposite of hedging.

(b) A foreign exchange speculator who expects the spot rate of a currency to be higher in three months could purchase the currency in the spot market today at today's spot rate, hold it for three months, and then resell it in the spot market after three months. If he is right, he will make a profit, otherwise he will break even or incur a loss. On the other hand, if the speculator expects the spot rate to be lower in three months, he can borrow the foreign currency and exchange it for the national currency at today's spot rate. After three months, if the spot rate on the foreign currency is sufficiently lower, he can earn a profit by being able to repurchase the foreign currency (to repay his foreign exchange loan) at the lower spot rate. (To make a profit, the new spot rate must be sufficiently lower to overcome the excess interest usually paid on the foreign currency *borrowed* for three months, over the interest received on an equal amount of the national currency *deposited* in a bank for three months.)

(c) Foreign exchange speculation usually takes place in the forward market because it is simpler and, at the same time, involves no borrowing of the foreign currency or tying up of the speculator's capital or funds (see Problems 7.15 and 7.16).

7.15 Suppose that a speculator feels that the spot rate of the pound in three months will be higher than today's three-month forward rate of the pound of $1.98.   (a) How can she use $198,000 for speculation in the forward exchange market?   (b) What happens if the spot rate of the pound in three months is $2.10? $1.90? $1.98?

(a) The speculator should buy £100,000 today in the forward market for delivery in three months, at today's forward rate of $1.98. [Note that here, as opposed to the case discussed in Problem 7.14(b) where foreign exchange speculation occurred in the spot market, the speculator is not actually using her funds now.]

(b) After three months, the speculator pays $198,000 and receives £100,000 on her matured forward contract. If the spot rate at that time is $2.10, she can immediately resell these £100,000 for $210,000 and earn $12,000 (minus a very small cost for the transaction). If, after three months, the spot rate of the pound is instead $1.90, she still pays $198,000 and receives £100,000 on her matured forward contract. But she can only resell the £100,000 now for $190,000, thus incurring a loss of $8,000. If after three months, the spot rate of the pound is $1.98, the speculator will earn no profit but will incur no loss either.

7.16 Suppose that a speculator believes that the spot rate of the pound in three months will be *lower* than today's three-month forward rate of the pound of $1.98.   (a) How can he use his dollars for speculation in the forward exchange market?   (b) What happens if the spot rate of the pound in three months is $1.90? $2.10? $1.98?

(a) The speculator should sell pounds today for delivery in three months at today's forward rate of the pound of $1.98. [Note that here, as opposed to the case discussed in Problem 7.14(b), the speculator is not borrowing the foreign currency.]

(b) If, after three months, the spot rate of the pound is $1.90, the speculator buys pounds at the price of $1.90 each, in the amount specified on his matured forward contract, and delivers them for the previously contracted rate of $1.98. The speculator thus earns 8¢ on each pound of the amount specified in the forward contract. If, on the other hand, the spot rate of the pound after three months is $2.10, the speculator will be forced to buy pounds at the price of $2.10 each and resell them at the previously contracted rate of $1.98. Thus, the speculator loses 12¢ on each pound of the amount specified in the forward contract. If after three months, the spot rate of the pound is $1.98, the speculator neither makes a profit nor takes a loss on the transaction.

7.17 (a) What is meant by stabilizing speculation? What is its effect?   (b) What is meant by destabilizing speculation? What is its effect?   (c) How can anyone who has to place an order abroad and/or make a payment in the foreign currency speculate if he or she expects the exchange rate to vary shortly?

(a) *Stabilizing speculation* refers to the purchase of a foreign currency with the domestic currency when the foreign exchange rate falls, in the expectation that it will soon rise and thus lead to a profit. Or, it refers to the sale of the foreign currency when its exchange rate rises in the expectation that it will soon fall. The effect of stabilizing speculation is to reverse or moderate the fall or rise in the foreign exchange rate. It will also and by itself tend to reduce the forward discount or premium on the foreign currency.

(b) *Destabilizing speculation*, on the other hand, refers to the sale of the foreign currency when its exchange rate falls in the expectation that it will fall even more, or to the purchase of the foreign currency when its exchange rate rises in the expectation that it will rise even more. Destabilizing speculation thus reinforces or magnifies fluctuations in foreign exchange rates and, if sufficiently large, may cause the forward discount on the foreign currency to differ greatly from its interest parity (see Section 7.6).

(c) If the individual expects the exchange rate to rise shortly, he or she can anticipate placing the order and/or making a payment to avoid the expected higher rate in the future. On the other hand, if the individual expects the exchange rate to fall shortly, he or she can postpone placing the order and/or making the payment so as to take advantage of the expected lower rate in the future. These are known as *leads and lags*, respectively, and are a form of speculation.

COVERED INTEREST ARBITRAGE

7.18 (a) What is meant by interest arbitrage? (b) Why does this lead to a foreign exchange risk? (c) How can this foreign exchange risk be covered?

(a) Interest arbitrage refers to the transfer of liquid funds from one monetary center (and currency) to another to take advantage of higher rates of return or interest.

(b) In order to make the foreign investment, the national currency must be converted into the foreign currency. Then, when the investment matures or is liquidated, the foreign currency must be reconverted back into the national currency. A foreign exchange risk arises because during the period of the investment, the (spot) exchange rate of the foreign currency may fall (so that the investor gets back fewer dollars per pound than were originally paid). This may wipe out most or all of the extra interest earned on the foreign over the domestic investment and may even lead to an actual loss.

(c) This foreign exchange risk can be covered, if at the same time that the investor exchanges the national for the foreign currency in order to make the foreign investment, she also engages in a forward sale of an equal amount of the foreign currency (plus the amount of interest that she will earn) to coincide with the maturity of the foreign investment. Since the foreign currency is likely to be at a forward discount (see Problem 7.22), she loses on the foreign currency transaction per se. But if the positive interest differential in favor of the foreign monetary center exceeds the forward discount on the foreign currency (when both are expressed in percentage per year), it pays to make the foreign investment.

7.19 Suppose that the rate on three-month treasury bills is (on a yearly basis) 12% in London and 8% in New York, and the spot rate of the pound is $2.00.   (a) How can a U.S. investor undertake uncovered interest arbitrage?   (b) What happens if the spot rate of the pound in three months is $1.99? $1.98? $1.96?   (c) How can the U.S. investor undertake covered interest arbitrage if the pound is at a three-month forward discount of 1% (per year)? How much would the U.S. investor earn on his foreign investment?

(a) The U.S. investor can exchange dollars for pounds at today's spot rate of $2.00 per pound, and then use these pounds to buy three-month British treasury bills in London and earn 4% more per year or 1% more for the three months than if he had used his dollars to purchase three-month U.S. treasury bills in New York.

(b) If in three months the spot rate of the pound is $1.99, the U.S. investor will earn an extra 1% interest for the three months, but since he originally bought pounds at $2.00 and resells them at $1.99, he will lose 1/2 of 1% on the foreign exchange transaction per se

$$\frac{\$2.00 - \$1.99}{\$2.00} = \frac{\$0.01}{\$2.00} = 0.005, \text{ or } 1/2 \text{ of } 1\%$$

Thus, he earns about 1/2 of 1% more on his foreign investment than if he had invested his money in U.S. treasury bills in New York. If in three months the spot rate is $1.98, he will lose 1% on the foreign exchange transaction, and so he earns nothing extra by investing abroad. Finally, if the spot rate in three months is $1.96, he loses 2% on the foreign exchange transaction against the extra 1% in interest earned. Thus, he earns about 1% *less* than if he had invested his money in U.S. treasury bills. It is to avoid risks of this type that interest arbitrage is usually covered.

(c) The U.S. investor can undertake covered interest arbitrage by (1) exchanging dollars for pounds at today's spot rate of the pound of $2.00, (2) using these pounds to buy three-month British treasury bills in London and (3) engaging today in a forward sale of an equal amount of pounds (plus the amount of interest he will earn) for dollars at today's three-month forward rate of the pound. The result is that he will gain an extra

1% in interest but will lose 1/4 of 1% for the quarter on the forward contract, for a net riskless extra gain of (about) 3/4 of 1% on his foreign investment. There is an incentive for covered interest arbitrage, as long as the positive interest differential in favor of London exceeds the forward discount on the pound (both expressed on a yearly basis).

7.20   Calculate exactly how many more dollars the U.S. investor of Problem 7.19(*c*) actually gains when he uses $200,000 for covered interest arbitrage in London rather than to purchase U.S. treasury bills in New York.

The U.S. investor exchanges his $200,000 for £100,000 at the spot rate of the pound of $2.00. He uses this £100,000 to buy British treasury bills in London. With the interest rate on U.K. treasury bills at 12% per year, the U.S. investor will earn 3% in interest for the quarter (£3,000 on his £100,000 investment). Since he knows that at the end of the three months he will have £103,000, he will sell these £103,000 today for dollars in the forward market for delivery in three months. But we were told that the pound is at a forward discount of 1% per year or 1/4 of 1% (0.0025) for three months with respect to the spot rate of the pound of $2.00. Thus, the three-month forward rate of the pound is: $2.00 − (0.0025)($2.00) = $2.00 − 0.005 = $1.995. After three months, the U.S. investor will sell his £103,000 at $1.995 per pound and receive $205,485. He earns $5,485 on his foreign investment of $200,000, or about 2.75% for the quarter. This is $1,485 more than the $4,000 (or 0.75 percentage points more than the 2%) that he would have earned for the quarter if he had instead used his $200,000 to buy U.S. treasury bills in New York.

7.21   As covered interest arbitrage continues under the conditions examined in Problem 7.19,   (*a*) explain what happens to the positive interest differential in favor of London. What are the market forces that tend to bring this about?   (*b*) Explain what happens to the forward discount on the pound. What are the market forces that bring this about? How far will covered interest arbitrage proceed?

(*a*)   As funds are transferred from New York to London, the supply of funds is reduced in New York and increased in London. This tends to cause the interest rate to rise in New York, say from 8% to 9%, and to fall in London, say from 12% to 11%, so that the positive interest differential in favor of London becomes 2% per year and 1/2 of 1% for a quarter.

(*b*)   At the same time, as the demand for spot pounds increases (so as to transfer pounds to London to earn the higher interest rate), the spot rate of the pound tends to increase. As the supply of forward pounds increases (to cover the exchange risk), the forward rate of the pound falls. For both reasons, the forward discount on the pound increases, say from 1% to 2% on a yearly basis or from 1/4 of 1% to 1/2 of 1% for a quarter. When this occurs, the forward rate of the pound is said to be at interest parity (the 1% extra interest for the quarter being exactly balanced by the 1% discount on forward pounds for the quarter) and covered interest arbitrage comes to an end. In the real world, the positive interest differential in favor of London may have to exceed the forward discount on the pound by at least 1/4 of 1% on a yearly basis for covered interest arbitrage to take place.

7.22   Suppose that the interest rate on three-month treasury bills is 12% in London and 10% in New York. (*a*) How much would a U.S. investor earn on covered interest arbitrage if the three-month forward pound is at a 1% premium? What happens as covered interest arbitrage proceeds?   (*b*) What would happen if the three-month forward pound is at 4% discount?   (*c*) What is the relationship between the spot and the forward rate of the foreign currency?

(*a*)   The U.S. investor will not only earn the extra 1/2 of 1% interest for the three months, but she will also earn another 1/4 of 1% on her foreign exchange transaction (by being able to resell pounds in the forward market for delivery in three months at a price 1/4 of 1% higher than she paid). Thus, her total extra gain is about 3/4 of 1%. However, as covered interest arbitrage proceeds, the positive interest differential in favor of London tends to fall [for the reason described in Problem 7.21(*a*)] from, say 2% to 1% per year. At the same time, the spot rate of the pound rises and the three-month forward rate of the pound falls [as in Problem 7.21(*b*)] until the forward premium on the pound becomes a forward discount of 1% per year and is at interest parity.

(b)   With a positive interest differential of 2% (per year) in favor of London but the three-month forward pound at 4% discount (per year), it does not pay for U.S. investors to undertake covered interest arbitrage in favor of London. On the contrary, it pays for *English investors to transfer funds to New York*. When they do that, they lose 2% interest but gain 4% on the foreign exchange transaction (by being able to buy back pounds with dollars at a rate 4% per year less than the rate at which they originally sold pounds for dollars). As this occurs, the positive interest differential in favor of London tends to *rise* (as funds are transferred from London to New York) and the forward discount on the pound falls (as British investors cover their exchange risk) until the forward discount on the pound is at interest parity.

(c)   Under normal conditions, the relationship between spot and forward rates is determined largely by covered interest arbitrage. If interest rates are higher abroad, covered interest arbitrage tends to keep the foreign currency at a forward discount with respect to the spot rate equal to the positive interest differential in favor of the foreign monetary center. If interest rates are higher domestically, covered interest arbitrage tends to keep the foreign currency at a forward premium relative to the spot rate (and the domestic currency at a forward discount) equal to the domestic positive interest differential. However, this may not hold even approximately when covered interest arbitrage is forbidden or with large destabilizing speculation (see Problem 7.17).

EXCHANGE RATE DYNAMICS

7.23   Explain why financial markets adjust much more quickly to a market disequilibrium and overwhelm adjustments in the real or trade sector in the short run.

A change in interest rates, wealth, expectations, and so on disturbs the equilibrium and leads each investor to reallocate financial assets to achieve a new equilibrium or balanced portfolio. The adjustment involves a change in the *stock* of the various financial assets in the portfolio. Having been accumulated over a long time, the total *stock* of financial assets in investors' portfolios in the economy is very large in relation to the yearly *flows* (additions to the stock) through usual savings and investments. Furthermore, any change in interest rates, expectations, or other forces that affect the benefits and costs of holding the various financial assets are likely to lead to an immediate or very rapid change in their stock, as investors attempt to quickly reestablish equilibrium in their portfolios.

For example, an increase in the interest rate abroad will lead investors to reduce their holdings of domestic money and domestic bonds and to increase their holdings of foreign bonds. This stock adjustment can be very large and usually occurs immediately or over a very short time. This is in contrast to a change in the *flow* of merchandise trade which results from, say, a depreciation of the nation's currency and which takes place only gradually and over a longer period (previous contracts have to be honored, and new orders may take many months to fulfill). Thus, *stock* adjustments in financial assets are usually much larger and quicker to occur than adjustments in trade *flows*.

7.24   Draw a figure showing that from a long-run equilibrium exchange rate $R = \$2/£1$, the dollar immediately depreciates by 16% and then gradually appreciates by 6% (for a net depreciation of 10%) to its new long-run equilibrium level.

Figure 7-5 shows that at the initial long-run equilibrium exchange rate of $R = \$2/£1$, the dollar depreciates immediately by 16% to $R = \$2.32/£1$ at time t_0 as a result of quick adjustments in financial markets and then gradually appreciates by 6% (for a net depreciation of 10%) to its new long-run equilibrium level of $R = \$2.20/£1$ as U.S. imports and exports gradually respond over time to the dollar depreciation.

7.25   Starting from interest parity, explain the exchange rate overshooting of the dollar that is likely to result from a reduction in the rate of interest in the U.S. relative to that in the U.K. (*Hint:* Use the theory of covered interest arbitrage.)

Starting from interest parity, the decline in the rate of interest in the U.S. makes the positive interest differential in favor of the U.K. larger than the forward discount on the pound. As a result, more investments flow from the U.S. to Britain under covered interest arbitrage. As investors purchase pounds on the spot market (to increase their investments in the U.K. in order to take advantage of the higher interest rate there) and at the same time sell pounds forward (to cover their exchange risk), the exchange or spot rate of the dollar rises (i.e., the dollar depreciates) and *the forward rate of the pound increases,* as required for interest parity to continue to hold. *A rising forward rate on the pound means that the market expects the pound to depreciate and the dollar to appreciate in the future!* The only way for the dollar to depreciate immediately and then appreciate over time as it moves toward its new long-run equilibrium level is for the dollar to immediately depreciate by more than required for the new long-run equilibrium level and then appreciate gradually over time to eliminate the overshooting.

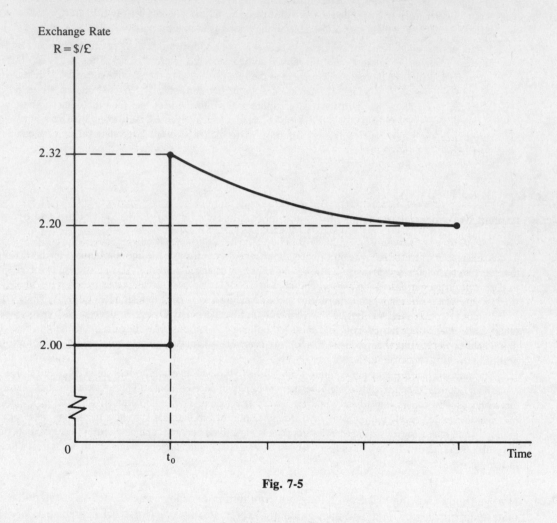

Fig. 7-5

THE EUROCURRENCY MARKETS

7.26   Give the reasons for the existence of the Eurocurrency market.

One reason for the existence of the Eurodollar market is relatively high interest rates that foreign banks pay on short-term dollar deposits. European banks seem able to operate on a smaller spread between borrowing and lending rates than U.S. banks. Another reason is that originally the U.S. dollar was the most important international currency, i.e., the vehicle currency, in which to make and receive international payments, so that multinational corporations (MNCs) found it very convenient to keep some dollar deposits abroad. Today, almost half of the total value of Eurocurrencies is in other leading currencies, such as the British pound, the German mark, the French and the Swiss francs and the Japanese yen. A third reason for the existence of the Eurodollar market is that MNCs could overcome domestic credit restrictions at home by borrowing in the Eurodollar market. A fourth reason is that communist nations prefer to keep dollar deposits outside the U.S. for fear that the U.S. might freeze their dollar deposits in the U.S. in a political crisis.

7.27   Explain   (*a*) how the Eurocurrency market can create money and   (*b*) why the U.S. money supply might not be affected by the creation of Eurodollar deposits.

(*a*)   The Eurocurrency market can create money in a manner analogous to the way the domestic banking system can create money in a fractional banking system, such as we have today (see Section 9.4 of Schaum's Outline of *Principles of Economics*). For example, Eurodollars are created when a bank outside the U.S. makes a dollar load to a firm that uses it to make a payment to another firm and the receiving firm deposits the dollars outside the U.S. Similarly, Eurodollars are created when a bank outside the U.S. that is short of dollars borrows dollars from another bank with unutilized dollars. Since there are no reserve requirements on Eurocurrency deposits, the money multiplier could be very large indeed. In reality, the money multiplier is instead believed to be very small because of leakages from the Eurocurrency market. These occur when dollars are converted into national currencies and end up in the nation's central bank or are deposited in the U.S.

(*b*)   When an individual or firm transfers dollar deposits from a New York to a London bank *having an account with a U.S. bank,* the U.S. money supply is not affected even though Eurodollars of an equal amount are created. If the London bank then lends these dollars in Europe, additional Eurodollars are created, but the U.S. money supply is still not directly affected.

7.28   Explain   (*a*) the problems created by the existence of Eurocurrency markets and   (*b*) the benefits resulting from this market.

(*a*)   One of the most serious problems arising from the existence of the Eurocurrency market is that the domestic stabilization efforts of national governments are reduced, particularly in small European nations. For example, a firm can overcome domestic credit restrictions by borrowing in the Eurocurrency market. Another problem is that short-term liquid funds can quickly and *en mass* move from one financial center to another (hot money flows), creating great instability in exchange rates and interest rates. These problems, however, are less serious today under a flexible exchange rate system than under the previous fixed exchange rate system. Finally, the Eurocurrency market is mostly unregulated, and so failure of a bank with large Eurocurrency deposits might trigger an international bank panic analogous to those created domestically by "runs" on important banks before the establishment of deposit insurance.

(*b*)   The benefits of the Eurocurrency market are the greater competition and efficiency in domestic banking that have resulted. Another benefit stems from the Eurocurrency market's ability to mediate. For example, the Eurocurrency market mediated the conflict caused by the huge deposits of petroleum-exporting countries after 1973 and the rapidly escalating import bills of petroleum-importing nations. It is very likely that by performing this function, the Eurocurrency market prevented a liquidity crisis in the middle and late 1970s.

Chapter 8

The Balance of Payments

8.1 BALANCE OF PAYMENTS ACCOUNTING

A nation's *balance of payments* is a summary statement of all its economic transactions with the rest of the world during a given year. Its main components are the current account, the capital account and the official reserve account. Each transaction is entered in the balance of payments as a credit or a debit. A *credit transaction* is one that leads to the receipt of a payment from foreigners. A *debit transaction* leads to a payment to foreigners.

8.2 THE CURRENT ACCOUNT

The *current account* includes trade in goods and services and unilateral transfers. The main categories of *service transactions* are travel and transportation, receipts and payments on foreign investments, and military transactions. *Unilateral transfers* refer to gifts made by individuals and the government to foreigners, and gifts received from foreigners. The exports of goods and services and the receipt of unilateral transfers are entered in the current account as credits (+) because they lead to the receipt of payments from foreigners. On the other hand, the import of goods and services and the granting of unilateral transfers are entered as debits (−) because they lead to payments to foreigners.

EXAMPLE 1. Table 8.1 presents a summary of the current account of the U.S. for the year 1988 as it appeared in a government publication (all values are expressed in billions of dollars).

Table 8.1

Exports of goods and services		530
Merchandise	319	
Services	211	
Imports of goods and services		−642
Merchandise	−447	
Services	−195	
Unilateral transfers, net		−15
U.S. Government grants	−10	
U.S. Government pensions and other transfers	−3	
Private remittances and other transfers	−2	
Balance on merchandise trade		−128
Balance on goods and services		−112
Balance on current account		−127

8.3 THE CAPITAL ACCOUNT

The *capital account* shows the change in the nation's assets abroad and foreign assets in the nation, other than official reserve assets. It includes direct investments (such as the building of a foreign plant), the purchase or sale of foreign securities (stocks, bonds and treasury bills), and the change in the nation's nonbank and bank claims on and liabilities to foreigners during the year. Increases in the nation's assets abroad and reductions in foreign assets in the nation (other than official reserve assets) are *capital outflows* or debits ($-$) in the nation's capital account because they lead to payments to foreigners. On the other hand, decreases in the nation's assets abroad and increases in foreign assets in the nation are *capital inflows* or credits ($+$) because they lead to the receipt of payments from foreigners (see Problems 8.7 to 8.9).

EXAMPLE 2.   Table 8.2 presents the U.S. capital account for 1988 (in billions of dollars).

Table 8.2

U.S. assets abroad, net [increase/capital outflow ($-$)]		-77
U.S. Government assets, other than official reserve assets, net	4	
U.S. private assets, net	-81	
Direct investment abroad	-17	
Foreign securities	-8	
Nonbank claims	-2	
Bank claims	-54	
Foreign assets in the U.S., net [increase/capital inflow ($+$)]		180
Direct investment	58	
U.S. treasury and other U.S. securities	47	
Nonbank liabilities	6	
Bank liabilities	69	
Balance on capital account		103

8.4 THE OFFICIAL RESERVE ACCOUNT

The *official reserve account* measures the change in a nation's official reserve assets and the change in foreign official assets in the nation during the year. A nation's *official reserve assets* include the gold holdings of the nation's monetary authorities, special drawing rights (SDRs), the nation's reserve position in the International Monetary Fund (IMF; see Problem 8.9), and the official foreign currency holdings of the nation. Increases in the nation's official reserve assets are debits ($-$), while increases in foreign official assets in the nation are credits ($+$) [see Problem 8.10(c)].

EXAMPLE 3.   Table 8.3 presents the U.S. official reserve account for 1988 (in billions of dollars).

Table 8.3

U.S. official reserve assets, net		-4
Gold	0	
Special drawing rights	0	
Reserve position in the IMF	1	
Convertible currencies	-5	
Foreign official assets in the U.S., net		39
Balance on U.S. official reserve account		35

8.5 DOUBLE-ENTRY BOOKKEEPING

Each international economic transaction is entered either as a credit or as a debit in the nation's balance of payments. But everytime a credit or a debit transaction is entered, an offsetting debit or credit, respectively, of the same amount is also recorded in one of the three accounts. This is referred to as *double-entry bookkeeping*.

The reason for double-entry bookkeeping is that, in general, every transaction has two sides. We sell something, and we receive payment for it. We buy something, and we must pay for it.

EXAMPLE 4. Some typical transactions are:

(a) A U.S. firm exports $500 of goods to the U.K. and is paid with a deposit of $500 worth of pounds sterling (England's currency) into its account with a London bank.

The U.S. credits the merchandise category of its current account for $500 and debits its capital account (an increase in U.S. bank assets abroad—a capital outflow) for $500.

(b) A U.S. tourist in London spends $300 for hotels and meals.

The U.S. debits the service category (travel) of its current account for $300 and credits its capital account (an increase in foreign holdings of U.S. assets or claims on the U.S.—a capital inflow) for $300.

(c) An Englishman buys $400 of American stocks and pays by drawing on his dollar deposits in a New York bank.

The U.S. both credits its capital account (an increase in foreign assets in the U.S.—a capital inflow) for $400 and debits its capital account (a decline in foreign bank assets in the U.S.—capital outflow) for $400.

(d) The U.S. government gives $200 cash aid to the government of India.

The U.S. debits unilateral transfers for $200 and credits its official reserve account (an increase in foreign official assets in the U.S.) for $200.

(e) The IMF allocates $100 of SDRs to the U.S.

The U.S. debits its official reserve account (an increase in its SDRs official reserves) by $100 (see Section 8.4) and, in order to preserve the equality of total credits to total debits, adds the credit entry, allocation of SDRs, for $100. In 1980, there was an allocation of SDRs of $1.2 billion to the U.S.

8.6 STATISTICAL DISCREPANCY

Theoretically, double-entry bookkeeping should result in total credits being equal to total debits when all three accounts of the balance of payments are taken together. However, because of recording errors and omissions, this equality does not usually hold. Thus, a special entry called *statistical discrepancy* is necessary to "balance" the nation's balance of payments statement.

EXAMPLE 5. When we sum the current account balance of $-\$127$ billion, the capital account balance of $\$103$ billion, and the official reserve account balance of $\$35$ billion, we get the overall credit balance of $(+)\$11$ billion in the international transactions of the U.S. for the year 1988. As a result, a statistical discrepancy of $-\$11$ billion must be included as a debit entry to ensure the overall accounting equality of total credits and total debits for the balance of payments statement as a whole. This statistical discrepancy is believed to have resulted primarily from unrecorded capital outflows from (debits of) the U.S.

8.7 MEASURING THE DEFICIT OR THE SURPLUS, OR OFFICIAL INTERVENTION

If total debits exceed total credits in the current and capital accounts (including the statistical discrepancy), the net debit balance measures the *deficit in the balance of payments* of the nation. This deficit must be settled with an equal net credit balance in the nation's official reserve account. The opposite is a *surplus in the balance of payments*. This measure of the deficit or surplus in the balance of payments (as well as the concept itself) is strictly correct only under a fixed exchange rate system. Under a *freely* flexible exchange rate system, the excess of expenditures over earnings abroad is automatically corrected by depreciation of the nation's currency (see Section 7.3). Under an exchange rate system which is not freely flexible but *managed* (as we have today; see Chapter 12), part of the excess of expenditures over earnings abroad is corrected by a depreciation of the nation's currency and part is settled by a net credit balance in the official reserve account of the nation. Huge trade deficits during the 1980s changed the U.S. from a creditor nation to the world's largest debtor nation by 1988 (see Problem 8.25).

EXAMPLE 6. Table 8.4 incorporates the information presented in Tables 8.1 to Table 8.3 and summarizes all U.S. international transactions for the year 1988, as presented in a U.S. government publication.

Table 8.4
Summary of U.S. International Transactions for 1988 (Billions of Dollars)

Exports of goods and services	**530**
Merchandise	319
Services	211
Imports of goods and services	**−642**
Merchandise	−447
Services	−195
Unilateral transfers, net	**−15**
U.S. government grants	−10
U.S. government pensions and other transfers	−3
Private remittances and other transfers	−2
U.S. assets abroad, net [increase/capital outflow (−)]	**−82**
U.S. official reserve assets, net	−4
U.S. government assets, other than official reserve assets, net	3
U.S. private assets, net	−81
Direct investment abroad	−17
Foreign securities	−8
Nonbank claims	−2
Bank claims	−54
Foreign assets in the U.S. net [increase/capital inflow (+)]	**219**
Foreign official assets in the U.S., net	39
Other foreign assets in the U.S., net	180
Direct investment in the U.S.	58
U.S. treasury and other U.S. securities	47
Nonbank liabilities	6
Bank liabilities	69
Allocation of special drawing rights	**0**
Statistical discrepancy	**−11**
Memoranda:	
Balance on merchandise trade	−128
Balance on goods and services	−112
Balance on current account	−127
Transactions in official reserve assets:	
Increase (−) in U.S. official reserve assets, net	−4
Increase (+) in foreign official assets in the U.S.	39

SOURCE: U.S. Department of Commerce, *Survey of Current Business* Washington, D.C.: U.S. Government Printing Office, June 1989.

Note that the capital account and the official reserve account are combined in Table 8.4. The net credit balance of (+)$35 billion obtained by summing the last two items of Table 8.4 measures the degree of U.S. official intervention in foreign exchange markets during 1988. Only under a fixed exchange rate system would it have referred to the U.S. balance of payments deficit.

Glossary

Balance of payments   A summary statement of all the economic transactions of a nation with the rest of the world during a given year.

Credit transaction   An economic transaction that leads to the receipt of a payment from foreigners.

Debit transaction   An economic transaction that leads to a payment to foreigners.

Current account   An account that includes trade in goods and services and unilateral transfers.

Service transaction   The part of the current account that includes travel and transportation, receipts and payments of income on foreign investments, and military transactions.

Unilateral transfers   Gifts made by individuals and the government to foreigners and gifts received from foreigners.

Capital account   An account showing the change in a nation's assets abroad and in foreign assets in the nation, other than official reserve assets.

Capital outflows   An increase in the nation's assets abroad and/or a reduction in foreign assets in the nation.

Capital inflows   A decrease in the nation's assets abroad and/or an increase in foreign assets in the nation.

Official reserve account   An account showing the change in the nation's official reserve assets and the change in foreign official assets in the nation during the year.

Official reserve assets   The gold holdings of the nation's monetary authorities, special drawing rights (SDRs), the nation's reserve position in the International Monetary Fund (IMF), and the official foreign currency holdings of the nation.

Double-entry bookkeeping   The accounting procedure whereby each international transaction is entered twice, once as a credit and once as a debit of an equal amount.

Statistical discrepancy   The special entry to "balance" a nation's balance of payments statement when all the three accounts of the balance of payments are taken together.

Deficit in the balance of payments   The excess of total debits over total credits in the current and capital accounts (and including the allocation of special drawing rights and the statistical discrepancy). It is also equal to the net credit balance in the nation's official reserve account.

Surplus in the balance of payments   The excess of total credits over total debits in the current and capital accounts (and including the allocation of SDRs and the statistical discrepancy). It is also equal to the net debit balance in the nation's official reserve account.

Review Questions

1. An economic transaction is entered in the balance of payments as a credit if it leads to   (*a*) the receipt of payment from foreigners,   (*b*) a payment to foreigners,   (*c*) either the receipt of a payment or the making of a payment,   (*d*) neither the receipt nor the making of a payment.

   Ans.   (*a*) See Section 8.1.

2. Which of the following transactions is a debit in the current account? (*a*) Export of merchandise, (*b*) export of services, (*c*) gift to foreigners, (*d*) gift from foreigners.

   Ans. (*c*) See Section 8.2.

3. The purchase of a U.S. stock by one of Britain's inhabitants represents (*a*) credit in the U.S. current account, (*b*) debit in the U.S. capital account, (*c*) credit in the U.S. official reserve account, (*d*) credit in the U.S. capital account.

   Ans. (*d*) See Section 8.3 and Table 8.2.

4. The payment of a dividend by an American company to a foreign stockholder represents (*a*) a debit in the U.S. capital account, (*b*) a credit in the U.S. capital account, (*c*) a credit in the U.S. official reserve account, (*d*) a debit in the U.S. current account.

   Ans. (*d*) See Section 8.2 and Table 8.1.

5. From the U.S. point of view, a drawing on (reduction of) foreign bank balances in a New York bank represents (*a*) capital inflow, (*b*) capital outflow, (*c*) outflow of official reserves, (*d*) debit in the current account.

   Ans. (*b*) See Section 8.3.

6. An increase in U.S. official reserve assets represents (*a*) credits in the U.S. official reserve account, (*b*) credits in the U.S. capital account, (*c*) debits in the U.S. official reserve account, (*d*) debits in the U.S. capital account.

   Ans. (*a*) See Section 8.4.

7. When a U.S. firm imports a good from England and pays for it by drawing on its pounds sterling balances in a London bank, the U.S. debits its current account and credits its (*a*) official reserve account, (*b*) unilateral transfers, (*c*) services in its current account, (*d*) capital account.

   Ans. (*d*) This is a decrease in U.S. bank assets abroad and so a U.S. capital inflow. See Section 8.5 and Example 4(*a*).

8. When an English tourist spends $200 worth of pounds in New York for hotels and meals, the U.S. credits the services category (travel) in its current account and debits (*a*) convertible currency in its official reserve account, (*b*) merchandise category in its current account, (*c*) capital account, (*d*) none of the above.

   Ans. (*c*) This is an increase in U.S. claims on foreigners and is equivalent to an increase in U.S. assets abroad, constituting a U.S. capital outflow. See Section 8.5 and Example 4(*b*).

9. The statistical discrepancy of $-$11 billion was entered in the 1988 statement of U.S. international transactions because (*a*) total credits exceeded total debits in the current and capital accounts by $11 billion, (*b*) total debits exceeded total credits in all three accounts taken together by $11 billion, (*c*) total credits exceeded total debits in all three accounts taken together by $11 billion, (*d*) total credits exceeded total debits in the capital and official reserve accounts by $11 billion.

   Ans. (*c*) See Section 8.6 and Example 5.

10. A deficit or surplus in the U.S. balance of payments is measured by the net balance of the (*a*) current account, (*b*) capital account, (*c*) allocation of SDRs, (*d*) statistical discrepancy, (*e*) all of the above.

    Ans. (*e*) See Section 8.7.

11. A deficit or surplus in the U.S. balance of payments can also be measured by the net balance of the change in (*a*) U.S. official reserve assets, (*b*) foreign official assets in the U.S., (*c*) U.S. private assets, (*d*) U.S. official reserve assets and foreign official assets in the U.S.

    Ans. (*d*) See Section 8.7.

12. The concept and the measure of a deficit and a surplus in the balance of payments are strictly appropriate only under (*a*) a fixed exchange rate system, (*b*) a freely flexible exchange rate system, (*c*) a managed floating exchange rate system, (*d*) all of the above.

   Ans. (*a*) See Section 8.7.

Solved Problems

BALANCE OF PAYMENTS ACCOUNTING

8.1 (*a*) What is meant by a nation's balance of payments? What is its purpose? (*b*) What is an international economic transaction? Who is a resident?

   (*a*) A nation's balance of international payments is a summary statement of all the economic transactions between the residents of the nation and the residents of other nations during a specified period of time, usually a calendar year. The U.S. and some other nations also keep such records on a quarterly basis. The main purpose of the balance of payments is to inform government authorities of the nation's international position and to help them formulate monetary, fiscal and commercial policies.

   (*b*) An international economic transaction refers to the exchange of a good, a service or an asset (for which payment is normally required) between the residents of one nation and the residents of other nations. Diplomats, military personnel, workers who temporarily emigrate and tourists are residents of the nation in which they hold citizenship. Similarly, a corporation is a resident of the nation in which it is incorporated, but its foreign branches and subsidiaries are not. These distinctions are somewhat arbitrary and may lead to difficulties. For example, a worker who starts out by emigrating temporarily may end up remaining permanently.

8.2 (*a*) What are the three main accounts in the U.S. balance of payments? What does each measure? (*b*) How are credits and debits entered in (the current and capital accounts of) the U.S. balance of payments?

   (*a*) The three main accounts of the balance of payments are the current account, the capital account and the official reserve account. The current account shows the flows of goods, services and transfer payments. The capital account shows the international flow of investments and loans. The official reserve account measures the change in U.S. official reserve assets and the change in foreign official assets in (the liabilities of) the U.S. during the year.

   (*b*) All economic transactions that lead to the U.S. receiving payments from foreigners are entered as credits (+) in the current account or in the capital account of the U.S. balance of payments. Thus, U.S. exports of goods and services, U.S. receipts of transfer payments from abroad, and capital inflows into the U.S. are entered as credits. On the other hand, all economic transactions which lead to the U.S. making payments to foreigners are entered as debits (−) in the current account or in the capital account. Thus, U.S. imports of goods and services, U.S. transfer payments to foreigners, and capital outflows from the U.S. are entered as debits.

THE CURRENT ACCOUNT

8.3 With reference to the services category of the current account in Table 8.1, explain in detail what is meant by and what is included in (*a*) travel and transportation, (*b*) receipts of income on U.S. assets abroad and payments of income on foreign assets in the U.S., (*c*) military transactions and (*d*) other services.

   (*a*) *Travel* refers to the expenditures of U.S. tourists abroad for meals, hotels and for the purchase of gifts (debits), and similar expenditures of foreign tourists in the U.S. (credits). *Transportation* refers to the expenditures of U.S. residents (tourists, business executives and firms) for the services of foreign carriers such as airlines, vessels, trains, etc. (debits), and similar expenditures of foreign residents for the services of U.S. carriers (credits). The U.S. had a net debit balance for travel and transportation of $(-)\$3$ billion in 1988.

(b) *Receipts of income on U.S. assets abroad* refers to the interest, dividends, earnings of unincorporated affiliates, reinvested earnings of incorporated affiliates and other earnings which U.S. residents earn on their foreign investments or which arise from their ownership of foreign assets (credits). Receipts of income on U.S. assets abroad were $108 billion in 1988.

   Payments of income on foreign assets in the U.S. refers to U.S. payments of interest, dividends and other earnings on foreign investments in the U.S. (debits). In 1988, this was $106 billion. These two entries are usually reported separately (rather than only their balance) because of their relatively greater importance.

(c) *Military transactions* refers to U.S. expenditures abroad for renting land, buildings and facilities for military installations, for the purchase of supplies for the military and for the expenditures of U.S. military personnel abroad. The credit counterparts are the foreign purchases of U.S. military materiel, the sharing of the cost of keeping U.S. troops and military installations abroad and the training of foreign militia. In 1988, the U.S. had a net debit balance of $(-)\$5$ billion in military transactions.

(d) *Other services* refers to banking, insurance, stock brokerage and similar services provided by U.S. institutions to foreign residents (credits) and purchases by U.S. residents from foreign institutions (debits). Also included here as credits are the expenditures to maintain foreign embassies in the U.S., and as debits, the U.S. expenditures to maintain embassies abroad. The U.S. had a balance on other services of $(+)\$20$ billion in 1988.

8.4 Define the meaning and scope of (a) unilateral private transfers and (b) government unilateral transfers.

(a) *Private unilateral transfers* refers to gifts made by individuals and nongovernmental institutions to residents of other nations. The private transfer payments made by U.S. residents (debits) may take the form of individuals' contributions to a famine relief fund for a less developed country, the remittances of an immigrant in the U.S. to relatives "back home," or a CARE package sent to undernourished children in a poor nation. As the richest nation in the world, the U.S. receives little if any transfer payments (credits) from the residents of other nations. The balance on private transfer payments for the U.S. was $-\$2$ billion in 1988.

(b) *Government unilateral transfers* refers to gifts or other payments (for which nothing direct is received in return) made by the government of one nation to individuals, institutions or the government of another nation. The transfer payments made by the U.S. government (debits) take the form of economic aid (such as grants of money, consumer goods, capital equipment or technical aid) to less developed nations; military aid (usually in the form of military materiel), and the remittance of old age pensions and other similar payments to foreign workers in the U.S. who retired abroad. U.S. residents receive few if any transfer payments from foreign governments. The balance on government unilateral transfers for the U.S. was $-\$13$ billion in 1988, and $-\$15$ billion for private and government unilateral transfers together.

8.5 Explain what is meant by (a) the merchandise trade balance. Was this balance favorable or unfavorable for the U.S. in 1988? (b) Do the same for the goods and services balance and (c) for the current account balance.

(a) The merchandise trade balance is obtained by subtracting the value of the goods imported by a nation from the value of the goods it exported. It is usually the first data of the nation's balance of payments to become available. In 1988, the value of U.S. exports of goods (credits) was $319 billion, while the value of U.S. imports of goods (debits) was $447 billion. Thus, the U.S. had a negative merchandise trade balance of $(-)\$128$ billion (see Table 8.1).

(b) The goods and services balance is obtained by adding the nation's merchandise trade balance and its balance on services. In 1988, the U.S. had a negative balance on goods and services of $(-)\$112$ billion. In the U.S. today, the goods and services balance receives exaggerated attention in relation to the other components of the U.S. balance of payments.

(c) The current account balance is obtained by adding the nation's goods and services balance to its balance on unilateral transfers. In 1988, the U.S. had a negative current account balance of $(-)\$127$ billion. Note that all the items entered in the current account are of a flow nature, referring to a certain amount per quarter or per year.

THE CAPITAL ACCOUNT

8.6   (*a*) What does the U.S. capital account measure?   (*b*) What forms can U.S. capital outflows take? (*c*) What forms can U.S. capital inflows take?

(*a*)   The U.S. capital account measures the change in U.S. assets abroad and foreign assets in the U.S., other than official reserve assets. Thus, while the current account measures the *flow* of goods, services and unilateral transfers, the capital account measures the *change in the stock* of all nonreserve financial assets. The justification for excluding official reserve assets from the capital account is that changes in reserves reflect government policies rather than market forces.

(*b*)   U.S. capital outflows can take the form of either increases in U.S. assets abroad (such as U.S. purchases of a foreign stock) or reductions in foreign assets in the U.S. (such as the sale by foreigners of a U.S. stock). Both are capital outflows and recorded as debits ($-$) because both lead to a payment to foreigners. Note that the capital account includes only the change in the stock of nonreserve financial assets. The changes in financial reserve assets or international reserves are included in the official reserve account (see Problem 8.10).

(*c*)   U.S. capital inflows can take the form of either reductions of U.S. assets abroad (such as the U.S. sale of a foreign stock) or increases in foreign assets in the U.S. (such as the purchase of a U.S. stock by foreigners). Both are capital inflows and recorded as credits ($+$) because both lead to the receipt of a payment from foreigners. Once again, the capital account includes only changes in nonreserve financial assets.

8.7   (*a*) What form do U.S. investments abroad take?   (*b*) Why does the U.S. invest abroad?   (*c*) What is the relationship between U.S. foreign investments and the flow of profits, dividends and interest to the U.S.?

(*a*)   U.S. investments abroad take the form of direct investments (such as the building of a plant or the purchase of real estate or land abroad), the purchase by U.S. residents of foreign securities (such as stocks, bonds and treasury bills) and increases in U.S. bank deposits abroad. Direct investments and portfolio investments with maturity of more than one year (e.g., stocks and bonds) are referred to as long-term investments to distinguish them from portfolio investments with maturity of one year or less (e.g., treasury bills) and bank deposits, which are referred to as short-term investments.

(*b*)   The U.S. invests abroad to take advantage of higher profit rates and higher interest rates (or the expectation of higher rates) abroad, to overcome trade barriers and/or to develop foreign sources of raw materials.

(*c*)   U.S. investments abroad give rise to the flow of profits, dividends and interest to the U.S. These represent foreign payments to the U.S. for the use of (or for the services received from the use of) U.S. capital and are appropriately entered as credits into the services category of the U.S. current account. Thus, capital movements must be clearly distinguished from the resulting flow of payments and returns. The former are entered into the capital account, the latter into the current account.

8.8   (*a*) What was the nature of U.S. private capital outflows and inflows in 1988?   (*b*) What was the balance in the U.S. capital account in 1988?

(*a*)   From Table 8.2, we can see that U.S. direct investments abroad ($17 billion) were much smaller than foreign direct investments in the U.S. ($58 billion), and so were U.S. purchases of foreign securities ($8 billion, compared with $47 billion for foreign purchases of U.S. securities) and the increase in U.S. bank liabilities abroad ($54 billion, compared with $69 billion for the increase in foreign bank deposits in the U.S.).

(*b*)   The U.S. capital account showed a total debit entry of $77 billion and a total credit entry of $180 billion, for a net credit balance of $103 billion. This is to be compared with a net debit entry of $127 billion in the U.S. current account.

THE OFFICIAL RESERVE ACCOUNT

8.9   What is meant by (*a*) gold reserves? (*b*) special drawing rights? (*c*) a nation's position in the International Monetary Fund? (*d*) convertible currencies?

    (*a*)   Gold reserves refer to the gold in the hands of the nation's monetary authorities. At the end of 1988, the U.S. held about $11 billion of gold reserves (at the old official price of $42.22 per ounce, but worth almost ten times more at the fluctuating free-market price of gold; see Chapter 12).

    (*b*)   Special drawing rights (SDRs or "paper gold") are international reserves created on the books of the International Monetary Fund or IMF (an international financial institution; see Chapter 12) and distributed to member nations in accordance with their importance in world trade. At the end of 1988, the U.S. had about $10 billion in SDRs.

    (*c*)   A nation's reserve position in the International Monetary Fund (IMF) refers to reserves paid by the nation in gold or convertible currencies upon joining the IMF. These are available to the nation on demand with no "strings" attached in the event of balance of payments difficulties (see Chapter 12). At the end of 1988, the U.S. reserve position in the IMF was $10 billion.

    (*d*)   Convertible currencies refer to U.S. dollars, British pound sterling, German marks, Swiss, French and Belgian francs, Japanese yen, Italian lire, Canadian dollars, Dutch guilders and a few other currencies which can be exchanged easily for one another and are normally acceptable in payment for international transactions. The U.S. dollar is by far the most important of the convertible currencies and represents a major portion of the reserves of most nations of the world. At the end of 1988, the U.S. held $17 billion of (foreign) convertible currencies. Thus, the U.S. overall total official international reserves were $48 billion ($11 billion in gold, $10 billion in SDRs, $10 billion in its reserve position at the IMF, and $17 billion in convertible currencies).

8.10   (*a*) What does the U.S. official reserve account measure? (*b*) What form do foreign official assets in the U.S. take? (*c*) How are changes in U.S. official reserve assets entered in the official reserve account of the U.S.? (*d*) How are changes in foreign official assets in the U.S. entered in the official reserve account of the U.S.?

    (*a*)   The official reserve account measures the change in U.S. reserve assets (gold, SDRs, the U.S. position in the IMF, and the U.S. holdings of foreign convertible currencies) and the changes in foreign official assets in the U.S. during the year.

    (*b*)   Foreign official assets in the U.S. usually take the form of U.S. dollars and U.S. treasury bills, U.S. bonds and U.S. notes in the hands of foreign monetary authorities.

    (*c*)   Increases in U.S. official reserve assets represent official *capital outflows* from the U.S. and are recorded as debits ($-$) in the U.S. official reserve account. Any decrease represents an official *capital inflow* and is recorded as a credit ($+$). Thus, the rule for deciding on debits and credits is the same as for private capital, except that we are now dealing with official capital. Thus, an inflow of (increase in) official reserves is a debit just like an inflow or import of goods and services, while an outflow of (decrease in) official reserves is a credit just like an outflow or export of goods and services. The reason for this seemingly strange way of entering changes in official reserve assets as credits or debits will become clear when we go on to define the deficit or surplus in the nation's balance of payments. Here, we are simply interested in learning how they are entered, rather than why they are entered that way.

    (*d*)   Increases in foreign official assets in the U.S. represent official *capital inflows* to the U.S. and are recorded as credits ($+$) in the U.S. official reserve account. For example, an increase in foreign official holdings of U.S. dollars can be thought of as "securities" giving foreigners claims on U.S. goods and services and equivalent to an increase in foreign official assets in the U.S. On the other hand, decreases in foreign official assets in the U.S. represent official *capital outflows* from the U.S. and are recorded as debits ($-$) in the U.S. official reserve account.

8.11   (*a*) What was the nature of the changes in the U.S. official reserve account during 1988? (*b*) What was the balance in the U.S. official reserve account in 1988? What was its significance?

(a) During 1988, U.S. official reserve assets increased (an official capital outflow from the U.S. and a debit) by $11 billion. Of this, $1 billion took the form of a decrease in the U.S. reserve position at the IMF and $5 billion represented an increase in U.S. official holdings of (foreign) convertible currencies. Also included in the U.S. official reserve account is the increase in foreign official assets in the U.S. (an official capital inflow to the U.S. and a credit) of $39 billion.

(b) With the increase in U.S. official assets of (−)$4 billion and the increase in foreign official assets in the U.S. of (+)$39 billion, there was a net credit balance of (+)$35 billion in the U.S. official reserve account. This means that there was an *overall* net increase in foreign official holdings of U.S. assets (e.g., of U.S. dollars) equal to $35 billion. It can, therefore, be inferred that there must have been an excess of U.S. expenditures abroad over U.S. earnings abroad equal to $35 billion on all but official transactions. This was settled by foreigners increasing their official holdings of U.S. (reserve) assets (i.e., dollars) equal to that amount.

DOUBLE-ENTRY BOOKKEEPING

8.12 (a) What is meant by double-entry bookkeeping? (b) Why is the single entry, statistical discrepancy, often required? (c) Identify the credit items and the debit items in *all three* accounts of the U.S. balance of payments.

(a) Double-entry bookkeeping refers to the accounting procedure whereby whenever a credit or debit transaction is entered in a nation's balance of payments, an offsetting debit or credit, respectively, of an equal amount is also entered. Thus, total credits should always equal total debits when the three accounts are taken together. The reason for double-entry bookkeeping is that, in general, every transaction has two sides. We sell something and we receive payment for it; we buy something and we have to pay for it.

(b) The special single entry, statistical discrepancy, is required whenever total credits in all three accounts of the balance of payments do not equal total debits. This often occurs because some items escape recording (due to oversight, secret capital movements or smuggling) while others may be incorrectly entered. Thus, if overall total credits equal 100 while overall total debits are 105, we need a credit entry for statistical discrepancy of (+)5.

(c) The credit items (+) in the U.S. balance of payments are (1) an export of goods and services and the receipt of unilateral transfers (in the current account), (2) capital inflows (in the capital account) and (3) an increase in foreign official assets in the U.S. and a decrease in U.S. official reserve assets (in the official reserve account). On the other hand, the debit items (−) are (1) an import of goods and services and the making of unilateral transfers, (2) capital outflows, (3) an increase in U.S. official reserve assets and a decrease in foreign official assets in the U.S. In short, a decrease in U.S. assets resulting from the export of goods, services and reserves, as well as capital inflows or imports into the U.S., are credits, while the opposite are debits.

8.13 How are the following transactions entered in the U.S. balance of payments? (a) A U.S. firm exports $100 worth of goods to the U.K., payable in three months. (b) After three months, the English importer pays by drawing down her dollar deposits in a New York bank. (c) What is left of transactions (a) and (b) if they occur within the same calendar year? If they do not?

(a) The U.S. credits merchandise in its current account for $100 and debits its capital account for $100. The reason for this is that by accepting payment in three months, the U.S. exporter is essentially extending a short-term loan to the foreign importer. This is a U.S. short-term private capital outflow (an increase in U.S. assets abroad) and is entered as a debit. (The exporter usually then rediscounts the importer's commercial obligation to pay at his bank. Thus, he gets his money immediately and his bank will collect the payment from the importer in three months.)

(b) When, after three months, the English importer pays by drawing on her dollar deposits or her bank's dollar deposits in a New York bank, the U.S. credits its capital account by $100 (a reduction in U.S. assets abroad—a capital inflow) and also debits its capital account by $100 (a decrease in foreign bank assets in the U.S.—a capital outflow).

(c) If transactions (a) and (b) occur during the same calendar year, the debit of transaction (a) in the U.S.

capital account is balanced or neutralized by the credit of transaction (*b*) in the U.S. capital account. Thus, what is left of transactions (*a*) and (*b*) in the U.S. balance of payments for that year is only the credit of $100 in the merchandise section of the current account [from transaction (*a*)] and the debit of $100 in the capital account [the reduction in foreign bank assets in the U.S. from transaction (*b*)]. If, on the other hand, transaction (*a*) occurred in October, November or December, transaction (*a*) would be included in the U.S. balance of payments for that year, while transaction (*b*) in the balance of payments for the following year.

8.14 Assuming that the U.S. exporter of Problem 8.13(*a*) ships his goods to England on an English ship, how would the transaction be recorded in the U.S. balance of payments if payment were made (*a*) by a $20 deposit in the shipping company's (or its bank's) account with a New York bank, (*b*) by drawing on his (i.e., the exporter's or his bank's) sterling balances in a London bank, (*c*) in cash with $20 worth of pounds sterling obtained from a New York bank, (*d*) in cash with a $20 bill which the shipping company then exchanges for pounds sterling in a London bank or (*e*) in cash with a $20 bill which the shipping company chooses to hold in its safe in the expectation that the dollar will soon increase in value in relation to pounds sterling.

(*a*) The U.S. debits by $20 the services category (transportation) of its current account and credits its capital account (an increase in foreign assets in the U.S.—a capital inflow) by $20.

(*b*) The U.S. credits its capital account (a decrease in U.S. assets abroad—a capital inflow) by $20.

(*c*) The same as in part (*b*).

(*d*) The same as in part (*a*).

(*e*) The same as in part (*a*).

8.15 How are the following transactions entered into the U.S. balance of payments? (*a*) An immigrant to the U.S. sends $100 to her relatives abroad, who exchange it for the local currency at a local bank. (*b*) The U.S. government ships $200 worth of food aid to India.

(*a*) The U.S. debits unilateral transfers (in its current account) for $100 and credits its capital account (an increase in foreign assets in the U.S.) for $100.

(*b*) The U.S. debits government unilateral transfers for $200 and credits merchandise exports, also in its current account, for $200.

8.16 How are the following transactions entered into the U.S. balance of payments? (*a*) The U.S. gives $200 cash aid to the government of India. (*b*) India uses the cash aid to import $200 worth of machinery from the U.S. (*c*) What remains of transactions (*a*) and (*b*) in the U.S. balance of payments if they both occur during the same year?

(*a*) The U.S. debits government unilateral transfers for $200 [see Example 4(*d*)] and credits foreign official assets in the U.S. in its official reserve account for $200.

(*b*) The U.S. credits merchandise exports in its current account for $200 and debits foreign official assets in the U.S. in its official reserve account for $200.

(*c*) The $200 credit and debit in the U.S. official reserve account cancel out, and what remains of transactions (*a*) and (*b*) in the U.S. balance of payments for that year is a credit of $200 in merchandise exports in its current account and a debit of $200 in government unilateral transfers, also in its current account [exactly as in Problem 8.15(*b*)]. The U.S. "real" aid to India takes the form of a shipment of machinery to India without any net change in the U.S. official reserve account. This aid represents a burden on U.S. taxpayers, but not on the U.S. balance of payments. This is the reason the U.S. often gives *tied aid* (i.e., cash aid to be spent in the U.S.).

8.17 How are the following transactions entered in the U.S. balance of payments? (*a*) A U.S. firm borrows $10 million in German marks from a U.S. bank and uses it to build a manufacturing plant in Germany. (*b*) A French citizen borrows $10,000 from a French bank and uses it to buy U.S. stocks.

(a)   The U.S. credits its capital account (a reduction in U.S. claims on foreigners and equivalent to a reduction in U.S. assets abroad—a capital inflow) for $10 million and debits its capital account (for direct investment abroad—a capital outflow) for $10 million.

(b)   The U.S. debits its capital account (a reduction in foreign claims on the U.S. and equivalent to a reduction in foreign holdings of U.S. assets—a capital outflow) for $10,000 and credits its capital account (for an increase in foreign holdings of U.S. securities—a capital inflow) for $10,000.

8.18   (a) How do English commercial banks generate a supply of dollars?   (b) How do they utilize them? (c) What happens if their dollar working balances rise above their desired level? Fall below their desired level?   (d) Repeat the entire process with pounds sterling balances for U.S. commercial banks.

(a)   English commercial banks generate a supply of dollars when English exporters of goods and services earn dollars abroad and exchange them for pounds sterling at English commercial banks, and when foreign investors exchange dollars for pounds sterling at English commercial banks in order to invest in England.

(b)   English commercial banks use their dollar balances when English importers of goods and services and English investors need dollars to pay for their foreign purchases and investments.

(c)   English commercial banks can exchange their excess dollar balances for pounds sterling at England's central bank. This increases England's official reserves of convertible currency (dollars). On the other hand, English commercial banks can replenish their depleted dollar balances from their central bank by paying in pounds sterling. This reduces England's official dollar reserves.

(d)   U.S. commercial banks generate a supply of pounds when U.S. exporters and foreign investors exchange pounds for dollars at U.S. commercial banks. These pound balances are used when U.S. importers and investors need them to make foreign payments. If the quantity of pounds supplied to U.S. commercial banks exceeds the quantity demanded. U.S. banks get rid of these excess pound balances by exchanging them for dollars at the Federal Reserve Bank in their district. Thus, U.S. official reserves of convertible currencies rise. When the opposite occurs, they obtain pounds by paying dollars and U.S. official reserves fall.

8.19   Are the following transactions entered in the U.S. balance of payments and, if so, how?   (a) An English commercial bank exchanges $100 of its dollar working balances for pounds at England's central bank.   (b) An English commercial bank buys $100 from its central bank with pounds.   (c) A U.S. commercial bank exchanges $100 worth of pounds for dollars at the Fed.   (d) A U.S. commercial bank buys $100 worth of pounds with dollars from the Fed.

(a)   Even though the U.S. is not directly involved in this transaction, it is entered in the U.S. balance of payments. This transaction is important from the U.S. point of view because it represents a switch from foreign private assets to foreign official assets in the U.S. Thus, the U.S. debits its capital account (a reduction in foreign private assets in the U.S.—a capital outflow) for $100 and credits (an increase in) foreign official assets in its official reserve account for $100.

(b)   The U.S. credits its capital account (an increase in foreign private claims on the U.S. and equivalent to an increase in foreign assets in the U.S.—a capital inflow) for $100 and debits (a decrease in) foreign official assets in the U.S. in its official reserve account for $100.

(c)   The U.S. credits its capital account (a reduction in U.S. claims on foreigners and equivalent to a decrease in U.S. private assets abroad—a capital inflow) for $100 and debits (an increase in) U.S. official reserve assets of convertible currencies (pounds) in its official reserve account for $100. (Note that foreign residents are not directly involved in this transaction.)

(d)   This entry is the opposite of the answer to part (c).

8.20   Are the following transactions entered in the U.S. balance of payments and, if so, how?   (a) A U.S. gold miner sells some newly mined gold to the New York Federal Reserve Bank.   (b) A U.S. firm imports some nonmonetary gold for industrial purposes.

(a)   Even though foreigners are not involved directly in this transaction, the increase in U.S. official holdings of gold represents, in a sense, a claim against foreigners since this gold can be used to make purchases abroad. Thus, this type of transaction is also entered in the U.S. balance of payments. The U.S. debits (an increase in) its official reserve (gold) assets and, in order to preserve the equality of total debits to total credits, credits (somewhat arbitrarily) the merchandise category of its current account. Note that gold is in an uncertain position as an international reserve since the U.S. government is trying to demonetize it (see Chapter 12).

(b) An import of nonmonetary gold for industrial uses is just like the import of any other commodity and is entered as a debit in the merchandise category of the U.S. current account. The corresponding credit entry to record the payment for this import can occur in a number of ways as indicated in Problem 8.14, depending on the form the payment takes.

MEASURING THE DEFICIT OR THE SURPLUS, OR OFFICIAL INTERVENTION

8.21   (a) If, for every debit or credit in the balance of payments, an offsetting credit or debit, respectively, of an equal amount is entered, how can a nation have a deficit or a surplus in the balance of payments? (b) How can a deficit or a surplus in the balance of payments be measured?

(a)   We have seen that because of double-entry bookkeeping, total credits always equal total debits when the three accounts are summed (including the allocation of SDRs and the statistical discrepancy). However, the deficit or surplus is measured by summing all items in the balance of payments except those in the nation's official reserve account. Only if the net balance on the nation's official reserve account were zero would the nation's balance of payments be in equilibrium.

(b)   If total debits exceed total credits in the current and capital accounts (including the statistical discrepancy), the net debit balance measures the deficit in the nation's balance of payments. This deficit must be settled (under a fixed exchange rate system) with an equal net credit balance in the official reserve account. On the other hand, if total credits exceed total debits in the current and capital accounts (and the statistical discrepancy), the net credit balance measures the surplus in the nation's balance of payments. This surplus must be settled (under a fixed exchange rate system) with an equal net debit balance in the official reserve account. All transactions in the current and capital accounts are called *autonomous items* because they take place for business or profit motives (except for unilateral transfers) and are independent of balance of payments considerations. On the other hand, the items in the official reserve account are called *accommodating items* because they result from or are needed to balance international transactions. Thus, a deficit in a nation's balance of payments is given either by the net debit balance in the nation's autonomous items or by the equal net credit balance in the nation's accommodating items. The opposite is true for a surplus.

8.22   (a) Why are the concepts and measurement of deficit or surplus not appropriate under a flexible exchange rate system?   (b) What is the difference between disequilibrium and a deficit in the balance of payments?

(a)   The concept and measurement of deficit or surplus in the balance of payments are not appropriate under a *freely* flexible exchange rate system because the tendency for a deficit to occur would be prevented by a depreciation of the nation's currency. Under a managed floating exchange rate system, part of the deficit would be corrected by a depreciation of the nation's currency and part would be financed by a net credit balance in the nation's official reserve account.

(b)   Disequilibrium refers to an actual or potential deficit. A nation has a potential deficit whenever it imposes import or other restrictions specifically designed to suppress an actual or open deficit. Then the nation is also in disequilibrium.

8.23   (a) Assuming a fixed exchange rate system, measure what the U.S. balance of payments deficit would be for 1988 by summing all the autonomous items in Table 8.4.   (b) Are the items in the balance of payments independent of one another, so that a change in one affects no other?

(a)   Summing (1) the current account balance of −$127 billion, (2) the net increase in U.S. assets abroad (other than U.S. official reserve assets) of −$77 billion, (3) the net increase in foreign assets in the U.S. (other than foreign official assets in the U.S.) of +$180 billion and (4) the statistical discrepancy of −$11 billion gives the net debit balance of (−)$35 billion for the 1988 U.S. balance of payments deficit. This was the *official settlements balance* deficit, to be distinguished from the *basic balance* deficit, which is measured by summing all the items in the current account and the long-term private capital items. The latter refers to direct investments and portfolio investments with maturity of more than one year. The IMF uses both balances and the U.S. neither.

(b)   The items in the balance of payments are interdependent rather than independent, so that a change in one has either a direct or indirect effect on the others. For example, an attempt to reduce the U.S. deficit by reducing U.S. imports or foreign aid is also likely to reduce U.S. exports, since foreigners will then have fewer dollars to spend on U.S. goods and services. Similarly, if the U.S. tried to reduce its long-term capital outflows, the income of U.S. investments abroad would also be reduced.

8.24   From the June issue of *Survey of Current Business* (available at your library), construct for the U.S. for the years 1980 to 1988 a table showing the total value of (1) exports of goods and services, (2) imports of goods and services, (3) balance on merchandise trade, (4) balance on goods and services, (5) balance on current account, (6) increase (−) in U.S. official reserve assets, and (7) increase (+) in foreign official assets in the U.S.

See Table 8.5. Note the sharp deterioration in the U.S. balance on merchandise trade, balance on goods and services, and balance on current account from 1980 to 1988.

Table 8.5
Summary of U.S. International Transactions, 1980–1988
(Billions of Dollars)

Year	Exports of Goods and Services (1)	Imports of Goods and Services (2)	Balance on Merchandise Trade (3)	Balance on Goods and Services (4)	Balance on Current Account (5)	Increase (−) in U.S. Official Reserve Assets (6)	Increase (+) in Foreign Official Assets in the U.S. (7)
1980	342	−333	−25	9	2	−8	15
1981	379	−363	−28	16	8	−5	5
1982	352	−350	−36	2	−7	−5	3
1983	337	−372	−67	−35	−44	−1	5
1984	371	−463	−113	−92	−104	−3	2
1985	371	−468	−122	−97	−113	−4	−2
1986	392	−509	−145	−117	−133	0	33
1987	446	−576	−160	−129	−144	9	48
1988	530	−642	−127	−112	−127	−4	40

8.25   Table 8.6 gives the *international investment position* of the U.S.   (a) How does this differ from the U.S. balance of payments?   (b) What does this tell us about the U.S. international position and its change over time?   (c) To what problems can the changed U.S. international position during the 1980s give rise?

(a)   The international investment position of a nation measures the total amount and the distribution of the nation's assets abroad and of foreign assets in the nation at the end of the year. Thus, while the balance of payments is a flow concept, the international investment position (often called the *balance of indebtedness*) of a nation is a stock concept. The latter allows the nation to project the future flow of income or earnings from the nation's foreign investments.

Table 8.6
International Investment Position of the U.S. in Selected Years, 1980–1988
(Billions of Dollars, book value at year-end)

Investment Category	1980	1984	1985	1986	1987	1988
Net U.S. international investment position	106	3	−111	−268	−378	−533
U.S. assets abroad	607	896	950	1,073	1,170	1,253
Official reserve assets	27	35	43	48	46	48
Gold	11	11	11	11	11	11
SDRs	3	6	7	8	10	10
Reserve position in the IMF	3	11	12	12	12	10
Foreign currencies	10	7	13	17	13	17
Other government assets	64	85	88	90	89	85
Private assets	517	776	819	935	1,035	1,120
Direct investments	215	211	230	260	308	327
Foreign securities	63	89	112	132	147	156
Bank claims	204	446	448	507	549	604
Other	35	30	29	36	31	33
Foreign assets in the U.S.	501	893	1,061	1,341	1,548	1,786
Official assets	176	199	203	242	284	322
Private assets	325	694	858	1,099	1,264	1,464
Direct investments	83	165	185	220	272	329
Other	242	529	673	879	992	1,135

SOURCE: U.S. Department of Commerce, *Survey of Current Business*, Washington, D.C.: U.S. Government Printing Office, October 1972 and June 1989.

(*b*) From Table 8.6 we can see that the U.S. changed from a net international creditor to the extent of $106 billion in 1980 to a very large (indeed the world's largest) debtor country (to the extent of over $500 billion) in 1988. This occurred because foreign assets in the U.S. more than tripled between 1980 and 1988 while U.S. assets abroad only doubled.

(*c*) The sharp deterioration in the U.S. international position during the 1980s can create serious problems for the U.S. in the future. For one thing, the U.S. will have to make huge net payments (interest, dividends, and profits) to foreigners in the future. This has led some to say that by incurring such huge and rising international debt, the U.S. is "mortgaging" its future (i.e., imposing a huge burden on future generations to service and repay the debt). Another problem is the danger of foreign domination.

Chapter 9

Adjustment in the Balance of Payments: Automatic

9.1 TYPES OF ADJUSTMENT

A deficit or surplus in a nation's balance of payments may arise for many reasons (see Problem 9.1) but cannot continue indefinitely (see Problem 9.2), thus giving rise to the need for adjustment.

Adjustment in the balance of payments may be classified as *automatic* (discussed in this chapter) or *policy* (Chapter 10). Automatic adjustments can be brought about by variations in external prices (Section 9.2), in internal prices (Section 9.3), in national income (Section 9.4), or in national income, prices and monetary changes (Sections 9.5 and 9.6).

For the sake of simplicity, we will limit our concept of the balance of payments to exports and imports only, unless otherwise indicated.

9.2 PRICE ADJUSTMENT MECHANISM UNDER A FLEXIBLE EXCHANGE RATE SYSTEM

Under a *flexible exchange rate system,* a deficit in a nation's balance of payments is automatically corrected by a depreciation of its currency, while a surplus is corrected by an appreciation (if the foreign exchange market is stable; see Problem 9.9). Assuming a stable market, a flexible exchange rate system is feasible in the real world only if the demand and supply of foreign exchange are relatively elastic.

EXAMPLE 1. In a two-nation world (the U.S. and the U.K.), a given deficit of £4 billion (*AB* in Fig. 9-1) in the U.S. balance of payments is corrected by a depreciation of the dollar from $2.00 = £1 to $2.40 = £1 with $D_£$ and $S_£$, but would require a depreciation to $3.60 = £1 with $D_£^*$ and $S_£^*$. Since a depreciation of the dollar also causes domestic or internal prices in the U.S. to rise (see Problems 9.5 and 9.6), a large depreciation of the dollar (as with $D_£^*$ and $S_£^*$) would not be feasible.

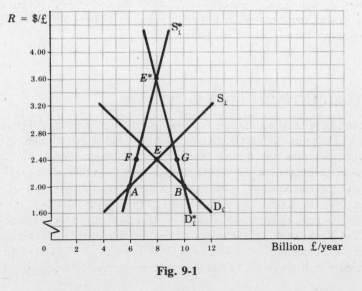

Fig. 9-1

The U.S. demand curve for pounds ($D_£$) is derived from the U.S. demand curve for imports (D_M) and the foreign supply curve of imports to the U.S. (S_M), both in terms of pounds (see Problem 9.7). Given S_M, the more elastic D_M is, the more elastic $D_£$ is. Also, the U.S. supply curve of pounds ($S_£$) is derived from the foreign demand curve for U.S. exports (D_X) and the U.S. supply curve of exports (S_X), both in terms of pounds. Given S_X, the more elastic D_X is, the more elastic $S_£$ is (see Problem 9.8). If D_X is inelastic, $S_£$ is negatively sloped and the foreign exchange market may be unstable (see Problems 9.9 and 9.10).

9.3   PRICE ADJUSTMENT MECHANISM UNDER THE GOLD STANDARD

Under the *gold standard* (1880–1914), the monetary authorities of each nation fix the price of gold in terms of the nation's currency and then stand ready to buy or sell any amount of gold at that price. This establishes a fixed relationship between any two currencies (*the mint parity*). Then, the exchange rate can only vary above and below the mint parity (the so-called *gold points*) by the cost of shipping gold between the two nations or monetary centers. Under the gold standard, the exchange rate is determined by the forces of demand and supply between the gold points, and is prevented from moving outside the gold points by gold shipments (see Example 2).

Adjustment under the gold standard was explained by the *price-specie-flow mechanism*. This rests on two basic assumptions: (1) the nation's money supply consists of gold or paper currency backed by gold and (2) a decrease in the nation's money supply leads to a decrease in its general price level, while an increase in its money supply leads to an increase in prices [the quantity theory of money; see Problem 9.16(*b*)]. Then, starting from a condition of equilibrium, a deficit or surplus in the nation's balance of payments will be automatically adjusted by a change in internal or domestic prices (see Example 3).

EXAMPLE 2.   The setting of the price of gold at \$35 per ounce by the U.S. and at £14 by the U.K. defines the fixed exchange rate of \$35/£14 = \$2.50/£1 (the mint parity). If the price of shipping £1 worth of gold between New York and London is 2.5¢, the exchange rate would be determined by demand and supply between \$2.525 and \$2.475 (the gold points) and prevented from moving outside this range by gold shipments (see Problems 9.12 to 9.15).

EXAMPLE 3.   Under the gold standard, a deficit in a nation's balance of payments leads to an outflow of gold and a decrease in the nation's money supply, which causes the general price level of the deficit nation to fall. This in turn stimulates the deficit nation's exports and leads to a reduction in its imports. The exact opposite occurs in the surplus nation. This process continues until the deficit (and surplus) have been completely eliminated. In addition, interest rates tend to rise in the deficit nation (because of the reduction in its money supply) and fall in the surplus nation (because of the increase in its money supply), causing short-term capital to flow from the surplus to the deficit nation and thus aid the adjustment process. Indeed, monetary authorities were expected to reinforce this process by further tightening credit in the deficit nation and expanding it in the surplus nation.

9.4   THE INCOME ADJUSTMENT MECHANISM

In examining the automatic price adjustment mechanisms, we implicitly assumed that national income remained constant. However, a change in the level of trade affects national income which, in turn, induces a change in the value of imports. For example, starting from an equilibrium position in the balance of trade and less than full employment domestically, an autonomous increase in the value of exports (X) causes real national income (Y) to rise by an amount equal to the increase in X times the *foreign trade multiplier, k*. If *the marginal propensity to save* or MPS $= \Delta S/\Delta Y = 0$, then $k = 1/$MPM, where MPM is *the marginal propensity to import,* or $\Delta M/\Delta Y$. In this case, the induced increase in M resulting from the increase in Y equals the original autonomous increase in X and so the adjustment in the balance of payments is complete (see Example 4). If, on the other hand (and more realistically), MPS > 0, $k = 1/($MPS $+$ MPM$)$ and the induced increase in M falls short of the increase in X and the adjustment is incomplete (see Example 5).

EXAMPLE 4.   Given that (1) Y is at less than full employment, (2) X = M originally, (3) X (which is exogenous or independent of Y) rises by \$100 and remains at this higher level (thus opening a surplus in the nation's balance of payments) and (4) MPS = 0 while MPM = 0.1, then

$$k = \frac{1}{\text{MPM}} = \frac{1}{0.1} = 10$$

$$\Delta Y = (\Delta X)(k) = (\$100)(10) = \$1,000$$

$$\Delta M = (\Delta Y)(\text{MPM}) = (\$1,000)(0.1) = \$100$$

Since the induced increase in M of \$100 equals the original autonomous increase in X of \$100, X = M once again (but at a level \$100 more than before) and so the adjustment is complete. Note that in order to isolate the automatic income adjustment mechanism, we implicitly assumed a fixed exchange rate system and also abstracted completely from other price and interest rate changes.

EXAMPLE 5.   Starting with the same given as in Example 4, except that now MPS = 0.15, we get

$$k = \frac{1}{\text{MPS} + \text{MPM}} = \frac{1}{0.15 + 0.10} = \frac{1}{0.25} = 4$$

$$\Delta Y = (\Delta X)(k) = (\$100)(4) = \$400$$

$$\Delta M = (\Delta Y)(\text{MPM}) = (\$400)(0.15) = \$60$$

Thus, an excess of X over M of \$40 (\$100 − \$60) will persist and the adjustment is incomplete. If the nation attempted to increase its X from a position of full employment, only prices would rise. Also, if X fell rather than rose, the nation might not be willing to let its real income fall and allow the automatic income adjustment mechanism to operate. The above discussion assumes a small nation. If the nation is large, *foreign repercussions* must also be considered (see Problem 9.30).

9.5   SYNTHESIS OF AUTOMATIC PRICE AND INCOME ADJUSTMENTS UNDER FLEXIBLE EXCHANGE RATES

We have seen in Section 9.2 that under a flexible exchange rate system, a deficit in the balance of payments is corrected by a depreciation of the nation's currency. This stimulates the nation's exports and discourages its imports (thus encouraging the production of import substitutes in the nation). The resulting increase in production and income in the nation induces imports to rise and neutralizes part of the original improvement in the nation's trade balance. If the deficit nation was already at full employment to begin with, the depreciation of its currency results in domestic inflation and no correction of its deficit, unless domestic absorption falls. Consideration of the income effects of a depreciation or devaluation is referred to as the *absorption approach*.

EXAMPLE 6.   We have seen in Fig. 9-1 that with $D_£$ and $S_£$, a 20% depreciation of the dollar from an exchange rate of R = \$2 to R = \$2.40 was required to correct the deficit of £4 billion (\$8 billion at R = \$2) in the U.S. balance of payments. But this did not take into account the resulting increase in income in the U.S. and induced rise in imports. Thus, a larger depreciation of the dollar would be required to correct the U.S. deficit [see Problem 9.31(a)]. If, however, the U.S. was at full employment to begin with, the depreciation of the dollar would be accompanied by inflation which entirely eliminates the competitive advantage that the depreciation of the dollar was supposed to give the U.S. As a result, the U.S. deficit would remain uncorrected [see Problem 9.31(b)], unless domestic absorption falls (see Problem 9.32).

9.6   SYNTHESIS OF AUTOMATIC ADJUSTMENTS UNDER THE GOLD-EXCHANGE STANDARD

The *gold-exchange standard* was established after World War II and lasted until 1971. This was a fixed exchange rate system in which the dollar was *pegged* or fixed in terms of gold and other currencies were pegged to the dollar. The exchange rates were then allowed to vary 1% above and below the fixed par values, and deficits or surpluses in the balance of payments could be settled in gold or in convertible foreign exchange, especially dollars.

Under the gold-exchange standard, the automatic adjustment mechanisms discussed, if allowed to operate, would to some extent reinforce each other and possibly lead to complete adjustment of balance of payments disturbances.

EXAMPLE 7. Suppose that a nation that was originally in balance of payment equilibrium starts importing (say, because of a change in tastes) a commodity previously produced at home. The nation will then face a decline in real income and a deficit in its balance of payments. The decline in the nation's real income will induce its M to fall, partly neutralizing the original autonomous increase in its M and deficit. The decline in real income is also likely to cause prices in the deficit nation to rise less rapidly than in the surplus nation. This encourages the deficit nation's X and discourages its M (see Section 9.3) and reinforces the adjustment process. In addition, the deficit nation's exchange rate is likely to depreciate (within the allowed limits), further encouraging its X and discouraging its M (see Section 9.2). Finally, the outflow of reserves from the deficit nation results (unless neutralized) in a contraction of its money supply and a rise in its interest rate. This, in turn, may lead to a reduction in investment (I), real national income (Y), and M, and also to a balancing short-term capital inflow (see Example 3), reinforcing the adjustment process still further. In the surplus nation, the exact opposite is likely to occur (see Problem 9.34).

Taken together, these automatic adjustment mechanisms, if allowed to operate, are likely to bring about complete adjustment in the balance of payments. The problem is that nations may not be willing to allow them to operate (if, for example, they lead to domestic unemployment or inflation), thus giving rise to the need for *policies* to complete the adjustment (see Chapter 10).

Glossary

Automatic adjustment   A mechanism that operates without government intervention to correct balance of payments disequilibria.

Adjustment policies   Specific measures adopted by a nation's monetary authorities for the purpose of correcting balance of payments disequilibria.

Flexible exchange rate system   An international monetary system in which balance of payments disequilibria are automatically corrected by exchange rate changes.

Gold standard   The international monetary system that operated from 1880 to 1914, under which gold was the only international reserve, exchange rates fluctuated only within the gold points, and balance of payments adjustments took place as described by the price-specie-flow mechanism.

Mint parity   The fixed exchange rates resulting under the gold standard from each nation defining the price of gold in its currency and passively standing ready to buy or sell any amount of gold at that price.

Gold points   The mint parity plus or minus the cost of shipping one unit of the currency worth of gold between the two nations.

Price-specie-flow mechanism   The automatic adjustment mechanism under the gold standard. It operated by the deficit nation losing gold and its money supply falling. This caused domestic prices to fall, thus encouraging the nation's exports and discouraging its imports until the deficit was corrected. A surplus was corrected by the opposite process.

Foreign trade multiplier (k)   The ratio of the change in income to the change in exports or investment, or $1/(MPS + MPM)$.

Marginal propensity to save (MPS)   The ratio of the change in saving to the change in income, or $\Delta S/\Delta Y$.

Marginal propensity to import (MPM)   The ratio of the change in imports to the change in income, or $\Delta M/\Delta Y$.

Foreign repercussions   The effect that a change in a large nation's income and trade has on the rest of the world and which the rest of the world has on the nation.

Absorption approach   Examines the effect of induced income changes of exchange rate variations.

Gold-exchange standard   The fixed exchange rate system that operated from the end of World War II until 1971, under which gold and convertible currencies (mostly U.S. dollars) served as international reserves.

Review Questions

1.   Automatic adjustment of balance of payments disequilibria can be brought about by variations in   (*a*) external prices, (*b*) internal prices,   (*c*) income,   (*d*) all of the above.

     Ans.   (*d*) See Section 9.1.

2.   Under a freely flexible exchange rate system (and stable foreign exchange market), a deficit in a nation's balance of payments is automatically corrected by   (*a*) a depreciation of its currency,   (*b*) an appreciation of its currency, (*c*) domestic inflation,   (*d*) a rise in national income.

     Ans.   (*a*) See Section 9.2.

3.   A depreciation of a nation's currency usually causes internal or domestic prices to   (*a*) fall,   (*b*) rise,   (*c*) remain unchanged,   (*d*) any of the above.

     Ans.   (*b*) See Example 1.

4.   A nation's demand curve for foreign exchange is derived from   (*a*) the foreign demand curve for the nation's exports, (*b*) the nation's supply curve of exports,   (*c*) the nation's demand curve for imports,   (*d*) the foreign supply curve of the nation's imports.

     Ans.   (*c*) and (*d*) See Example 1.

5.   The supply curve of foreign exchange of a nation is derived from   (*a*) the foreign demand curve for the nation's exports,   (*b*) the nation's supply curve of exports,   (*c*) the nation's demand curve for imports,   (*d*) the foreign supply curve of the nation's imports.

     Ans.   (*a*) and (*b*) See Example 1.

6.   Under the gold standard,   (*a*) each nation defines the price of gold in terms of its currency and then stands ready to buy and sell any amount of gold at that price,   (*b*) there is a fixed relationship between any two currencies called the mint parity,   (*c*) the exchange rate is determined by demand and supply between the gold points and is prevented from moving outside the gold points by gold shipments,   (*d*) all of the above.

     Ans.   (*d*) See Section 9.3 and Example 2.

7.   According to the price-specie-flow mechanism, which sequence of events was supposed to bring about adjustment in a deficit nation under the gold standard?

     (*a*) Reduction in its money supply, falling internal prices, falling exports and rising imports,
     (*b*) Reduction in its money supply, rising internal prices, rising exports and falling imports,
     (*c*) Reduction in its money supply, falling internal prices, rising exports and falling imports,
     (*d*) Increase in its money supply, rising internal prices, falling exports and rising imports.

     Ans.   (*c*) See Section 9.3 and Example 2.

8.   Under the gold standard, the loss of gold and reduction in the money supply in the deficit nation lead to

     (*a*) a reduction in its interest rate and a capital inflow
     (*b*) a reduction in its interest rate and a capital outflow

(c) an increase in its interest rate and a capital outflow
(d) an increase in its interest rate and a capital inflow

Ans.   (d) See Example 3.

9.   In examining the automatic income adjustment mechanism, we assume   (a) less than full employment,   (b) a fixed exchange rate system,   (c) constant internal prices and interest rates,   (d) all of the above.

Ans.   (a) See Section 9.4 and Example 4.

10.   In the real world, the automatic income adjustment mechanism, if allowed to operate, will bring about   (a) incomplete adjustment,   (b) complete adjustment,   (c) perverse adjustment,   (d) any of the above.

Ans.   (a) This is so because MPS > 0 (see Example 5).

11.   The improvement in a nation's balance of trade and payments resulting from a depreciation of its currency is   (a) reinforced by the induced fall in imports in the nation,   (b) partly neutralized by the induced rise in imports,   (c) partly neutralized by the induced fall in imports,   (d) any of the above.

Ans.   (b) See Section 9.5.

12.   In the real world, the automatic income, price and interest adjustment mechanisms, if allowed to operate, are likely to

(a) reinforce each other but still result in incomplete adjustment
(b) reinforce each other and result in complete adjustment
(c) work at cross purposes from each other and result in incomplete adjustment
(d) work at cross purposes from each other and result in perverse adjustment

Ans.   (b) See Section 9.6 and Example 7.

Solved Problems

CAUSES AND TYPES OF DISEQUILIBRIA: NEED AND CLASSIFICATION OF ADJUSTMENTS

9.1   Discuss briefly   (a) the short-run or cyclical reasons and   (b) the long-run or structural reasons for disequilibria in a nation's balance of payments.

(a)   A *cyclical* expansion of national income at home and contraction abroad will increase the nation's imports, reduce its exports and lead to a deficit. Similarly, a higher rate of inflation at home than abroad will encourage imports and discourage exports. A crop failure or strike may have the same effect and lead to a deficit. A deficit may also arise from international capital flows.

(b)   Some of the long-run or structural reasons for disequilibria are: a difference in the rate of growth at home and abroad, changes in tastes or demand preferences, different rates of technological progress and changing factor endowments (conditions of production or supply) and changes in the economic and political framework within which trade and payments are conducted (such as the type and level of protection, formation of trading blocs, wars, etc.).

9.2   Explain why   (a) a deficit nation cannot continue to run deficits continuously and   (b) a surplus nation is not willing to continue to run surpluses indefinitely.

(a)   A deficit nation can finance or settle the deficit in its balance of payments by drawing on its international reserves, by borrowing abroad or both. Since each nation has limited reserves and its ability to borrow abroad on a continuous basis is also limited by its ability to repay, the nation cannot continue to run deficits indefinitely. The U.S. was in this position in 1971.

(b)   Once a surplus nation feels that its international reserves are adequate, it becomes more and more reluctant to continue running surpluses and accumulating international reserves. After all, it would then be giving up real goods and services in exchange for sterile gold or foreign exchange. Germany and Japan found themselves in this situation in 1971. Similarly, surplus nations are reluctant to continue lending to deficit nations indefinitely for fear of default. The oil-exporting nations have already reached this position. Though the need for and the burden of adjustment are greater and more immediate for deficit nations, they are also felt by surplus nations.

9.3   Distinguish between   (a) automatic and policy adjustment mechanisms and   (b) automatic price and income adjustment mechanisms.

(a)   Automatic adjustment mechanisms are those which are activated by a balance of payments disequilibrium itself without any government action and which operate to reduce or eliminate the disequilibrium (unless the government takes steps specifically designed to prevent their operation). These are to be distinguished from adjustment policies adopted by the government for the specific purpose of correcting the disequilibrium in the balance of payments. Note that while automatic adjustment mechanisms are triggered off as soon as the disequilibrium occurs, it usually takes some time to recognize the need for adjustment policies, to adopt them and for them to begin to operate.

(b)   The automatic price adjustment mechanism relies on price changes in the deficit and surplus nations to bring about adjustment. This operates differently under a flexible exchange rate system than under the gold standard. On the other hand, the automatic income adjustment mechanism relies on induced variations in national income in the deficit and surplus nations to be activated. For pedagogical reasons, each of these automatic adjustment mechanisms is originally studied separately. In the real world, this is unrealistic since to some extent they all operate simultaneously, as explained in Sections 9.5 and 9.6.

ADJUSTMENT WITH FLEXIBLE EXCHANGE RATES

9.4   With respect to Fig. 9-1 (repeated below for easy reference in Fig. 9-2),   (a) indicate what percentage depreciation of the dollar would eliminate deficit AB in the U.S. balance of payments if $D_\pounds$ and $S_\pounds$ were the relevant curves.   (b) How large a deficit would remain in the U.S. balance of payments when the dollar depreciated as much as in part (a) but the relevant curves were instead $D_\pounds^*$ and $S_\pounds^*$? (c) What percentage depreciation of the dollar would be required to eliminate deficit AB with $D_\pounds^*$ and $S_\pounds^*$?

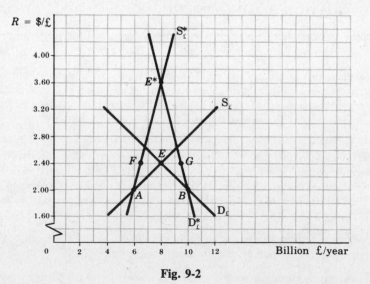

Fig. 9-2

(a)   With $D_£$ and $S_£$, a depreciation of the dollar from \$2.00 = £1 to \$2.40 = £1 is required to eliminate deficit *AB* (of £4 billion) completely in the U.S. balance of payments. Using \$2.00 as the base, this represents a 20% depreciation of the dollar with respect to the pound [(\$2.40 − \$2.00)/\$2.00 = \$0.40/\$2.00 = 20%].

(b)   With a 20% depreciation, the quantity demanded of pounds by the U.S. would fall only from £10 billion to £9.5 billion (the movement from *B* to *G* along $D_£^*$ in Fig. 9-2), while the quantity supplied would rise only from £6 billion to £6.5 billion (the movement from *A* to *F* along $S_£^*$), leaving a deficit of £3 billion per year (*FG* in Fig. 9-2) in the U.S. balance of payments.

(c)   With $D_£^*$ and $S_£^*$, 80% depreciation of the dollar (to point *E**) would be required to eliminate completely the same original deficit of *AB* in the U.S. balance of payments [(\$3.60 − \$2.00)/\$2.00 = \$1.60/\$2.00 = 80%].

9.5   Given Fig. 9-3, (a) explain, with respect to Panel A, why the foreign supply curve of imports to the U.S. (S_M) shifts up when the dollar depreciates. (b) Why is the shift not parallel? (c) State, with respect to Panel B, the equilibrium price of U.S. imports in terms of dollars before the depreciation of the dollar, with a 20% depreciation and with an 80% depreciation (D_M refers to the U.S. demand curve for imports).

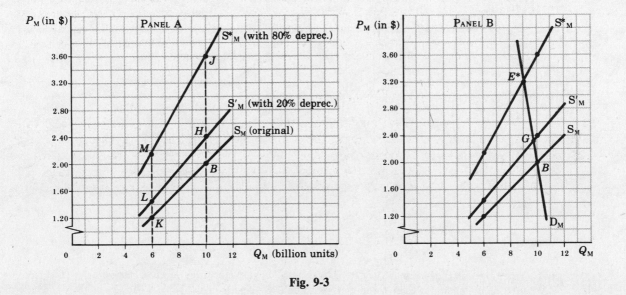

Fig. 9-3

(a)   When the dollar depreciates, English exporters who supply the U.S. imports receive less in terms of pounds for each dollar earned in the U.S. If the dollar depreciates 20% or 80%, they receive 20% or 80% less, respectively. This is like a 20% or an 80% tax, respectively, on each dollar that English exporters earn in the U.S. and results in an upward shift in S_M which is, in percentage terms, of the same magnitude as the percentage devaluation of the dollar with respect to the pound. Thus, S_M (when measured in dollars) shifts upward to S_M' with a 20% depreciation of the dollar and to S_M^* with an 80% depreciation (see Fig. 9-3, Panel A). To be noted is that D_M (when measured in dollars) is not affected by a depreciation of the dollar.

(b)   Since S_M is positively sloped, the same given percentage calculated from rising supply prices gives rising absolute amounts and a nonparallel shift. For example, point *H* (in Fig. 9-3, Panel A) is 20% above point *B* and so is *L* over *K*. Similarly, *J* is 80% above *B* and so is *M* over *K*.

(c)   The price of U.S. imports (P_M) in dollars is determined as usual at the intersection of D_M and S_M (both in dollars). Thus, with D_M and S_M, $P_M = \$2.00$ and $Q_M = 10$ billion units (point B in Panel B). With S'_M, $P_M \cong \$2.36$ and $Q_M \cong 9.6$ billion units (point G). With S^*_M, $P_M = \$3.20$ and $Q_M = 9$ billion units (point E^*). Note that we have implicitly assumed that the U.S. imports only a single commodity from the U.K.; otherwise, P_M and Q_M would refer to price and quantity indexes. (The more advanced student should also be able to show that points B, G and E^* along D_M correspond to points B, G and E^* along $D^*_\pounds$ in Fig. 9-2.)

9.6   Given Fig. 9-4,   (a) explain why a depreciation of the dollar causes the foreign demand for U.S. exports (D_X) to shift up. Why is the shift not parallel?   (b) What is the equilibrium P_X (in \$) before the depreciation of the dollar, with a 20% depreciation and with an 80% depreciation? (S_X refers to the U.S. supply of exports.)   (c) Why is depreciation not feasible to correct a deficit when $D_\pounds$ and $S_\pounds$ are inelastic?

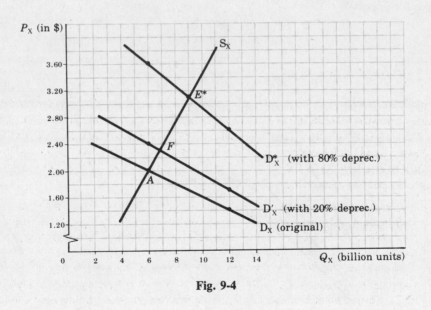

Fig. 9-4

(a)   When the dollar depreciates, say by 20% or 80%, English importers receive, respectively, 20% more or 80% more dollars for each pound they spend on U.S. exports. This is like a subsidy on their purchase of U.S. exports and causes their D_X (in terms of dollars) to shift up respectively, by 20% to D'_X or by 80% to D^*_X. Since D_X is negatively sloped, a given percentage calculated from falling demand prices gives falling absolute amounts and a nonparallel shift. Note that S_X (in terms of dollars) is not affected at all by a depreciation of the dollar.

(b)   With D_X, the equilibrium $P_X = \$2.00$ and $Q_X = 6$ billion units (point A in Fig. 9-4). With D_X, $P_X = \$2.30$ and $Q_X = 6.8$ (point F). With D^*_X, $P_X = \$3.10$ and $Q_X = 9$ (point E^*). Note that we have implicitly assumed that the U.S. exports only a single commodity to the U.K.; otherwise, P_X and Q_X would refer to price and quantity indexes. (The more advanced student should also be able to show that points A, F and E^* along S_X correspond to points A, F and E^* along $S^*_\pounds$ in Fig. 9-2.)

(c)   In Problem 9.4, we saw that the more inelastic $D_\pounds$ and $S_\pounds$, the greater the depreciation necessary to correct a deficit of a given size. But the greater the depreciation of the domestic currency, the greater the increase in P_M and P_X [see Problems 9.5(c) and 9.6(b)] and the increase in the domestic general price level. Thus, depreciation becomes less feasible to correct a deficit in the nation's balance of payments. In addition, the greater the depreciation necessary, the more likely it is to induce destabilizing speculation.

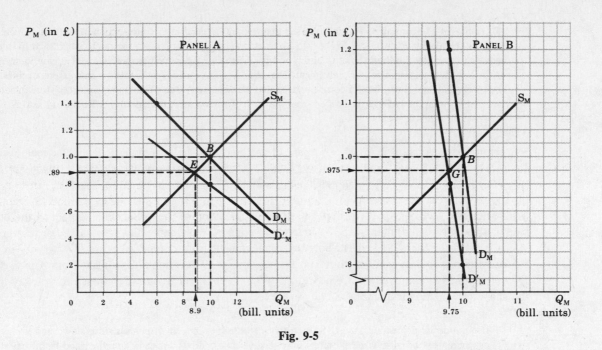

Fig. 9-5

9.7 With reference to Fig. 9-5, (*a*) explain why a depreciation of the dollar with respect to the pound causes a downward shift in the U.S. D_M *in terms of pounds*. What depreciation of the dollar is indicated by the shift from D_M to D_M' in Panels A and B?   (*b*) Show that a movement from point *B* to point *E* down S_M in Panel A corresponds to a movement from *B* to *E* along $D_\pounds$ in Fig. 9-2, while a movement from *B* to *G* along S_M in Panel B corresponds to a movement from *B* to *G* along $D_\pounds^*$.   (*c*) Given S_M, what can you say about the shapes of D_M and $D_\pounds$?

(*a*) When the dollar depreciates, the U.S. demand for imports (D_M) in terms of pounds shifts down and to the left because U.S. importers receive fewer pounds for each dollar spent on English imports. In Panels A and B of Fig. 9-5, D_M' is 20% below D_M and thus it refers to a 20% depreciation of the dollar with respect to the pound. The shift is not parallel because it is a constant percentage. Note that the English supply of U.S. imports (S_M) in terms of pounds is not affected by a depreciation of the dollar.

(*b*) At point *B* in Panel A, $P_M = \pounds 1$ times $Q_M = 10$ billion units equals £10 billion (point *B* on $D_\pounds$ in Fig. 9-2), while at point *E* in Panel A, $P_M \cong \pounds 0.89$ times $Q_M \cong 8.9$ billion units equals £8 billion (point *E* on

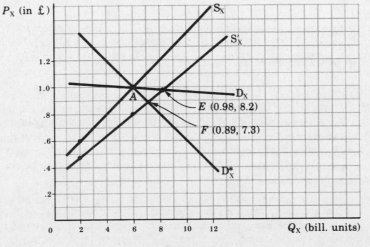

Fig. 9-6

$D_£$ in Fig. 9-2). Turning to Panel B, we see that at point B, $P_M = £1$ times $Q_M = 10$ billion units equals £10 billion (point B on $D_£^*$ in Fig. 9-2), while at point G, $P_M \cong £0.975$ times $Q_M \cong 9.75$ billion units equals (about) £9.5 billion (point G on $D_£^*$ in Fig. 9-2). Thus, a movement from B to E down S_M in Panel A of Fig. 9-5 corresponds to a movement from B to E up $D_£$ in Fig. 9-2, while a movement from B to G down S_M in Panel B of Fig. 9-5 corresponds to a movement from B to G up $D_£^*$ in Fig. 9-2. More generally, we can say that the U.S. $D_£$ is derived from the U.S. D_M from the U.K. and the U.K. S_M to the U.S., both in terms of pounds.

(c)   From Panels A and B in Fig. 9-5, we can say that given S_M, the more inelastic D_M is, the more inelastic $D_£$ is. Note that $D_£$ is always negatively sloped, except when D_M is vertical (in which case a downward shift in D_M resulting from a depreciation of the dollar cannot be seen) and so $D_£$ is also vertical.

9.8   With reference to Fig. 9-6, (a) explain why a depreciation of the dollar with respect to the pound causes a downward shift in the U.S. S_X in terms of pounds. What depreciation of the dollar is indicated by the shift from S_X to S_X'? (b) Show that a movement from point A to point E down D_X in Fig. 9-6 corresponds to a movement from A to E up $S_£$ in Fig. 9-2, while a movement from A to F down D_X^* corresponds to a movement from A to F up $S_£'$. (c) Given S_X and S_X', what can you say about the shape of D_X and the shape of $S_£$?

(a)   When the dollar depreciates, the U.S. supply of exports (S_X) in term of pounds shifts down and to the right (i.e., increases) because U.S. exporters now receive more dollars for each pound earned from exports. In Fig. 9-6, S_X' is 20% below S_X and thus refers to a 20% depreciation of the dollar with respect to the pound. The shift is not parallel because it is a constant percentage. Note that when the dollar depreciates, the English demand for U.S. exports (D_X) in terms of pounds is not affected.

(b)   At point A in Fig. 9-6, $P_X = £1$ times $Q_X = 6$ billion units equals £6 billion (point A and $S_£$ and $S_£^*$ in Fig. 9-2). At point E on S_X' and D_X in Fig. 9-6, $P_X \cong £0.98$ times $Q_X \cong 8.2$ billion units equals (about) £8 billion (point E on $S_£$ in Fig. 9-2). Thus, a movement from A to E down D_X in Fig. 9-6 corresponds to a movement from A to E up $S_£$ in Fig. 9-2. On the other hand, at point F on S_X' and D_X^* in Fig. 9-6, $P_X \cong £0.89$ times $Q_X = 7.3$ billion units equal (about) £6.5 billion (point F on $S_£^*$ in Fig. 9-2). Thus, a movement from A to F down D_X^* in Fig. 9-6 corresponds to a movement from A to F up $S_£$ in Fig. 9-2. More generally, we can say that the U.S. $S_£$ is derived from the U.K. D_X from the U.S. and the U.S. S_X to the U.K., both in terms of pounds.

(c)   From Fig. 9-6, we can say that, given S_X and S_X', the more inelastic D_X is, the more inelastic $S_£$ is. Since $QS_£$ increases as we move from A to E down D_X and from A to F down D_X^*, both the coefficient of price elasticity of D_X and that of D_X^* exceed 1 (i.e., $n_x > |-1|$ and $n_x^* > |-1|$) and so $S_£$ and $S_£^*$ are both positively sloped.

9.9   With reference to Fig. 9-7, (a) explain why a movement from point A to point H down D_X^{**} in Panel A corresponds to a movement from A to H up $S_£^{**}$ in Panel B. (b) With $D_£$ the same as in Fig. 9-2, explain why the foreign exchange market in Panel B of Fig. 9-7 is stable.

(a)   At point A in Panel A, $P_X = £1$ times $Q_X = 6$ billion units equals £6 billion (point A on $S_£^{**}$ in Panel B, at $R = \$2.00 = £1$). When the dollar depreciates by 20%, S_X in Panel A shifts down to S_X' (as in Fig. 9-6) and results in the new equilibrium point H. At point H in Panel A, $P_X = £0.85$ times $Q_X = 6.5$ billion units equals £5.525 (point H on $S_£^{**}$ in Panel B, at $R = \$2.40 = £1$). Since a movement from A to H down D_X^{**} results in a fall in $QS_£$, $n_X^{**} < |-1|$ and $S_£^{**}$ is negatively sloped. (If $n_X^{**} = |-1|$, $S_£^{**}$ would be vertical; $S_£^{**}$ would also be vertical if S_X is vertical so that a shift in S_X with a depreciation cannot be seen and $QS_£$ remains unchanged.)

(b)   The foreign exchange market of Panel B is stable because when $QD_£ > QS_£$, R automatically rises to E^{**} (i.e., the dollar depreciates) and the U.S. deficit is eliminated. If $QD_£ < QS_£$, R automatically falls to E^{**} and the surplus is eliminated. Even though $S_£^{**}$ is negatively sloped, the foreign exchange market is still stable here.

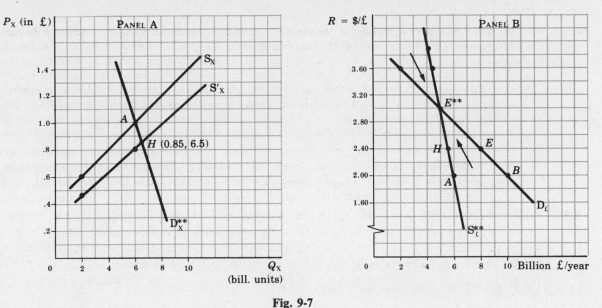

Fig. 9-7

9.10 (*a*) Explain why the foreign exchange market of Fig. 9-8 is unstable. ($D_£$ in Fig. 9-8 is the same as in Panel B of Fig. 9-7.) (*b*) What are the general conditions for an unstable foreign exchange market?

(*a*) If for some reason there is a displacement from equilibrium point E' in Fig. 9-8 so that $R > \$1.20 = £1$, $QD_£ > QS_£$ and a deficit is opened in the U.S. balance of payments. Then, R automatically rises (i.e., the dollar depreciates) and the U.S. deficit becomes even larger. On the other hand, if $R < \$1.20 = £1$, $QS_£ > QD_£$ and the U.S. has a surplus. This causes R to fall (i.e., the dollar to appreciate) and the surplus rises. Thus, a movement away from E' automatically moves us even further away from E' and so the foreign exchange market is unstable.

(*b*) In order to have an unstable foreign exchange market, (1) $S_£$ must be negatively sloped and (2) $S_£$ must be flatter and more elastic than $D_£$ in the vicinity of the equilibrium point. The stability of the foreign exchange market can also be expressed in terms of the coefficient of the price elasticity of D_X (i.e., n_X) and the coefficient of price elasticity of D_M (i.e., n_M), with D_X and D_M expressed in terms of either the domestic or foreign currency. Given infinite or very large coefficients of price elasticity of S_X and S_M (i.e., $\varepsilon_X = \varepsilon_M = \infty$), the foreign exchange market is stable only if $n_X + n_M > |-1|$. (If $n_X + n_M = 1$, a depreciation or appreciation leaves the deficit or surplus unaffected.) This is known as the Marshall-Lerner condition. (If ε_X and ε_M are relatively small, the foreign exchange market may be stable even if $n_X + n_M < |-1|$.) Foreign exchange markets are usually stable and n_X and n_M sufficiently elastic to make flexible exchange rates feasible.

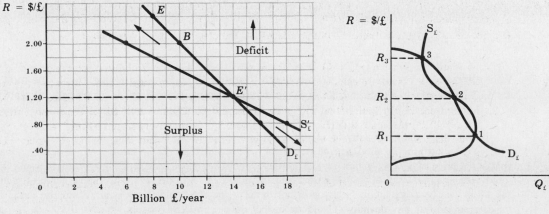

Fig. 9-8

Fig. 9-9

9-11 With reference to Fig. 9-9, (a) indicate whether the foreign exchange market is stable or unstable at equilibrium points 2, 3 and 1.   (b) Explain why at a high enough R, $QD_£ = 0$ and at a low enough R, $QS_£ = 0$.

(a) At equilibrium point 2, $S_£$ is negatively sloped and flatter or more elastic than $D_£$. Therefore, the foreign exchange market is unstable and a small displacement from equilibrium point 2 will automatically push the economy even further away from point 2, until stable equilibrium points 3 or 1 are reached. However, this requires such a large change in R that it is unfeasible to rely on fluctuating exchange rates to correct balance of payments disequilibria.

(b) The U.S. $D_£$ touches the vertical axis (i.e., $QD_£ = 0$) at a high enough R because with a high enough depreciation of the dollar, the U.S. finds imports so expensive that eventually it imports nothing and so $QD_£ = 0$. The U.S. $S_£$ touches the vertical axis (i.e., $QS_£ = 0$) at a low enough R because with a high enough appreciation of the dollar. U.S. exports become so expensive that eventually the U.S. will be unable to export anything and its $QS_£ = 0$.

ADJUSTMENT UNDER THE GOLD STANDARD

9.12 Suppose that, under the gold standard, the price of 1 ounce of gold is set at \$35 by U.S. monetary authorities and at £14 by the U.K. monetary authorities.   (a) What is the relationship between the dollar and the pound? What is this called?   (b) If to ship any amount of gold between New York and London costs 1% of the value of the gold shipped, define the U.S. gold export point or upper limit in the exchange rate between the dollar and the pound ($R = \$/£$). Why is this so?   (c) Define the U.S. gold import point or the lower limit in the exchange rate ($R = \$/£$). Why is this so?

(a) Since \$35 = 1 ounce of gold = £14, the dollar price of £1 or the exchange rate ($R = \$/£$) is fixed at \$35/14 = \$2.50. Thus, fixing the price of gold in terms of national currencies under the gold standard establishes a fixed relationship or exchange rate between any two currencies. This is called *the mint parity*.

(b) Since to ship \$2.50 worth of gold from New York to London costs 1% or 2.5¢), the U.S. gold export point or the upper limit of the exchange rate ($R = \$/£$) equals \$2.50 plus 2.5¢ or \$2.525. The reason for this is that no U.S. resident would pay more than \$2.525 to obtain £1, since he or she could buy \$2.50 worth of gold from the U.S. treasury, ship it to the U.K. at a cost of 2.5¢ and sell it to the U.K. treasury for £1. Thus, under the gold standard, the exchange rate of the pound can never rise above (and the dollar depreciate past) the U.S. gold export point of \$2.525.

(c) Similarly, the exchange rate can never fall below (and the dollar appreciate past) the U.S. gold import point of \$2.475. The reason for this is that no U.S. resident would accept less than \$2.475 for each pound sold, since he or she could always buy a pound's worth of gold from the U.K. treasury at the fixed price, import this gold into the U.S. at a cost of 2.5¢ and resell it to the U.S. treasury for \$2.50. Thus, the U.S. resident can get pounds at \$2.475 (\$2.50 minus 2.5¢) and will not accept less upon selling them. Note that the shipping cost of gold includes not only the transportation cost but also all other handling charges, insurance and the interest forgone while the gold is in transit.

9.13 With reference to Problem 9.12, draw a figure from the U.S. point of view, showing the mint parity, the U.S. gold export point and the U.S. gold import point, as well as a U.S. supply curve of and a U.S. demand curve for pounds that intersect within the gold points and above the mint parity.

In Fig. 9-10, the mint parity of \$2.50 only serves to define the U.S. gold export point of \$2.525 and the U.S. gold import point of \$2.475. Since under the gold standard, the U.S. stands ready to sell any quantity of gold at the price of \$35 per ounce, no U.S. resident would pay more than \$2.525 per pound, because he or she could obtain any quantity of pounds at that price by gold exports. Thus, the U.S. supply curve of pounds ($S_£$) has a kink and becomes infinitely elastic or horizontal at the U.S. gold export point. Similarly, since the U.S. stands ready to buy any quantity of gold at \$35 per ounce, no U.S. resident would sell pounds for less than \$2.475, because he or she could sell any quantity of pounds at that price by importing gold. Thus, $D_£$ has a kink

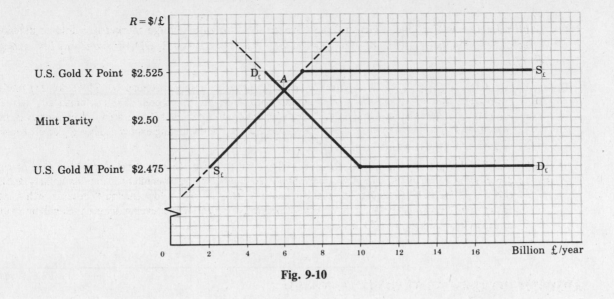

Fig. 9-10

and becomes infinitely elastic at the U.S. gold import point. Under the gold standard, the portions of $S_£$ and $D_£$ outside the gold points (dashed in Fig. 9-10) are irrelevant.

9.14 Figure 9-11 is the same as Fig. 9-10 except that two alternative and higher demand curves, $D_£'$ and $D_£''$, have been added. With reference to Fig. 9-11, indicate what the exchange rate would be under a flexible exchange rate system and under the gold standard with   (a) $D_£$,   (b) $D_£'$ (c) $D_£''$,   (d) What is the size of the deficit in the U.S. balance of payments under the gold standard and with $D_£'$? How is this deficit settled?

(a)   Under a flexible exchange rate system, the equilibrium exchange rate is determined exclusively by the forces of demand and supply. Under the gold standard, the exchange rate is determined by the forces of demand and supply within the gold points, and is prevented from moving outside the gold points by gold shipments. Thus, with $D_£$, the equilibrium exchange rate is $2.515 and the equilibrium quantity is £6 billion per year (point A in Fig. 9-11) under both a flexible exchange rate system and the gold standard. The U.S. balance of payments is in equilibrium and there are no gold shipments.

(b)   If for some reason $D_£$ shifts up to $D_£'$, the equilibrium exchange rate rises to $2.525 and the equilibrium quantity increases to £7 billion per year (point B in Fig. 9-11) under both a flexible exchange rate system and the gold standard. The U.S. balance of payments is in equilibrium and there are no gold shipments.

(c)   With $D_£''$ and a flexible exchange rate system, the equilibrium exchange rate is $2.535 and the equilibrium quantity is £8 billion per year (point C in Fig. 9-11). On the other hand, with the gold standard, gold arbitrageurs see to it that the dollar does not depreciate past the U.S. gold export point and the exchange rate will be $2.525.

(d)   At the exchange rate of $2.525, $QD_£'' = £9$ billion (point F in Fig. 9-11) and exceeds $QS_£ = £7$ billion on normal or autonomous transactions (point B). The excess demand for pounds of £2 billion per year (BF) represents the size of the deficit in the U.S. balance of payments for the year and is satisfied by £2 billion worth of U.S. gold exports [as described in Problem 9.129b)]. Note that the U.S. treasury does not actively support the dollar but simply and passively sells any amount of gold required to keep the exchange rate from rising above (and the dollar depreciating past) $2.525. However, with a limited supply of gold reserves, a need arises to correct the deficit.

9.15 Figure 9-12 is the same as Fig. 9-10 except that two alternative supply curves, $S_£'$ and $S_£''$, have been added. With reference to Fig. 9-12, indicate what the exchange rate would be under a flexible exchange rate system and under the gold standard with   (a) $S_£'$ and   (b) $S_£''$.   (c) What is the size of the surplus in the U.S. balance of payments under the gold standard and with $S_£''$? How is this surplus settled?

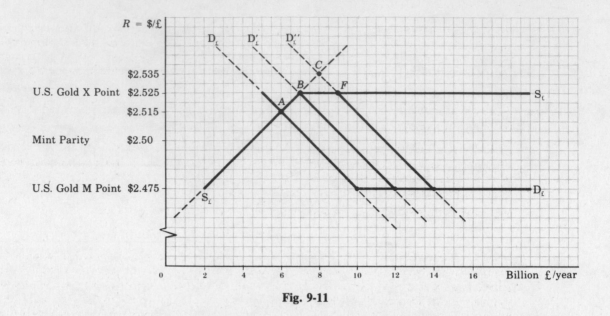

Fig. 9-11

(a) If, with an unchanged $D_£$, $S_£$ shifts down (increases) to $S'_£$, the equilibrium exchange rate falls from \$2.515 (point A in Fig. 9-12) to \$2.485 (point G), and the equilibrium quantity rises from £6 billion to £9 billion per year—under both a flexible exchange rate system and the gold standard. The U.S. balance of payments remains in equilibrium and there are still no gold shipments.

(b) With $S''_£$ and a flexible exchange rate system, the equilibrium exchange rate is \$2.455 and the equilibrium quantity is £12 billion per year (point H). On the other hand, with the gold standard, gold arbitrageurs see to it that the dollar does not appreciate past the U.S. gold import point and the exchange rate will be \$2.475. (If both $D_£$ and $S_£$ shift at the same time, the result is obtained in an analogous way and is left as an exercise for the reader.)

(c) However, at the exchange rate of \$2.475, $QS''_£$ = £14 billion (point K) and exceeds $QD_£$ = £10 billion on normal or autonomous transactions (point J). The excess supply of pounds of £4 billion per year (JK) represents the size of the surplus in the U.S. balance of payments for the year and is satisfied by £4 billion

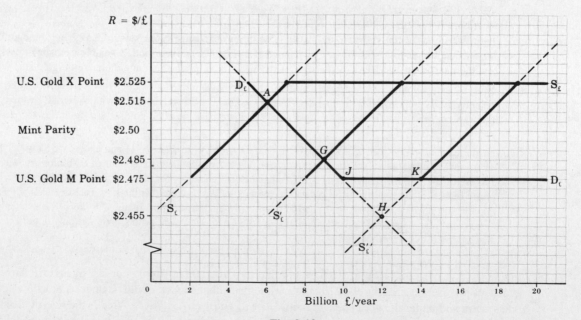

Fig. 9-12

worth of gold imports into the U.S. [as described in Problem 9.12(c)]. Note that the U.S. treasury passively buys any amount of gold required to keep the exchange rate from falling below (and the dollar appreciating past) $2.475. Since a surplus nation may not wish to continue accumulating gold reserves past a certain amount, a need arises to correct the surplus. The gold standard operated from about 1880 to 1914.

9.16 State (a) the assumptions of the gold standard and the price-specie-flow mechanism and   (b) the quantity theory of money.

(a) (1) Each nation fixes the price of gold in terms of its currency and stands ready to buy and sell passively any amount of gold at that price, (2) each nation's money supply consists of gold or paper currency backed by gold, (3) the quantity theory of money holds so that the price level of a nation varies directly with its money supply and (4) exports and imports readily respond to price changes.

(b) We start with the so-called *equation of exchange*,

$$MV = PQ$$

where M refers to the nation's money supply, V to the velocity of circulation of money, P to the price level and Q to physical output. At the time of the gold standard, most economists (as characteristic of the classical school) believed that aside from temporary disturbances, an automatic tendency toward full employment was built into the economy (based on their assumption of perfect and instantaneous flexibility in all prices, wages and interest rates). Thus, they took Q to be fixed at the full-employment level. They also believed that V depended on institutional factors and was constant. With V and Q relatively constant, a change in M causes a direct (and proportionate) change in P.

9.17 (a) Explain how a change in prices under the gold standard was supposed to eliminate the surplus in a nation's balance of payments.   (b) How did David Hume use his price-specie-flow mechanism to show that the attempt of a nation to accumulate gold continuously, as advocated by the mercantilists, was self-defeating?

(a) Under the gold standard, a surplus in a nation's balance of payments leads to an inflow of gold and an increase in the nation's money supply. The increase in the money supply leads to an increase in the general price level of the surplus nation. This in turn stimulates the surplus nation's imports and discourages its exports, until the surplus is entirely eliminated. This adjustment process can be visualized in Fig. 9-13. This shows that the $2 billion surplus of exports (X) over imports (M) at point A results in a continuous inflow of gold and an increase in the nation's money supply until its price index has risen 20% and X = M at point B. If the nation were instead originally at point C, its deficit of $3 billion would be corrected automatically by a continuous gold loss and reduction in its money supply until its price index had fallen from 150 to 120 and X = M at point B. This adjustment process is reinforced by the reverse price movement in the trade partner.

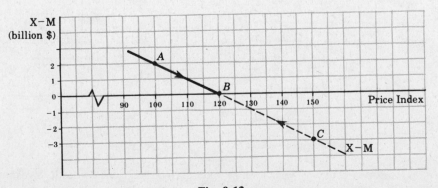

Fig. 9-13

(b) The mercantilists believed that a nation could continue accumulating gold by exporting more than it imported (see Section 1.3). However, David Hume explained that an inflow of gold increased the money supply of the nation and its price level. This discouraged the nation's exports, encouraged its imports and led to gold outflows. Thus, the nation's attempt to accumulate gold continuously by stimulating its exports and restricting its imports was futile or self-defeating.

9.18 (a) Explain how interest changes in the deficit and surplus nations help the adjustment process under the gold standard. (b) What were the "rules of the gold standard?"

(a) The inflow of gold from the deficit to the surplus nation automatically results in an increase in the money supply of the surplus nation and a decrease in the deficit nation. This causes interest rates to fall in the surplus nation and to rise in the deficit nation and induces a balancing short-term capital flow from the surplus to the deficit nation. Although this induced short-term capital flow is of a once-and-for-all nature rather than continuous, it helps the adjustment process.

(b) Under "the rules of the gold standard," nations were supposed to reinforce the adjustment process by further expanding credit in the surplus nation and tightening it in the deficit nation. The adjustment process under the gold standard was remarkably smooth, and it now seems to have resulted primarily from stabilizing short-term capital movements rather than from price changes (as it was once believed, and as described in Problem 9.17). See Section 12.1.

THE INCOME ADJUSTMENTS MECHANISM

9.19 Given: (1) a closed economy with no foreign trade, at less than full employment with a constant price level and interest rates, (2) Savings (S) = domestic investment (I_d) = \$100 at the equilibrium level of real national income (Y_E) of \$1,000 and (3) MPS = $\Delta S/\Delta Y$ = 0.25, while I_d is a constant at every level of national income and is determined exogenously (i.e., outside the model). If I_d now increases autonomously by \$100 and remains at this higher level, find (a) the domestic multiplier, k, (b) the new equilibrium level of national income, Y_E', and (c) the induced change in S. (d) Show the results to parts (a), (b) and (c) graphically.

(a)
$$k = \frac{\Delta Y}{\Delta I_d} = \frac{1}{MPS} = \frac{1}{0.25} = 4$$

(b)
$$\Delta Y = (\Delta I_d)(k) = (\$100)(4) = \$400$$
$$Y_E' = Y_E + \Delta Y = \$1,000 + \$400 = \$1,400$$

(c)
$$\Delta S = (\Delta Y)(MPS) = (\$400)(0.25) = \$100$$

(d) See Fig. 9-14.

Note that the S function has a negative vertical intercept (i.e., S < 0 at Y = 0).

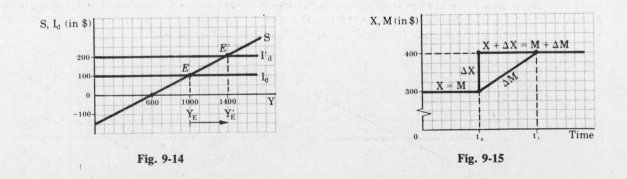

Fig. 9-14   Fig. 9-15

9.20 Given: (1) an open economy with foreign trade but no saving or domestic investment (i.e., $S = I_d$ = 0 = MPS), (2) a fixed exchange rate system and no change in internal prices or interest rates, (3) X = M = \$300 at Y_E = \$1,000, which is well below full employment and (4) MPM = $\Delta M/$

$\Delta Y = 0.25$ while X is a constant at every level of national income and is determined exogenously (i.e., outside the model by the level of national incomes and tastes abroad). If X now increases autonomously by \$100 and remains at this higher level (so the nation now has a surplus in its balance of payments), find   (a) the foreign trade multiplier, k,   (b) the new equilibrium level of national income, Y'_E and   (c) the induced change in M, X, S, and I_d.   (d) Is the adjustment in the balance of payments complete?   (e) Why did we make assumption (2) above?

(a) $k = \Delta Y/\Delta X = 1/MPM$, since M are a leakage, as are S. Here, $k = 1/MPM = 1/0.25 = 4$.

(b) $\Delta Y = (\Delta X)(k) = (\$100)(4) = \$400$, since an autonomous increase in X is an injection into the system just as is an autonomous increase in I_d. $Y'_E = Y_E + \Delta Y = \$1,000 + \$400 = \$1,400$.

(c) $\Delta M = (\Delta Y)(MPM) = (\$400)(0.25) = \$100$. $\Delta X = \Delta I_d = 0$ since X and I_d are independent of Y. In addition, since MPS has been assumed to be zero in this problem, induced $\Delta S = 0$.

(d)   Since at Y_E, $X = M = \$300$ and the autonomous increase in X of \$100 results in an induced increase in M also of \$100, the adjustment in the balance of payments is complete. The time sequence of the adjustment can be visualized with Fig. 9-15.

(e)   Assumption (2) is unrealistic but necessary in order to isolate (for purposes of study) the income adjustment mechanism from other automatic adjustment mechanisms. It will later be relaxed.

9.21   (a) Draw a figure for Problem 9.20 similar to Fig. 9-14.   (b) What would have happened if there had been an autonomous fall rather than a rise in X of \$100 in Problem 9.20?

(a)   See Fig. 9-16. Note that the M function has a positive vertical intercept (i.e., M > 0 at Y = 0) since the nation may still purchase some imports with its international reserves.

(b)   We can see from Fig. 9-16 that if X fell autonomously by \$100 from the original level of \$300, Y_E would fall to \$600 at which adjustment is complete with X = M = \$200.

9.22   (a) What would happen in Fig. 9-16 if at the same time that X increased autonomously by \$100, there were also an *autonomous* increase in M of \$100?   (b) What is the difference between an autonomous change in M and an induced change in M? How do these differ from each other and from an increase in MPM?

(a)   An autonomous increase in M of \$100 causes the entire M function to shift up by \$100 to M' and leads to $Y''_E = \$1,000$ and $X' = M' = \$400$ (point E'' in Fig. 9-17). If there had been an autonomous decrease in M of \$100 instead, we can see from Fig. 9-17 that this would have led to $Y''_E = \$1,800$ and $X' = M' = \$400$.

(b)   A change in M is autonomous if it is independent of Y. That is, the entire M function shifts up or down so that more or less M will be purchased at each Y. This may result from a change in tastes for imports. On the other hand, a change in M is induced if it results from a change in Y. This is reflected in a movement along an unchanged M function. $MPM = \Delta M/\Delta Y$ and refers to the slope of the M function. Thus, an increase in MPM refers to an increase in the slope of the M function and results in a decline in k (since k is the reciprocal or inverse of the MPM). The MPM for the U.S. is about 0.13; it has increased since the 1950s and is generally lower than the MPM in other industrialized nations.

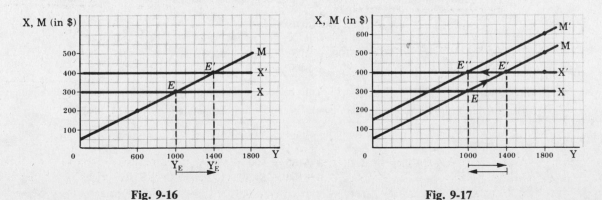

Fig. 9-16   Fig. 9-17

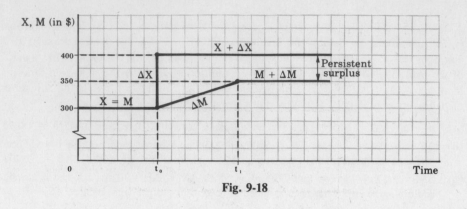

Fig. 9-18

9.23 Given: (1) an open economy with a fixed exchange rate system and constant internal prices and interest rates, (2) $S = I_d = \$100$ and $X = M = \$300$ at $Y_E = \$1,000$ which involves widespread unemployment and (3) MPS $=$ MPM $= 0.25$ where I_d and X are independent of Y and exogenously determined. Now X increases autonomously by $\$100$ and remains at this higher level. Find (a) k, (b) Y_E' and (c) ΔM and ΔS. (d) Is the adjustment in the balance of payments complete? (e) Show the time sequence of the adjustment with a figure similar to Fig. 9-15.

(a)
$$k = \frac{\Delta Y}{\Delta X} = \frac{1}{MPS + MPM} = \frac{1}{0.25 + 0.25} = \frac{1}{0.5} = 2$$

(b)
$$\Delta Y = (\Delta X)(k) = (\$100)(2) = \$200$$
$$Y_E' = Y_E + \Delta Y = \$1,000 + \$200 = \$1,200$$

(c)
$$\Delta M = (\Delta Y)(MPM) = (\$200)(0.25) = \$50$$
$$\Delta S = (\Delta Y)(MPS) = (\$200)(0.25) = \$50$$

(d) The adjustment in the balance of payments is incomplete. Specifically, a surplus of $\$50$ will remain in the nation's balance of trade (and payments) because the autonomous increase in X of $\$100$ resulted in an induced increase in M of only $\$50$.

(e) See Fig. 9-18.

9.24 With reference to Problem 9.23, state the equilibrium condition for Y (a) before X rose and (b) after X rose.

(a) The equilibrium condition for Y before X rose is given by

$$\text{Injections} = \text{Leakages}$$
$$I_d + X = S + M$$
$$\$100 + \$300 = \$100 + \$300$$
$$\$400 = \$400$$

Since at $Y_E = \$1,000$, $X = M = \$300$, the balance of trade (and payments) is simultaneously in equilibrium.

(b) Starting from Y_E, the equilibrium condition for Y after X rose is given by

$$\text{Change in injections} = \text{Change in leakages}$$
$$\Delta I_d + \Delta X = \Delta S + \Delta M$$
$$0 + \$100 = \$50 + \$50$$
$$\$100 = \$100$$

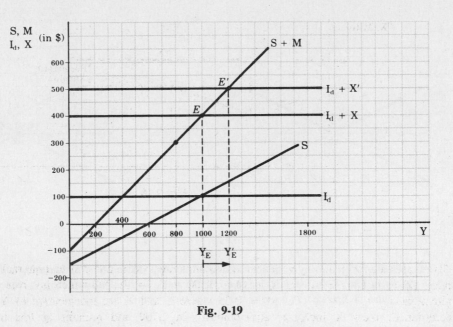

Fig. 9-19

Note that I_d is independent of Y, so that when Y rises from Y_E to Y_E', there is no induced change in domestic investment (i.e., $\Delta I_d = 0$). Since $\Delta X = \$100$ while $\Delta M = \$50$, the nation faces a persistent surplus in its balance of payments of $50 per time period at $Y_E' = \$1,200$.

9.25 (a) Draw a figure for Problem 9.23 similar to Fig. 9-16.   (b) What would happen if X had fallen rather than risen autonomously by $100?

   (a)   The slope of the S + M function in Fig. 9-19 equals MPS + MPM = 0.25 + 0.25 = 0.5. Also, at point E and $Y_E = \$1,000$, $I_d = S = \$100$, $X = M = \$300$ and $S + M = I_d + X = \$100 + \$300 = \$400$. At point E' and $Y_E' = \$1,200$, $S + M = I_d + X' = \$500$ but $X' > M$ by $50, the same amount by which $S > I_d$. Note that for simplicity, we have implicitly assumed throughout that the I_d, S, X and M functions are straight lines (i.e., the marginal propensities remain constant). Note that the horizontal and vertical scales in Fig. 9-19 are different.

   (b)   If X had instead fallen autonomously by $100, we can see from Fig. 9-19 that now $Y_E' = \$800$, at which $S + M = I_d + X' = \$300$ with $M > X'$ by $50, the same amount by which $I_d > S$.

9.26 (a) Derive the X − M function from Fig. 9-16 (before the autonomous increase in X) and the S − I_d function from Fig. 9-14 (before the autonomous increase in I_d) and plot them on a graph. (b) What is the equilibrium Y in Fig. 9-20? Why?   (c) What is the usefulness of Fig. 9-20 as compared to Fig. 9-19?

   (a)   From Fig. 9-16, we get that at Y = 0, X = $300 and M = $50; therefore, X − M = $250 (the vertical intercept in Fig. 9-20). The values of X − M at other levels of Y are similarly obtained. The X − M function is negatively sloped because we are subtracting rising M from constant X. That is, the balance of trade deteriorates as Y rises. From Fig. 9-14, we get that at Y = 0, S = −$150 and $I_d = \$100$; therefore, $S − I_d = −\$150 − \$100 = −\$250$ (the vertical intercept in Fig. 9-20). The values of $S − I_d$ at other levels of Y are similarly obtained. The $S − I_d$ function is positively sloped because we are subtracting a constant I_d from rising S.

   (b)   In Problem 9.24(a), we saw that the equilibrium condition for Y is given by

$$I_d + X = S + M$$

which, by transposing I_d and M, gives

$$X − M = S − I_d$$

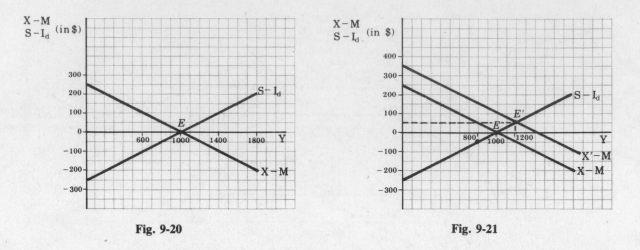

Fig. 9-20   Fig. 9-21

Graphically, Y_E is given at the intersection of the $X - M$ and $S - I_d$ functions and equals $1,000 (the same as in Fig. 9.19). $X - M$ is often referred to as *net foreign investment* (I_f) since a trade surplus or deficit must be financed by some sort of capital movement. Thus, the above equilibrium condition of

$$X - M = S - I_d$$

can be rewritten as

$$I_f = S - I_d$$

which equals

$$I_d + I_f = S$$

(c)   The usefulness of Fig. 9-20 over Fig. 9-19 is that in Fig. 9-20, we can read off more clearly and readily what the balance of trade is at Y_E. Since in Fig. 9-20, the $X - M$ and $S - I_d$ functions cross on the horizontal or income axis, $X - M = I_f = 0$ (i.e., $X = M$, as at point E in Fig. 9-19).

9.27   (a) Redraw Fig. 9-20, showing what happens if there is an autonomous increase in X of $100. (b) What happens if there is instead an autonomous decrease in X of $100?

(a)   An autonomous increase in X of $100 causes the $X - M$ function to shift up vertically by $100 to $X' - M$ in Fig. 9-21. This gives $Y'_E = $1,200$, at which $X' - M = I_f = S - I_d = 50 (as at point E' in Fig. 9-19). Thus, the original autonomous increase in X and trade surplus of $100 were partially neutralized by the induced increase in M resulting from the increase in Y_E to Y'_E.

(b)   Starting from equilibrium point E in Fig. 9-21, if there is an autonomous fall in X of $100, we can see that now $Y'_E = 800, at which $X' - M = I_f = S - I_d = -50 [the same as in Problem 9.25(b)]. Thus, the original autonomous decrease in X and trade deficit of $100 are partially neutralized by the induced fall in M resulting from the fall in Y. Note also that an autonomous fall in X has the same effect as an autonomous rise in M, and vice versa.

9.28   Starting from equilibrium point E in Fig. 9-20 and widespread domestic unemployment,   (a) show what happens if I_d increases autonomously by $200 and remains at this higher level.   (b) What if there is instead an autonomous decrease in I_d of $100?   (c) What if there is instead an autonomous increase in S of $100? An autonomous decrease of $100?

(a)   An autonomous increase in I_d of $200 causes the $S - I_d$ function to shift down vertically by $200 to $S - I'_d$ in Fig. 9.22 because the negative term is increased. This gives $Y^*_E = $1,400$, at which $X - M = I_f = S - I_d = -100.

(b)   If there is instead an autonomous decrease in I_d of $100, $S - I_d$ shifts up vertically by $100, and we can see that now $Y^*_E = 800, at which $X - M = I_f = S - I_d = 50.

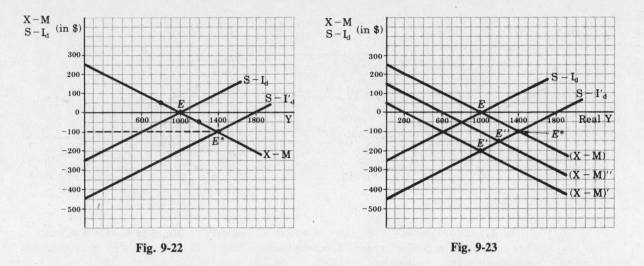

Fig. 9-22   Fig. 9-23

(c) An autonomous increase in S of $100 causes the $S - I_d$ function to shift up vertically by $100 just as in the case of an autonomous decrease in I_d of $100, and the result is the same. Starting from equilibrium point E in Fig. 9.22, if there is instead an autonomous decrease in S of $100, we can see that now $Y_E^* = $1,200$, at which $X - M = I_f = S - I_d' = -100 (net foreign disinvestment). Note that increases in X and S help the balance of payments, while increases in M and I_d hurt it.

9.29   Starting from equilibrium point E in Fig. 9-22,   (a) show what happens if there is an autonomous increase in I_d by $200, but the full-employment level of national income, $Y_F = $1,000$.   (b) What if Y_F were $1,200?

(a) Since we are told that $Y_E = Y_F = $1,000$ to begin with, *real* national income cannot now rise above $Y_F = $1,000$ to $Y_E^* = $1,400$ as in Problem 9.28(a), when $S - I_d$ shifts down to $S - I_d'$. The result is that only the domestic price level will rise. But as prices rise, the nation's X fall and its M rise. Both of these changes cause the $(X - M)$ function to shift down until it intersects the $S - I_d'$ function at $Y_F = $1,000$. This occurs when the $(X - M)$ function has shifted down to $(X - M)'$. (See Fig. 9-23.) The result is equilibrium point E', at which $Y_E' = Y_F = Y_E = $1,000$ and $(X - M)' = I_f = S - I_d' = -200. Thus, starting from full employment and equilibrium in the balance of payments (point E in Fig. 9-23), an autonomous increase in investment causes domestic inflation which opens a deficit in the nation's balance of payments.

(b) Starting from equilibrium point E in Fig. 9-23 but with $Y_F = $1,200$ instead, the downward shift in the $S - I_d$ function to $S - I_d'$ causes real national income to rise from $Y_E = $1,000$ to $Y_F = $1,200$. However, domestic prices will also have to rise sufficiently to cause the $(X - M)$ function to shift down to $(X - M)''$ to give equilibrium point E''. At E'', $Y_E'' = Y_F = $1,200$ and $(X - M)'' = I_f = S - I_d' = -150. So far, we have implicitly assumed that domestic prices remain constant until real Y_F is reached, after which, they rise. In the real world, we know that prices can rise even at less than full employment and rise faster as we approach full employment (refer to the Phillips curve in your principles text).

9.30   So far in our discussion, we have also implicitly assumed that the nation is small, so that there are *no foreign repercussions*. We have also assumed no *accelerator*.   (a) What is meant by foreign repercussions?   (b) What are the foreign repercussions resulting from an autonomous increase in the exports of nation 1 and nation 2?   (c) What are the foreign repercussions on nation 1 resulting from an autonomous increase in I_d?   (d) What is meant by the accelerator. How would its inclusion affect the above analysis?

(a) In a world of two large nations (nation 1 and nation 2), a change in the level of trade of nation 1 also affects the level of national income of nation 2. This in turn affects the level of trade and national income of nation 1 and is a foreign repercussion for nation 1.

(b)

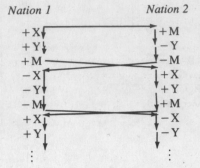

These foreign repercussions peter out and dampen the original autonomous increase in X of nation 1. When foreign trade multiplier for nation 1 for an autonomous increase in its exports which replace domestic production in nation 2 is given by

$$k = \frac{1}{MPS_1 + MPM_1 + MPM_2(MPS_1/MPS_2)}$$

which is smaller than k without foreign repercussions.

(b)

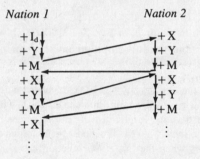

These foreign repercussions peter out and dampen the effect of the original autonomous increase in I_d in nation 1. For nation 1, then

$$k = \frac{1 + (MPM_2/MPS_2)}{MPS_1 + MPM_1 + MPM_2(MPS_1/MPS_2)}$$

which is larger than the multiplier in part (b). Note that this is how the business cycle is propagated from one nation to others. Foreign repercussions can be safely neglected only if the nation is very small.

(d) The accelerator refers to the rise in I_d as Y rises, so that the I_d function is positively sloped rather than horizontal. Accelerators have fallen somewhat into disuse, and so they have not been included. There is also a possibility that X fall as Y rise or that X come out of past rather than current production. These complications have also been implicitly ignored.

SYNTHESIS OF AUTOMATIC PRICE AND INCOME ADJUSTMENTS UNDER FLEXIBLE EXCHANGE RATES

9.31 Assume that (1) a nation's $S - I_d$ function is a straight line with slope of 1 while its $X - M$ function is a straight line with slope of -1; (2) the $S - I_d$ and $X - M$ functions intersect at $Y_E = \$1,000$, showing a deficit of \$100 in the nation's balance of trade and payments; (3) the full-employment level of income $Y_F = \$1,400$; and (4) the foreign exchange market is stable.   (a) Draw a figure showing how the nation can reach equilibrium in its balance of trade and payments under a flexible exchange rate system; by how much will the X − M function have to shift up in order to correct the $100 deficit?   (b) Show what happens if the full-employment level of income $Y_F = Y_E = \$1,000$.

(a)   The nation is originally at point E in Fig. 9-24, with $Y_E = \$1,000$ and a deficit of $100. With a stable foreign exchange market, the nation's currency will depreciate sufficiently to shift its X − M function up to (X − M)′, so that it intersects the unchanged S − I_d function on the horizontal axis at Y = $1,200 (point E′ in Fig. 9-24). The X − M function had to shift up by $200 (EA in Fig. 9-24) because the rise in the nation's real income induces its imports to rise (which reduces the original improvement).

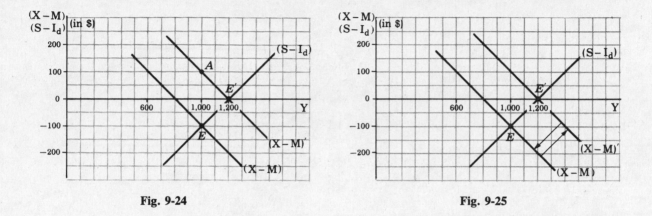

Fig. 9-24   Fig. 9-25

(b)   If the nation were already at full employment at $Y_E = \$1,000$, the depreciation of its currency tends to shift its X − M function up to (X − M)′ and correct the deficit as in part (a). However, the resulting demand-pull inflation will eliminate the price advantage that the depreciation of the currency was supposed to give the nation, so that the nation's X − M function shifts back to its original position and the deficit remains uncorrected (see Fig. 9-25).

9.32   Suppose that a nation is at full employment without inflation but has a deficit in its balance of payments. (a) Explain why a depreciation of the nation's currency will not correct the deficit unless real output rises or domestic expenditures or absorption fall.   (b) How can the nation's output rise as a result of the depreciation?   (c) How can domestic absorption fall automatically as a result of the depreciation? (d) How can the government help reduce domestic absorption and make the devaluation effective?

(a)   Depreciation of the nation's currency stimulates the nation's exports and its production of import substitutes. However, unless real output can somehow be expanded and/or domestic absorption reduced, this will lead to excess aggregate demand. The resulting inflation will then wipe out the price advantage of the devaluation and the deficit will remain uncorrected.

(b)   Even if the nation is already at full employment, depreciation of the nation's currency could lead to higher real national output through the better utilization and the more economic allocation of existing resources. Though possible, this is by no means certain or sufficient. Thus, for depreciation to be effective, domestic absorption must fall.

(c)   Domestic absorption can fall automatically as the nation's currency depreciates because of a real cash balance effect, money illusion and redistributive effect. The real cash balance effect operates as follows: When a nation's currency depreciates, domestic prices rise; if the money supply remains constant, real cash balances fall and can be replenished only by reducing consumption or absorption. The money illusion cuts absorption if consumers spend less when prices rise, even though their incomes have also risen. Finally, absorption falls if the depreciation redistributes income to consumers with higher marginal propensities to save. However, these effects may be inoperative or insufficient.

(d)   The government can help reduce domestic absorption (and allow the depreciation to be effective) by adopting expenditure-reducing policies. These are discussed in Chapter 10.

SYNTHESIS OF AUTOMATIC ADJUSTMENTS UNDER THE GOLD-EXCHANGE STANDARD

9.33 (a) Draw a figure similar to Fig. 9-10 and explain how the gold-exchange standard would operate if the par value is set or pegged at $2.50 = £1 and U.S. monetary authorities actively intervene in the foreign exchange market and sell or buy pounds for dollars to prevent the exchange rate from moving more than 1% above or below the par value. (b) Could we have a fixed exchange rate system without any connection with gold?

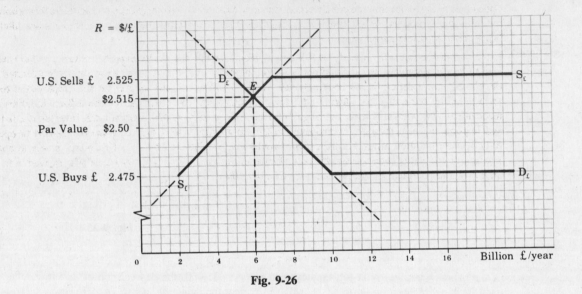

Fig. 9-26

(a) Figure 9-26 is identical to Fig. 9-10 except that we now have the par value instead of the mint parity and the U.S. selling or buying price of pounds instead of the U.S. gold export and gold import points. At $R = \$2.525$, the U.S. sells pounds (out of its reserves) to prevent any further increase in R (or further depreciation of the dollar). Thus, $S_£$ has a kink and becomes infinitely elastic at $R = \$2.525$. On the other hand, at $R = \$2.475$, the U.S. buys pounds (adding to its international reserves) to prevent any further decrease in R (or appreciation of the dollar). Thus, $D_£$ becomes infinitely elastic at $R = \$2.475$. Under this system, the exchange rate is determined by $D_£$ and $S_£$ within the support prices (point E in Fig. 9-26), and is prevented from moving outside the allowed band of fluctuation by active intervention by the monetary authorities (in a way analogous to that discussed in Problems 9.14 and 9.15). The size of the intervention required determines the size of the nation's deficit or surplus and points to the need for adjustment. Under the gold-exchange standard, it actually was nations other than the U.S. that generally intervened in foreign exchange markets with purchases or sales of dollars to keep exchange rates within the allowed band of fluctuation. For its part, the U.S. stood ready to exchange foreign official holdings of dollars for gold on demand and at the fixed price of $35 per ounce. This system operated from the end of World War II until 1971, when it collapsed (see Chapter 12).

(b) We could have a fixed exchange rate system without any connection with gold if national monetary authorities use only convertible currencies as international reserves to intervene in foreign exchange markets in order to keep exchange rates within the agreed band of fluctuation. This is essentially the system that operated from the collapse of the gold-exchange standard in 1971 until 1973, when a flexible exchange system of sorts came into existence (see Chapter 12).

9.34 (a) Explain in detail how a surplus in a nation's balance of payments, resulting from an autonomous increase in its exports (from a position of less than full employment), may be corrected automatically under the gold-exchange standard. (b) Explain why the surplus and deficit nations may not be willing to allow the automatic adjustment mechanisms to operate under the gold-exchange standard. What is the result of their unwillingness?

(a) Unless neutralized, the autonomous increase in exports causes the nation's real national income to rise. This induces an increase in the nation's imports, which only partially offsets the surplus (since MPS > 0 in the real world). The increase in the real national income of the surplus nation is also likely to cause its prices to rise in relation to prices abroad. In addition, its exchange rate is likely to appreciate (within the allowed limits). These encourage the surplus nation's imports and discourage its exports and so reinforce the income adjustment mechanism. Furthermore, the inflow of reserves to the surplus nation, unless neutralized, increases the nation's money supply and may lead to lower interest rates. This tends to increase investment, income and imports and also stimulates a capital outflow, all of which help the adjustment process. The exact opposite is likely to occur in the deficit nation, and this, together with foreign repercussions, further reinforces the adjustment process. When considered together, these automatic adjustment mechanisms are likely to bring about complete adjustment.

(b) If the surplus nation were already at full employment, an increase in its exports (*ceteris paribus*) would lead to excess aggregate demand and demand-pull inflation—and this is usually not passively tolerated. On the other hand, a deficit nation is usually not willing to allow its national income and employment to fall as required by the automatic income adjustment mechanism. The other part of the automatic adjustment mechanism—the one that operates through a change in the money supply, interest rates, investments, income and imports and also through international short-term capital flows—may also not be allowed to operate fully because it would mean that the nations would have to give up their use of monetary policy to correct unemployment and/or inflation for the sake of external balance. The only way out of this impasse is to rely on *policies* to complete the adjustment (see Chapter 10).

Chapter 10

Adjustment Policies: Open Economy Macroeconomics

10.1 ECONOMIC OBJECTIVES OF NATIONS

Among the most important economic objectives of nations are the maintenance of internal and external balance. *Internal balance* refers to domestic full employment with price stability. *External balance* refers to equilibrium in the nation's balance of payments. If a conflict arises, internal balance usually takes precedence over external balance.

With at least two objectives, a minimum of two policy instruments are usually necessary to achieve both objectives *completely*. Each policy tool should be paired with the target on which it is most effective.

10.2 INTERNAL BALANCE WITH EXPENDITURE-CHANGING POLICIES

Domestic unemployment can be corrected with expenditure-increasing (i.e., expansionary fiscal and monetary) policies. Expansionary *fiscal policy* refers to an increase in government expenditures and/or reduction in taxes. Easy *monetary policy* refers to an increase in the nation's money supply and leads to a reduction in the nation's interest rates, which stimulates investments. If unemployment is accomplished by a deficit in the nation's balance of payments, the expansion in national income (to eliminate unemployment) induces a rise in imports and the reduction in interest rates may lead to a larger short-term capital outflow (or reduced inflow), both of which increase the deficit. If unemployment is accompanied by a surplus, reducing unemployment will also reduce the surplus.

On the other hand, expenditure-reducing (i.e., restrictive fiscal and monetary) policies to curb inflationary pressures in the economy would increase a surplus but reduce a deficit.

EXAMPLE 1. Table 10.1 gives the four possible combinations of internal and external imbalance, the *expenditure-changing policies* to achieve internal balance in each case, and their effects on the external imbalance.

Table 10.1

Case	Policy for Internal Balance	Effect on External Balance
I Unemployment with deficit	Expansionary	Worsens
II Unemployment with surplus	Expansionary	Improves
III Inflation with surplus	Restrictive	Worsens
IV Inflation with deficit	Restrictive	Improves

Note that in cases I and III there is a conflict between internal and external balance. Even if there is no conflict (cases II and IV), the use of fiscal and monetary policies to achieve internal balance will improve the external balance, but are not likely to completely eliminate the external imbalance. Similarly, if external balance were given priority, internal balance could not be achieved (see Problem 10.5). To achieve both simultaneously, we need two policy tools.

10.3 EXTERNAL BALANCE WITH EXPENDITURE-SWITCHING POLICIES

External balance can usually be achieved with *expenditure-switching policies*. These refer primarily to devaluation and revaluation. *Devaluation* refers to an increase in the exchange rate from one par value to another.

This normally stimulates the devaluing nation's exports, reduces its imports and improves the nation's balance of trade and payments, and so it could be used to correct a deficit. A *revaluation* refers to the opposite and could be used to correct a surplus.

EXAMPLE 2.   Figure 10-1 shows an economy operating at point E, with unemployment and a deficit of $100 in its balance of trade and payments (case I in Table 10.1). To correct the deficit, the nation could devalue its currency sufficiently to shift the $X - M$ function up to $(X - M)'$, so that it intersects the unchanged $S - I_d$ function on the horizontal axis (so $X = M$) at the higher real income of $Y_E' = \$2,400$. Note that to correct a deficit of $100, the $X - M$ function had to shift up by $200 ($EA$ in Fig. 10-1) because the rise in the nation's real income (from Y_E to Y_E') induces its M to rise (which reduces the original improvement). We can sometimes get a rough indication of the size of the devaluation required by the purchasing-power-parity theory (see Problem 10.9). However, if the economy were already at full employment at point E, the devaluation would be effective only if domestic expenditures or absorption were reduced, automatically (by a real cash balance effect, money illusion, and redistributive effect) or by expenditure-reducing policies (see Problem 10.10).

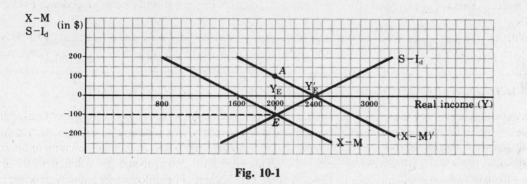

Fig. 10-1

10.4   INTERNAL AND EXTERNAL BALANCE WITH EXPENDITURE-CHANGING AND -SWITCHING POLICIES

By using an expenditure-changing (i.e., fiscal) policy for internal balance and an expenditure-switching policy (i.e., devaluation or revaluation) for external balance, both objectives of internal and external balance can be achieved simultaneously. (Monetary policy will be reintroduced in the next section so that we may now avoid dealing with changes in short-term international capital movements.)

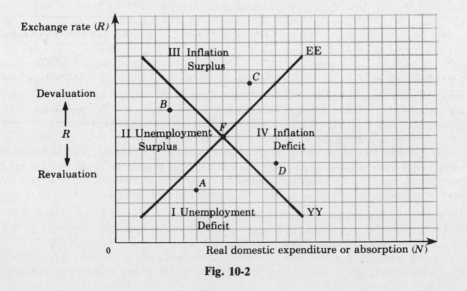

Fig. 10-2

EXAMPLE 3. In Fig. 10-2, the various combinations of exchange rates (R) and real domestic expenditure or absorption (N) that give internal balance are shown by the YY curve. The YY curve is negatively inclined, showing that an increase in N must be balanced by a decrease in the nation's R (to reduce its trade balance) in order to remain at full employment without inflation. Points above the curve refer to inflation, while points below to unemployment. On the other hand, the EE curve gives all points of external balance X = M (for zero net capital movements). The EE curve is positively inclined, showing that a devaluation (which improves the nation's trade balance) must be balanced by an increase in N (to induce the nation's imports to rise sufficiently) to remain in external balance. Points above the EE curve refer to surplus, while points below to deficit. The crossing of the two curves defines the four cases of internal and external imbalance shown in Table 10.1. Table 10.2 gives the fiscal and expenditure-switching policies needed to reach internal and external balance simultaneously (point F in Fig. 10-2), starting from points A, B, C and D.

Table 10.2

Point	Fiscal Policy for Internal Balance	Policy for External Balance
A (Unemployment with deficit)	Expansionary	Devaluation
B (Unemployment with surplus)	Expansionary	Revaluation
C (Inflation with surplus)	Restrictive	Revaluation
D (Inflation with deficit)	Restrictive	Devaluation

10.5 INTERNAL AND EXTERNAL BALANCE WITH FISCAL AND MONETARY POLICIES

During the post-World War II period, nations were extremely reluctant to change the par value of their currencies to reach equilibrium, and did so only rarely, after long delays and when practically forced upon them, rather than as a matter of policy (see Problem 10.16). One possible way out of this impasse was to view fiscal policy and monetary policy as two *distinct* policy instruments and use fiscal policy for internal balance and monetary policy for external balance, so that both objectives could be achieved simultaneously without any change in exchange rates. This can be shown with *IS, LM and FE curves* (see Example 4), by having the IS and LM curves cross on the FE curve at the full employment level of national income (see Example 5).

EXAMPLE 4. The *IS curve* shows the various combinations of interest rates (r) and national income (Y) that result in equilibrium in the goods market (i.e., at which the quantity demanded of goods and services equals the quantity supplied). The IS curve is negatively inclined because a lower r is associated with a higher level of investment and Y for equilibrium in the goods market. The *LM curve* shows the various combinations of r and Y at which the money market is in equilibrium (i.e., at which the transaction and the speculative demand for money equal the given and fixed supply of money). The speculative demand for money is inversely related to r, while the transaction demand for money is proportional to Y [see Problem 10.18(a)]. The LM curve is positively inclined because the higher r is, the smaller is the quantity of money demanded for speculative purposes and the resultant larger supply of money available for transaction purposes will only be held at higher Y. The *FE curve* shows the various combinations of r and Y at which the nation's balance of payments is in equilibrium at a given exchange rate. The FE curve is positively inclined because a higher r leads to greater capital inflows (or smaller outflows) and must be balanced with a higher Y and imports (M) for the balance of payments to remain in equilibrium. Fiscal policy shifts the IS curve to the right if it is expansionary and to the left if it is contractionary [see Problem 10.17(d)]. Monetary policy shifts the LM curve to the right if it is easy and to the left if it is tight [see Problem 10.18(d)]. Equilibrium in the goods market, in the money market and in the balance of payments can be achieved simultaneously by using fiscal policy and monetary policy in such a way as to have the IS and the LM curves cross on the FE curve at the full employment level of national income.

EXAMPLE 5. In Fig. 10-3, the nation is in equilibrium in the goods and money markets at point E (with r = 10% and Y_E = 1,000) but faces recession or unemployment since the full employment level of national income is Y_F = 1,400. The nation also faces a balance of payments deficit because at Y_E = 1,000, r would have to be 12% (point H') to be on the FE curve. Alternatively, Y would have to be 800 (point H) to be on the FE curve at r = 10%. Starting at point E with unemployment and a deficit in its balance of payments, the nation can use expansionary fiscal policy to shift

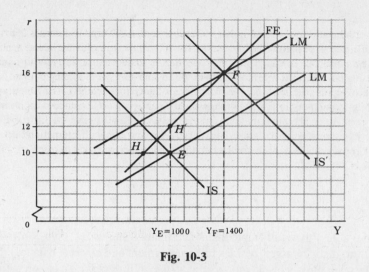

Fig. 10-3

the IS curve to the right to IS′ and tight monetary policy to shift the LM curve to the left to LM′ so that the IS′ and the LM′ curves cross at point F on the FE curve, with $r = 16\%$ and $Y_F = 1,400$. Then, the nation is in equilibrium in all three markets simultaneously. To see how the nation can reach equilibrium in all three markets simultaneously at Y_F when capital flows are perfectly elastic and under flexible exchange rates, see Problems 10.20 and 10.21, respectively.

10.6   THE POLICY MIX FOR INTERNAL AND EXTERNAL BALANCE

In the previous section, we have seen that to achieve internal and external balance simultaneously without changing the exchange rate, the nation must direct fiscal policy to achieve internal balance and monetary policy to achieve external balance. If the nation did the opposite, the nation would move further away from both balances. This can be shown with an internal balance *(IB) line* and an external balance *(EB) line*.

EXAMPLE 6.   In Fig. 10-4, movements along the horizontal axis away from the origin refer to expansionary fiscal policy (i.e., to higher government expenditures and/or taxes), while movements along the vertical axis away from the origin refer to tight monetary policy (i.e., to reductions in the nation's money supply and increases in interest rate). The IB line shows the various combinations of fiscal policy (G) and monetary policy (r) that result in internal balance. There is inflation below the IB line and unemployment above it. The IB line is positively inclined because expansionary fiscal policy must be balanced with a sufficiently tight monetary policy to remain on the IB line. On the other hand, the EB

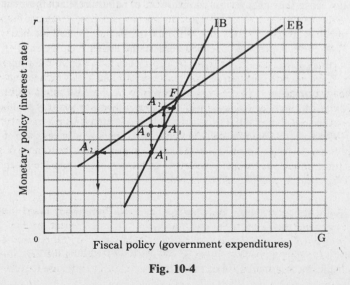

Fig. 10-4

line shows the various combinations of G and r that result in external balance. There is a deficit below the line and a surplus above it. The EB line is positively inclined because a higher G increases the level of national income (Y) and imports (M) and must be balanced with higher capital inflows (or smaller outflows), which require a higher r, for the nation to remain on the EB line. The EB line is flatter than the IB line because monetary policy also induces international short-term capital flows. Only at point F, where the IB and EB lines cross, is the nation simultaneously in internal and external balance. Starting at point A_0 in Fig. 10-4 showing unemployment and deficit, if the nation uses expansionary fiscal policy to reach point A_1 on the IB line, then tight monetary policy to reach A_2 on the EB line, and so on, the nation's policies will converge on point F (where the IB and EB lines cross). If the nation uses instead easy monetary policy to reach point A_1' on the IB line, then contractionary fiscal policy to reach A_2', and so on, the nation will move farther away from point F.

10.7   DIRECT CONTROLS

With prices rising even at less than full employment and rising faster as full employment is approached, price stability becomes a third, distinct target (besides full employment and external balance). Since there is usually a trade-off between the unemployment and inflation rates (the Phillips curve), a nation with stronger inflationary pressures may have to accept a higher rate of unemployment than a nation with weaker inflationary tendencies. If this is not sufficient or acceptable, domestic price and wage controls (incomes policy) may be necessary to curb inflation.

On the other hand, if short-term international capital movements do not readily respond to interest rate changes, or if monetary policy is used along with fiscal policy for internal balance, then an external imbalance can only be corrected with flexible exchange rates or suppressed with *trade and exchange controls*. The latter are interferences with the free international flow of goods, services and capital and are of many kinds [see Problem 10.31(b)]. Finally, a nation could strive to also achieve a "reasonable" rate of growth by changing its interest rate structure (see Problem 10.32).

Glossary

Internal balance   The objective of having full employment with price stability.

External balance   The objective of having equilibrium in the nation's balance of payments.

Fiscal policy   A policy based on changes in government expenditures, taxes or both.

Monetary policy   A policy based on the nation's monetary authorities making changes in the nation's money supply and the effect that these changes have on domestic interest rates.

Expenditure-changing policies   Fiscal and monetary policies to change the level of aggregate demand.

Expenditure-switching policies   Policies based primarily on a devaluation or revaluation of the nation's currency in order to switch the nation's expenditures from foreign to domestic producers or vice-versa.

Devaluation   The increase in the exchange rate from one par value to another made by the nation's monetary authorities.

Revaluation   A decrease in the exchange rate from one par value to another made by the nation's monetary authorities.

IS curve   The negatively inclined curve showing the various combinations of interest rates and national income levels at which the goods market is in equilibrium.

LM curve   The positively inclined curve showing the various combinations of interest rates and national income levels at which the money market is in equilibrium.

FE curve   The (usually) positively inclined curve showing the various combinations of interest rates and national income levels at which the nation's balance of payments is in equilibrium.

IB line   The positively inclined line showing the various combinations of fiscal and monetary policies that result in internal balance.

EB line   The positively inclined line showing the various combinations of fiscal and monetary policies that result in external balance.

Trade and exchange controls   A reference to tariffs, quotas, multiple exchange rates and restrictions on international capital movements.

Review Questions

1. The most important economic objective of the U.S. and most other developed nations is usually   (*a*) internal balance,   (*b*) external balance,   (*c*) a *reasonable* rate of growth,   (*d*) an equitable distribution of income.

   Ans.   (*a*) See Section 10.1.

2. To achieve three economic objectives simultaneously and completely, we usually need at least the following number of economic policy instruments: (*a*) one,   (*b*) two,   (*c*) three,   (*d*) four.

   Ans.   (*c*) See Section 10.1.

3. If a nation faces domestic unemployment and a deficit in its balance of payments, the use of expenditure-increasing policies to correct the unemployment will make the deficit   (*a*) smaller,   (*b*) larger,   (*c*) zero,   (*d*) any of the above.

   Ans.   (*b*) See Section 10.2 (case I in Table 10.1).

4. The use of expenditure-reducing policies to correct inflationary pressures in the economy will make   (*a*) a surplus smaller,   (*b*) a surplus larger,   (*c*) a deficit smaller,   (*d*) a deficit larger.

   Ans.   (*b*) and (*c*) See Section 10.2 (cases III and IV in Table 10.1).

5. The appropriate expenditure-switching policy to correct a deficit in the balance of payments is   (*a*) revaluation,   (*b*) devaluation,   (*c*) monetary policy,   (*d*) fiscal policy.

   Ans.   (*b*) See Section 10.3.

6. If the nation in Fig. 10-2 is on the YY curve above point *F*, the nation faces   (*a*) unemployment and surplus,   (*b*) inflation and surplus,   (*c*) internal balance and surplus,   (*d*) internal balance and deficit.

   Ans.   (*c*) Since the nation is on the YY curve, the nation is in internal balance. Since the nation is above the EE curve, the nation has a surplus.

7. If the nation in Fig. 10-2 is on the YY curve above point *F*, the nation can reach point *F* by   (*a*) devaluation and expansionary fiscal policy,   (*b*) revaluation and restrictive fiscal policy,   (*c*) devaluation and restrictive fiscal policy,   (*d*) revaluation and expansionary fiscal policy.

   Ans.   (*d*) To reach *F*, the nation has to move down (revaluation) and to the right to increase *N* (and this requires expansionary fiscal policy).

8. Points above the LM curve refer to   (*a*) excess demand for money,   (*b*) excess supply of money,   (*c*) unemployment,   (*d*) inflation.

   Ans.   (*b*) See Section 10.5.

9. To eliminate unemployment and a deficit in the balance of payments, the nation must employ   (a) contractionary fiscal policy and easy monetary policy,   (b) expansionary fiscal policy and tight monetary policy,   (c) contractionary fiscal policy and tight monetary policy,   (d) expansionary fiscal policy and easy monetary policy.

   Ans.   (b) See Section 10.5 and Fig. 10-3.

10. If the nation in Fig. 10-4 is on the EB line below point F, the nation faces   (a) unemployment and surplus,   (b) unemployment and deficit,   (c) external balance and unemployment,   (d) internal balance and surplus.

   Ans.   (c) Since the nation is on the EB line, the nation is in external balance. Since the nation is above the IB line, the nation faces unemployment.

11. If the nation in Fig. 10-4 is on the EB line below point F, the nation can reach point F by   (a) easy monetary policy and restrictive fiscal policy,   (b) tight monetary policy and expansionary fiscal policy,   (c) easy monetary policy and expansionary fiscal policy,   (d) tight monetary policy and restrictive fiscal policy.

   Ans.   (b) To reach point F, the nation has to move upward (tight monetary policy) and to the right (expansion of fiscal policy).

12. Trade and exchange controls refer to   (a) tariffs,   (b) quotas,   (c) multiple exchange rates,   (d) restrictions on international capital movements,   (e) all of the above.

   Ans.   (e) See Section 10.7.

Solved Problems

ECONOMIC OBJECTIVES OF NATIONS

10.1   (a) Identify several of the most important economic objectives or targets of nations. Which of these is normally given priority?   (b) What are some of the most important policy instruments or tools that a nation can employ to achieve these targets?   (c) How many policy instruments or tools does a nation need to reach its objectives?   (d) How does the nation decide which tool to use for each specific target?

   (a)   Some of the most important economic objectives are (1) internal balance, which refers to full employment (or an unemployment rate of no more than, say, 2 or 3%) and price stability (or a rate of inflation of no more than 2 or 3% per year); (2) external balance or equilibrium in the balance of payments; (3) a *reasonable* rate of growth and (4) an *equitable* distribution of income. Most nations normally regard internal balance as their most important economic objective, but they are sometimes forced to switch their priority to the external balance in the face of large and persistent balance of payments disequilibria.

   (b)   Some of the most important policy instruments available to a nation are (1) expenditure-changing or demand policies, which refer to fiscal policy (conducted by changing government expenditures and/or taxes) and monetary policy (which changes the money supply and affects interest rates); (2) expenditure-switching policies, which refer to devaluation and revaluation (however, nations have often been unwilling to utilize them) and (3) direct controls, or interferences with the operation of market forces and refer to price and wage controls, and trade and exchange controls. Direct controls are a last resort and are usually employed when other policies have been found to be ineffective.

   (c)   A nation generally needs an effective policy instrument or tool for each independent objective or target that it wants to reach. Sometimes a single tool will help the nation approach more than one target, but it is generally rare and coincidental that a nation will completely and simultaneously achieve more than one target with a single tool—or more targets than the number of tools at its disposal.

   (d)   Each tool should be paired with the target on which it is most effective. This is sometimes referred to as the *principle of effective market classification*.

INTERNAL BALANCE WITH EXPENDITURE-CHANGING POLICIES

10.2 Suppose a nation faces domestic unemployment and a surplus in its balance of payments.   (a) Explain in detail the expenditure-changing policies required to cure the unemployment.   (b) What would happen to the nation's external imbalance? Why?

(a) Domestic unemployment can be corrected with expenditure- or demand-increasing policies. These refer to expansionary fiscal and monetary policies. Expansionary fiscal policy refers to an increase in government expenditure and/or a reduction in taxes. A reduction in taxes leads to an increase in consumption, which as an increase in government expenditures, results in a multiple expansion in national income. On the other hand, easy monetary policy refers to an increase in the money supply and reduction in interest rates. These stimulate investment and also result in a multiple expansion in national income.

(b) If domestic unemployment was accompanied by a surplus in the nation's balance of payment (case II in Table 10.1), the expansion in national income (to eliminate unemployment) induces a rise in imports, and the reduction in interest rates (from the easy monetary policy) may lead to a larger short-term capital outflow (or reduced inflow), both of which reduce the surplus. Sometimes the original surplus could even turn into a deficit. This is more likely to occur when the original surplus is small, unemployment is large (so that strongly expansionary fiscal and monetary policies are needed), the marginal propensity to import is high, domestic prices rise as the economy approaches full employment, and capital movements readily respond to the fall in the interest rate. Only rarely and by coincidence will the elimination of unemployment also lead to complete external balance.

10.3 Suppose a nation faces domestic inflationary pressures (due to excess aggregate demand) and a surplus in its balance of payments.   (a) Explain in detail the expenditure-changing policics required to curb the inflationary pressures in the economy.   (b) What would happen to the nation's external imbalance? Why?

(a) Domestic inflationary pressures resulting from excess aggregate demand can be corrected with expenditure- or demand-decreasing policies. These refer to restrictive fiscal and monetary policies. Restrictive fiscal policy refers to a decrease in government expenditures and/or an increase in taxes. An increase in taxes leads to a reduction in consumption, which as a decrease in government expenditures, results in a multiple contraction in national income. On the other hand, tight monetary policy leads to higher interest rates, lower investments and a multiple contraction in national income.

(b) If the domestic inflation was accomplished by a surplus in the nation's balance of payments (case III in Table 10.1), curbing the inflation stimulates the nation's exports and discourages its imports, both of which improve the nation's trade balance. In addition, the increase in domestic interest rates (from the tight monetary policy) may lead to a larger short-term capital inflow (or reduced outflow). With an improved trade balance and a larger capital inflow or a reduced outflow, the original surplus in the nation's balance of payments will become even larger. Thus, the use of expenditure- or demand-increasing policies to achieve internal balance will worsen the external imbalance.

10.4 Suppose a nation faces domestic inflationary pressures due to excess aggregate demand and a deficit in its balance of payments.   (a) What expenditure-changing policies are required to achieve internal balance?   (b) What would happen to the nation's external imbalance? Why?

(a) Domestic inflationary pressures resulting from excess aggregate demand can be corrected with expenditure- or demand-decreasing policies. These refer to restrictive fiscal and monetary policies which operate exactly as described in Problem 10.3(a).

(b) If the domestic inflation was accompanied by a deficit in the nation's balance of payments (case IV in Table 10.1), curbing the inflation improves the nation's trade balance and also leads to a larger short-term capital inflow or reduced outflow [exactly as described in Problem 10.3(b)]. These cause the nation's deficit to be reduced, eliminated entirely or even turned into a surplus. A surplus is more likely to arise the smaller the original deficit, the more restrictive the fiscal and monetary policies required to curb the inflation, the more the nation's trade balance improves as a result of curbing inflation and the more responsive short-term capital movements are to a rise in interest rates. Only rarely and by coincidence will the expenditure- or demand-reducing policies imposed to correct the domestic inflation also and at the same time lead to complete external balance.

10.5 Suppose that a nation used its expenditure-changing policies to achieve external rather than internal balance. (*a*) Explain how a nation facing unemployment and a deficit in its balance of payments (case I in Table 10.1) can eliminate its deficit. What would happen to its level of unemployment? (*b*) Construct a table similar to Table 10.1, showing the type of policy required to achieve external balance and its effect on the internal imbalance for each of the four possible combinations of internal and external imbalance. (*c*) In which case does a conflict arise between external and internal balance?

(*a*) The nation can correct the deficit in its balance of payments by expenditure-decreasing (i.e., restrictive fiscal and monetary) policies. The resulting reduction in national income induces a decline in the nation's imports which improves its trade balance. In addition, the increase in the nation's interest rate (from its restrictive monetary policy) results in a larger short-term capital outflow or reduced outflow. In this way, the nation can pursue the precise expenditure-decreasing policies to achieve complete external balance. However, this will, at the same time, make the domestic recession worse.

(*b*)

Table 10.3

Case	Policy for External Balance	Effect on Internal Balance
I Unemployment with deficit	Restrictive	Worsens
II Unemployment with surplus	Expansionary	Improves
III Inflation with surplus	Expansionary	Worsens
IV Inflation with deficit	Restrictive	Improves

(*c*) In cases I and III in Table 10.3, there is a conflict between external and internal balance. Even if there is no conflict (cases II and IV), the use of fiscal and monetary policies to achieve external balance will improve the internal imbalance, but only rarely and by chance will they completely eliminate it. A situation similar to case I was faced by the U.S. in the early 1950s, 1960s and 1970s and by the U.K. in the mid-1960s, and while the U.S. gave priority to the internal balance, the U.K. gave it to the external balance. In 1961, Germany faced case III and also gave priority to the external balance. In general, however, it is internal balance that is given priority when a conflict arises.

EXTERNAL BALANCE WITH EXPENDITURE-SWITCHING POLICIES

10.6 (*a*) Explain what is meant by devaluation. Does this differ from depreciation? (*b*) Explain what is meant by revaluation. Does this differ from appreciation? (*c*) Why are devaluation and revaluation referred to as expenditure-switching policies? (*d*) Under what condition is a devaluation or a revaluation effective in correcting a deficit or a surplus in a nation's balance of payments? When are they feasible?

(*a*) Devaluation refers to an increase in the exchange rate from one par value to another and could be used as a policy instrument by a nation under a fixed exchange rate system to correct a deficit in its balance of payments. On the other hand, depreciation refers to an increase in the exchange rate [see Problem 7.6(*b*)] resulting from the free operation of the market forces of demand and supply under a flexible exchange rate system. Sometimes this distinction is not made and the two terms are used interchangeably.

(*b*) Revaluation refers to a decrease in the exchange rate from one par value to another and could be used as a policy instrument by a nation under a fixed exchange rate system to correct a surplus in its balance of payments. On the other hand, appreciation refers to a decrease in the exchange rate [see Problem 7.7(*b*)] resulting from the free operation of the market forces of demand and supply under a flexible exchange rate system. Sometimes the two terms are used interchangeably.

(c)   Devaluation and revaluation are referred to as expenditure-switching policies because they switch expenditures from foreign to domestic goods and services and vice versa. More specifically, by increasing the price of a unit of the foreign currency, devaluation will make a nation's imports more expensive in terms of the domestic currency (see Problem 9.5) and its exports cheaper to foreigners in terms of the foreign currency (see Problem 9.8). This causes expenditures to be switched from foreign to domestic goods as the nation satisfies more of its needs by domestic production rather than through imports, and as the nation's exports rise. Similarly, a revaluation stimulates the nation's imports and discourages its exports, thus switching expenditures from domestic to foreign goods and services.

(d)   As with depreciation or appreciation, devaluation or revaluation can correct a deficit or surplus in a nation's balance of payments only if the foreign exchange market is stable (see Problem 9.10). If the foreign exchange market were unstable, a revaluation (not a devaluation) would be required to correct a deficit, and a devaluation (not a revaluation) would be needed to correct a surplus (see Fig. 9-8). Assuming a stable market, expenditure-switching policies become more feasible as policy instruments to correct balance of payments disequilibria, the more elastic is the demand and supply of foreign exchange [see Problem 9.6(c)].

10.7   Assume that (1) a nation's $S - I_d$ function is a straight line with slope of 1 while its $X - M$ function is a straight line with slope of -1, (2) the $S - I_d$ and $X - M$ functions intersect at $Y_E = \$2,000$ showing a deficit of $200 in the nation's balance of trade and payments and (3) the foreign exchange market is stable.   (a) Draw a figure showing how the nation can reach equilibrium in its balances of trade and payments by altering the exchange rate.   (b) If, at $Y_E = \$2,000$, the nation also faces unemployment, what would happen to its level of unemployment as the nation's deficit is corrected? (c) What would happen if the nation altered the exchange rate sufficiently to correct its deficit, but the nation initially faced excess aggregate demand and demand-pull inflation at $Y_E = \$2,000$?

(a)   The nation is originally at point E in Fig. 10-5, with $Y_E = \$2,000$ and a deficit of $200. With a stable foreign exchange market, the nation could correct the deficit by devaluing its currency sufficiently to shift its $X - M$ function up to $(X - M)'$, so that it intersects the unchanged $S - I_d$ function on the horizontal axis (so $X = M$) at the higher real income of $2,400 (point E' in Fig. 10-5). Note that to correct a deficit of $200, the $X - M$ function had to shift up by $400 ($EA$ in Fig. 10-5) because the rise in the nation's real income induces its imports to rise (which reduces the original improvement).

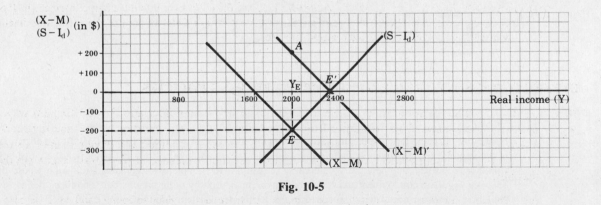

Fig. 10-5

(b)   If, at point E, the nation faces unemployment with a deficit (case I in Tables 10.1 and 10.3), the elimination of the deficit with a devaluation would reduce or eliminate unemployment and the nation may even face inflation. Specifically, if the full-employment level of real national income with price stability, $Y_F > \$2,400$, then unemployment would be reduced when the deficit is eliminated with the devaluation. If instead $Y_F = \$2,400$, the devaluation that eliminates the deficit will also and at the same time completely eliminate unemployment. If $Y_F < \$2,400$, say $2,200, then the devaluation that seems to be required to correct the deficit will not only eliminate unemployment, but will turn it into excess aggregated demand and demand-pull inflation. This in turn reduces the price advantage that nation receives from the devaluation.

(c) If the nation faced inflation with deficit at point E in Fig. 10-5 (case IV in Tables 10.1 and 10.3), the devaluation would add to the excess aggregate demand and the resulting higher inflation rate would quickly undo the price advantage of the devaluation [i.e., the $(X - M)'$ function would shift back to its original position]. In this case, a devaluation by itself would be the wrong policy. Expenditure-reducing policies are now required. These would eliminate or reduce the inflation, and thereby reduce the nation's deficit (see Problem 10.4).

10.8   Assume that (1) a nation's $S - I_d$ function is a straight line with slope of 1/2 while its $X - M$ function is a straight line with slope of $-1/2$; (2) the $S - I_d$ and $X - M$ functions intersect at $Y_E = \$2,000$ showing a surplus of $100 in the nation's balance of trade and payments; and (3) the foreign exchange market is stable.   (a) Draw a figure showing how the nation can reach equilibrium in its balance of trade and payments by altering the exchange rate.   (b) If, at $Y_E = \$2,000$, the nation also faces unemployment, what would happen to its level of unemployment as the nation's surplus is corrected? (c) What type of internal imbalance would the nation face (together with the surplus) if the full-employment level of real national income with price stability, $Y_F < Y_E = \$2,000$?   (d) What would happen to the internal balance if $Y_F = \$1,400$, $\$1,600$ or $\$1,800$ and the nation altered the exchange rate sufficiently to achieve external balance?

(a)   The nation is originally at point E in Fig. 10-6, with $Y_E = \$2,000$ and a surplus of $100. With a stable foreign exchange market, the nation could correct the surplus by revaluing its currency sufficiently to shift its $X - M$ function down to $(X - M)'$, so that it intersects the unchanged $S - I_d$ function on the horizontal axis (so $X = M$) at the lower real income of $1,600 (point E' in Fig. 10-6). Note that to correct a surplus of $100, the $X - M$ function must shift down by $200 ($EA$ in Fig. 10-6), because as the $X - M$ function shifts down, Y falls and induces a fall in the nation's imports which neutralizes part of the original effect of the revaluation.

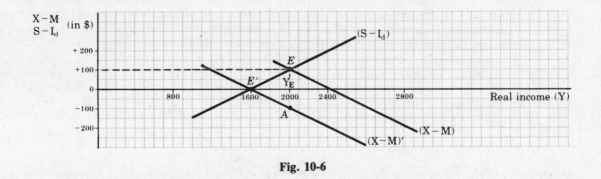

Fig. 10-6

(b)   If, at point E, the nation faces unemployment with a surplus (case II in Tables 10.1 and 10.3), the elimination of the surplus with a revaluation would increase domestic unemployment. On the other hand, a devaluation would reduce unemployment but would cause the surplus to become even greater. The nation would then be *exporting* its unemployment and this would invite retaliation by other nations that also faced deflationary tendencies. This is indeed what happened in the 1930s (see Chapter 12).

(c)   If the full-employment level of real national income with price stability, $Y_F < Y_E = \$2,000$, then the nation would initially face excess aggregate demand and demand-pull inflation together with a surplus at point E (case III in Tables 10.1 and 10.3). The elimination of the surplus with a revaluation then reduces the inflation, eliminates it or results in unemployment.

(d)   If $Y_F = \$1,400$, the nation ends up with a lower excess aggregate demand and rate of inflation as it revalues its currency sufficiently to eliminate the surplus. If $Y_F = \$1,600$, the nation eliminates the surplus and the inflation completely with the revaluation. If $Y_F = \$1,800$, the inflation would give way to unemployment as the surplus is eliminated with the revaluation. This once again points to the conclusion that to achieve complete internal and external balance simultaneously, two policy tools are normally needed. Note also that we have implicitly assumed that domestic prices remain constant until full employment is reached.

10.9 In the real world, nations usually do not know the shape of the demand and the supply curve of foreign exchange and so they do not know how much to devalue or revalue their currencies to correct a deficit or surplus in the balance of payments. They can, sometimes, get a rough indication from *the purchasing-power-parity* (PPP) theory. In its absolute version, this states that the exchange rate between two currencies should equal the ratio of the price indexes in the two nations. In its more refined, relative formulation, it states that the change in the exchange rate should equal the relative change in relative prices in the two nations. With regard to the above, restate in symbols   (a) the absolute version of this doctrine and   (b) the relative version. What is their usefulness?

(a)   Letting a = our country (the U.S.) and b = the foreign country (the U.K.), then R_{ab} = the price of foreign exchange in terms of our currency (or \$/£). The absolute formulation of the purchasing-power-parity doctrine can then be stated as

$$R_{ab} = \frac{P_a}{P_b}$$

where P_a = the price index in nation a and P_b = the price index in nation b. This says, for example, that if the price level in the U.S. is double the price level in the U.K., then the exchange rate should be \$2 = £1. The absolute formulation of the PPP theory is grossly incorrect and cannot be taken seriously because it fails to take into account transportation costs and other obstructions to the free flow of trade, and it does not consider capital flows and nontraded goods.

(b)   Letting 0 = the base period and 1 = period 1, then according to the relative formulation:

$$\frac{R_{ab1}}{R_{ab0}} = \frac{P_{a1}/P_{a0}}{P_{b1}/P_{b0}}$$

This says that the change in the exchange rate should be the same as the change in relative prices in the two nations. For example, assuming that P_{b1}/P_{b0} is fixed and is not affected by what nation a does (i.e., nation a is very small), if nation a were in equilibrium before its prices rose by 100%, nation a should devalue by 100% to return to equilibrium. This relative formulation holds, as a first approximation, only if the disturbance results exclusively from different rates of inflation in the two nations. Even then, serious index number problems remain. With structural changes (i.e., with changes in technology, resource supplies, tastes, long-term capital movements or with war), even this formulation is useless. In these cases, the nation could allow the exchange rate to freely fluctuate for a while to find its own equilibrium level before repegging it.

10.10 Suppose that a nation is at full employment without inflation but has a deficit in its balance of payments. (a) Explain why a devaluation will not correct the deficit unless real output rises or domestic expenditures or absorption fall.   (b) How can the nation's output rise as a result of the devaluation? (c) How can domestic absorption fall automatically as a result of the devaluation?   (d) How can the government help reduce domestic absorption and make the devaluation effective?

(a)   A devaluation stimulates the nation's exports and its production of import substitutes. However, unless real output can somehow be expanded and/or domestic absorption reduced, this will lead to excess aggregate demand. The resulting inflation will then wipe out the price advantage of the devaluation and the deficit will remain uncorrected.

(b)   Even if the nation is already at full employment, a devaluation could lead to higher real national output through the better utilization and the more economic allocation of existing resources. Though possible, this is by no means certain or sufficient. Thus, for a devaluation to be effective, domestic absorption must fall.

(c)   Domestic absorption can fall automatically as a result of a devaluation because of a real cash balance effect, money illusion and redistributive effect. The real cash balance effect operates as follows: When a nation devalues, domestic prices rise; if the money supply remains constant, real cash balances fall and can be replenished only by reducing consumption or absorption. The money illusion cuts absorption if consumers spend less when prices rise, even though their incomes have also risen. Finally, absorption falls if the devaluation redistributes income to consumers with higher marginal propensities to save. However, these effects may be inoperative or insufficient.

(d) The government can help reduce domestic absorption (and allow the devaluation to be effective) by adopting expenditure-reducing policies. Thus, once again we see that to achieve simultaneous internal and external balance, two policy tools are required. Note that up to the last sentence, the answer to this problem is identical to that of Problem 9.32, except that we are now examining the effect of a devaluation rather than of a depreciation.

INTERNAL AND EXTERNAL BALANCE WITH EXPENDITURE-CHANGING AND -SWITCHING POLICIES

10.11 With reference to Fig. 10-7 (the same as Fig. 10-2 but repeated here for ease of reference), indicate (a) what the YY curve shows, (b) why points A and B refer to unemployment, (c) why points C and D refer to inflation and (d) why the YY curve is negatively inclined.

(a) Each point on the YY curve refers to a particular combination of exchange rate (R) and real domestic expenditure (N) that involves internal balance or full employment with price stability.

(b) Point A involves the same R but lower N than the point directly across on the YY curve. Thus, A involves unemployment or recession. The same is true for point B and for any other point to the left and below the YY curve.

(c) Point C involves the same R but higher N than the point directly across on the YY curve. Thus, C involves excess aggregate demand and inflation. The same is true for point D and for any other point to the right and above the YY curve.

(d) Starting from a point on the YY curve, a revaluation by itself (a downward movement) leads to a deterioration in the nation's trade balance and unemployment, which to be corrected requires an increase in real domestic expenditures (a movement to the right). Thus, the YY curve is negatively sloped. Alternatively, a devaluation (an upward movement) from a point on the YY curve improves the nation's trade balance and leads to excess aggregate demand and inflation. Since to correct the inflation, N must be reduced (a movement to the left), the YY curve must be negatively inclined.

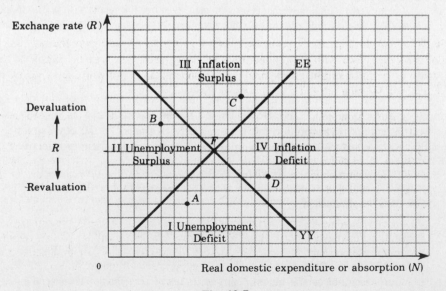

Fig. 10-7

10.12 With reference to Fig. 10.7, indicate (a) what the EE curve shows, (b) why A and D refer to deficit, (c) why B and C refer to surplus and (d) why the EE curve is positively inclined.

(a) Each point on the EE curve refers to a particular combination of exchange rate (R) and real domestic expenditure (N) that involves external balance or equilibrium in the balance of payments.

(b) Point A involves the same N but lower R than the point directly above on the EE curve. Thus, A involves an overvalued domestic currency and a deficit in the balance of payments. The same is true for point D and for any other point below and to the right of the EE curve.

(c) Point B involves the same N but higher R than the point directly below on the EE curve. Thus, B involves an undervalued domestic currency and a surplus in the balance of payments. The same is true for point C and for any other point above and to the left of the EE curve.

(d) Starting from a point on the EE curve, an increase in real domestic expenditures (a movement to the right in Fig. 10-7) by itself induces a rise in imports and opens a deficit in the nation's balance of payments which can be corrected with a devaluation (an upward movement). Thus, the EE curve is positively sloped. Alternatively, a decrease in N (a movement to the left) from a point on the EE curve induces a fall in imports and opens a surplus in the nation's balance of payments which can be corrected with a revaluation (a downward movement). Thus, once again we see that the EE curve must be positively inclined.

10.13 With reference to Fig. 10-7, (a) explain the type of fiscal and expenditure-switching policy required to achieve internal and external balance simultaneously, starting from points A, B, C and D. (b) Why was monetary policy omitted?

(a) The nation is simultaneously in internal and external balance at point F, where the YY and EE curves cross. To reach point F from A, the nation must move to the right and up. This involves expansionary fiscal policy (to increase real domestic expenditure) and devaluation. From point B, the nation must move to the right (with expansionary fiscal policy) and down (with revaluation). From C, the nation must move to the left (with restrictive fiscal policy) and down (with revaluation). From D, the nation must move to the left (with restrictive fiscal policy) and up (with devaluation). These policies are summarized in Table 10.2.

(b) Monetary policy could also have been used to achieve internal balance. However, by affecting interest rates, monetary policy not only affects the level of investments but also induces changes in international capital movements. Since this would greatly complicate our presentation in this section, we postpone the introduction of monetary policy until Problem 10.17. Thus, at each point on the EE curve, X − M equals a given autonomous level of net capital movement. There is a different EE curve for each level of net capital movement.

10.14 With reference to Fig. 10-7, indicate whether a nation can achieve internal and external balance simultaneously, (a) with an expenditure-switching policy only, if the nation is in internal balance but faces a deficit or surplus in its balance of payments and (b) with fiscal policy only, if the nation is in external balance but faces recession or inflation.

(a) If the nation is on the YY curve below point F (so that the nation is in internal balance but faces a deficit in its balance of payments), a devaluation by itself could move the nation to a point straight up and on the EE curve. However, this would lead to inflation (see Fig. 10-7). To reach point F, the nation should use restrictive fiscal policy together with devaluation. On the other hand, if the nation is on the YY curve above point F, a revaluation by itself could move the nation to a point straight down and on the EE curve. This, however, would lead to recession. The nation can reach point F with expansionary fiscal policy together with a smaller revaluation.

(b) If the nation is on the EE curve below point F, expansionary fiscal policy by itself could move the nation to a point directly across and on the YY curve, but this would lead to a deficit (see Fig. 10-7). To reach point E, the nation should use a weaker expansionary fiscal policy and devaluation. On the other hand, if the nation is on the EE curve above point F, the nation could reach the YY curve with restrictive fiscal policy. However, this would lead to a surplus. The nation can reach point F with a weaker restrictive fiscal policy and revaluation.

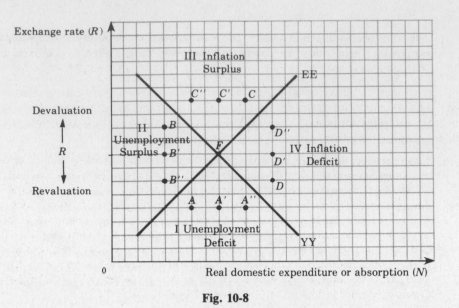

Fig. 10-8

10.15 Starting from each point in Fig. 10-8 (the same as Fig. 10-7, except for the additional points), (*a*) set up a table indicating the fiscal and expenditure-switching policies required to bring the economy to internal and external balance simultaneously (point *F*). (*b*) What causes the difference in the required policies to reach point *F* from the three points in each case?

(*a*)   **Table 10.4**

Case	Point	Fiscal Policy for Internal Balance	Policy for External Balance
	A	Expansionary	Devaluation
I	*A′*	None	Devaluation
	A″	Restrictive	Devaluation
	B	Expansionary	Revaluation
II	*B′*	Expansionary	None
	B″	Expansionary	Devaluation
	C	Restrictive	Revaluation
III	*C′*	None	Revaluation
	C″	Expansionary	Revaluation
	D	Restrictive	Devaluation
IV	*D′*	Restrictive	None
	D″	Restrictive	Revaluation

(*b*) Since point *A′* is directly below point *F*, devaluation alone will correct the deficit and unemployment. From *C′*, a revaluation alone will bring the nation to *F*. Since *B′* is at the equilibrium *R*, expansionary fiscal policy alone will bring the nation to *F*. From *D′*, restrictive fiscal policy alone is needed to reach *F*. These, however, occur only rarely. On the other hand, from *A″*, a devaluation alone could be used to reach EE, but this would not only eliminate unemployment but would also cause inflation, which could be corrected with restrictive fiscal policy. Point C'' is the opposite of A'' and requires the opposite policies. From B'', expansionary fiscal policy to eliminate unemployment not only eliminates the surplus but turns it into a deficit, requiring a devaluation for correction. The exact opposite is true for D''.

10.16 (a) Why were nations generally reluctant to use expenditure-switching policies to correct external imbalances during the post-World War II period?   (b) To what problem did this give rise? How could this problem be resolved?

   (a) Under the rules of the international monetary system set up after World War II, nations in *fundamental disequilibrium* were allowed to change the par value of their currencies (see Chapter 12). However, industrial nations found themselves very reluctant to do so. Surplus nations enjoyed the prestige of the surplus and the accumulation of reserves. Deficit nations refused to devalue out of national pride, since a devaluation was viewed as a sign of weakness. In addition, the U.K. and especially the U.S. felt that a devaluation would impose an unacceptable burden on foreign holders of their currencies. Too frequent changes in exchange rates were also believed to lead to instability. Thus, exchange rate changes occurred only infrequently, when practically forced upon the nation, and certainly not as a matter of deliberate policy. Since 1950, the U.K. devalued only in 1967, France in 1957, 1969 and 1982, the U.S. not before 1971, while Germany revalued in 1961, 1969, 1971 and 1973 (see Chapter 12).

   (b) Since nations were generally unwilling to use expenditure-switching policies for external balance, they were left with expenditure-changing policies to correct both internal and external imbalances. This could be done by using fiscal policy for internal balance and monetary policy for external balance.

INTERNAL AND EXTERNAL BALANCE WITH FISCAL AND MONETARY POLICIES

10.17 With reference to Fig. 10-9 (adapted from Fig. 10-3), indicate   (a) what the IS curve shows,   (b) why the IS curve is negatively inclined,   (c) the type of disequilibrium of points to the right and to the left of the curve,   (d) the effect of expansionary and contractionary fiscal policies on the IS curve.

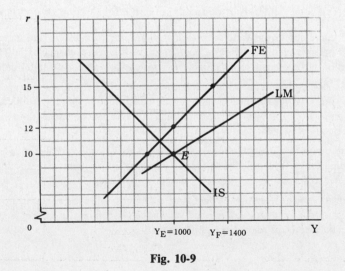

Fig. 10-9

   (a) The IS curve shows the various combinations of interest rates (r) and national income (Y) at which the quantity demanded of goods and services is equal to the quantity supplied (i.e., at which $I + X = S + M$), so that the nation is in equilibrium in the goods market.

   (b) The IS curve is negatively inclined because a lower r is associated with higher levels of investment and Y (through the multiplier process).

(c) Points to the right of the IS curve refer to situations at which $I + X < S + M$. Points to the left refer to $I + X > S + M$.

(d) Expansionary fiscal policy increases government expenditures and/or reduces taxes (which increase private consumption) and shifts the IS curve to the right because at each r the goods market is in equilibrium at higher Y. On the other hand, contractionary fiscal policy shifts the IS curve to the left.

10.18 With reference to Fig. 10-9, indicate (a) what the LM curve shows, (b) why the LM curve is positively inclined, (c) the type of disequilibrium of points to the right and to the left of the curve, (d) the effect of easy and tight monetary policies on the LM curve.

(a) The LM curve shows the various combinations of interest rates (r) and national income (Y) at which the quantity demanded of money for transaction and speculative purposes is equal to the given and fixed supply of money, so that the money market is in equilibrium. The *transaction demand for money,* which refers to the active money balances to carry on business transactions, varies directly with Y. The *speculative demand for money,* which refers to the inactive money balances maintained to take advantage of future (financial) investment opportunities, varies inversely with r.

(b) The LM curve is positively inclined because, starting from a point on the LM curve, increasing r will reduce the quantity of money demanded for speculative purposes. The resultant larger supply of money available for transaction purposes will only be held at higher Y.

(c) To the right of the LM curve the total demand for money exceeds the given and fixed supply of money, so that the money market is not in equilibrium. To the left of the LM curve, there is an excess quantity of money supplied.

(d) Easy monetary policy in the form of an increase in the nation's money supply shifts the LM curve to the right, so that at each r, Y must be higher to absorb the increase in the money supply.

10.19 With reference to Fig. 10-9, indicate (a) what the FE curve shows, (b) why the FE curve is positively inclined, (c) the type of disequilibrium of points to the right and to the left of the curve, (d) the effect of a devaluation or depreciation and a revaluation or appreciation on the FE curve.

(a) The FE curve shows the various combinations of interest rates (r) and national income (Y) at which the nation's balance of payments is in equilibrium at a given exchange rate. The balance of payments is in equilibrium when a positive trade balance is matched by an equal capital outflow or vice versa.

(b) The FE curve is usually positively inclined because a higher r leads to a greater capital inflow (or smaller outflow) and must be balanced with a higher Y and imports (M) for the balance of payments to remain in equilibrium. The FE curve is vertical if capital flows do not respond at all to a change in r and are horizontal with perfectly elastic capital flows.

(c) Points to the right of the FE curve refer to deficit in the nation's balance of payments because at a given r and capital flows, Y and M are too high for balance of payments equilibrium. Points to the left of the FE curve refer to surplus in the nation's balance of payments.

(d) A devaluation or depreciation of the nation's currency shifts the FE curve down because the nation's trade balance improves and so a lower r and smaller capital inflows (or greater outflows) are needed to keep the nation's balance of payments in equilibrium.

10.20 (a) Draw a figure similar to Fig. 10-9 showing that the nation is in equilibrium in the goods market, in the money market and in the balance of payments at $r = 10\%$ and $Y_E = 1,000$, but $Y_F = 1,400$. (b) Draw a figure showing how the nation of part (a) can use fiscal and monetary policies to reach equilibrium in all three markets simultaneously without changing its exchange rate.

(a) See Fig. 10-10.

(b) See Fig. 10-11.

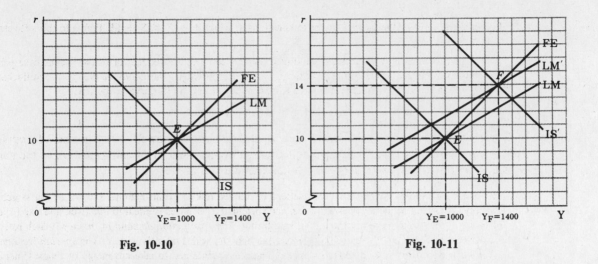

Fig. 10-10   Fig. 10-11

10.21 (*a*) Draw a figure similar to Fig. 10-10, but with FE horizontal to reflect perfectly elastic capital flows, and show how the nation can reach full employment and equilibrium in all three markets with fiscal policy only.   (*b*) What would happen if the nation used monetary policy instead?

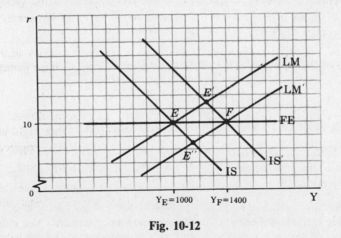

Fig. 10-12

(*a*)   The nation of Fig. 10-12 can reach $Y_F = 1,400$ with the expansionary fiscal policy that shifts the IS curve to IS'. The tendency of *r* to rise (point E') induces capital inflows that shift the LM curve to LM' so that all three curves cross on the FE curve at point *F*. This case is particularly relevant to small industrialized countries of Western Europe.

(*b*)   If to reach $Y_F = 1,400$ the nation of Fig. 10-12 used an easy monetary policy that shifts the LM curve to the right to LM', *r* would tend to fall (point E''). This leads to capital outflows that shift the LM' curve back to LM, so that monetary policy would be completely ineffective in this case.

10.22 Starting from Fig. 10-12,   (*a*) show how the nation can reach $Y_F = 1,400$ with easy monetary policy only under flexible exchange rates or with devaluation or revaluation.   (*b*) What would happen if the nation used instead fiscal policy and changes in exchange rates?

(*a*)   Starting from point *E* in Fig. 10-13, the nation could use the easy monetary policy to shift the LM curve to the right to LM' so as to cross the IS curve at point E' at $Y_F = 1,400$. However, at point E' the nation has a deficit in its balance of payments because point E' is to the right of the FE curve. Thus, the nation's currency depreciates. This shifts the FE curve to the right, say, to FE'. Since with a depreciation, the nation's exports (X) and imports (M) fall, the IS curve also shifts to the right, say, to IS'. The depreciation

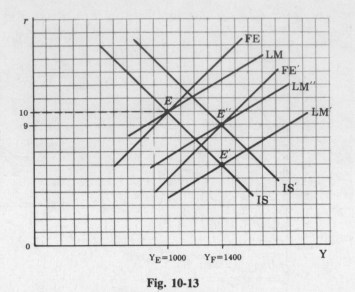

Fig. 10-13

will also increase domestic prices and the transaction demand for money so that the LM′ curve shifts back to the left part of the way, say, to LM″ because the nation's *real* money supply declines. In Fig. 10-13, the IS′, LM″ and FE′ curves cross at point E″ and all three markets are in equilibrium simultaneously at $Y_F = 1,400$. This is the end result of a process that may take several steps and doses of easy monetary policy to actually reach.

(b) If the nation used fiscal rather than monetary policy and exchange rate changes to reach internal and external balance, we would then be back to the analysis of Section 10.4.

THE POLICY MIX FOR INTERNAL AND EXTERNAL BALANCE

10.23 With reference to Fig. 10-14 (from Fig. 10-4), indicate   (*a*) what the IB line shows,   (*b*) why points *A* and *B* refer to unemployment,   (*c*) why points *C* and *D* refer to inflation and   (*d*) why the IB line is positively inclined.

(*a*) Each point on the IB line refers to a particular combination of fiscal policy (G) and monetary policy (*r*) that yields internal balance or full employment with price stability.

(*b*) Point *A* involves the same G but higher *r* than the point directly below on the IB line. Thus, *A* involves unemployment or recession. The same is true for point *B* and for any other point above and to the left of the IB line.

(*c*) Point *C* involves the same G but lower *r* than the point directly above on the IB line. Thus, *C* involves excess aggregate demand and inflation. The same is true for point *D* and for any other point below and to the right of the IB line.

(*d*) Starting from a point on the IB line representing unemployment, an increase in *r* or a tighter monetary policy by itself (an upward movement in Fig. 10-14) leads to unemployment, which to be corrected requires an increase in G or expansionary fiscal policy (a rightward movement). Thus, the IB line is positively inclined. Alternatively, a reduction in *r* (a downward movement) from a point on the IB line results in inflation, which to be corrected requires a decrease in G (a leftward movement). Thus, once again we see that the IB line must be positively inclined.

10.24 With reference to Fig. 10-14, indicate   (*a*) what the EB line shows,   (*b*) why points *A* and *D* refer to deficit,   (*c*) why *B* and *C* refer to surplus and   (*d*) why the EB line is positively inclined.

(*a*) Each point on the EB line refers to a particular combination of fiscal policy (G) and monetary policy (*r*) that yields external balance or equilibrium in the balance of payments.

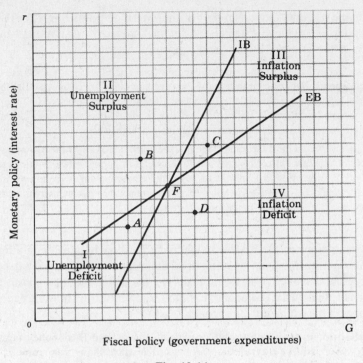

Fig. 10-14

(*b*) Point *A* involves the same G but lower *r* (and therefore smaller short-term capital inflows or larger outflows) than the point directly above on the EB line. Thus, *A* involves a deficit in the nation's balance of payments. The same is true for point *D* and for any other point below and to the right of the EB line.

(*c*) Point *B* involves the same G but higher *r* (and therefore smaller short-term capital outflows or larger inflows) than the point directly below on the EB line. Thus, *B* involves a surplus in the nation's balance of payments. The same is true for point *C* and for any other point above and to the right of the EB line.

(*d*) Starting from a point on the EB line, expansionary fiscal policy (a rightward movement in Fig. 10-14) induces the nation's imports to rise, leading to a deficit in the nation's balance of payments. To correct the deficit in the nation's balance of payments, an increase in *r* (an upward movement) is required to induce a smaller capital outflow or a larger inflow into the nation. Thus, the EB line must be positively inclined.

10.25 With reference to Fig. 10-14, explain the type of fiscal and monetary policy required to achieve simultaneous internal and external balance, starting from points *A, B, C* and *D*.

The nation is simultaneously in internal and external balance at point *F* where the IB and EB lines cross. To reach point *F* from point *A*, the nation must move to the right and upward. This involves expansionary fiscal policy and tight monetary policy. From point *B*, the nation must move to the right (expansionary fiscal policy) and downward (easy monetary policy). From *C*, the nation must move to the left (restrictive fiscal policy) and downward (easy monetary policy). From *D*, the nation must move to the left (restrictive fiscal policy) and upward (tight monetary policy). These policies are summarized in Table 10.5.

Table 10.5

Point	Fiscal Policy for Internal Balance	Monetary Policy for External Balance
A (Unemployment with deficit)	Expansionary	Tight
B (Unemployment with surplus)	Expansionary	Easy
C (Inflation with surplus)	Restrictive	Easy
D (Inflation with deficit)	Restrictive	Tight

10.26 (*a*) Why is the EB line flatter than the IB line? What does this imply for the relative effectiveness of monetary policy to achieve external and internal balance?   (*b*) When would the EB line have the same slope as the IB line? What would happen in that case?

(*a*)   We saw in Section 10.2 that to correct unemployment or inflation, we could use fiscal policy and/or monetary policy. The EB line is flatter than the IB line because monetary policy, by altering interest rates, also induces changes in short-term international capital movements. The more responsive capital movements are to interest rate changes, the flatter is the EB line relative to the IB line. This makes monetary policy relatively more effective in correcting external rather than internal imbalances.

(*b*)   The EB line would have the same slope (and be coincidental with) the IB line only if short-term international capital movements did not respond at all to changes in interest rates. In this case, monetary policy, as fiscal policy, can only affect the balance of payments through changes in national income. Therefore, no useful purpose would be served by treating fiscal and monetary policies as two distinct policy instruments. The nation would once against be facing two targets with a single policy instrument.

10.27 Starting from a point on the EB line below point F, show by arrows on a figure similar to Fig. 10-14 how a nation can reach point F by using fiscal policy to achieve internal balance and monetary policy to achieve external balance. What would happen if the nation did the opposite? On the same figure, but starting from a point on the IB line above point F, show by arrows how the nation can reach point F. What would happen if the nation did the opposite?

In Fig. 10-15, if the nation started from point A_0 and used fiscal policy to achieve internal balance and monetary policy to achieve external balance, the nation would move from point A_0 to point A_1, A_2, and so on, converging on point F (see the directions of the arrows). If the nation did the opposite, it would move from A_0 to A_1', A_2', and so on, moving further away from point F. Starting from point C_0, the nation will converge on point F with the appropriate policy mix and move further away from point F with the wrong policy mix (see the direction of the arrows from point C_0 in Fig. 10-15).

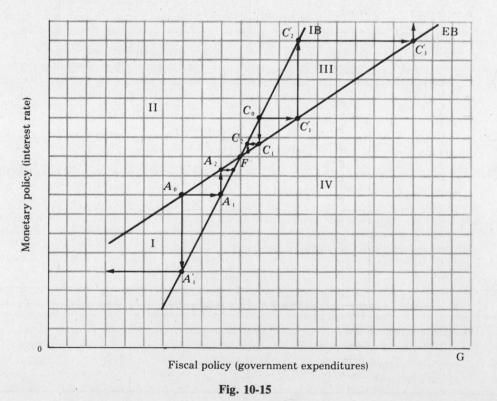

Fig. 10-15

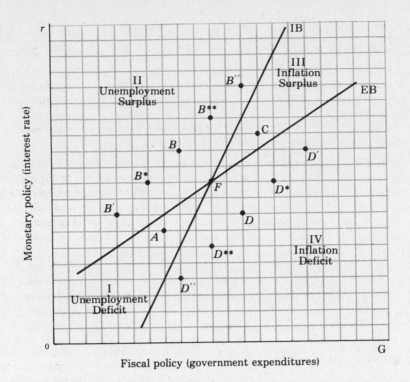

Fig. 10-16

10.28 Starting from each point in Fig. 10-16 (the same as Fig. 10-14, except for the additional points for cases II and IV), (a) set up a table indicating the fiscal and monetary policies necessary to reach point F. (b) What causes the difference in the required policies to reach point F from the five points in each case? (c) Would different policies be required to reach point F from different points in cases I and III? Why?

(a)   **Table 10.6**

Case	Point	Fiscal Policy for Internal Balance	Monetary Policy for External Balance
	B	Expansionary	Easy
	B*	Expansionary	None
II	B**	None	Easy
	B'	Expansionary	Tight
	B''	Restrictive	Easy
	D	Restrictive	Tight
	D*	Restrictive	None
IV	D**	None	Tight
	D'	Restrictive	Easy
	D''	Expansionary	Tight

(b) Since points B* and D* are on a horizontal line through point F, only fiscal policy will be sufficient to reach point F. Since B** and D** are on a vertical line through F, only monetary policy is required to reach F. These, however, occur only rarely. On the other hand, from B', an expansionary fiscal policy alone could be used to reach IB, but this would turn the surplus in the balance of payments into a deficit, which requires tight monetary policy to correct. Point D' is the opposite of B' and requires the opposite policies. From B'', the easy monetary policy to correct the surplus will result in inflation which, to correct, requires restrictive fiscal policy. Point D'' is the opposite of B'' and requires the opposite policies.

(c)   Since all points in case I are below and to the left of point F, they all require expansionary fiscal policy and tight monetary policy to reach F (see Fig. 10-16). The exact opposite is true for all points in case III.

10.29   Discuss briefly some of the major shortcomings of the analysis of internal and external balance with monetary and fiscal policies.

With respect to Section 10.6, short-term international capital movements may not respond to changes in interest rates, their responsiveness may be erratic, or it may be a once and for all reaction rather than the continuous process assumed by the model. In the real world, we do not have exact knowledge as to the precise effect of fiscal and monetary policies. In the case of the U.S., it may be difficult to coordinate fiscal and monetary policies since they are conducted by different governmental authorities. Time lags between the decision to adopt a policy and its operation further complicate matters. The analysis also assumes no offsetting changes occurring in other nations. Some of these same shortcomings also apply to the analysis in Section 10.4.

DIRECT CONTROLS

10.30   (a) What complication arises when we allow for the possibility of inflation before the full-employment level of national income is reached?   (b) How can the nation achieve simultaneous internal and external balance in this case?

(a)   In the absence of inflation before full employment, internal balance or full employment with price stability can be regarded as a single target requiring a single policy instrument to achieve. But when this is not the case, full employment and price stability must be treated as two distinct targets requiring two distinct policy instruments to achieve. Then the nation faces at least three targets: full employment, price stability and external balance. These cannot all be achieved simultaneously with only fiscal and monetary policies.

(b)   Since there is usually a trade-off between the rate of unemployment and the rate of inflation (the Phillips curve), a nation facing stronger inflationary pressures may have to accept a higher rate of unemployment than a nation facing weaker inflationary tendencies. The alternative is domestic wage and price controls or income policy to curb the (structural) inflation. The U.S. did just this in 1971–1972 but without much success.

10.31   (a) With monetary policy available for correcting external imbalance, how can we explain the persistence in some nations of balance of payments deficits, year after year, during the gold-exchange standard period?   (b) What other measure besides monetary policy, devaluation or flexible rates could the deficit nation adopt to correct its deficit?   (c) What objections could be raised against this.

(a)   Even though monetary policy was available for correcting external imbalances during the gold-exchange standard period (1946–1971), monetary policy was not generally used for that purpose. Thus, the U.S., during most of the postwar period, seemed to have used monetary policy primarily to reinforce fiscal policy for internal balance. Even if monetary policy is used for external balance, short-term international capital movements may not respond to interest rate changes, may not respond sufficiently or may even be destabilizing.

(b)   If the nation did not use monetary policy for external balance or if it were ineffective, and if the nation were also reluctant to devalue its currency or unable or unwilling to adopt fluctuating exchange rates, then a persistent deficit could be suppressed with trade and exchange controls. These may take the form of import restrictions, restrictions on foreign travel and tourist expenditures abroad, restrictions on speculative short-term capital outflows, on the purchase of foreign securities and on direct investments abroad. Under the most extreme form of exchange controls, all foreign exchange earned must be sold or turned over to government authorities, which then allocate it to users according to government priorities. This can completely suppress the deficit but usually leads to black markets and corruption. Another form of exchange control is *multiple exchange rates* (i.e., the use of a lower exchange rate for essential imports, such as machinery, and a higher one for nonessentials).

(c)   In general, trade and exchange controls have been greatly reduced since the early 1950s, and the imposition of new ones is prohibited, except temporarily and in special cases, under the present international monetary system (see Chapter 12). In any event, there are strong objections to trade and exchange controls because they distort resource allocation, impair economic efficiency and generally reduce the gains from trade.

10.32 A nation could also attempt to achieve a *reasonable* rate of growth by changing its interest rate *structure* and using short-term interest rates for external balance while using long-term interest rates for economic growth.   (a) What is meant by the interest rate structure? What is meant by distorting it? How can this be accomplished?   (b) Explain how a nation with a deficit in its balance of payments can correct the deficit and at the same time achieve a reasonable rate of growth.

(a)   In the real world, there is no single rate of interest. Rather, there are many, depending on the risk involved, on the length of time to maturity, etc. These different interest rates are not independent of each other but interdependent, so that a change in one rate will affect to a greater or lesser extent all the others. For example, rising short-term rates generally exert a rising influence on long-term rates. The interest rate structure refers to the relationship between all these different rates of interest at a particular point in time. If the government attempted to increase short-term rates but at the same time prevented this from pulling long-term interest rates up, the government would be distorting or twisting the *natural* interest rate structure. The government could do this by open market sales of treasury bills (which would depress their price and result in higher short-term rates) while at the same time making more funds available for long-term investments (in order to prevent long-term rates from being pulled up).

(b)   A deficit in the nation's balance of payments could be corrected with tight monetary policy. This would increase short-term interest rates, which would reduce short-term capital outflows or increase inflows and so correct the deficit. However, the rise in short-term interest rates would also exert a rising influence on long-term interest rates, which would discourage long-term domestic investments and the long-term economic growth of the national economy. This could be prevented by making, at the same time, more funds available for long-term investments. Thus, by breaking up monetary policy into its effect on short-term and long-term interest rates, the nation can strive for the fourth target of a *reasonable* rate of economic growth. The U.S. seemed to have done this during the 1960s.

10.33 (a) Summarize the various measures that a nation could use to correct an external imbalance under a fixed exchange rate system.   (b) Why is cooperation among nations often required in order for these measures to be successful?

(a)   Aside from domestic deflation, a nation can correct a deficit in its balance of payments with a devaluation (aimed at improving its trade balance), by forcing up its interest rates with tighter monetary policy (in order to induce a larger short-term capital inflow or reduce the outflow), by holding its rate of inflation lower than abroad or by direct controls on trade and payments (usually as a last resort to correct a persistent deficit). A surplus nation could do the opposite to correct its surplus.

(b)   The above measures could be effective only if other nations cooperate and do not retaliate. If a devaluation by a nation leads to a comparable devaluation by other nations, the trade balance will not improve. The only result will be a reduction in the volume of trade and in the gains from trade. Such competitive devaluations actually occurred during the 1930s (see Chapter 12). Similarly, a nation's attempt to attract foreign short-term capital by forcing its interest rates up may be completely neutralized by a similar increase in interest rates abroad. The same would be true if the nation achieved a lower rate of domestic inflation, but this reduction was matched by other nations. Finally, for the direct controls on trade and payments imposed by one nation to be effective, other nations must not retaliate with controls of their own.

Chapter 11

The Monetary Approach
to the Balance of Payments and Flexible
versus Fixed Exchange Rates

11.1 THE MONETARY APPROACH UNDER FIXED EXCHANGE RATES

The *monetary approach to the balance of payments* views the balance of payments as an essentially monetary phenomenon, with money playing the key role in the long run both as a disturbance and adjustment in the nation's balance of payments. According to the monetary approach, a deficit in a nation's balance of payments results from an excess in the stock of money supplied that is not eliminated or corrected by the nation's monetary authorities. A surplus results from an uncorrected excess demand for money in the nation. Under a fixed exchange rate system, the deficit or surplus is automatically corrected in the long run by an outflow or inflow of money (international reserves) that eliminates the excess supply of or demand for money.

EXAMPLE 1. The monetary approach postulates that the *demand for money* is given by $M_d = kPY$, where k is the desired ratio of nominal money balances to nominal national income, P is the domestic price level and Y is real output (so that PY is the nominal national income). Thus, with $k = 1/4$ and $PY = 800$, $M_d = (1/4)(800) = 200$. The demand for money is also inversely related to the rate of interest in the nation, but for simplicity this is disregarded here. On the other hand, the nation's total *supply of money*, $M_s = m(D + F)$, where m is the money multiplier given by the reciprocal of the legal reserve requirement (LRR) in the nation of 1/LRR, D is the domestic credit created by the nation's authorities and F is the nation's international reserves. $D + F$ is the nation's *monetary base*. Thus, with LRR $= 0.2$ (so that $m = 5$), $D = 32$ and $F = 10$, $M_s = (5)(32 + 10) = 210$. Since $M_s > M_d$, the nation has a deficit in its balance of payments, which in the long run is automatically corrected under a fixed exchange rate system by an outflow of money (reserves) equal to 2, so that $M_s = (5)(32 + 8) = 200 = M_d$.

11.2 POLICY IMPLICATIONS OF THE MONETARY APPROACH
UNDER FIXED EXCHANGE RATES

According to the monetary approach, a policy can only affect a nation's balance of payments through its effect on the demand for and supply of money in the nation. Any policy that increases a nation's demand for money relative to its supply leads to an inflow of money or reserves from abroad (an improvement in the nation's balance of payments) under a fixed exchange rate system. On the other hand, an increase in the nation's money supply relative to its demand results in an outflow of money or reserves, which worsens the nation's balance of payments. However, the effect of these policies is only temporary because of the monetarists' belief that there is an automatic tendency toward equilibrium in the balance of payments in the long run.

EXAMPLE 2. A devaluation of its currency by a deficit nation increases domestic prices and results in an increased demand for money in the nation. This helps absorb the excess supply of money causing the deficit. However, according to the monetary approach, the devaluation does no more than speed the adjustment process in the short run and is entirely unnecessary in the long run because of the automatic tendency toward equilibrium in the balance of payments in the long run. If the nation's monetary authorities meet the increased demand for money resulting from the devaluation with an equal increase in the supply of money, the devaluation is completely ineffective, even in the short run. With a larger increase in the supply of money, the nation's balance of payments deficit will actually increase.

11.3 THE MONETARY APPROACH UNDER FLEXIBLE EXCHANGE RATES

According to the monetary approach, the depreciation of a deficit nation's currency under a freely flexible exchange rate system increases the nation's demand for money and absorbs the excess supply of money (which was the cause of the deficit) without any outflow of money or reserves from the nation. On the other hand, the appreciation of a surplus nation's currency automatically eliminates the excess demand for money in the nation without any inflow of money or reserves. Thus, nations retain a large degree of control over their money supply under a freely flexible exchange rate system. Under a managed exchange rate system (as we have today), balance of payments disequilibria are partly corrected by exchange rate changes (which affect the demand for money in the deficit and surplus nations) and are partly corrected by international money flows (which change the supply of money in the deficit and surplus nations).

EXAMPLE 3.   During the middle and late 1970s, the tendency for the U.S. to have balance of payments deficits was partly corrected by a depreciation of the dollar (which increased the U.S. demand for money and absorbed part of the excess supply of money) and was partly corrected by an outflow of dollars (which eliminated the remaining excess supply of money in the U.S.). In a surplus nation such as Germany, the nation's currency appreciated (reducing the excess demand for money) and the nation received an inflow of money or reserves (satisfying the remaining excess demand for money). According to monetarists, it was the *continuous* tendency for excessive money creation in the U.S. and insufficient money creation in Germany that resulted in the continuous depreciation of the dollar and outflow of dollars from the U.S. and appreciation of the mark and inflow of dollars to Germany during the middle and late 1970s.

11.4 TYPES OF EXCHANGE RATE SYSTEMS

Besides the fixed and flexible exchange rate systems examined in Chapter 9, there are a number of hybrid systems that combine various characteristics of both. An *adjustable peg system* requires nations to periodically change par values when in balance of payments disequilibrium. Under a *crawling peg system,* par values are changed by small amounts at frequent and specified intervals until the equilibrium exchange rate is reached. A *managed floating system* is one under which monetary authorities intervene in foreign exchange markets to smooth out short-run fluctuations without attempting to affect the long-run trend in exchange rates. There are also *optimum currency areas,* which are composed of a group of nations that have permanently fixed the exchange rates among themselves.

EXAMPLE 4.   The gold-exchange standard that operated during the postwar period until 1971 was originally set up as an adjustable peg system, but ended up operating as a truly fixed exchange rate system (see Section 9.6). Since 1973, we have had a managed exchange rate system, except for most developing nations which operate essentially under an adjustable peg system. Since the end of 1981, Brazil, Colombia, Peru and Portugal have had a crawling peg system. Since 1973, the European Economic Community has attempted to set itself up as an optimum currency area, but without much success.

11.5 THE CASE FOR FLEXIBLE EXCHANGE RATES

A flexible exchange rate system has the following alleged advantages over a fixed exchange rate system. (1) Balance of payments adjustments are continuous, small and smooth rather than occasional, large and disruptive. (2) Only the exchange rate needs to change to bring about balance of payments adjustment rather than the required change in all internal prices under a fixed exchange rate system such as the gold standard. (3) Since exchange rates are at or close to equilibrium at all times, the comparative advantage of the nation is clearly evident and the nation's trade pattern is not distorted. (4) Nations are freed from using monetary policy to achieve external balance, which enables them to focus on domestic goals. (5) Flexible exchange rates allow each nation to pursue its own desired inflation-unemployment trade-off. (6) The cost of foreign exchange intervention is avoided. (7) The risk of policy mistakes is also reduced since under a flexible exchange rate system, balance of payments disequilibria are automatically corrected.

EXAMPLE 5.   Under the gold-exchange standard, exchange rate changes were indeed occasional, large and disruptive because internal prices were "sticky" rather than flexible, especially downward (see Chapter 12). Many developing nations began to export some heavily subsidized manufactured goods which clearly did not reflect their comparative advantage. Nations which attempted to use monetary policy to reinforce fiscal policy to achieve internal balance or aimed at the goal of having a "reasonable" rate of growth or an equitable distribution of income generally faced serious balance of payments disequilibria. Nations such as the U.S., the U.K., France and Italy, which seemed willing to tolerate higher inflation rates to keep unemployment rates lower, were constrained by the resulting large balance of payments deficits, while the opposite was generally true for nations such as Germany, Japan and Switzerland. A great deal of the effort of national monetary authorities was directed into foreign exchange market interventions under the gold-exchange standard and some policy mistakes were inevitable.

11.6   THE CASE FOR FIXED EXCHANGE RATES

A fixed exchange rate system has the following alleged advantages over a flexible exchange rate system. (1) It results in a smaller degree of uncertainty in international trade and finance. (2) It is more likely to lead to stabilizing rather than destabilizing speculation. (3) It results in greater price discipline (i.e., it is less inflationary). Advocates of flexible exchange rates disagree with these arguments (see Problem 11.14).

EXAMPLE 6.   The interwar (i.e., the period between world wars) experience with flexible exchange rates seemed to indicate that they introduced such a degree of uncertainty as to disrupt the regular flow of international trade and investments and to result in destabilizing speculation. On the other hand, the last years of the gold-exchange standard were marred by chaotic conditions in foreign exchange markets and destabilizing speculation. The experience since 1973 with managed exchange rates has generally been positive on most accounts, except for inflation control. However, the great volatility and large and persistent misalignment of the U.S. dollar during the 1980s are now leading expert opinion to favor restraints on exchange rate fluctuations (see Section 12.7).

Glossary

Monetary approach to the balance of payments   The theory that postulates that the balance of payments is an essentially monetary phenomenon, with money playing the key role in the long run as both the cause and the cure of balance of payments disequilibria.

Demand for money   According to the monetary approach, the nation's demand for nominal money balances is stable in the long run and is directly related to the nation's nominal income but inversely related to the rate of interest in the nation.

Supply of money   The nation's monetary base $(D + F)$ times the money multiplier (m).

Monetary base   The domestic credit created by the nation's monetary authorities plus the nation's international reserves, or $D + F$.

Adjustable peg system   The exchange rate system under which par values are periodically changed to correct balance of payments disequilibria.

Crawling peg system   The exchange rate system under which par values are changed by small amounts at frequent and specified intervals until the equilibrium exchange rate is reached.

Managed floating system   The exchange rate system under which monetary authorities intervene in foreign exchange markets to smooth out short-run fluctuations without attempting to affect the long-run trend in exchange rates.

Optimum currency area   A group of nations with permanently fixed exchange rates among themselves.

Review Questions

1. Which of the following is true with respect to the monetary approach to the balance of payments? (*a*) It views the balance of payments as an essentially monetary phenomenon. (*b*) A balance of payments deficit results from an excess supply of money in the nation. (*c*) A balance of payments surplus results from an excess demand for money. (*d*) Balance of payments disequilibria are automatically corrected in the long run. (*e*) All of the above.

   Ans. (*e*) See Section 11.1

2. If the nation's money income or GNP is 100 and the desired ratio of nominal money balances to nominal national income is 1/4, the quantity demanded of money in the nation is (*a*) 20, (*b*) 25, (*c*) 50, (*d*) 100.

   Ans. (*b*) See Example 1.

3. A nation's monetary base is equal to (*a*) the domestic credit created by the nation's monetary authorities, (*b*) the nation's international reserves, (*c*) the nation's money supply, (*d*) the domestic credit created by the nation's monetary authorities plus the nation's international reserves, (*e*) the nation's money supply plus its international reserves.

   Ans. (*d*) See Example 1.

4. According to the monetary approach, a revaluation of a nation's currency (*a*) increases the nation's demand for money, (*b*) increases the nation's supply of money, (*c*) reduces the nation's demand for money, (*d*) reduces the nation's supply of money.

   Ans. (*c*) See Section 11.2 and Example 2.

5. According to the monetary approach, if at the same time that a surplus nation revalues its currency to correct a balance of payments surplus the nation reduces its money supply, the revaluation will be (*a*) ineffective in the short run, (*b*) effective in the short run, (*c*) effective in the long run, (*d*) any of the above.

   Ans. (*b*) See Section 11.2 and Example 2.

6. According to monetarists, a balance of payments deficit is automatically corrected under a freely flexible exchange rate system by a depreciation of the deficit nation's currency, which (*a*) reduces its excess demand for money, (*b*) reduces its excess supply of money, (*c*) increases its excess demand for money, (*d*) increases its excess supply of money.

   Ans. (*a*) See Section 11.3.

7. Which of the following is a hybrid exchange rate system? (*a*) Adjustable peg system, (*b*) crawling peg system, (*c*) managed floating system, (*d*) all of the above.

   Ans. (*d*) See Section 11.4.

8. Under a managed floating exchange rate system, the nation's monetary authorities intervene in foreign exchange markets to (*a*) smooth out short-run fluctuations in exchange rates, (*b*) smooth out long-run fluctuations in exchange rates, (*c*) smooth out short-run and long-run fluctuations in exchange rates, (*d*) keep exchange rates fixed among a group of nations.

   Ans. (*a*) See Section 11.4.

9. Which of the following is an alleged advantage of a flexible over a fixed exchange rate system? (*a*) Balance of payments adjustments are continuous and smooth. (*b*) Internal prices need not change to bring about balance of payments adjustment. (*c*) The nation's trade pattern is not distorted. (*d*) All of the above.

   Ans. (*d*) See Section 11.5.

10. Which of the following is *not* an alleged advantage of a flexible over a fixed exchange rate systems? (*a*) It frees

monetary policy for other domestic goals. (*b*) It is less inflationary. (*c*) It leads to fewer policy mistakes. (*d*) All of the above.

Ans. (*b*) See Sections 11.5 and 11.6.

11. Which of the following is *not* an alleged advantage of a fixed over a flexible exchange rate system? (*a*) It introduces less uncertainty into international trade and finance. (*b*) It leads to stabilizing speculation. (*c*) It allows each nation to follow its desired inflation-unemployment trade-off. (*d*) It results in greater price discipline.

Ans. (*c*) See Sections 11.5 and 11.6.

12. The 1980s experience with managed exchange rates (*a*) strongly supports a fixed exchange rate system, (*b*) strongly supports a freely flexible exchange rate system, (*c*) mildly supports a flexible exchange rate system, (*d*) supports some restriction on exchange rate fluctuations.

Ans. (*d*) See Example 6.

Solved Problems

THE MONETARY APPROACH UNDER FIXED EXCHANGE RATES

11.1 Explain what is meant by the (*a*) monetary approach to the balance of payments, (*b*) demand for money, (*c*) supply of money, (*d*) money multiplier and (*e*) monetary base.

(*a*) The monetary approach to the balance of payments views the balance of payments as an essentially monetary phenomenon, with money playing the key role in the long run both as a disturbance and adjustment in the nation's balance of payments. This approach was conceived toward the end of the 1960s as an extension of domestic monetarism and was fully developed during the 1970s, when it was advanced as a superior alternative to the elasticity, absorption and policy approaches (discussed in Chapters 9 and 10). The predictions and policy implications of this approach often contradict those of the traditional approaches.

(*b*) According to the monetary approach, the demand for nominal money balances (M_d) is stable in the long run and directly related to the nation's nominal national income level but inversely related to the rate of interest (r) in the nation. Abstracting from r for simplicity, $M_d = kPY$, where k is the desired ratio of nominal money balances to nominal national income (this is the inverse of the velocity of circulation of money; i.e., $k = 1/v$), P is the domestic price level in the nation and Y is the real output (so that PY is the nominal national income). It is assumed that Y is at or tends toward full employment.

(*c*) A nation's total money supply, $M_s = m(D + F)$, where m is the money multiplier, D is the domestic credit created by the nation's monetary authorities or the domestic assets backing the nation's money supply and F is the international reserves of the nation.

(*d*) The money multiplier, m, is given by the reciprocal of the legal reserve requirements (LRR) in the nation or 1/LRR. That is, each new dollar deposited in any commercial bank increases the nation's money supply by a multiple of $1 under a fractional banking system. The money multiplier is a concept analogous to the income multiplier discussed in Section 9.4 (for a review, refer to *Schaum's Outline of Principles of Economics* or your principles text).

(*e*) The monetary base of the nation is equal to $D + F$, where D is the domestic component and F is the international component. The monetary base of the nation is also referred to as "high-powered money."

11.2 Given $v = 5$, $PY = 2,000$, LRR $= 0.25$, $D = 70$, and $F = 20$, find (*a*) M_d and (*b*) M_s. (*c*) Does the nation have a deficit or a surplus in its balance of payments? (*d*) If D remains unchanged, by how much must F change in the long run in order for the nation's balance of payments to be in equilibrium under a fixed exchange rate system?

(a)
$$k = \frac{1}{v} = \frac{1}{5}$$
$$M_d = kPY = (1/5)(2,000) = 400$$

(b)
$$m = \frac{1}{LRR} = \frac{1}{0.25} = 4$$
$$M_s = m(D + F) = 4(70 + 20) = 360$$

(c) Since $M_d > M_s$, the nation has a surplus in its balance of payments.

(d) The surplus in the nation's balance of payments will be automatically corrected in the long run under a fixed exchange rate system by an inflow of money (international reserves) to the nation equal to 10, so that F will rise from 20 to 30 in the nation. Then, $M_s = 4(70 + 30) = 400 = M_d$.

11.3 Explain (a) in what way the adjustment process postulated by the monetary approach under a fixed exchange rate system is similar and different from the price-specie-flow mechanism advanced by David Hume, (b) why a non-reserve-currency country has no control over its money supply in the long run. (c) why a reserve-currency country retains a great degree of control over its money supply.

(a) The adjustment mechanism postulated by the monetary approach is similar to the price-specie-flow mechanism advanced by David Hume (see Section 9.3) in that both rely on an international flow of money or reserves from the deficit to the surplus nation to automatically correct the balance of payments disequilibria of both nations. However, while the international flow of money or reserves tends to reduce prices in the deficit nation and increase prices in the surplus nation to bring about adjustment according to the price-specie-flow mechanism, it is the international flow of reserves itself that eliminates the excess supply of money in the deficit nation and the excess demand for money in the surplus nation, without any change in prices, according to the monetary approach. Indeed, according to "global monetarists," the *law of one price* prevails, with prices in different nations differing only by transportation costs, tariffs, and so on.

(b) Starting from the condition $M_d = M_s$ and equilibrium in the balance of payments, if a non-reserve-currency country attempted to increase its M_s (i.e., to conduct easy monetary policy), $M_s > M_d$ and the excess money supply will flow out, and the nation would lose an equal amount of F. Thus, D will rise and F will fall by an equal amount, leaving the nation's money base $(D + F)$ unchanged in the long run. The opposite would happen if the nation attempted to reduce its M_s (i.e., to conduct tight monetary policy). Thus, according to monetarists, a non-reserve-currency country has no control over its money supply in the long run under a fixed exchange rate system.

(c) According to monetarists, a reserve-currency country, such as the U.S., retains a great deal of control over its money supply. The reason is that if the U.S. increases its money supply (so that $M_s > M_d$) a portion of its money supply will flow out of the nation but, to the extent that receiving nations increase their international reserves in the form of dollar deposits in the U.S., the attempt on the part of the U.S. to increase its M_s will be successful. The same is true if the U.S. attempted to reduce its money supply in order to conduct tight monetary policy.

POLICY IMPLICATIONS OF THE MONETARY APPROACH UNDER FIXED EXCHANGE RATES

11.4 (a) Explain how, according to the monetary approach, the imposition of an import tariff or quota can speed up the process of correcting a nation's balance of payments deficit under a fixed exchange rate system. (b) What is the effect of an exogenous increase in domestic prices on a nation's balance of payments? (c) What is the effect of an exogenous increase in domestic interest rates on the nation's balance of payments?

(a) The imposition of an import tariff or quota increases domestic prices in the nation and, as such, it increases the nation's demand for money. On the assumption that the nation had a deficit in its balance of payments to begin with, the increase in the nation's demand for money helps absorb the excess supply of money, which is the cause of the deficit. For this to have any effect on the nation's balance of payments, however, the nation's monetary authorities must not match the increased demand for money with an equal increase in the nation's supply of money, otherwise the devaluation will have no effect. In any event, the improvement would be only of temporary importance (i.e., it would do no more than speed up the adjustment process) and be entirely unnecessary in the long run, because according to the monetary approach there is an automatic tendency toward equilibrium in the balance of payments in the long run.

(b) An exogenous increase in domestic prices in a nation, say, as a result of an increase in the price of its petroleum imports, increases the nation's demand for money and, in general, has the same effect on the nation's balance of payments as a devaluation of the nation's currency.

(c) An exogenous increase in interest rates in the nation reduces the speculative demand for money (since the opportunity foregone in holding inactive money balances increases). Given the nation's money supply, the reduced demand for money results either in an increased excess supply of money and deficit or in a reduced excess demand for money and surplus.

11.5 Explain how continuous growth affects a nation's balance of payments under a fixed exchange rate system according to (a) the monetary approach and (b) the traditional income-multiplier approach. (c) Which of these two approaches seems to better explain the experience of Germany during the 1960s, when Germany faced high growth and balance of payments surplus?

(a) Continuous growth leads to a continuous increase in a nation's demand for money. If the nation's monetary authorities do not change the domestic component of the nation's money supply or increase it by less than the increase in demand, the excess demand for money will be met by a continuous inflow of money or reserves and improvement in the nation's balance of payments under a fixed exchange rate system. On the other hand, if the nation's monetary authorities increase the nation's money supply to match or exceed the increased demand for money, the nation's balance of payments will remain unaffected or will worsen.

(b) According to the traditional income-multiplier approach, continuous growth induces a continuous rise in the nation's imports and, by itself, tends to result in continuous balance of payments deficits for the nation. This result is the opposite of that postulated by the monetary approach, under which continuous growth, by itself, tends to result in a continuous balance of payments surplus for the nation.

(c) Germany's experience of high growth and balance of payments surplus under the fixed exchange rate system prevailing in the 1960s is rather easily explained by monetarists in terms of the smaller increase in the money supply of Germany relative to its increased demand for money resulting from growth. Though explanations are not lacking for Germany's experience along the traditional income-multiplier approach, they seem somewhat strained and complex.

THE MONETARY APPROACH UNDER FLEXIBLE EXCHANGE RATES

11.6 Explain why according to monetarists (a) nations retain control over their money supply under a flexible exchange rate system but not under a fixed exchange rate system, (b) nations could not sterilize continuous money outflows or inflows under a fixed exchange rate system in order to retain control over their money supply.

(a) According to monetarists, balance of payments disequilibria are corrected by exchange rate changes without any international flow of money or reserves under a flexible exchange rate system. Thus, the nation retains control over its money supply in the long run. For example, if a nation in balance of payments equilibrium increased its money supply (easy monetary policy), its currency would depreciate and absorb the excess supply of money, without any outflow of money or reserves from the nation. Thus, the increase in the nation's money supply would be retained in the nation. On the other hand, if the nation reduced its money supply (tight monetary policy), the excess demand for money would be eliminated by an appreciation of the nation's currency, without any inflow of money or reserves to the nation. As a result, the nation's attempt to reduce its money supply would succeed. Under a fixed exchange rate system, the attempt of a nation to increase its money supply and conduct easy monetary policy would simply lead to the outflow of the excess supply of money in the long run, while a nation's attempt to reduce its supply of money and conduct tight monetary policy would simply lead to an inflow of money or reserves. As a result, non-reserve-currency nations have little or no control over their money supply in the long run under a fixed exchange rate system.

(b) A deficit nation could not sterilize continuous international money outflows in the long run under a fixed exchange rate system because the nation would run out of international reserves. On the other hand, a surplus nation would run out of domestic assets backing the nation's money supply if it attempted to prevent a continuous inflow of money or reserves from increasing the nation's money supply. In the long run, a surplus nation would either have to give up its goal of domestic price stability or revalue its currency. This is, in fact, what happened to Germany during the 1960s, when the large inflow of reserves led to some domestic inflation and to a revaluation of the mark in 1961 and 1969.

11.7 From a monetarist point of view, explain   (a) the world-wide inflation during the middle and late 1970s,   (b) the reason for the relatively higher inflationary rates in the U.S., the U.K., France and Italy than in Germany, Japan and Switzerland,   (c) the relationship between rates of inflation and exchange rates.

(a) According to monetarists, the world-wide inflation prevailing during the middle and late 1970s resulted primarily from increases in the money supply of the world as a whole exceeding the real rate of growth of the world economy.

(b) Monetarists explain the high inflation rates in nations such as the U.S., the U.K., France and Italy by pointing out the fact that monetary authorities in these nations increased money supply faster than the real rate of growth of these nations. On the other hand, Germany, Japan and Switzerland faced much lower inflationary rates because their money supply growth was slower than their real rate of growth. These latter nations still faced some inflation because they did not allow their exchange rates to freely appreciate under the managed exchange rate system presently in effect and they did not succeed in completely sterilizing inflows of money or reserves from nations facing excessive money growth.

(c) Nations increasing their money supply faster than their real rate of growth face domestic inflation under a fixed exchange rate system and depreciating currency under a flexible exchange rate system. Under the present managed exchange rate system, they usually face a little of both. On the other hand, surplus nations face some domestic inflation (if the world supply of money grows faster than the growth of the world economy) and some currency appreciation. Exchange rates are also affected by expectations of the relative rates of inflation in different nations, with nations expected to have higher than average inflationary rates facing depreciation of their currency and those expected to have lower than average inflation rates experiencing appreciation of their currency (*ceteris paribus*). Note that the monetary approach stresses the role of monetary variables and the long run, while traditional approaches stress real variables and the short run. Some empirical tests support the monetary approach, some do not. But the number of economists adhering to the monetary approach is growing.

TYPES OF EXCHANGE RATE SYSTEMS

11.8 Identify and indicate the most important characteristics of   (a) a fixed exchange rate system,   (b) a freely flexible exchange rate system,   (c) hybrid exchange rate systems.

(a) The fixed exchange rate system *par excellence* is the gold standard (1880–1914). Under it, the exchange rate can only fluctuate within the gold points about the fixed mint parity (see Section 9.3) and gold is the only reserve asset. Another fixed exchange rate system is the gold-exchange standard that operated during the postwar period until it collapsed in 1971. Under this system, monetary authorities determine the band of allowed fluctuation in exchange rates about fixed par values, and both gold and convertible currencies are used as international reserve assets. We can also have a fixed exchange rate system without any connection with gold. Here, monetary authorities determine the band of allowed fluctuation of exchange rates about fixed par values, and only convertible currencies are used as international reserves. The system that operated from August 1971 until March 1973 was of this type. Since the dollar was by far the most important reserve currency, this system was close to a dollar standard.

(b) Under a freely flexible exchange rate system, a deficit or surplus in a nation's balance of payments is automatically corrected by a depreciation or appreciation, respectively, in the nation's currency. There is no government intervention in foreign exchange markets and no loss or accumulation of international reserves by the nation. Indeed, international reserves are entirely unnecessary under such a system. This system was never adopted in its purest form in the real world.

(c) Hybrid exchange rate systems refer to adjustable pegs, crawling pegs and managed floating, all of which combine various characteristics of fixed and flexible exchange rate systems. An adjustable peg system requires nations to periodically change par values when in balance of payments disequilibrium. To avoid large discrete changes, a crawling peg system changes par values by small amounts at frequent, specified intervals until the equilibrium exchange rate is reached. Under a managed exchange rate system, monetary authorities intervene in foreign exchange markets to smooth out short-run fluctuations without attempting to affect the long-run trend in exchange rates.

11.9 (a) Are international reserves needed in hybrid exchange rate systems? (b) How can monetary authorities smooth out short-run fluctuations in exchange rates?

(a) As opposed to a freely flexible exchange rate system in which exchange rate changes automatically and quickly eliminate balance of payments disequilibria so that there is no need for international reserves, hybrid exchange rate systems still require nations to hold international reserves. But their need for international reserves is much smaller than under a truly fixed exchange rate system because changes in par values or exchange rates under hybrid systems correct part of balance of payments disequilibria.

(b) Under a managed floating system, monetary authorities can smooth out short-run fluctuations in exchange rates by intervening in foreign exchange markets and supplying out of a nation's international reserves a portion of the short-run excess demand for foreign exchange in the market (thus moderating the tendency for the nation's currency to depreciate) and absorbing (and adding to its reserves) a portion of any short-run excess supply of foreign exchange in the market (thus moderating the tendency for the nation's currency to appreciate). The feasibility of this policy of "leaning against the wind" rests on the fact that it does not require national monetary authorities to know the long-run trend in exchange rates (which they are often in no better position to know than international speculators).

11.10 (a) What is the purpose of the small band of fluctuation about the established par value under a fixed exchange rate system? (b) What happens if the allowed band of fluctuation under a fixed exchange rate system is made wider and wider? (c) What is the relationship of an optimum currency area to fixed and flexible exchange rate systems?

(a) The advantage of the small band of fluctuation about the established par value under a fixed exchange rate system is that the nation's monetary authorities will not have to intervene constantly in foreign exchange markets to maintain the established par value, but only when exchange rates tend to move outside the allowed band of fluctuation. This simplifies the maintenance of the fixed exchange rate system and reduces the cost of intervention in foreign exchange markets.

(b) If the allowed band of fluctuation about a par value under a fixed exchange rate system is made wider and wider, more and more of required balance of payments adjustments take place by exchange rate changes, leaving less and less to be corrected by other means or financed by international reserve flows. At the limit, the band of allowed fluctuation can be so large that practically all balance of payments adjustments are made automatically by exchange rate changes, thereby eliminating the need for any official intervention in foreign exchange markets. This is essentially a flexible exchange rate system.

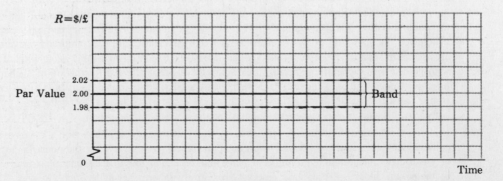

Fig. 11-1

(c) An optimum currency area refers to a group of nations whose currencies are linked through permanently fixed par values. The currencies of member nations could then be linked with the currency of nonmembers through a fixed, flexible or a hybrid exchange rate system. Regions of a nation obviously form an optimum currency area. On the international level, the European Monetary System (EMS) is similar to an optimum currency area (see Section 12.7).

11.11 Starting from a par value of $2 = £1 and with exchange rates allowed to fluctuate by 1% on either side of the par value, draw a figure showing (a) a fixed exchange rate system, (b) an adjustable peg system under which a deficit nation devalues by 6% or revalues by 6% at the end of three months, (c) a crawling peg system under which the nation increases its par value by 2% at the end of each of three months.

(a) See Fig. 11-1.

(b) See Fig. 11-2.

(c) See Fig. 11-3.

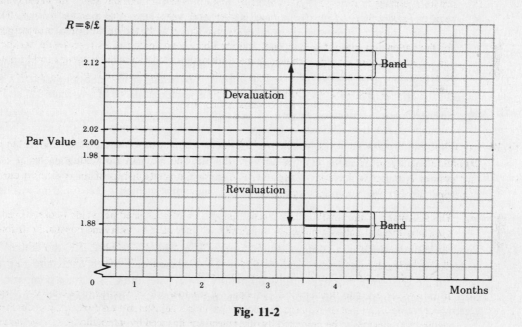

Fig. 11-2

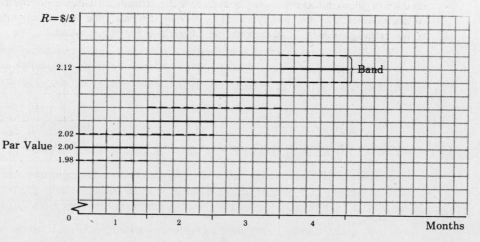

Fig. 11-3

THE CASE FOR FLEXIBLE EXCHANGE RATES

11.12 Identify and comment on each of the alleged advantages of a flexible over a fixed exchange rate system.

(1) Balance of payments adjustments are continuous, small and smooth under a flexible exchange rate system. Balance of payments disequilibria are never allowed to become so large and cumulative, as may happen under a fixed exchange rate system, that a large and disruptive change in par values is required.

(2) Only the exchange rate needs to be changed in order to bring about a balance of payments adjustment under a flexible exchange rate system. This is much more efficient than changing all domestic prices, as is required under a fixed exchange rate system. (The reasoning here is the same as that used for changing to daylight savings time during summer months, i.e., it is easier to reset the nation's clock than reschedule all events for an hour earlier.)

(3) With exchange rates at all times at or near equilibrium, the nation's comparative advantage is clearly evident. On the other hand, under a fixed exchange rate system, the exchange rate may be too low so that a commodity may seem unduly cheap to foreigners. As a result, the nation may export a commodity in which it does not have a comparative advantage. The opposite is true when the exchange rate is too high.

(4) Monetary policy is freed for use in achieving domestic goals other than external balance. This is no small benefit in view of the limited range of effective policy tools at the nation's disposal and the generally greater number of national goals than policies.

(5) Flexible exchange rates also allow each nation to strive to achieve its own inflation-unemployment trade-off. Under a fixed exchange rate system, a nation wishing to tolerate high unemployment to keep the inflation rate lower than in other nations is constrained by the resulting balance of payments deficits.

(6) No intervention in foreign exchange markets is required to keep exchange rates within allowed limits. Foreign exchange market interventions are generally very complex, require highly skilled technicians to undertake, are time consuming and can have uncertain results.

(7) With balance of payments disequilibria automatically adjusted under a flexible exchange rate system, the possibility of policy mistakes is avoided. For example, under a fixed exchange rate system, a nation may be forced to change its par value after strenuous and costly attempts to keep it. This was usually the case under the gold-exchange standard.

11.13 Suppose that the price of a commodity is \$5 in the U.S. and £2 in the U.K., the actual exchange rate under a fixed exchange rate system is \$3 = £1, but the equilibrium exchange rate is \$2 = £1. (*a*) Will the U.S. import or export this commodity?   (*b*) Does the U.S. have a comparative advantage or disadvantage in this commodity?   (*c*) What per-unit tax or subsidy does the actual exchange rate involve?

(*a*) The U.S. will export this commodity because $P = \$5$ in the U.S. and $P = \$6$ in the U.K. at the actual exchange rate of \$3 = £1.

(*b*) At the equilibrium exchange rate of \$2 = £1, the price of the commodity is $P = \$5$ in the U.S. and $P = \$4$ in the U.K. Thus, the U.S. has a comparative disadvantage in this commodity even though the U.S. exports it. As a result, the pattern of trade is distorted by the prevailing disequilibrium exchange rate.

(*c*) The actual exchange rate of \$2 = £1 involves a \$1 per-unit subsidy on exports of the commodity by the U.S.

COMPARISON OF FIXED AND FLEXIBLE EXCHANGE RATE SYSTEMS

11.14 Explain how advocates of flexible exchange rates might counter the argument that a fixed exchange rate system   (*a*) results in a smaller degree of uncertainty in international trade and finance,   (*b*) is more likely to lead to stabilizing speculation,   (*c*) results in greater price discipline.

(*a*) Advocates of flexible exchange rates point out that while exchange rates are certainly more stable on a day-to-day basis under a fixed exchange rate system, the large discrete changes in par values that periodically become necessary under a fixed exchange rate system are even more damaging and disruptive to the smooth flow of international trade and investments than the small continuous changes in exchange rates under a flexible exchange rate system.

(b)   Advocates of flexible exchange rates feel that stabilizing speculation is much more likely to take place when exchange rates are free to adjust continuously, automatically, and by small amounts than when they are prevented from adjusting until a large discrete change becomes unavoidable. Under a fixed exchange rate system, speculators will sell the currency when they expect it to be devalued and purchase the currency when they expect it to be revalued, thus amplifying exchange rate fluctuations (destabilizing speculation).

(c)   Advocates of flexible exchange rates concede that a fixed exchange rate system leads to more monetary discipline (i.e., to a lower inflation rate) than a flexible exchange rate system. However, they point out that some of this greater price discipline is achieved at the expense of the nation being unable to pursue its desired inflation-unemployment trade-off.

11.15 (a) What overall conclusion can be reached as to the advantages and disadvantages of fixed versus flexible exchange rates?   (b) What are the advantages and disadvantages of hybrid exchange rate systems?

(a)   When all relevant factors are considered, flexible exchange rates do not compare unfavorably to fixed exchange rates as far as the degree of uncertainty in international trade and finance is concerned. Flexible exchange rates do seem more inflationary, but they also allow governments to pursue their desired inflation-unemployment trade-off, unhampered by balance of payments considerations. Although the present system is a managed float rather than a freely flexible exchange rate system, it is the closest of the hybrid systems to a freely flexible exchange rate system. While many experts have become somewhat dissatisfied with the present managed exchange rate system (primarily as a result of the large volatility and large and persistent misalignment of the U.S. dollar during the 1980s), it is generally recognized that no fixed exchange rate system could have survived the turmoil of the early 1970s.

(b)   An adjustable peg system is the closest of the hybrid systems to a fixed exchange rate system and, as such, it shares some of its disadvantages, particularly the increased uncertainty and the possibility of destabilizing speculation arising from the large periodic exchange rate changes that become necessary to correct balance of payments disequilibria. A crawling peg system can avoid this disadvantage with small preannounced exchange rate changes, but only at the expense of being somewhat more inflationary. A managed floating system is also more inflationary than fixed exchange rates. In addition, a nation can manage its exchange rates to be higher than equilibrium in order to stimulate its exports (a beggar-thy-neighbor policy). The ability of a nation to do this is limited by the amount of international reserves of the nation and the possibility of retaliation by the nation's trade partners.

11.16 How do   (a) hedging and   (b) speculation take place under a fixed exchange rate system?

(a)   Since, under a fixed exchange rate system, the exchange rate can also fluctuate (within the allowed limits), there usually still arises a need for hedging. This generally takes place as described in Section 7.4, except if the exchange rate is at or very close to the allowed limits of fluctuation. If the exchange rate is at the upper limit allowed, then importers and all others with foreign exchange payable at a future date need not hedge since the exchange rate can only fall in the future. On the other hand, if the exchange rate is at the lower limit allowed, then exporters and all others with foreign exchange receivable need not hedge since the exchange rate can only rise. This is true except when there is a feeling that the limits themselves may be changed in the near future. In that case, all should hedge.

(b)   If speculators believe that the allowed limits of foreign exchange fluctuation will be maintained, they will sell the foreign currency when its exchange rate is at or near its upper limit (in the expectation that it will fall in the future) and buy it when at or near its lower limits (in the expectation that it will rise in the future). In this case, speculation is stabilizing and eliminates or reduces the need of intervention (by the monetary authorities) to keep the exchange rate within the allowed limits. If, on the other hand, speculators feel that the monetary authorities will not be able or willing to continue to prevent a currency from depreciating past its upper limit, or appreciating past its lower limit, then speculation will be destabilizing. This increases the need of intervention and increases the probability that the speculators' expectations will be fulfilled (see Chapter 12).

Chapter 12

The International Monetary System:
Past and Present

12.1 THE CLASSICAL GOLD STANDARD PERIOD

The classical gold standard operated from about 1880 to 1914 and was characterized by relatively free trade and unrestricted international capital movements. Adjustment under the classical gold standard was rather quick and smooth but is now believed to have occurred primarily through stabilizing short-term capital movements and changes in national income rather than through price changes, as described by the price-specie-flow mechanism.

EXAMPLE 1. During the classical gold standard period, London was the undisputed center of international trade and finance. In such a world, England usually financed a deficit in its balance of payments by increasing its interest rate and attracting short-term capital rather than by a gold outflow. Furthermore, a gold outflow (to the extent that there was one) improved the nation's trade balance primarily by reducing national income, rather than by causing a decline in domestic prices (which even then were somewhat inflexible downward). The opposite was true when England had a surplus in its balance of payments (see Problem 12.2).

12.2 THE INTERWAR PERIOD

World War I brought the classical gold standard to an end. The interwar period was characterized by generally chaotic conditions in international trade and finance. There were fluctuating exchange rates from the end of the war to 1925 (except for the U.S., which returned to gold in 1919). Starting in 1925, an attempt was made to reestablish the gold standard, but it collapsed by 1931 at the time of the Great Depression. There followed a period of competitive devaluations, as nations tried to *export* their unemployment (beggar-thy-neighbor policies). Tariffs, quotas and exchange controls also became widespread, with the result that the volume of world trade was cut almost in half. Deflationary tendencies were completely overcome only as nations rearmed for World War II.

EXAMPLE 2. After World War I, London lost its position as the single undisputed center of international trade and finance. With a multicentered international financial system (London, New York, Paris) international short-term capital movements were often destabilizing. This forced England off gold in 1931 and was an important reason for the collapse of the gold standard. Furthermore, nations generally did not follow the so-called rules of the game but sterilized or neutralized international capital and gold movements, preventing them from affecting the nation's money supply and initiating the adjustment process (see Problem 12.6). There were also a number of serious policy mistakes. For example, in 1933–1934, the U.S. devalued the dollar to stimulate its economy even though it had a surplus in its balance of payments.

12.3 THE BRETTON WOODS SYSTEM

The basis for the post-World War II international monetary system was laid at Bretton Woods, New Hampshire in 1944 by the U.S. and the U.K. It can best be understood as an attempt to prevent a recurrence of the chaotic conditions in international trade and finance that prevailed after World War I. The new system called for the establishment of the *International Monetary Fund* (IMF) to oversee that nations followed an agreed-upon code of rules in their conduct of international trade and finance (see Example 3) and also to set up borrowing facilities for nations facing temporary balance of payments difficulties (see Example 4). The Bretton Woods System operated until 1971, when it collapsed.

EXAMPLE 3.   Upon joining the IMF, each nation was to fix the value of its currency in terms of gold or dollars and then keep its exchange rate within 1% of its par value (the gold-exchange standard). The par value could be changed only in case of *fundamental* (i.e., large and persistent) *disequilibrium* and with the permission of the IMF (except for changes of 10% or less). Temporary deficits were to be financed out of the nation's reserves and borrowing from the IMF. (For long-term development assistance, the *World Bank* was created). After a period of transition, *convertibility of currencies* into one another was to be resumed and trade restrictions were to be gradually removed under the *General Agreement on Tariffs and Trade* (GATT).

EXAMPLE 4.   Each nation was assigned a quota to the Fund. The size of a nation's quota was based on its economic importance and determined the nation's voting power and its ability to borrow from the Fund. The nation was to pay 25% of its quota in gold and the remainder in its own currency. In borrowing from the Fund, the nation would get convertible currencies in exchange for depositing more of its currency, until the Fund held no more than 200% of the nation's quota in the nation's currency. The nation could borrow no more than 25% of its quota per year, for a total of 125% over five years. The nation's borrowing of the first 25% of its quota (the so-called *gold tranche*) was practically automatic. For each further borrowing (the *credit tranches*), rising interest rates were charged and more supervision of the Fund imposed. Repayments were to be made within three to five years and involved purchase of the nation's currency with gold or other convertible currencies approved by the Fund.

12.4   OPERATION AND EVOLUTION OF THE BRETTON WOODS SYSTEM

In many ways, the Bretton Woods System operated as intended, but in some, it did not (see Example 5). Furthermore, the system evolved over the years in several important directions in response to changing conditions (see Example 6). In general, the Bretton Woods System served the world well—during its operation, world output rose rapidly and world trade even faster.

EXAMPLE 5.   Nations in fundamental disequilibrium found themselves very reluctant to change their par values. From 1950 to 1971, the U.K. devalued only in 1967, France only in 1957 and 1969; Germany revalued in 1961 and 1969; the U.S., Japan and Italy never changed their par values, while Canada (defying the rules of the IMF) had fluctuating rates from 1950 to1961 and then again from 1970. The convertibility of the dollar was resumed soon after the war; major European currencies became formally convertible in 1961 and the Japanese yen in 1964. Several rounds of negotiations under GATT reduced tariffs on manufactured goods to about 7% nominally and 12% effectively by 1971. After several increases in quotas, the total resources of the Fund reached $28.5 billion by 1971 (of which $6.7 billion or about 23.5% was the U.S. quota). By 1971, the Fund had lent $22 billion (most of it after 1956), of which $4 billion was outstanding. The communist nations, with the exception of Yugoslavia, were not members of the IMF; nor was Switzerland.

EXAMPLE 6.   To supplement its resources, the Fund negotiated in 1962 the *General Arrangements to Borrow* (GAB) up to $6 billion from the *group of ten* (most important industrial nations). Nations could supplement their regular IMF borrowing facilities by negotiating *standby arrangements* with the Fund to borrow additional amounts in case of need, and by *swap arrangements* with other nations. The Fund also began to allow nations to borrow up to 50% of their quota in a year (up from 25%). International reserves were supplemented by a total of $9.5 billion of *special drawing rights* (SDRs) or *paper gold* distributed by the Fund to nations according to their quotas, in three installments in January 1970, 1971, and 1972. In 1961, the U.S. and a group of industrial nations established the *gold pool* to sell gold on the London market to prevent the gold price from rising above the official level of $35 per ounce. This was discontinued in 1968 when a two-tier system was established, with the private price of gold determined by conditions of demand and supply and allowed to rise above the official price. A *Eurodollar* market centered in London also came into existence. Eurodollars are dollar deposits in banks outside the U.S. They amounted to about $46 billion at the end of 1970.

12.5   THE U.S. BALANCE OF PAYMENTS PROBLEM

The U.S. balance of payments has been in deficit in almost every year since 1950. U.S. deficits were rather small, averaging about $1 billion per year from 1950 to 1957 but rose to over $3 billion per year from 1958 to 1970. The U.S. financed its deficits from 1950 to 1970 with a $13 billion loss of its gold reserves (which declined from $24 to $11 billion) and with over $40 billion by dollar outflows. The U.S. would not or could not adopt some policies to correct its deficit, and the policies that it did adopt failed to eliminate the deficit.

EXAMPLE 7.   Up to about 1949, the U.S. ran huge trade balance surpluses with Europe and extended Marshall aid to help Europe pay for them. With European recovery more or less complete by 1950, the U.S. trade surplus declined and the U.S. balance of payments turned into deficit. Up to 1957, these deficits were small and allowed European nations to build up their reserves. This was the period of the *dollar shortage*. Contributing to the much larger U.S. deficits since 1958 were first the huge increase in capital outflows, then the Vietnam War, and beginning with 1968, the virtual disappearance of the U.S. trade balance surplus. The U.S., quite understandably, would not deflate its economy for the sake of external balance, and with dollars used as international reserves, it felt that it could not devalue. Instead, it stimulated U.S. exports, reduced military and other government expenditures abroad, tied foreign aid, imposed a tax on the purchase of foreign securities in 1963 and extended it to long-term bank loans to foreigners in 1965. Finally, in 1968 it imposed mandatory controls over U.S. direct investment abroad. It also intervened in the forward and spot markets and sold *Roosa bonds* [see Problem 12.12(*c*)].

12.6   THE COLLAPSE OF THE BRETTON WOODS SYSTEM

The *immediate* cause for the collapse of the Bretton Woods System was the expectation, beginning in March 1971 in the face of huge and persistent deficits, that the U.S. would soon be forced to devalue the dollar. This led to a massive flight of liquid capital from the U.S. When some small European central banks attempted to convert part of their dollar reserves into gold at the Fed, the U.S. suspended the gold convertibility of the dollar (August 15, 1971) and imposed a 10% import surcharge. Had the U.S. not done this, it would soon have exhausted all of its gold reserves. The *fundamental* cause of the collapse is to be found in the problems of liquidity, adjustment and confidence. Most of the increase in liquidity (i.e., international reserves) under the Bretton Woods System was in the form of dollars arising from U.S. balance of payments deficits. But, as the U.S. was unable to adjust its deficits and too many unwanted dollars accumulated in foreign hands, confidence in the dollar was lost and the system collapsed.

EXAMPLE 8.   The *Smithsonian Agreement* in December 1971 provided for an increase in the official price of gold from $35 to $38 per ounce (a dollar devaluation of about 9%), and a further revaluation of a few currencies, especially the yen and the mark. Currencies were allowed to fluctuate by $2\frac{1}{4}$% above or below their new par value (up from 1%), the U.S. removed the 10% import surcharge, while the dollar remained inconvertible into gold. But with another huge deficit in the U.S. balance of payments in 1972, massive speculation against the dollar resumed in February 1973 and led to another devaluation of the dollar, this time by 10% (achieved by an increase in the official price of gold to $42.22 per ounce). When speculation against the dollar flared up again in March 1973, exchange rates were left free to float except for some official intervention and are still floating today.

12.7   THE PRESENT INTERNATIONAL MONETARY SYSTEM

Since March 1973, all the large developed nations and many of the largest developing nations have operated under a managed floating exchange rate system. Under this system, nations' monetary authorities intervene in foreign exchange markets to smooth out "excessive" short-run fluctuations in exchange rates. The *Jamaica Accords* (ratified in April 1978) formally recognized this arrangement and allowed nations the choice of the exchange rate regime. The present international monetary system has also evolved in a number of important ways, including new allocations of SDRs, increased nations' quotas in the IMF, renewal of the General Agreements to Borrow (GAB), the abolishment of the official gold price, and the formation of the *European Monetary System* (EMS). Throughout most of the 1980s, the dollar faced great volatility and gross misalignments, and by the end of the 1980s the U.S. had become the world's largest debtor nation (see Problem 12.20). A number of other international economic problems also remain (see Problem 12.21).

EXAMPLE 9. By 1990, one-third of the 151 member nations of the IMF had opted for a managed float. These included all the large industrial nations and many of the large developing nations, so that about 4/5 of world trade moved among nations with either independently or jointly managed exchange rates. Other developing nations pegged their exchange rates to the U.S. dollar, other major currency, or SDRs. A new allocation in 1979 and 1981 increased the total SDR holdings of member nations of $20 billion. Since 1981, the value of one SDR is based on a weighted average of the U.S. dollar, the British pound, the German mark, the French franc, and the Japanese yen. In 1989, one SDR was worth $1.35. Through increased membership and periodic increases in member nations' quotas, IMF total resources reached $120 billion, and the total reserve position of member nations at the IMF was $28 billion in 1989. The IMF increased its loans to cover balance of payments deficits resulting from temporary short-falls in exports. In 1979, GAB was renewed and expanded. The gold price rose to over $800 per ounce in January 1980 but fell to below $400 by the end of 1982 and remained at that level throughout the rest of the 1980s.

EXAMPLE 10. In 1979, the European Economic Community (EEC) announced the formation of the European Monetary System (EMS) as part of the EEC's aim toward greater monetary integration. The main features of the EMS are (1) the creation of the *European Currency Unit* (ECU), defined as a weighted average of the EEC currencies, (2) having EEC currencies (with some exception) fluctuate no more than 2.25% with respect to established central rates or par values, and (3) the establishment of the *European Monetary Fund* (EMF) to provide short-term balance of payments assistance to EEC nations. The U.K. has thus far refused to join.

Glossary

International Monetary Fund (IMF)   The international institution created under the Bretton Woods System for the purposes of (1) overseeing that nations followed a set of agreed rules of conduct in international trade and finance and (2) providing borrowing facilities for nations facing balance of payments difficulties.

Fundamental disequilibrium   Large and persistent balance of payments deficits or surpluses.

World Bank   The international institution established after World War II to provide long-run development assistance to developing nations.

Currency convertibility   The ability to exchange one national currency for another without any restrictions or limitations.

General Agreement on Tariffs and Trade (GATT)   An international organization devoted to the promotion of freer trade through multilateral trade negotiations.

Gold tranche   The 25% of a nation's quota paid into the IMF in gold and which the nation can borrow from the Fund automatically.

Credit tranche   The amount that a member nation can borrow yearly from the IMF over and above the gold tranche.

General Arrangements to Borrow (GAB)   The arrangements under which the IMF negotiated to borrow up to $6 billion from the "group of ten" (most important industrial nations) and Switzerland to augment its resources if needed to help nations in balance of payments difficulties.

Standby arrangements   The advance permission for future borrowings from the IMF by a nation at the IMF.

Swap arrangements   The arrangements under which national central banks negotiate to exchange each other's currency, to be used to intervene in foreign exchange markets to combat international hot money flows.

Smithsonian Agreement   The agreement, reached in December 1971 in Washington, under which the dollar was devalued by about 9% (by increasing the price of gold from $35 to $38 per ounce), other strong currencies were revalued by various amounts with respect to the dollar, the dollar convertibility into gold remained suspended, and exchange rates were allowed to fluctuate by 2.25% on either side of the new par values.

Jamaica Accords   The agreements, reached in January 1976 and ratified in April 1978, that officially recognized the managed float and led to the abolishment of the official price of gold.

European Monetary System (EMS)   The organization, formed in 1979 by EEC members, that has the responsibility of defining the European Currency Unit (ECU) of account, maintaining the fluctuation of exchange rates within 2.25% on either side of established central rates or par values, and overseeing the operations of the European Monetary Fund (EMF). The U.K. is presently not a member.

European Currency Unit (ECU)   The unit of account, defined by the European Monetary System, based on the weighted average of the currencies of the EEC members.

European Monetary Fund (EMF)   The institution of the European Monetary System that provides short- and medium-term balance of payments assistance to member nations.

Review Questions

1. Which of the following statements with regard to the classical gold standard is false?   (*a*) London was the undisputed center of international trade and finance.   (*b*) There was relatively free trade and unrestricted international capital movements.   (*c*) International short-term capital movements were stabilizing.   (*d*) Prices were highly flexible, both upward and downward.

   Ans.   (*d*) See Section 12.1.

2. Adjustment to balance of payments disequilibria under the classical gold standard is now believed to have occurred primarily through   (*a*) the price-specie-flow mechanism,   (*b*) gold shipments,   (*c*) price changes,   (*d*) stabilizing short-term capital movements and changes in national income.

   Ans.   (*d*) See Section 12.1.

3. Which of the following statements with regard to the interwar period is correct?   (*a*) The gold standard operated over the entire period.   (*b*) Adjustment to balance of payments disequilibria was rather quick and smooth.   (*c*) Generally chaotic conditions prevailed in international trade and payments.   (*d*) There was relatively free trade and unrestricted capital movements.

   Ans.   (*c*) See Section 12.2.

4. Adjustment to balance of payments disequilibria during the interwar periods was brought about by   (*a*) stabilizing capital movements,   (*b*) the price-specie-flow mechanism,   (*c*) changes in national incomes,   (*d*) none of the above.

   Ans.   (*d*) See Example 2.

5. The Bretton Woods System was   (*a*) a gold standard,   (*b*) a flexible exchange rate system,   (*c*) a gold-exchange standard,   (*d*) none of the above.

   Ans.   (*c*) See Example 3.

6. The Bretton Woods System   (*a*) set up a code of rules for nations to follow in their conduct of international trade and finance,   (*b*) set up borrowing facilities for nations in temporary balance of payments difficulties,   (*c*) evolved over the years in several important ways,   (*d*) served the world fairly well,   (*e*) all of the above.

   Ans.   (*e*) See Sections 12.3 and 12.4.

7. Which of the following does not represent an evolution of the Bretton Woods System as it operated until 1971? (*a*) The General Arrangements to Borrow,   (*b*) standby arrangements,   (*c*) flexible exchange rates,   (*d*) special drawing rights,   (*e*) the gold pool.

Ans.   (*c*) See Example 6.

8. The U.S. balance of payments was generally   (*a*) in surplus from 1946 to 1949,   (*b*) in deficit from 1950 to 1957, but the deficits were rather small,   (*c*) in deficit from 1958 to 1970 and deficits were large,   (*d*) all of the above.

Ans.(*d*) See Section 12.5.

9. On which of the following methods did the U.S. rely most during the 1960s to correct the deficit in its balance of payments? (*a*) Domestic deflation,   (*b*) devaluation of the dollar,   (*c*) direct controls of specific items in the balance of payments,   (*d*) official intervention in the foreign exchange market.

Ans.   (*c*) See Example 7.

10. The immediate cause for the collapse of the Bretton Woods System was   (*a*) the expectation that the U.S. would soon be forced to devalue the dollar,   (*b*) the massive flight of liquid capital from the U.S.,   (*c*) the attempt by three small European central banks to convert part of their dollar holdings into gold at the Fed,   (*d*) all of the above.

Ans.   (*d*) See Section 12.6.

11. The fundamental cause for the collapse of the Bretton Woods System was   (*a*) the liquidity problem,   (*b*) the adjustment problem,   (*c*) the confidence problem,   (*d*) all of the above.

Ans.   (*d*) See Section 12.6.

12. The present international monetary system is   (*a*) a gold standard,   (*b*) a freely flexible exchange rate system, (*c*) a fixed exchange rate system but with more frequent exchange rate changes and a wider band of allowed fluctuations,   (*d*) a fluctuating exchange rate system but with some intervention by monetary authorities to help maintain orderly foreign exchange markets (managed float).

Ans.   (*d*) See Section 12.7.

Solved Problems

THE CLASSICAL GOLD STANDARD PERIOD

12.1   (*a*) How would a deficit in England's balance of payments be adjusted if the price-specie-flow mechanism operated?   (*b*) How did England in fact adjust a deficit in its balance of payments during the classical gold standard period?

(*a*)   According to the price-specie-flow mechanism, a deficit in England's balance of payments would lead to a gold outflow and decrease in its money supply. England would then remain at full employment but would face declining domestic prices (the quantity theory of money). This would stimulate England's exports and discourage its imports. The exact opposite would occur in the surplus nation. This process would continue until the improvement in England's balance of trade was sufficient to eliminate the deficit in its balance of payments.

(*b*)   When England faced a deficit in its balance of payments during the gold standard period, it reacted by deliberately increasing its interest rate (then called the *bank rate*). With London the undisputed center of international trade and finance, short-term capital movements responded quickly and in a stabilizing manner. Thus, it is now widely believed that England financed its deficits primarily by short-term capital inflows rather than by gold outflows. To the extent that there were gold outflows, these had a deflationary impact on the domestic economy which discouraged imports rather than causing a decline in domestic prices, as described by the price-specie-flow mechanism. The reason for this is that even during the classical gold standard period, prices were hardly flexible downward, as theoretically assumed.

12.2   Explain briefly how England seems to have corrected surpluses in its balance of payments during the classical gold standard period.

When England faced a surplus in its balance of payments during the classical gold standard period, it usually reacted by reducing its interest rates. This resulted in a short-term capital outflow from England in place of a gold inflow to settle the surplus. Furthermore, to the extent that England did experience a gold inflow from a position of less than full employment, its trade balance worsened primarily as a result of an increase in national income rather than because of a rise in domestic prices. Only if England were at full employment or faced inflation would a surplus in its balance of payments settled by a gold inflow be eliminated by an increase in domestic prices, as described by the price-specie-flow mechanism.

12.3   The reestablishment of the gold standard today could not work well. Discuss.

During the heyday of the gold standard, settlement of the balance of payments disequilibria took the form of stabilizing short-term capital movements rather than gold shipments in the majority of cases. With London as the undisputed center of international trade and finance, there were no speculative or destabilizing capital movements. However, in today's multicentered world (New York, London, Zurich, Frankfurt, Paris, Milan, Tokyo) international short-term capital flows are likely to move erratically and in a destabilizing fashion from one monetary center to another. In such a situation, adjustment to balance of payments disequilibria would have to come about through changes in internal prices and/or national income. A deficit nation would have to deflate and a surplus nation inflate, and thus give priority to external over internal balance. This is entirely unacceptable in today's world. Primarily because of this, the reestablishment of the gold standard today should be considered as only a remote possibility.

THE INTERWAR PERIOD

12.4   (a) Why did nations let their exchange rates fluctuate for several years immediately after World War I?   (b) How is this related to the purchasing-power-parity doctrine?

(a)   Because of the inflationary and structural changes that took place during World War I, nations did not know at what level to repeg their exchange rates after the war. Thus, they allowed their exchange rates to fluctuate for several years in hopes of getting some idea from the market as to the appropriate level at which to repeg them.

(b)   The purchasing-power-parity (PPP) theory was developed by Gustav Cassell at the end of World War I for the specific purpose of estimating the equilibrium exchange rates to be reestablished after the war. However, because of the major structural changes that occurred in England and other major trading nations during the war, the PPP theory gave very biased results (see Problem 10.9). For example, since England had liquidated a great deal of its foreign investment to pay for the war and had lost a great deal of its competitiveness in international markets (especially to the U.S.), the estimated exchange rate of the pound with respect to many other major currencies was grossly overvalued.

12.5   (a) What was the immediate cause of the collapse of the gold standard in 1931?   (b) What were the fundamental causes?   (c) What happened after 1931?

(a)   By 1931, many nations were holding sterling (and to some extent dollars and francs) in addition to gold as part of their international reserves. These sterling holdings were backed and convertible into gold at the Bank of England (so that this was really a gold-exchange standard). In 1931, massive flows of speculative funds led to fears as to the continued gold convertibility of the overvalued pound. This caused a run on the very small gold reserves of England, forcing it off gold in 1931 and dealing a death blow to the system.

(b)   The fundamental causes of the collapse of the new system are to be found in the breaking out of the Great Depression (to which the new system contributed) and in the lack of an adequate adjustment mechanism. Specifically, in the multicentered world then in existence, short-term international capital movements were often destabilizing. In addition, nations sterilized or neutralized changes in their money supplies arising from balance of payments disequilibria. This prevented adjustment through changes in prices and national incomes. However, it is likely that even a well-functioning international monetary system would have broken down under the strain of the world depression.

(c)   The year 1931 was followed by a period of competitive devaluations (even from positions of surplus) as nations attempted to export their unemployment. By the time this process came to an end in 1936, the exchange rates among the major currencies were essentially the same as in 1930. This was also a period when many restrictions were imposed on international trade and finance, with the result that the volume of world trade was cut almost by half. By 1939, depression had given way to full employment—and war.

12.6   (a) Explain how a decline in a nation's money supply caused by a deficit in its balance of payments can be sterilized. Why did nations usually do this during the interwar period?   (b) Explain how an increase in the money supply caused by a surplus can be sterilized. Why did nations usually do this during the interwar period?

(a)   A nation could sterilize a decline in its money supply caused by a deficit in its balance of payments by open market purchases of treasury bills from the public. This decreases private holdings of treasury bills and puts more money in circulation. During the interwar period, nations generally did not follow the rules of the game but sterilized deficits, preventing them from decreasing the nation's money supply. Since wages and prices were generally inflexible downward, a decline in the money supply would have had a further deflationary effect on the economy, and nations wanted to avoid this.

(b)   A nation could sterilize an increase in its money supply caused by a surplus in its balance of payments by open market sales of treasury bills to the public. This increases private holdings of treasury bills and was used by surplus nations during the interwar period to prevent the surplus from increasing their money supplies. Increases in the nation's money supply from a condition of recession and surplus would have helped to correct both. Nations, such as the U.S. in 1934, chose instead to stimulate their economies by devaluing their currencies. This added to deflationary pressures around the world and represented a serious policy mistake.

THE BRETTON WOODS SYSTEM

12.7   With respect to the Bretton Woods System, explain   (a) what type of an exchange rate system it was and how it was set up and maintained,   (b) how nations were supposed to finance and correct balance of payments deficits and   (c) the rules on convertibility and trade restrictions.

(a)   The Bretton Woods System was a gold-exchange standard. Each nation was to fix the value of its currency in terms of gold or dollars and then actively intervene in the foreign exchange market to keep its exchange rate from moving by more than 1% above or below its par value. The dollar was practically the only *intervention currency* (so that we truly had a gold-dollar standard) until the latter part of the 1950s and early 1960s when the currencies of most other industrial nations became convertible into dollars. Within the band of allowed fluctuations, the equilibrium exchange rate was determined by the forces of demand and supply.

(b)   Nations were supposed to finance temporary deficits in their balance of payments out of their international reserves and by borrowing from the IMF—without domestic deflation (which was unacceptable), without devaluation (which could lead to competitive devaluations) or import restrictions (which would also lead to retaliation). Borrowings from the IMF were to be for short periods (three to five years) so as not to tie up the resources of the IMF into long-term loans. For long-term development assistance, the International Bank for Reconstruction and Development, or simply the World Bank and its affiliates, the International Finance Corporation and the Agency for International Development, were created. A change in the nation's exchange rate was to be used only to correct a fundamental disequilibrium (which was never clearly defined, but which we may take to mean a *large and persistent* disequilibrium). Thus, the Bretton Woods System, at least as conceived, combined stability with some flexibility.

(c)   After a period of transition following the war, currencies were to be made convertible into one another and into dollars. Nations were generally forbidden to impose additional trade restrictions (otherwise convertibility would not have much meaning) and were encouraged by the IMF to remove unilaterally existing trade restrictions and to negotiate multilateral reductions under the sponsorship of the General Agreement on Tariffs and Trade (GATT).

12.8   If a nation's quota in the IMF was set at $100 million,   (*a*) how and in what was this amount to be paid? How much could the nation borrow in any one year under the original rules?   (*b*) Explain the procedure whereby this nation borrows from the Fund the maximum amount allowed for the first year.   (*c*) How much could the nation borrow in subsequent years? For how many years could this take place? Explain the procedure whereby this nation borrows the maximum amount allowed in each subsequent year.

(*a*)   The nation has to pay 25% of its quota, or $25 million, in gold and the remaining 75% ($75 million) in the nation's currency. Under the original rules of the IMF, a nation could borrow only 25% of its quota in any one year.

(*b*)   The first year this nation can borrow $25 million from the Fund in any convertible currency approved by the Fund. This is the gold tranche and can be drawn from the Fund almost automatically, without any restrictions or conditions. Upon borrowing this $25 million, the nation pays or deposits an additional $25 million of its currency with the Fund, increasing the Fund's holdings of this nation's currency from the original $75 million (75% of the nation's quota) to $100 million (100% of this nation's quota).

(*c*)   The nation can borrow a maximum of 25% of its quota in each subsequent year until the Fund holds no more than 200% of the nation's quota in the nation's currency. Since after the first borrowing (the gold tranche), the IMF is already holding 100% of the nation's quota in the nation's currency, the nation can borrow a maximum of 25% of its quota in each of four subsequent years (the credit tranches) before reaching its borrowing limit. As the nation borrows under each additional credit tranche, it deposits $25 million of its currency with the Fund and faces increasing interest charges and supervision from the Fund. Thus, the overall maximum that a nation could borrow over a period of five years was one gold tranche and four credit tranches for a total of 125% of its quota.

12.9   (*a*) How and when was a nation to repay its IMF loans?   (*b*) What would happen if the nation in Problem 12.8 (henceforth referred to as nation A) stopped borrowing from the Fund after the first year, but before it repaid its loan, nation B borrowed $25 million from the Fund in nation A's currency?

(*a*)   The nation repays its loans by repurchasing its currency from the Fund with other convertible currencies approved by the Fund, until the Fund is once again holding no more than 75% of the nation's quota in the nation's currency. The Fund allows repayment to be made in currencies of which the Fund holds less than 75% (and up to 75%) of the issuing nations' quota. Repayment must be made within three to five years.

(*b*)   If nation B borrows $25 million of nation A's currency, after nation A has borrowed but not yet repaid its gold tranche, nation A's repayment becomes unnecessary since the Fund will once again hold no more than 75% of nation A's quota in nation A's currency. If nation B instead borrowed $50 million of nation A's currency, then not only need nation A not repay its gold tranche, but it can also borrow another $25 million (its *super gold tranche*) without repayment.

OPERATION AND EVOLUTION OF THE BRETTON WOODS SYSTEM

12.10   How did the Bretton Woods System operate with respect to   (*a*) adjustment to fundamental disequilibria,   (*b*) convertibility of currencies and   (*c*) trade restrictions?

(*a*)   Under the Bretton Woods System, industrial nations found themselves reluctant to devalue or revalue even when in fundamental disequilibrium. They regarded a devaluation as a sign of weakness and tried to avoid it until it was practically forced upon them. Similarly, they resisted a needed revaluation, preferring instead to continue accumulating reserves. By doing so, these nations gave up most of the flexibility envisioned by the Bretton Woods System, as far as adjustment to balance of payments disequilibria was concerned. On the other hand, Canada had flexible exchange rates from 1950 to 1961 and then from 1970, while developing nations devalued all too often. But the fact that the major industrial nations chose not to use exchange rate changes as a policy instrument for external balance was crucial for the survival of the system (see Section 12.6).

(b)   The major European currencies became convertible for current account purposes, *de facto* in 1958 and *de jure* or formally in 1961. The Japanese yen became formally convertible in 1964. Restrictions on capital account transactions were allowed in order to protect nations against the possibility of huge amounts of destabilizing liquid capital movements (*hot money*). These became larger, more frequent and more disruptive toward the end of the 1960s and early 1970s.

(c)   Encouraged by the IMF, nations gradually dismantled the maze of trade restrictions imposed during the war, so that tariffs on manufactured goods fell to about 7–12% by 1971. Negotiations to reduce barriers to trade in agricultural commodities and on light manufactures (which are of particular importance to developing nations) were not so successful. By 1971, nontariff trade barriers such as quotas and health and safety regulations were probably more important, quantitatively, than tariffs as obstacles to trade.

12.11 Discuss briefly the evolution of the Bretton Woods System with regard to   (*a*) the General Arrangements to Borrow,   (*b*) standby arrangements,   (*c*) swap arrangements,   (*d*) special drawing rights,   (*e*) the gold pool and   (*f*) Eurodollars.

(a)   The General Arrangements to Borrow (GAB) was negotiated by the IMF with the "group of ten" and Switzerland to supplement its resources if needed to help nations with balance of payments difficulties. The amount involved was $6 billion. (This was over and above the periodic increases in the member nations' quotas which were envisioned in the Articles of Agreement that set up the Fund.)

(b)   Nations negotiated standby arrangements with the IMF in order to supplement their international reserves and the regular borrowing facilities available to them at the Fund. Once negotiated, the nation could count, if and when the need arose, on the immediate availability of the amount agreed upon, without any further questioning or restrictions. A commitment charge of 1/4 of 1% was imposed on the amount earmarked, while an interest charge of up to 5.5% or more per year was imposed on the portion actually drawn. These standby arrangements were usually negotiated for a first line of defense against unanticipated, huge and destabilizing hot money flows. In time, the IMF also began to allow nations to borrow up to 50% of their quotas in any one year.

(c)   Swap arrangements are negotiated between central banks to exchange each other's currency, often to be used to intervene in the forward exchange market to protect the nations' currencies against hot money flows. They are negotiated for specified periods of time and with an exchange rate guarantee. When they become due, they can either be renegotiated or settled by a reverse transaction. The U.S. has negotiated many of these swap arrangements with the central banks of most industrial nations since the early 1960s.

(d)   Special drawing rights (SDRs) or paper gold are accounting entries into the books of the IMF. Under an international agreement reached in 1967, $9.5 billion of them were distributed (in January 1970, 1971 and 1972) to IMF members according to their quotas. They were intended to supplement existing international reserves, in hopes that the U.S. would be successful in curbing its deficits and dollar outflows.

(e)   The gold pool was an attempt, started in 1961 by a group of industrial nations under the leadership of the U.S., to feed gold into the London gold market in order to prevent the private price of gold from rising above its official price of $35 per ounce. In 1962, the gold pool was extended on the buying side also. The effort was discontinued in 1968, when a two-tier system came into existence.

(f)   Eurodollars are dollars deposited in European banks to earn higher rates of interest. Total deposits of Eurodollars grew rapidly in the 1960s and by the end of 1970 amounted to over $46 billion. Eurodollars, together with other European currencies deposited outside their domestic market (Eurocurrencies), amounted to over $60 billion in 1970. The existence of a Eurodollar market can reduce the effectiveness of monetary policy in the U.S., as U.S. firms (especially multinational corporations) borrow in this market, when short-term interest rates rise in the U.S. as a result of a tight monetary policy.

THE U.S. BALANCE OF PAYMENTS PROBLEM

12.12 How did the U.S. use   (*a*) monetary policy and   (*b*) official intervention in the foreign exchange market in an attempt to eliminate the deficit in its balance of payments?   (*c*) Why did U.S. monetary authorities sell Roosa bonds to foreign official holders of dollars? (Roosa bonds are medium-term Treasury instruments denominated in dollars but with an exchange guarantee.)

(*a*)   Throughout the 1960s, the U.S. generally adopted a tighter monetary policy and maintained higher short-term interest rates than were justified by internal conditions, in order to reduce the short-term capital outflow from the U.S. or stimulate an inflow. At the same time, it strived to keep long-term interest rates relatively low in order not to discourage domestic growth [see Problem 10.32(*b*)].

(*b*)   U.S. official intervention in the foreign exchange market took the form of forward sales of strong European currencies, such as the German mark, for dollars so as to increase the forward discount on these strong currencies and thus discourage an outflow of liquid funds from the U.S. under covered interest arbitrage (see Section 7.6). U.S. monetary authorities also intervened in the spot market by purchasing dollars with other currencies. The foreign exchange for these interventions in the forward and spot markets was usually obtained by swap arrangements with other central banks.

(*c*)   Starting in the early 1960s, U.S. monetary authorities sold Roosa bonds in order to absorb the excess dollars in the hands of foreign central banks and thus avoid conversion into gold at the Fed. Such conversions would have further reduced U.S. official gold reserves and further weakened the dollar (see Section 12.6). Thus, Roosa bonds only indirectly helped the U.S. balance of payments.

12.13   What were   (*a*) the major benefit of and   (*b*) the major cost to the U.S. resulting from the fact that the dollar was the central reserve currency in the Bretton Woods System?   (*c*) Did this benefit exceed the cost?

(*a*)   The major benefit received by the U.S. as a result of the fact that the dollar was used as an international reserve asset was that the U.S. could finance its deficits by using its own currency (and so receive *seignorage*). If the U.S. had faced the same discipline as other nations (which could finance their deficits only from their gold reserves and other convertible currencies accumulated through surpluses), the U.S. would have exhausted gold reserves in the early 1960s and would have been forced to correct its deficits then. As it was, the U.S. could continue to run deficits by paying with its own currency, until by the end of 1970s, foreigners held over $50 billion in dollars against the $11 billion of U.S. gold reserves.

(*b*)   The major cost or disadvantage for the U.S. resulting from the use of the dollar as the central reserve currency was that the U.S. faced much greater serious policy limitations than most other nations in correcting its balance of payments deficits. Thus, the U.S. freedom to use monetary policy for internal balance was more restricted than in most other nations [see Problem 12.12(*a*)], so that the U.S. had to rely more heavily on fiscal policy. Furthermore, with other nations holding huge amounts of dollars as international reserves, the U.S. felt that it could not devalue its currency (as for example, the U.K. did in 1949, 1957 and 1967).

(*c*)   Whether the use of the dollar as an international reserve asset conferred more benefits than costs on the U.S. is a difficult, perhaps impossible, question to answer objectively, and there are conflicting opinions. One thing is certain—the U.S. did not encourage the use of the dollar as an international reserve asset after World War II. It just occurred.

THE COLLAPSE OF THE BRETTON WOODS SYSTEM

12.14   Had the U.S. agreed to convert dollars into gold for the European central banks that demanded such a conversion in August 1971, the U.S. would have soon exhausted all of its gold reserves. Comment.

Just before August 15, 1971, some small European central banks presented part of their dollar holdings at the Fed to be converted into gold. They did this in the belief that a devaluation of the dollar was imminent. Such a devaluation would have reduced the value of their dollar reserves. Since the amount of dollars held as official reserves abroad was two or three times larger than U.S. gold reserves, if the U.S. had agreed to convert into gold the dollars presented to it in August 1971, other central banks would have rushed in to convert their dollar holdings into gold before U.S. gold reserves were exhausted. Thus, the U.S. was forced to suspend the gold convertibility of the dollar on August 15, 1971. This put an end to the gold-exchange standard and essentially put the world on a pure dollar standard. At the same time, the U.S. imposed a 10% import surcharge, which it promised to remove when other nations, particularly Japan and Germany, revalued their currencies to correct the overvaluation of the dollar.

12.15 (*a*) Why were foreigners eager to accept dollars in payment for U.S. deficits in the early 1950s rather than demand gold in the first place and from the very beginning?   (*b*) How did all this change in the 1960s?   (*c*) How did the U.S. respond to the changed conditions of the 1960s?   (*d*) What were the immediate causes for the collapse of the Bretton Woods System?

    (*a*)   As part of the Articles of Agreement setting up the Bretton Woods System after World War II, the U.S. made a standing commitment to exchange into gold and on demand any dollar presented to the Fed, at the fixed gold price of $35 per ounce. This commitment, together with the fact that the U.S. came out of World War II with by far the strongest economy in the world and holding most of the world's gold reserves, made the dollar "as good as gold." In addition, dollar deposits earned interest, while gold did not. Furthermore, dollars were much more convenient than gold as a medium of exchange for international transactions. For all of these reasons, nations were eager to accept payments in dollars and accumulate them as international reserves. This was true until the late 1950s, which became known as the *dollar shortage* period.

    (*b*)   As a result of the large and persistent U.S. balance of payments deficits since 1958 and the continuing decline in the U.S. gold stock, foreign official dollar holdings became equal to U.S. gold reserves in the early 1960s and became much larger with each passing year. It then became evident that, if the need arose, the U.S. would no longer be able to honor its commitment to exchange all foreign held dollars into gold at $35 per ounce. This made foreigners less eager to accept dollars.

    (*c*)   As European central banks became nervous about continuing to accumulate more dollars and threatened conversion into gold, the U.S. created Roosa bonds (see Problem 12.12) and took stronger measures to correct its balance of payments deficits.

    (*d*)   When the U.S. balance of payments deficits persisted and actually increased in 1970, the feeling became widespread that the U.S. would soon be forced to devalue the dollar. This caused a massive flight of liquid capital from the U.S. and led the central banks of Belgium, the Netherlands and Switzerland to demand the conversion of dollars into gold, forcing the U.S. on August 15, 1971 to suspend the gold convertibility of the dollar.

12.16 (*a*) What was decided by the "group of ten" under the Smithsonian Agreement in December 1971?   (*b*) What happened in February 1973?   (*c*) In March 1973?

    (*a*)   In meetings held at the Smithsonian Institution in Washington in December 1971, the "group of ten" (most important industrial nations) decided to increase the price of gold from $35 to $38 per ounce (this implied a devaluation of the dollar of about 9%) and to revalue by various amounts the yen, the mark, the Belgian franc and the Dutch guilder. The result was a realignment of the exchange rate of the dollar by about 17% with respect to the yen, 14% with respect to the mark, 12% with the Belgian franc and Dutch guilder, 9% with the pound and the franc, and by various smaller percentages with respect to all other currencies, for an overall trade-weighted devaluation of the dollar of about 8%. The effect of this was to remove part of the overvaluation of the dollar. In addition, the allowed band of fluctuations above and below the new par values was increased to $2\frac{1}{4}$%, and the U.S. rescinded the 10% import surcharge that it had imposed on August 15, 1971. Nixon hailed this as "the most significant monetary agreement in the history of the world" and promised that "the dollar would never again be devalued." This essentially put the world on a pure dollar standard.

    (*b*)   As a result of another huge deficit in the U.S. balance of payments in 1972, it was felt that the Smithsonian Agreement was not working and that another devaluation of the dollar would be needed. Even though this inference was questionable (since it normally takes from two to three years for a devaluation to be fully effective), it was nevertheless widely held. This led to renewed speculation against the dollar and became self-fulfilled in February 1973 when the U.S. was once again forced to devalue the dollar, this time by about 10% (achieved by an increase in the official price of gold to $42.22 per ounce). In the meantime, the dollar remained inconvertible into gold.

    (*c*)   In March 1973, speculation against the dollar flared up again and left most of the world's major currencies fluctuating, with exchange rates determined by conditions of demand and supply but with some intervention by monetary authorities to maintain orderly markets.

12.17 (*a*) What is meant by international liquidity? Why is liquidity needed? How was it provided during the postwar period until 1973?   (*b*) How is the problem of providing adequate liquidity related to the adjustment problem?   (*c*) How were the problems of liquidity and adjustment related to the problem of confidence? Why did these represent the fundamental causes of the collapse of the Bretton Woods System?

(*a*)   International liquidity refers mainly to official international reserves. These include official holdings of gold, convertible currencies, SDRs, and the reserve positions in the IMF (see Problem 8.4). International liquidity is needed so that nations can temporarily finance deficits, without direct trade restrictions, and while allowing other more acceptable adjustment measures, to operate to correct balance of payments deficits. "Too little" liquidity hampers the expansion of world trade; "too much" leads to world inflationary pressures. Until 1973, most of the increase in international liquidity was provided by dollars and other convertible currencies (see Table 12.1).

Table 12.1
International Reserves
(Billions of Dollars, End of Year)

	1949	1959	1969	1970	1971	1972	1973
Gold (at official price)	33	38	39	37	39	39	43
Foreign exchange	11	16	33	45	81	104	123
SDRs	—	—	—	3	7	10	11
Reserve positions in the IMF	2	3	7	8	7	7	7
Totals	46	57	79	93	134	160	184

SOURCE: IMF, *International Financial Statistics Yearbook*, 1979 and 1981.

(*b*)   Convertible currencies become part of international reserves when the issuing nations run balance of payments deficits and pay for them with their own currencies. Most of the increase in international liquidity until 1973 was provided by convertible currencies (see Table 12.1). This is a reflection of the fact that the adjustment mechanism did not work well in the postwar period so that nations, especially the U.S., continued to run huge deficits and add to world liquidity.

(*c*)   The less adequate is the adjustment mechanism, the larger are the balance of payments deficits incurred by the major industrial nations, the longer they persist in time, and thus the more they add to world liquidity (to the extent that nations finance the deficits with their own currencies). But as the world's holdings of any currency continue to increase, confidence in the currency decreases. These closely related problems of liquidity, adjustment and confidence were the fundamental causes for the collapse of the Bretton Woods System in 1971.

THE PRESENT INTERNATIONAL MONETARY SYSTEM

12.18 How are the international monetary arrangements in existence since 1973 different from the pre-1971 system, with regard to   (*a*) exchange rates and   (*b*) price and ownership of gold?   (*c*) How well is the present international monetary system operating?

(*a*)   As opposed to the Bretton Woods System, the exchange rate of most major currencies such as the dollar, the pound, the mark, the yen, and the franc have been fluctuating since 1973. Some currencies, particularly Latin American ones, are tied to the dollar, other currencies are tied to the pound, while still others are fluctuating with the mark, thus beginning to form currency blocks. Still other currencies are tied to SDRs. Most monetary authorities intervene in foreign exchange markets to prevent unnecessarily wide fluctuations in their exchange rates. As a result, there is still a need for international reserves, although it is not as great as under the fixed exchange rate system prevailing before 1971.

(b) Since 1968 there has been a free market price of gold, but until 1971, this did not move too far from the official gold price of $35 per ounce. In 1971, the official price of gold was raised to $38 per ounce and the free market price began to rise well above it. Starting in 1975, U.S. residents were allowed for the first time since 1933 to buy gold, but in the face of an almost nonexistent demand, the price of gold fell below $200 per ounce. The price of gold rose to over $800 per ounce in January 1980 but fell below $400 per ounce by the end of 1982 and remained at that level throughout the rest of the 1980s.

(c) The managed floating exchange rate system in operation since 1973 [see Problems 11.8(c) and 11.9(b)] worked remarkably well, considering the sharp increase in petroleum prices since the Fall of 1973, the huge problem of recycling petrodollars, and the double-digit, world-wide inflation and recession during the late 1970s and early 1980s. Throughout all of these upheavals, foreign exchange markets remained relatively calm and world trade continued to expand. The great volatility and large and persistent misalignment of the U.S. dollar during the 1980s, however, are now leading expert opinion to favor the imposition of some restraints on exchange rate fluctuations.

12.19 The establishment of a freely flexible exchange rate system today is unlikely. Discuss.

Under a freely flexible exchange rate system, exchange rates are determined exclusively by the forces of demand and supply without any foreign exchange market intervention on the part of monetary authorities. Under such a truly self-adjusting system, the need for international reserves would virtually disappear and monetary authorities could devote most of their energies to achieve internal balance. However, flexible exchange rates are inflationary, and exchange rates may fluctuate too widely for the smooth conduct of international trade and finance. This may unduly distort the world's specialization pattern. As a result, it is rather unlikely that the present managed exchange rate system will evolve into a truly *freely* flexible exchange rate system. Indeed, it is more likely that more restrictions will be imposed in the future on exchange rate fluctuations.

12.20 (a) What are the most serious *monetary* problems facing the world economy today? (b) How do these involve the United States? (c) What is proposed to solve these problems?

(a) The most serious monetary problems facing the world economy today are the excessive volatility of exchange rates and the persistence of large disequilibria in exchange rates. Since 1973 exchange rates have been characterized by very large volatility and overshooting. This can discourage the flow of international trade. More serious is the fact that under the present managed floating exchange rate system, large exchange rate disequilibria can arise and persist for several years. This was clearly the case for the U.S. dollar during the 1980s.

(b) The excessive appreciation of the dollar during the first half of the 1980s has been associated with huge trade deficits for the U.S. and almost irresistible calls for increased trade protection. Indeed, by the middle of 1985, large budget deficits and capital inflows had turned the U.S. from a creditor nation into a debtor nation, for the first time since 1914. By 1989, the U.S. was by far the world's largest debtor nation. This requires huge payments to service the debt and leads to fears of foreign domination in the United States.

(c) The persistence of disequilibrium and the great volatility of exchange rates have led to renewed calls for reform of the present international monetary system along the lines of establishing target zones of allowed fluctuations for the major currencies and for more international cooperation and coordination of policies among the leading nations. The earlier debate on the relative merits of fixed versus flexible rates has been superseded by discussions of the optimal degree of exchange rate flexibility and policy cooperation. In February 1987, the leading five industrial nations agreed at Louvre to cooperate closely to foster stability of exchange rates around the then prevailing levels. Despite the heavy intervention in foreign exchange markets by these countries' central banks, exchange rates continued to fluctuate by wide margins from the rates prevailing at the time of the Louvre agreement.

12.21 Identify the major problems (other than that examined in Problem 12.20) facing the world economy today, and explain why they are problems.

The major problems facing the world economy today (besides excessive exchange rate volatility and misalignments) are (1) the rising protectionism in developed countries, (2) the huge international debt of developing countries, and (3) the slow growth and poverty of the poorest developing countries.

(1) *Rising protectionism in developed countries*. Since the mid-1970s, there has been a rapid proliferation of nontariff trade barriers (NTBs). This tendency was reinforced during the 1980s by the growing trade deficits of the U.S. vis-à-vis Japan and Germany. Today the spread of NTBs represents the most serious threat to the postwar trading system and world welfare and is also encouraging the formation of huge trading blocks. The Uruguay Round of trade negotiations (1986–1990) sought to reverse the rise of the new protectionism, bring services and agriculture into GATT and improve GATT dispute-settlement mechanisms.

(2) *The international debt problem of developing countries*. During the 1970s, developing countries accumulated a huge international debt that they found impossible to repay or even service during the 1980s. The debt arose as many developing countries borrowed heavily from private banks in developed nations to finance their growing capital needs and to pay for sharply higher oil bills during the 1970s. Large-scale defaults were avoided only by repeated interventions by the IMF. Such defaults could make some of the largest commercial banks in the U.S. insolvent and possibly even lead to a world financial collapse reminiscent of the 1930s. For the debt problem to be overcome and for sustained growth to resume in developing countries, a large increase in the flow of equity capital in the form of direct investments and the opening of developed countries' markets more widely to their exports are required.

(3) *Poverty and development problems of developing countries*. The average real per capita GNP in low-income developing nations is far below that in middle-income developing nations and extremely low in relation to that in developed nations. In addition, absolute differences in GNP per person continue to widen. An international economic system that has spread the benefits from international trade and specialization so unevenly can hardly be said to be functioning properly—not to say equitably. A world where millions of people starve not only is unacceptable from an ethical point of view but also can hardly be expected to be a world in which peace and tranquility can prevail. Many proposals have been advanced by the World Bank, the United Nations, and other international forums on how to improve living conditions in developing nations and stimulate their development. There is, however, little hope that massive programs (which require sharp increases in foreign aid) will be undertaken soon.

Final Examination

1. *Assume that* (1) the return on three-month treasury bills is 9% (on a yearly basis) in Frankfurt and 5% in New York, (2) the spot exchange rate of the deutsche mark (DM) is $0.40, (3) the three-month forward DM is at a 2% discount (per year), and (4) you have $1,000,000 that you want to use for covered interest arbitrage for three months.

    Calculate the earnings in dollars on your foreign investment.

2. With reference to the U.S. balance of payments, explain briefly (*a*) what it measures and what its purpose is, (*b*) what each of its three main accounts measures, (*c*) which are the credit items and which are the debit items, (*d*) how a deficit and surplus in the balance of payments is measured and why these measures as well as the concepts themselves are appropriate only under a fixed exchange rate system. (*e*) What overall conclusion can you reach with respect to the U.S. international transactions for the year 1988?

3. *Given:* (1) the gold-exchange standard under the Bretton Woods system, (2) the equilibrium level of income of a nation, $Y_E = \$1,000$ which represents full employment without inflation, (3) exports (X) = imports (M) = \$200, (4) the marginal propensity to save (MPS) = 0.15, while the marginal propensity to import (MPM) = 0.25 and (5) there is an autonomous *decrease* in X of \$100 and X remains at the lower level.

    (*a*) Find the foreign trade multiplier, k.

    (*b*) Find the new equilibrium level of income, Y_E'.

    (*c*) Would the adjustment in the balance of payments of the nation be complete or incomplete if we relied only on the automatic income adjustment mechanism?

    (*d*) Discuss how the other automatic adjustment mechanisms (besides the income adjustment mechanism) would also operate (if unchecked) in the deficit and surplus nations. Will all these automatic adjustment mechanisms, if allowed to operate, bring about complete adjustment in the balance of payments of the deficit and surplus nations?

    (*e*) Discuss briefly why the deficit and surplus nations may not be willing to allow these automatic adjustment mechanisms to operate? What would be the result of this?

4. (*a*) Identify the various policies that a nation could adopt to correct a deficit in its balance of payments under a fixed exchange rate system.

    (*b*) Explain briefly how these measures are supposed to operate to correct the deficit.

    (*c*) What conditions are required for these measures to be effective?

    (*d*) What measures can the nation use to correct a deficit in its balance of payments and domestic unemployment?

    (*e*) How can the nation correct a deficit, inflation and unemployment?

    (*f*) How can the nation simultaneously achieve internal and external balance under a flexible exchange rate system?

5. (*a*) What are the most serious *monetary* problems facing the world economy today?

    (*b*) How do these involve the U.S.?

    (*c*) What is proposed to solve these problems?

ANSWERS

1. You should use your $1,000,000 to buy deutsche marks. At the spot rate of $0.40, you will get DM2,500,000. Use these to buy German treasury bills. With the interest rate at 9% per year, you will earn 2.25% for the quarter on DM2,500,000. This amounts to DM56,250. Thus, at the end of three months you will have DM2,500,000 + DM56,250 = DM2,556,250. In order to cover the foreign exchange risk, at the same time that you exchange dollars for deutsche marks and use them to buy German treasury bills, you should sell DM2,556,250 forward for delivery in three months. Since the three-month forward DM is at a 2% discount per year or 1/2 of 1% for the quarter, the three-month forward rate of the DM is $0.40 − (0.005)($0.40) = $0.40 − 0.002 = $0.398. After three months, you will get DM2,556,250 and by selling them at the rate of $0.398 as agreed on the forward contract, you get $1,017,387.50. Thus, you earned $17,387.50 on your foreign investment. If instead of using your $1,000,000 for covered interest arbitrage you bought U.S. treasury bills, after three months, you could have earned only 1/4 of the annual rate of 5% per year prevailing in New York, or 1.25%. This amounts to $12,500. Thus, you earned $4,887.50 more on your foreign investment.

2. (a) The U.S. balance of payments for any year measures the international position of the U.S. during the year. Its main purpose is to inform government authorities and to help them formulate momentary, fiscal and commercial policies for the nation. It is also important for firms and banks in formulating their business decisions.

   (b) The current account measures the international flow of goods, services and unilateral transfers. The capital account measures the flow of investments and loans while the official reserve account measures the change in the nation's official reserve assets and the change in foreign official assets in the nation during the year.

   (c) The credit items (+) in the U.S. balance of payments are (1) the export of goods and services and the receipt of unilateral transfers (in the current account), (2) capital inflows (in the capital account), and (3) the increase in foreign official assets in the U.S. and the decrease in U.S. official reserve assets (in the official reserve account). On the other hand, the debit items (−) are (1) the import of goods and services, (2) the making of unilateral transfers, (3) capital outflows, (4) the increase in U.S. official reserve assets and the decrease in foreign official assets in the U.S. In short, a decrease in U.S. assets resulting from the export of goods, services and reserves, as well as capital inflows or imports into the U.S. are credits, while the opposite are debits.

   (d) If total debits exceed total credits in the current and capital accounts (and including the allocation of SDRs and the statistical discrepancy), the net debit balance measures the deficit in the nation's balance of payments. This deficit must be settled (under a fixed exchange rate system) with an equal net credit balance in the official reserve account. Thus, a deficit is given either by the net debit balance in the nation's autonomous items or by the equal net credit balance in the nation's accommodating items. The opposite is true for a surplus. This is true only under a fixed exchange rate system because under a flexible exchange rate system, the tendency for a balance of payments deficit or surplus is prevented entirely or in part by a depreciation or an appreciation, respectively, of the nation's currency.

   (e) The $35 billion net credit balance in the U.S. official reserve account for the year 1988 indicates the extent of U.S. official intervention in foreign exchange markets to prevent a larger depreciation of the dollar under the managed floating exchange rate system then in operation.

3. (a)
$$k = \frac{1}{\text{MPS} + \text{MPM}} = \frac{1}{0.15 + 0.25} = \frac{1}{0.4} = 2.5$$

   (b)
$$\Delta Y = (\Delta X)(k) = (-\$100)(2.5) = -\$250$$
$$Y'_E = Y_E + \Delta Y = \$1,000 - \$250 = \$750$$

   (c) $\Delta M = (\Delta Y)(\text{MPM}) = (-\$250)(0.25) = -\$62.50$. Since X fell by $100 while M are induced to fall only by $62.50, the nation will have a continuing deficit of $37.50, and so the adjustment is incomplete.

   (d) Because of the reduction in real national income in the deficit nation, its domestic prices are likely to fall in relation to prices in the surplus nation (*ceteris paribus*). This is likely to encourage the exports of the deficit nation, discourage its imports and so reinforce the adjustment process. In addition, the exchange rate is likely to depreciate (within the allowed limits of the gold-exchange standard) for the deficit nation and appreciate for the surplus nation, further encouraging the exports and discouraging the imports of the deficit nation. Finally, the outflow of reserves from the deficit nation and the inflow into the surplus nation, unless neutralized, are likely to increase interest rates in the former and lower them in the latter. This will have two effects. First, it tends to reduce investments, income and imports in the deficit nation and do the opposite in the surplus nation. Second, it tends to stimulate a short-term capital inflow into the deficit nation from the surplus nation. Both of these effects tend to reinforce the adjustment process. There are, in addition, foreign repercussions which also work in the same direction. When all of these automatic adjustment mechanisms are considered together, adjustment in the balance of payments is likely to be complete.

(*e*) The deficit nation is usually not willing to allow its national income and employment to fall as required by the operation of the automatic income adjustment mechanism. On the other hand, if the surplus nation were already at full employment, the increase in its exports (*ceteris paribus*) would lead to excess aggregate demand and demand-pull inflation—and this is usually not passively tolerated. The other part of the automatic adjustment mechanism—the one that operates through a change in the money supply, interest rates, investments, income and imports and also through international short-term capital flows—may also not be allowed to operate because it would mean that the nations would have to give up their use of monetary policy to correct domestic unemployment or inflation (or both) for the sake of external balance. The only way out of this impasse is to rely on *policies* to complete the adjustment.

4. (*a*) A nation could correct a deficit in its balance of payments by devaluing its currency, by holding its inflation rate lower than abroad, by increasing its short-term interest rates, or by direct controls on trade and payments.

(*b*) A devaluation will make the nation's imports more expensive to domestic buyers and its exports cheaper to foreigners. This usually improves the balance of trade and payments of the nation. The same results could be achieved by holding the domestic rate of inflation lower than abroad. On the other hand, an increase in the nation's short-term interest rate usually reduces short-term capital outflows from the nation or increases inflows, thus improving its balance on capital account and payments. Finally, and usually as a last resort to correct its deficit, a nation could impose restrictions on imports and capital outflows (direct controls) while giving subsidies and other inducements to its exports and capital inflows.

(*c*) For a devaluation to be effective to correct a deficit, the foreign exchange market must be stable (otherwise the devaluation will increase the deficit, and a revaluation would be required instead). A devaluation is also a feasible policy if the demand and supply for foreign exchange are "relatively" elastic. Finally, for a devaluation to be effective from a condition of full employment, domestic absorption must be reduced, either automatically or with expenditure- or demand-decreasing policies. The same is true if the nation attempts to correct the deficit by holding down its rate of inflation. For an improvement to occur in the capital account, capital movements must be responsive to higher domestic rates of interest. Finally, for all the above measures and for direct controls to be effective, other nations must cooperate and not retaliate.

(*d*) The nation could devalue its currency to correct the deficit and use expenditure-increasing policies to eliminate unemployment—unless the devaluation turns the unemployment into excess aggregate demand and inflation, in which case expenditure-decreasing policies are required. A devaluation rarely eliminates precisely both the deficit and unemployment. In any event, both targets must be approached with coordinated policies. If on the other hand, the nation is unwilling to devalue, then it could use expansionary fiscal policy to eliminate unemployment and tight monetary policy (to attract foreign short-term capital) to correct its deficit. If short-term international capital movements do not respond sufficiently or respond in the wrong direction, the nation may have to impose direct controls on capital movements and trade.

(*e*) If the nation faces unemployment, inflation and a deficit, the nation may have to accept a higher rate of unemployment to hold its inflation lower than abroad. If this is unacceptable, wage and price controls (incomes policy) may be necessary to curb inflation. Holding down the domestic inflation below the rate of inflation abroad will also reduce the deficit. If the deficit persists, the nation will either have to devalue its currency (to improve its trade balance) and/or increase its short-term interest rates (to attract foreign short-term capital). If these do not work, restrictions on capital outflows and trade may be necessary to eliminate the deficit.

(*f*) Fluctuating exchange rates will correct the deficit automatically if the foreign exchange market is stable and if domestic absorption is reduced when the nation is at full employment. In that case, the nation is free to use all the policy instruments at its disposal to achieve internal balance and its other goals.

5. (*a*) The most serious monetary problems facing the world economy today are the excessive volatility of exchange rates and the persistence of large disequilibria in exchange rates. Since 1973 exchange rates have been characterized by very large volatility and overshooting. This can discourage the flow of international trade. More serious is the fact that under the present managed floating exchange rate system, large exchange rate disequilibria can arise and persist for several years. This was clearly the case for the U.S. dollar during the 1980s.

(*b*)   The excessive appreciation of the dollar during the first half of the 1980s has been associated with huge trade deficits for the U.S. and almost irresistible calls for increased trade protection. Indeed, by the middle of 1985, large budget deficits and capital inflows had turned the U.S. from a creditor nation into a debtor nation, for the first time since 1914. By 1989, the U.S. was by far the world's largest debtor nation. This requires huge payments to service the debt and led to fears of foreign domination in the U.S.

(*c*)   The persistence of disequilibrium and great volatility of exchange rates have led to renewed calls for reform of the present international monetary system along the lines of establishing target zones of allowed fluctuations for the major currencies and for more international cooperation and coordination of policies among the leading nations. The earlier debate on the relative merits of fixed versus flexible rates has been superseded by discussions of the optimal degree of exchange rate flexibility and policy cooperation. In February 1987, the leading five industrial nations agreed at Louvre to cooperate closely to foster stability of exchange rates around then prevailing levels. Despite heavy intervention in foreign exchange markets by these countries' central banks, exchange rates continued to fluctuate by wide margins from the rates prevailing at the time of the Louvre agreement.

Index

The letter *p* following a page number refers to a Problem